Palgrave Studies of Internationalization in Emerging Markets

Series Editors
Marin Marinov
Aalborg University
Aalborg, Denmark

Svetla Marinova
Aalborg University
Aalborg, Denmark

Emerging market nations such as Russia, Brazil, China, South Africa and India as well as Eastern European territories, are in the process of changes and growth that require specific study and attention. The international business strategies employed in these territories target new opportunities, the study of which provides scholars the opportunity to evolve international business theory.

Covering three main themes - international business, management and marketing – **Palgrave Studies of Internationalization in Emerging Markets** will encompass a multiplicity of topics. Examining the new ways in which firms from emerging economies develop and implement their internationalization strategy, as well as their management and marketing strategies, the series will encompass specific issues such as social entrepreneurship, operations and regional specifics of internationalization. Looking closer at the specifics underlying the development of emerging market nations and their firms, this series aims to shed light on the current and future issues associated with the challenges and opportunities offered by the varying contexts of emerging markets.

More information about this series at
http://www.palgrave.com/gp/series/15456

Marina Latukha
Editor

Talent Management in Global Organizations

A Cross-Country Perspective

Editor
Marina Latukha
Graduate School of Management
St. Petersburg State University
St. Petersburg, Russia

Palgrave Studies of Internationalization in Emerging Markets
ISBN 978-3-319-76417-7   ISBN 978-3-319-76418-4   (eBook)
https://doi.org/10.1007/978-3-319-76418-4

Library of Congress Control Number: 2018957848

© The Editor(s) (if applicable) and The Author(s) 2018
This work is subject to copyright. All rights are solely and exclusively licensed by the Publisher, whether the whole or part of the material is concerned, specifically the rights of translation, reprinting, reuse of illustrations, recitation, broadcasting, reproduction on microfilms or in any other physical way, and transmission or information storage and retrieval, electronic adaptation, computer software, or by similar or dissimilar methodology now known or hereafter developed.
The use of general descriptive names, registered names, trademarks, service marks, etc. in this publication does not imply, even in the absence of a specific statement, that such names are exempt from the relevant protective laws and regulations and therefore free for general use.
The publisher, the authors and the editors are safe to assume that the advice and information in this book are believed to be true and accurate at the date of publication. Neither the publisher nor the authors or the editors give a warranty, express or implied, with respect to the material contained herein or for any errors or omissions that may have been made. The publisher remains neutral with regard to jurisdictional claims in published maps and institutional affiliations.

Cover illustration: tabuday / Alamy Stock Vector

This Palgrave Macmillan imprint is published by the registered company Springer Nature Switzerland AG
The registered company address is: Gewerbestrasse 11, 6330 Cham, Switzerland

Acknowledgment

This book, *Talent Management in Global Organizations: A Cross-Country Perspective*, is the collective work presenting our accumulative knowledge born from many discussions, reflections, inspirations and observations. Being part of an international team of researchers, I know that the global environment is the platform for our collaboration, driving our research possibilities and opportunities in this global world.

Several contributions made in this book were supported by St. Petersburg State University, Graduate School of Management. Within the project, aiming to study the influence of talent management practices on a company's absorptive capacity in modern economic conditions in Brazil, Russia, India and China (Project ID 16.23.1456.2017), Chapters 3, 4, 11 and 12 were developed. Research presented in Chapter 16 has been conducted also with financial support from St. Petersburg State University, Graduate School of Management (Project ID 16.23.1457.2017).

The Central and Eastern European International Research Team (CEEIRT) composed of researchers from different universities from the Central and Eastern European Region—has begun a long-term research project investigating the transition of human resource management practices and its roles in multinational organizations' subsidiaries, as these challenges occur in the countries of the region. Chapter 9 reflects the results of CEEIRT surveys and my appreciation goes to the support we obtained from distinguished Eastern European colleagues who took part in this research.

vi   Acknowledgment

I would like also to acknowledge the opportunity to belong to the Center for the Study of Emerging Markets and Russian Multinational Enterprises, where lots of insights and fruitful ideas were gained, and extend my gratitude to colleagues who co-authored this book.

Finally, I express my appreciation to Svetla Marinova, who helped in the editing and contributed her efforts and assistance during the preparation of this book.

Contents

Part I	**Talent Management in the Asia-Pacific Region**	1

1 Talent Management in a Global Environment: New Challenges for Regions, Firms and Managers   3
Marina Latukha

2 Talent Management in the Asia-Pacific: A Story of Cultural Diversity   9
Anna Veselova and Liudmila Veselova

3 China: Managing the Global Talent Market   15
Anna Veselova and Liudmila Veselova

4 India: Growth Embedded in Tradition   41
Anna Veselova and Liudmila Veselova

5 Korea: Culture and Reality   63
Anna Veselova and Liudmila Veselova

viii   Contents

Part II   Talent Management in Central and Eastern Europe   87

6   Talent Management in Central and Eastern Europe:
     Similarities and Differences   89
     Victoria Tikhonova, József Poór, János Fehér, and Valeria Dvornikova

7   Poland: How to Become a Leader   95
     Victoria Tikhonova

8   Czech Republic: Making Differences Important   119
     Victoria Tikhonova and Valeria Dvornikova

9   Hungary: Creating New Opportunities for Talent   143
     József Poór, János Fehér, and Victoria Tikhonova

**Part III   The Commonwealth of Independent States: Soviet
     Heritage in Action   167**

10   CIS: Soviet Heritage in Action   169
      Louisa Selivanovskikh

11   Kazakhstan: Leaving the Past Behind   175
      Louisa Selivanovskikh

12   Belarus: Moving Forward   207
      Louisa Selivanovskikh

13   Ukraine: Challenges for Further Development   237
      Louisa Selivanovskikh

Contents   ix

Part IV   Talent Management in Latin America   267

14 Latin America: Talent Management in the New Reality   269
Maria Laura MacLennan, Gabriel Vouga Chueke, Andrei Panibratov, Svetla Marinova, and Daria Klishevich

15 Brazil: Catching Up and Moving Forward   277
Maria Laura MacLennan and Gabriel Vouga Chueke

16 Argentina: Learning to Tango with Talent Management   299
Svetla Marinova and Daria Klishevich

17 Chile: Terra Incognita   321
Andrei Panibratov, Maria Laura MacLennan, and Gabriel Vouga Chueke

18 Creating a Talent Management Agenda for a Global Environment   343
Marina Latukha, Anna Veselova, Liudmila Veselova, József Poór, János Fehér, Victoria Tikhonova, Louisa Selivanovskikh, Maria Laura MacLennan, Gabriel Vouga Chueke, Svetla Marinova, Andrei Panibratov, and Daria Klishevich

Index   351

Notes on Contributors

Valeria Dvornikova is a doctoral student at the Organizational Behavior and Human Resource Management Department of the Graduate School of Management in St. Petersburg State University, Russia. She holds Master's degree in management from St. Petersburg State University's Graduate School of Management. She is a graduate of Vienna University of Economics and Business and ESC Rennes Business School. Dvornikova's research interests focus on talent management and talent migration in emerging markets.

János Fehér is Associate Professor and Academic Director of Human Resources at the BA Program of Károli Gáspár University of the Reformed Church in Hungary, with the Institute of Economics and Management, and a Private Professor at Szent István University in Gödöllő, Hungary. His earlier positions include Associate Professor and Department Head at Szent István University, Associate Professor and Program Director at IMC/International Management Center in Budapest, and Visiting Associate Professor at Temple University Philadelphia, Case Western Reserve University, Cleveland (Budapest Campus), and Budapest Corvinus University. His teaching areas are Management, Human Resource Management and Organizational Behavior. He has been a Consultant for and Program Developer, Director and Instructor of Upper Level Management Programs in leading Hungarian and international companies.

Daria Klishevich is a doctoral student at the Graduate School of Management of St. Petersburg State University, Russia. She is also Research Assistant at the

Centre for the Study of Emerging Markets and Russian Multinational Enterprises at GSOM. Klishevich holds Master's degree in sociology and European Studies from St. Petersburg State University and Universität Bielefeld (Germany). Klishevich's research interests focus on international business, cross-cultural analysis, emerging multinationals and non-market strategies of companies.

Marina Latukha is Doctor of Science and Associate Professor of Organizational Behaviour and Human Resources Management at the Graduate School of Management, St. Petersburg State University, Russia. She is also the lead researcher at the Centre for the Study of Emerging Market and Russian Multinational Enterprises. Latukha holds a PhD and doctoral degree in management from St. Petersburg State University, GSOM, and also has graduated from several postdoctoral programs in leading European and American business schools (the Harvard Business School, the Haas School of Business, the London Business School and the HEC School of Business). She is the author of a number of case studies (more than 30) and academic articles published in top-ranked academic journals (more than 50), such as *Human Resource Management, The International Journal of Human Resource Management, Thunderbird International Business Review* and *European Management Journal*. Lathuka's research interests and teaching areas focus on international and strategic human resource management, talent management and emerging multinationals.

Maria Laura MacLennan is Adjunct Professor in Business Studies at Centro Universitario FEI in Brazil. She holds a PhD in Business Studies from the University of Sao Paulo, where she conducted research on international HRM and strategy. She is an active member of the Academy of International Business and the European Academy of International Business. Her main research interest is in interdisciplinary studies bounding HRM and strategy.

Svetla Marinova is Professor of International Business and Marketing at Aalborg University in Denmark. She is expert on the transition and post-transition development of Central and Eastern European economies with a special interest in business restructuring, transformation and emergence. Her research covers generic business growth and foreign direct investments as means for promoting new business models and innovation that can foster firm-level international competitiveness. Publications include nine books and more than 100 academic papers on internationalization of emerging economies and firms, the role of contextual combinations in this process, and the interplay between institutional and business entrepreneurship in promoting outward foreign direct investments. Marinova is a proponent of targeted integration of research and

Notes on Contributors   **xiii**

innovation with education, institutional support and business initiative, that could enable emerging economies remodel their competitive position in the world.

Andrei Panibratov is Professor of Strategic and International Management at the Graduate School of Management, and the Head of the Center for the Study of Emerging Markets and Russian Multinational Enterprises at St. Petersburg State University, Russia. His research interests and lecturing area focus on internationalization of emerging market firms, outward FDI from emerging economies, and Russian multinationals. He has participated in consulting and research projects in a number of international and Russian organizations, universities and companies. Panibratov is the author/co-author of several books, series of case studies, and articles published in Russia and abroad.

József Poór is Professor of Management at Szent István University in Hungary, where he teaches a variety of management courses. He is also Professor of Management at J. Selye University Komarno (Slovakia). He served as Guest Professor at five US universities and taught 14 short summer semesters. He was Senior Manager at different internationally recognized professional service firms (Mercer, HayGroup and Diebold) and at the International Management Center in Budapest. His scholarly publications have appeared in more than 10 internationally referred journals. He has authored and co-authored books and book chapters in Hungarian, English and Romanian.

Louisa Selivanovskikh is a doctoral student of the Organizational Behavior and Human Resource Management Department of the Graduate School of Management and a research assistant at the Centre for the Study of Emerging Markets and Russian MNEs, St. Petersburg University, Russia. Her research interests lie in the area of strategic human resource management, knowledge management and emerging markets. Selivanovskikh has had several publications in international and Russian journals, including *Journal of East-West Business* and *Russian Management Journal*. Selivanovskikh is also a member of the Academy of International Business (AIB) and the European International Business Academy (EIBA).

Victoria Tikhonova is Assistant Professor of Public Administration at the Graduate School of Management of St. Petersburg State University in Russia. She is writing her PhD at Lappeenranta University of Technology in Finland. Tikhonova is a graduate of the dual diploma Master's Program in Technology and Innovation Management at St. Petersburg State University, GSOM and xiv **Notes on Contributors**

Lappeenranta University of Technology. Tikhonova's academic interests focus on international human resource management and career research.

Anna Veselova is Senior Lecturer at the Operations Management Department of the Graduate School of Management, St. Petersburg State University, Russia. She is also a researcher at the Centre for the Study of Emerging Markets and Russian Multinational Enterprises. Veselova has publications in international academic journals (e.g. International Journal of Emerging Markets). Veselova is a member of the Academy of International Business (AIB), the European International Business Academy (EIBA) and the European Association of Chinese Studies (EACS). Veselova's research interests focus on the international activities of emerging market firms, interrelations between firm's strategic and structural characteristics, context-related specificities of human resource management, among others.

Liudmila Veselova is Senior Lecturer at the European Studies Department of the School of International Relations at St. Petersburg State University. She is also a member of the working group of the Center for Chinese Studies (Russia) and the European Association of Chinese Studies (EACS). Her areas of interest include the modern history of China, Chinese social policy, the middle class in China, Sino-Russian relations, competitive advantages of the Chinese companies and talent management in China. Veselova is involved in both teaching and research; she has conducted research at Peking University, the Free University of Berlin, University of Turku and Wuhan Normal University. Her research has been published in Russian and international academic journals.

Gabriel Vouga Chueke is the founder of the Photo-Gabriel Brazilian Multinationals Observatory, a research center engaged in generating and disseminating knowledge about Brazilian FDI worldwide. Vouga Chueke holds Master's degree in International Management from ESPM in Brazil and will receive his PhD in business from the University of Sao Paulo. Vouga Chueke was an MBA exchange student at the University of Chicago, and he is a Global Mindset Facilitator through the Thunderbird School of Global Management. Vouga Chueke is a member of the Academy of International Business (AIB) and the European International Business Academy (EIBA). His research interests include emerging market multinationals, host-country institutional environment and entry mode strategy. He was Assistant Editor of the *Review of International Business* published by ESPM, and he is Professor in the same school. Vouga Chueke has acted as consultant to the Brazilian government, the Switzerland Chamber of Commerce in Brazil and others.

Part I

Talent Management in the Asia-Pacific Region

1

Talent Management in a Global Environment: New Challenges for Regions, Firms and Managers

Marina Latukha

The world has experienced dramatic changes in the past decade or so: borders have become less important and barriers for the movement of people and goods have been eased. Despite these fast changes, local cultures and traditions, historic roots and origins still remain important across the globe. In the rapidly changing global environment, regions and countries need to adjust and adapt to globalization processes to be able to survive, compete and lead in turbulent times of overwhelming changes. Talent management in the global environment focuses on developing the most effective configurations of managerial practices aiming to ensure a constant talent flow, to and within organizations, in order to enable them to sustain competitive advantages in the domestic and international markets within and across countries and regions. Those companies that have embraced the design, implementation and systematic development of their talent management practices have consistently achieved high efficiency and effectiveness in their operations.

M. Latukha (✉)
Graduate School of Management, St. Petersburg State University,
St. Petersburg, Russia
e-mail: marina.latuha@gsom.pu.ru

© The Author(s) 2018
M. Latukha (ed.), *Talent Management in Global Organizations*,
Palgrave Studies of Internationalization in Emerging Markets,
https://doi.org/10.1007/978-3-319-76418-4_1

Talent management is currently one of the most popular concepts worldwide. Yet, it is a management concept that has emerged only recently and the diversity of management approaches and practices across the globe leads to different talent management manifestations in various organizations. Moreover, different meanings and interpretations of the concept have emerged, which has created some challenges and divergent perspectives on its development. From a business and economic perspective, the ability to attract, develop and retain talented employees, interns, idea generators and implementers has become vital for companies' sustained domestic, regional and international competitiveness. The forces driving firms to develop their talent management strategies and practices are reasons that transcend national boundaries, such as increasing global competition, dominance of new global economic systems, emergence of new economic initiatives and regional economic alliances, industry consolidation, and the rapid increase in the number of multinational enterprises, which operate not only in local markets, but in any viable markets overseas. This inevitably has consequences for a firms' talent management. With increasing talent mobility trends—essentially meaning that countries, regions and cities have no longer any unique claims to talented people who originate in a given home location, but are globally mobile and sought after—talent management strategies, approaches and practices appear to be of extreme importance for the long-term survival not only of individual companies, but even for regions and individual countries. This makes us turn our attention to talent management and its practices that on the one hand should reflect existing global experience, but on the other, need to be integrated and embedded in local contextual specificity. By drawing further attention to global talent management and its role in organizational success, it is important to mention that economic dynamics, regional-level strong competition and talent mobility across countries have given talent management influential power and transformed it into a vitally global issue for companies and countries. This fact pushes researchers, organizations and managers to discuss the key internal and external factors affecting talent management systems in different countries, to find adequate mechanisms for the adaptation of talent management to existing national cultures, to build talent attraction and retention tools that can enable firms to overcome the challenges of talent shortages, and to seek a balance between the advanced talent management practices developed by developed market firms and those aligned with a country-specific environment. From a global point of view, demand and competition for talent is getting more intensive. This makes it crucial for firms to develop sophisticated talent management systems that can act across geographical and cultural barriers, and which can convert global challenges into opportunities for innovation and creativity for the long-term success of a firm. Thus talent management can be seen as a mechanism and enabler of the long-term success of a firm.

The main tasks of global talent management include management recruitment, selection, training and development, performance appraisal and compensation, labor relations and career development of future managers that should be better explored and understood in culturally, historically and economically diverse environments. Talent management is nowadays partially discussed in more traditional textbooks on human resource management and leadership or on organizational behavior, where talent management is investigated mainly through the examples of human resource management practices of companies in developed economies. Some textbooks, handbooks and edited books have also reflected on the strategic issues of talent management showing the importance of the topic in general and offer examples of talent management practices of companies from developed countries, but rarely such from those in emerging markets.

In this book, we focus on companies representing contexts that have been neglected by researchers, but these companies and the countries from which they originate play an ever-increasing economic and cultural role in the contemporary world. We have based the contributions in this book on examples from the Asia-Pacific region, Central and Eastern Europe, Latin America and the countries of the CIS, thus creating a unique opportunity to enhance the understanding of talent management employed by companies operating in these regions.

By providing insights on the talent management strategies and practices of companies from the regions mentioned above, two main objectives are met. Firstly, the discussion of talent management incorporates a more region-specific perspective which, with the currently emerging and developing regional integration blocs, has gained greater significance.

Secondly, unveiling unknown experiences of talent management in organizations from dynamic and fast-changing economies demonstrates the challenges faced by researchers in building a more all-round understanding of contextually embedded aspects of talent management. Many emerging economy companies have become global players in the past decade or so and, in doing so, they have created new knowledge, new experiences and new approaches to talent management, which make up one of the key pillars of their global rise. These have remained overlooked by mainstream researchers who often find it easier to focus mainly on firms from developed market economies instead of emerging ones, or/ and on hard performance indicators rather than on soft issues such as talent management.

Organization of this Book

This book consists of four parts and each one of them represents a particular context. All parts have three main chapters bringing examples of talent management in firms from three individual countries. Each chapter starts with an initial discussion of talent management country-specific issues, which is followed by case studies highlighting key aspects of organizational talent management practices.

Part I presents an Asia-Pacific perspective in which the talent management practices of companies from China, India and Korea are discussed. Being in the Asia-Pacific region, these companies are heavily dependent on economic growth and cultural background. Country-specific talent management practices are elaborated on and regional trends that create a background for the effective management of talent are deliberated. Chapter 3 is focused on managing the talent market in China by exploring how Chinese companies create their competitive advantages through talent management strategies and practices adopted by leading Chinese companies. Chapter 4 presents the Indian context and critically discusses talent management practices and challenges in Indian companies. The chapter elaborates on what the best talent management strategy is and what else is important for firms from India in managing talented employees in comparison with other countries in the Asia-Pacific region. Chapter

5 presents the role of talent management in creating and supporting sustainable competitive advantage in firms from Korea. Different examples showing how talent management practices may contribute to a firm's competitive advantage in the Korean context are provided. Special attention is paid to identifying specific talent management practices, which influence the competitive advantages of firms in this particular context.

Part II introduces an overview of the main talent management practices, such as talent attraction, evaluation, training, development, rewarding and so on, and stresses the importance of regional and country practices for better understanding the phenomenon of talent management in the CEE context. Examples of CEE firms are set in the context of the most important challenges firms face in their human resource management and talent management practices. Moreover, based on the analysis of companies from three countries we resolve the issue of how similar or different talent management in CEE companies is from companies elsewhere. Chapter 7 discusses talent management in Poland, in particular, how talent attraction, talent development and talent retention help Polish companies to align their organizational strategic goals. The chapter highlights the connection between talent management practices and the financial results of companies, revealing the contribution that managing talent in enhancing firm performance plays. Chapter 8 explores how existing talent management approaches can be implemented in the context of the Czech Republic. This chapter also analyzes the specifics and similarities of talent management practices in Czech firms comparing them with firms in other CEE countries. Chapter 9 discusses the talent management practices of firms from Hungary and provides a detailed analysis of their background. The historical development of talent management in Hungary reveals interesting approaches that have made Hungarian companies successful in the global environment.

Part III contends that the country-specific environment shapes the peculiarities of talent management practices by discussing the interplay of Westernized and localized approaches in the CIS context. It shows how talent management is influenced by a number of factors, some of which are specific to Kazakhstan, Belorussia and Ukraine, yet others are quite common in the CIS context. Chapter 11 reflects on talent management in Kazakhstan's firms and suggests that despite the dynamic economic growth of the national economy, talent management practices are either in transition from those of the Soviet past to the ones that exist in Western multinational corporations or are a mixture of these. As Belorussian companies are less studied in respect to talent management, Chapter 12 explores the experience of Belorussian companies and identifies development perspectives of talent management practices in this context. Chapter 13 provides a comprehensive view of talent management practices in Ukrainian companies. Ukrainian firms have been trying not to lose their competitive advantage and to further develop their human resources. This chapter discusses how talent management can be considered as a source of a firm's success in this turbulent context.

Part IV emphasizes the new tasks in managing people and talent in Latin America by exploring talent management in countries such as Argentina and Chile. Chapter 15 concentrates on the analysis of talent attraction, development and retention in Brazilian companies. The chapter discusses what Brazilian companies should be focused on in order to create innovative talent management practices to advance extant talent management approaches that may not be applicable to the Brazilian context. Chapter 16 presents talent management in Argentina and explores how the internal and external environment shapes talent management strategy, which is aligned with the overall strategic objectives of Argentinian companies. Chapter 17 explores talent management lessons from Chilean companies by including cases that illustrate how talent attraction, development and retention may be a basis for organizational growth, change, continuous improvement and career development in the Chilean context and how these enable long-term competitive advantages for firms. In Chapter 18 we summarize the main trends in talent management in global world and provide our vision on how talent management can help companies to be more effective.

2

Talent Management in the Asia-Pacific: A Story of Cultural Diversity

Anna Veselova and Liudmila Veselova

The past few decades have witnessed the continuous integration of the Asia-Pacific region into the global economy. While most of the developed countries have struggled to overcome the consequences of the recent financial crisis, the Asia-Pacific region has continued to experience stable development and growth. The expanding markets of China and India, in particular, have provided prospective opportunities for businesses. The business development in these two most populous countries in the world has led to the increasing relevance of human capital and has stimulated the evolution of human resource management strategies and approaches (McDonnell et al. 2012).

A. Veselova (✉)
Graduate School of Management, St. Petersburg State University,
St. Petersburg, Russia
e-mail: a.s.veselova@gsom.pu.ru

L. Veselova
School of International Relations, St. Petersburg State University,
St. Petersburg, Russia

© The Author(s) 2018
M. Latukha (ed.), *Talent Management in Global Organizations*,
Palgrave Studies of Internationalization in Emerging Markets,
https://doi.org/10.1007/978-3-319-76418-4_2

When considering talent management in the Asia-Pacific region, it is important to take into account existing variations in geographical and economic conditions, the diversity of cultures and the traditional, culturally embedded, management approaches. Many Asian companies miss enjoying the strategic benefits of talent management due to the dominance of traditional management styles, a lack of clear understanding of the human resource management function, existing non-transparent practices of staff hiring and a dearth of competent human resource managers (De Guzman et al. 2011). While there are significant variations in talent management practices among the countries in the region, overall, there are substantial, culturally defined differences between talent management in the whole region and the rest of the world. Talent management in this region is informed by long-termism, a high power distance, collective behavior, a much more interdependent relationship between the individual, community and society, and permeating religious and philosophical beliefs.

In this part, we discuss talent management practices in companies from the three most influential Asia-Pacific economies: China, India and Korea. These countries are rather unique in the economic growth they have achieved over a relatively short period of time. We will elaborate on their country-specific talent management practices and will discuss regional trends as a background for the effective management of talent. The focus on these particular countries is determined by the fact that they offer significant business opportunities, which bring about human resource issues, in general, and talent management concerns, in particular (McDonnell et al. 2012). China and India together make up over one-third of the world's population; both have a large, young workforce that is increasingly well educated and eager to succeed. This has a tremendous effect on competition for jobs, employment and talent retention.

Talent management practices are strongly dependent on a country's institutional environment and its cultural traditions (Cooke et al. 2014). Though emerging economies are often treated as a homogeneous group of countries, such an approach loses sight of context specificities, which do exist. Among the problems that are shared by most Asia-Pacific countries is the loss of their home-grown talent. Many qualified and experienced professionals, instead of working for domestic firms, emigrate to other countries, move to foreign-owned multinational enterprises or accept offshore appointments (Cooke 2011). A lack of integration between authorities, businesses and educational institutions in terms of the up-bringing of new generations of employees makes the situation even worse (Chatterjee et al. 2014).

Nevertheless, it has become obvious both for local employers and governments that without proper human capital companies cannot build competitive advantage to compete successfully in their domestic markets and overseas. In particular, in 2008 the Chinese government launched the Thousand Talents Plan initiative, which aimed to attract both local and foreign talent to compensate for the lack of a qualified labor force in the country. The program was aimed at recruiting full professors from prestigious institutions worldwide or senior managers for key Chinese organizations. By 2014, the planned number of recruits was exceeded by four times (Recruitment Program of Global Experts 2017). South Korea also developed a comprehensive set of measures to attract back talented people who had left the country. In contrast, despite the fact there has been great concern about the availability and retention of knowledge workers in India (Bhatnagar 2007), the Indian authorities have not implemented any coherent policy to control and regulate labor migration. These polity differences have influenced the unequal development of human resources in the three countries (Kuptsch and Pang 2006).

Chinese and Indian talent management practices are similarly focused on financial incentives, training and development, as well as performance management and fast-track promotion. The introduction of these practices has been stimulated to a large extent by the increasing number of Western companies which have penetrated the Chinese and Indian markets and introduced their management approaches (Appelbaum et al. 2000). As China and India share some cultural traditions, this is also reflected in their talent management practices. Thus, in both countries the use of workplace-based voluntary benefits to incentivize employees is found to be especially efficient (Nankervis et al. 2013). Employers are expected to care for their employees' welfare through the provision of extensive workplace benefits, which is driven by the deeply rooted, traditional, paternalistic culture (Cooke 2008). In contrast to Indian and Korean companies, Chinese firms are still more attentive to employees' living conditions and their family and social life. They often provide employees with housing or better financial arrangements to compensate for housing expenditures. This tradition has its roots in the Chinese past and relates to the "iron bowl" concept. Korean companies, as opposed to Chinese and Indian ones, are less mindful about the financial appraisal of and rewards to their employees, but have a stronger focus on creating comfort in the internal environment that is associated with a feeling of harmony and trust.

Further on, we elaborate on country-specific talent management practices and gain an understanding of regional trends as a background for the effective management of talent in local firms.

References

Appelbaum, Eileen, Thomas R. Bailey, Peter Berg, and Arne L. Kalleberg. 2000. *Manufacturing Advantage: Why High-Performance Work Systems Pay Off.* Ithaca: ILR Press.

Bhatnagar, Jyotsna. 2007. Talent Management Strategy of Employee Engagement in Indian ITES Employees: Key to Retention. *Employee Relations* 29 (6): 640–643.

Chatterjee, Samir, Alan Nankervis, and Julia Connell. 2014. Framing the Emerging Talent Crisis in India and China. *A Human Capital Perspective* 1 (1): 25–43.

Cooke, Fang L. 2008. *Competition, Strategy and Management in China.* Basingstoke: Palgrave Macmillan.

———. 2011. Talent Management in China. In *Global Talent Management*, ed. Hugh Scullion and David G. Collings, 132–154. New York: Routledge.

Cooke, Fang L., Debi S. Saini, and Jue Wang. 2014. Talent Management in China and India: A Comparison of Management Perceptions and Human Resource Practices. *Journal of World Business* 49 (2): 225–235.

De Guzman, Gloria M., James P. Neelankavil, and Kaushik Sengupta. 2011. Human Resources Roles: Ideal Versus Practiced: A Crossed-Country Comparison among Organizations in Asia. *The International Journal of Human Resource Management* 22 (13): 2665–2682.

Kuptsch, Christiane, and Eng F. Pang. 2006. *Competing for Global Talent.* Geneva: International Institute for Labour Studies.

McDonnell, Anthony, David G. Collings, and John Burgess. 2012. Guest Editor's Note: Talent Management in the Asia Pacific. *Asia Pacific Journal of Human Resources* 50: 391–398.

Nankervis, Alan R., Fang L. Cooke, Samir Chatterjee, and Malcolm Warner. 2013. *New Models of Human Resource Management in China and India.* Abingdon, Oxon: Routledge.

Recruitment Program of Global Experts. 2017. www.1000plan.org/en/. Accessed 15 July 2017.

3

China: Managing the Global Talent Market

Anna Veselova and Liudmila Veselova

Human resource management, in general, and talent management, in particular, has a long history and tradition in China, and this significantly affects business and organizational relationships. It is impossible to consider the Chinese human resource management system and talent management strategies without looking at China's unique historical path and cultural idiosyncrasies. Radical changes in Chinese economic and cultural life started at the end of the 1970s when Deng Xiaoping launched economic reforms in the country. Since then, China has achieved a steady economic growth that has enabled it to respond to the challenges of the new global business and economic environment. In order to be able to develop and implement the unprecedented economic changes, China has

---

A. Veselova (✉)
Graduate School of Management, St. Petersburg State University, St. Petersburg, Russia
e-mail: a.s.veselova@gsom.pu.ru

L. Veselova
School of International Relations, St. Petersburg State University, St. Petersburg, Russia

© The Author(s) 2018
M. Latukha (ed.), *Talent Management in Global Organizations*,
Palgrave Studies of Internationalization in Emerging Markets,
https://doi.org/10.1007/978-3-319-76418-4_3

transformed its human resource management system. After the Cultural Revolution (1966–1976), the country experienced a lack of talent, many universities were closed and many professors and teachers were killed or sent to prison, while a large part of the intellectual community tried to emigrate. This was recognized as a serious problem as well-educated people were greatly needed for the country's economic transformation. The significance of education has always been acknowledged as something exceptional and a key determinant of success: as the Chinese philosopher Confucius put it, "all are low-brow activities, except education" (Cooke et al. 2014).

After the launch of the "Four Modernizations" and "Open-Door" policy, Chinese firms had to implement significant changes in their structure and management, which resulted in decentralization of planning and decision-making, a toughening of personal accountability for performance, fast knowledge acquisition and so on (Iles et al. 2010). To bring these changes to life, Chinese firms had to look for qualified and talented personnel who were competent and savvy enough to learn. Despite the fact that the Chinese government always tried to grow and cultivate talent and paid considerable attention to human resources (HR), China faced a number of challenges when trying to meet the demands of Western multinationals that invested in the country's economy at the end of the 1990s and the beginning of the 2000s.

The promotion of foreign investment by the Chinese government and the overall attractiveness of the huge Chinese market brought thousands of Western companies to China in the late 1990s (Vorhauser-Smith 2012). China's integration into the world economy has been accompanied by an intensive knowledge and competence inflow that was additionally stimulated by the investment of foreign companies in local production as they had to transfer the full range of advanced managerial practices in the area of human resource management and talent management. However, the adoption of these Western practices was not smooth or easy (Björkman and Lu 1999). Several studies on the implementation of Western-transferred human resource management practices in Chinese firms have confirmed the limited applicability of such a direct approach due to the particular cultural and institutional idiosyncrasies (Li and Scullion 2006). Among these are the gap between theory and practice in educational programs, the state-owned enterprise mentality, the "iron rice bowl" heritage, and the high costs of living in other countries (Tung 2007). Considering that the curricula of most Chinese business schools and universities have always been heavily sanctioned by the Chinese government, Chinese managers have been skeptical about the applicability of Western human resource management theories and approaches to the Chinese context where Confucian values remain dominant (Cooke 2012).

For some time, Western multinationals had an advantage over local companies in terms of talent attraction as they offered better compensation packages and work conditions. However, their advantages were not well received as Chinese employees felt frustrated in a non-traditional environment of fierce competition where they were challenged by language and cultural nuances (Vorhauser-Smith 2012). Moreover, specific Chinese customs and habits have proved to be serious constraints for international companies in terms of degree of convergence, which has effectively led to increasing levels of divergence (Rowley and Benson 2002). Confucian values of high moral standards, harmonious relationships and social obligations to those who are higher in authority are very different from those postulated in Western companies. However, in China they largely determine intra-organizational interactions and form the ideological basis for management approaches (Latukha 2016).

Recruitment and talent attraction processes in China are often implemented through network-based recruitment practices, especially in large companies and state-owned enterprises. It is believed that network-based recruitment practices can provide effective pre-hire outcomes, such as faster attraction of prospective applicants and highly competent employees (Warner 2009). Despite nepotism, which exists in certain industries, in modern China there is a growing tendency toward greater transparency and objectivity in recruitment processes, as this is the only way to obtain effective and talented employees. Most successful in this regard have been large Chinese firms with an international presence.

Under the strong influence of Confucian values and collectivist philosophy, Chinese employees are more inclined to life-long learning and advancement. They demonstrate a strong desire for learning and personal development—a key criterion of talent—making talent management practices critical for organizational learning and knowledge sharing. Recent research shows that Chinese companies make large investments in various developmental and training programs which create conditions that allow the quite extensive use of an unskilled labor force and bring up talent internally through on-the-job development. Very often professional training is oriented at delivering basic knowledge, skills and abilities to employees that are required for fulfilling their working tasks (Ng and Ciu 2004). Such an approach results in a more general knowledge base rather than special skills, which does not allow individual employees to form a strong competitive position either on individual level or for the whole organization. Another important aspect of such training is the constant maintenance and enhancement of the ideological and political consciousness of employees through moral education (Zhu et al. 2012). Reflecting this, Chinese companies tend to emphasize moral conduct as a key attribute of talent.

Performance appraisal systems in traditional Chinese companies are also context specific. Characterized by a risk-averse cultural environment with high levels of "power distance" and clear hierarchies, in such companies promotion and reward is carried out more on the basis of tenure, status and ranks, rather than on performance (Connell and Stanton 2014).

Nevertheless, it should be noted that recent trends in Chinese talent management and the approaches adopted by the largest and most influential Chinese companies could bring about new perspectives. The fact, that a new generation of Chinese talent has more social and economic advantages, and higher expectations of career development, has pushed Chinese firms to provide well-grounded and complex talent management policies and practices to attract the best talent. On average, Chinese senior managers are five years younger than senior managers in other Asian countries and they can benefit from finding the best company for career building. Moreover, the decisive role of wages when choosing a place in which to work and the willingness of Chinese talent to change jobs if there are better conditions (Xue 2014) have created a need for developing effective talent retention tools.

Further in this chapter, we consider the major talent management practices implemented by the most successful Chinese companies. We specifically focus on three different industries—car manufacturing, tele-communications and investment—to show that current changes are not limited to any particular sector of the economy, but rather have an all-embracing nature.

Geely Automobile Holdings (Geely): The Talent Management Revolution

Geely is an automobile company located in the Zhejiang province, which operates in research, production, marketing and sales of sedans and related automobile components. Being part of a huge conglomer-ate, Zhejiang Geely Holding Group Co., it is one of China's top auto-mobile producers (Top 10 Domestic Car Manufacturers in China 2016). The company operates in several Asian, European and American markets (i.e. China, Hong Kong, Korea, the Middle East, Europe, Africa, Central and South America). Geely owns six manufacturing plants in Linhai, Ningbo/Cixi, Luqiao, Xiangtan, Jinan and Chengdu and produces 13 models of cars under three product brands: Emgrand, GLEagle and Englon.

The company was founded by Li Shufu in 1986 as a refrigerator pro-ducer. In 1994, Geely started to produce motorcycles and in 1997 it entered the automobile industry, introducing its first vehicle, the Geely HQ (GlobalCarBrands 2015). In 2001, the Chinese government certi-fied Geely's model JI-6360, and this allowed Geely to become the first Chinese private organization certified to manufacture automobiles (Wang 2011). In 2002, there were several claims that Geely's cars were just cop-ies of existing models by other producers or a mix of different automo-biles produced by foreign companies. The company reacted almost immediately and started to manufacture new distinctive cars with the use of advanced technologies in order to eliminate further comparison. In 2003, Geely went outside the Chinese market for the first time and started its international expansion (Wang 2011). Geely's cars have suc-ceeded due to their fuel efficiency, performance and reliability, especially in Asian and European markets.

The first public showing of Geely in the international arena took place in 2005 during the 61st Frankfurt Auto Show where Geely was the first Chinese automobile company to participate in this event (Alon et al. 2012). In 2006, the company made an agreement with the Rolf Group of Russia to import and sell Geely sedans to the Russian market (Panibratov 2017). In the same year, Geely tried for the first time to enter the British market through a joint venture with MB Holdings to produce the iconic London taxi in Shanghai.

The international expansion of Geely was supplemented by stronger vertical integration, which created a basis for enhancing the firm's competitive advantage. In 2009, Geely acquired the operating assets of Drivetrain Systems International, an Australian-based company and the world's second-largest manufacturer of automatic gearboxes that it supplied to Ford and Chrysler, for a total of USD 40.22 million. Geely acquired the company in order to focus on supplying automatic transmission for original equipment manufacturers (Reuters 2009). The main strategic goal of this deal was to gain access to technologies for automatic gearboxes and to boost Geely's production of more complex and sophisticated cars.

To diversify its portfolio with something that adds value for the European market, by mid-2008 Geely negotiated the acquisition of Volvo with the Ford Motor Company. In 2010, the deal was completed and with this acquisition Geely Holding Group became the first multinational automotive corporation in China (Geely 2017). This deal stimulated a significant technological upgrading of Geely's globalization strategy and strengthened its position and image as a producer of eco-friendly and safe cars. In 2012, Geely and Volvo signed a Technology Transfer Agreement aimed at building a research and development (R&D) center in Gothenburg (Christian 2012). Understanding the necessity of encouraging and developing HR that will correspond to the company's vision and strategy, Geely has also established numerous schools, colleges and universities, including the Zhejiang Automotive Vocational and Technical College, Hanna University Sanya College, Zhejiang Automotive Engineering Institute and Beijing Geely University, which were oriented at creating a talent pool for the company's needs.

Geely sees its key long-term objective as being "a leading global automobile group with good reputation and integrity, winning respect from its customers" which produces "good cars that are the safest, most environment-friendly and most energy-saving" (Geely Annual Report 2016). As a result of gaining a strong position on the world automobile market, Geely has changed its direction from competing on price to competing on quality, service, customer satisfaction and brands, which is implemented through substantial investment in R&D. As a part of its development, Geely implemented a quality control system in accordance with international standards. Additionally, the firm restructured its supplier network based on its new emphasis on safety and efficiency (Alon et al. 2012).

In order to differentiate itself in the worldwide arena Geely has developed several innovative technologies. It introduced the first Chinese electronic steering system and two unique technologies known as the "low-out monitoring and breaking system" and the "energy efficient building system" (Alon et al. 2012). This focus on differentiation and innovation significantly influenced Geely's HR policy, stimulating more active talent attraction, targeted selection and development of its personnel.

One of Geely's corporate values is to make all Geely's stakeholders happy. In particular, Geely strives that its staff should enjoy the process of discovering and solving problems and hence experience continuous improvement, "enjoying the success that let[s] Geely cars go around the world instead of international cars go[ing] around China" (Geely 2017). These values are reflected in Geely's corporate culture which has been evolving for more than 20 years and has allowed the firm to develop a uniqueness that enables it to innovate and carefully grow its business. To date, Geely's corporate culture is based on six core principles: entrepreneurship, diversity, adaptability, humanity, nerve-like management and "military-style-efficient execution". Entrepreneurial orientation stimulates research and innovation, and maintains Geely's leading position among Chinese car manufacturers. Diversity and adaptability work as key factors of Geely's success through improved performance and quality, careful commitment, planning and teamwork. Moreover, Geely's corporate culture also has Chinese traditional attributes such as humanity where, on the one hand, staff members can feel part of a huge loving family, and on the other, the company urges every employee to observe and respect the rules consciously. Nerve-like management is also a reflection of the traditional Chinese approach and philosophy which consider that every single aspect and activity has an effect on the others. The uniqueness of Geely's corporate culture is also expressed in complementing the above-mentioned features with a clear hierarchical approach where leaders care for their subordinates, while the subordinates respect their leaders and superiors pleading to learn modestly from others and from criticism as well. Moreover, Geely has some of the features of adhocracy which makes the company oriented toward long-term growth and change. Such an unusual mixture makes Geely a unique and attractive employer for young and prospective local talent.

Geely is one of the largest employers in China. Its structure, the organization of its human resource management, and its organizational behavior are untypical of Chinese companies. While most Chinese firms look for a cheap workforce and try to maximize their profits without investing in modern technologies and human capital, Geely resorts to a different, forward-looking strategy. Being considered as a corporate citizen, Geely promotes its own performance mainly by focusing on the most important aspects, such as personnel training, cultural sponsorship, giving help to disabled people, and trying to fulfill its economic, social, legal and business integrity responsibilities.

At the initial stage of introduction and development of the corporate talent management system, Geely used the prototypes offered by Western and Japanese car manufacturers. Geely took a track on learning from other successful car producers Thus it benchmarked the organization of work processes in Toyota and adopted some of them. By doing this, the company tried to avoid difficulties associated with the creation of a stable system of work processes.

Through maintaining a highly trained and skilled workforce, Geely can stay competitive in today's technologically dynamic world and support growth. Therefore, Geely partnered with NetDimensions, a global provider of performance, knowledge and learning management systems, to implement a three-phase learning and talent management strategy. The first stage includes the establishment of a robust and flexible talent management platform to deliver online training programs, foster a collaborative environment and enhance a knowledge-sharing culture among employees. The second stage assumes a leverage of the system to include all employees in Geely's subsidiaries as well as the whole supply chain in an extended enterprise model. Finally, in the third stage, the company can enjoy benefits from the multi-language functionality of the NetDimensions Talent Suite to cover all Geely's overseas employees in five countries, including Indonesia, Uruguay, Cuba, Belarus and Russia (NetDimensions 2013).

To meet the constantly increasing need for qualified personnel caused by its rapid growth and development, Geely has to develop qualified workers with its own resources. Trying to apply German engineering educational and training standards, Geely extensively invests in the education and development of its employees. Unlike many Western companies, which turn to vocational high schools or traditional universities for educational services, Geely Group founded its own corporate university, Beijing Geely University (BGU), in 2000 (eBeijing 2017). The high quality of education provided by BGU is confirmed by the fact that it has been accredited by the Beijing People's Municipal Government and the Ministry of Education of the People's Republic of China. Moreover, in 2006 professors and trainers at the university were certified at the German Chamber for Industry and Commerce (IHK), acknowledging that BGU training corresponds to the standards of German engineering education (Beijing Geely University 2017).

The university plays a great role both in recruiting and developing talent for Geely. Apart from offering educational programs, which are specially designed to develop Geely's personnel, it also operates to compensate for the lack of qualified employees. The recruitment process for BGU graduates is much easier than for outsiders, as prospective talent can be identified during the educational process. Geely's recruitment process also comprises its own corporate career portal, job search and recruitment websites, so high efficiency is achieved through combining all these methods, which are oriented at standardization and automation of the corporate recruitment system and its integration with other recruitment channels in order to accelerate candidates' reviewing and evaluation processes.

Apart from corporate university education and training, there are also on-site educational activities; for example, new manufacturing workers usually start in a special training area near the plant where they learn the fundamentals of the job tasks under the supervision of experienced specialists. This program, based on intensive on-the-job training, assumes that a supervisor assesses the on-the-job results of a new worker for three months and only after that is the worker allowed to start working for the company. Such an approach guarantees a high level of quality and performance. Geely also promotes the long-term skill development of workers, and its wage level correlates to the level of occupational certification according to a system of industry-wide occupational skills, governed by the Chinese Ministry for Human Resources and Social Security.

To make the selection and evaluation processes for managerial personnel more transparent, in 2010 Geely introduced a distinctive, competitive, assessment procedure called a "sunshine platform" based on managers' key performance indicators (KPIs). The assessment system includes a problem-solving task and a group interview, where managers from different departments perform as interviewers. Those managers who successfully pass the assessment are publicly announced; those who fail have the chance to improve their departmental performance in the next period; however, if a team fails to meet the KPIs several times in a row, its manager could be displaced and competition for the vacant position announced (Jürgens and Krzywdzinski 2013). This approach is not traditional for Chinese companies as they are traditionally more inclined to use conduct and loyalty than KPIs in performance assessment. Moreover, the public announcement of poor performance could lead to "losing face", which is detrimental in Chinese culture, so although being a traditional practice in Western companies, such an approach is very harsh on Chinese employees.

In 2015, Geely introduced remuneration packages for its employees based on individual experience and work profile. These packages are annually reviewed by top management and depend both on overall company performance and external market conditions. There are also specific retirement packages provided by the company within the Mandatory Provident Fund Scheme (in Hong Kong) and state-managed retirement benefit scheme (in the People's Republic of China), along with other motivation initiatives adopted by the company (Geely Announcement 2015).

To some extent, Geely has effected a talent management revolution in that it has found its own way of implementing advanced Western practices and keeping its employees happy. According to feedback from Geely's employees, it has created favorable conditions which inspire employees to perform better within the team of talent and provide many opportunities for self-realization and career development (Geely Linkein Profile 2017).

China Mobile: Adaptation and Implementation

China Mobile is the largest mobile operator in the world. It was rated as one of the most wealthy and influential public companies in the world according to the FT Global 500(FT 500 2015) and the Forbes Global 2000 (The Global 2000 2017). The company was founded in 1997 in Hong Kong as a result of the Chinese state-owned telecommunications monopoly ceasing. By 2006, China Mobile had acquired over 30 companies and had become the first telecommunications company that was listed as a PRC (primary reference clock), operating in 31 provinces (China Mobile Limited Annual Report 2006). In 2009, China Mobile acquired a license to expand its business into 3G networks, using the Chinese standard TD-SCDMA (time division-synchronous code division multiple access) (GSM Arena 2017). In 2013, the company obtained the right to expand to 4G networks. Firstly, China Mobile introduced 4G networks in 16 cities in China, and right after getting confirmation that customers were satisfied, it continued to expand the network all over the country (Apple 2013). By 2010, China Mobile controlled about 70% of the Chinese market, while its competitors China Unicom and China Telecom has 20% and 10% respectively (Morningstar 2011).

During the past 15 years, China Mobile has been changing its mission and strategy depending on its competitive position. At the beginning of this century, it aimed to implement service and business leadership and achieve a world-class position as an expert in mobile communications among communications corporations. Since 2006, it has diversified its interests and ambitions to information systems through a "leap-frogging" strategy; and starting from 2011, sustainable development was announced as a priority. China Mobile aims to achieve sustainable development in two ways: by recognizing risks, acquiring more strategic resources and achieving the best performance, and by promoting sustainability as a whole with the help of responsible operations and the promotion of equality in society.

China Mobile has built a strong corporate governance structure and a top-down organizational structure from the Council at the top down to specific positions with various responsibilities for internal control. The corporate structure is quite complex and includes more than 10 departments and "special departments" that help to educate people for further work in the company. It has created a three-tier system of internal controls, which enables monitoring of the entire process of marketing, production and management. China Mobile focuses on risk and core management areas in order to align all its rules of internal control in everyday operations. Moreover, the company has introduced special information technology (IT) systems to assign tasks, deliver requirements and control results.

Stating its key values as responsibility and pre-eminence, the company aims to improve the public lives of outsiders and its employees. Similar to Geely, China Mobile puts a lot of effort into organizing its employees so that they feel part of a family, oriented toward one common goal. China Mobile strives to continuously improve its personnel commitment through, for example, special programs, a three-year plan titled "Establishment and implementation plan for corporate culture" (China Mobile Limited Corporate Social Responsibility Report 2006), competitions for employees in writing essays on the topic of "How to become an excellent company", and so on.

Employing more than 400,000 people (Statista 2017), China Mobile highlights the key role of its employees in its overall corporate development and organizes its processes of recruitment, work and dismissal to meet both regulations and stakeholders' expectations, as well as offering adequate rights and welfare to employees. Recently, China Mobile introduced a transparent and open, multi-layered and three-dimensional, recruitment system, which includes uniform written examinations and a fair and just environment for employee selection (China Mobile Limited Sustainability Report 2016).

China Mobile applies a wide range of practices to motivate its employees and retain talent. Apart from competitive remuneration, it provides its employees with insurance and welfare coverage, a psychological consultation service, as well as the "Happiness 1+1" activity to enhance employees' physical and mental well-being. The company also supports employees who are suffering from serious diseases and offers them help.

Understanding dynamism and change in the external environment and trying to keep its competitive position as an employer, China Mobile has developed and introduced an Outstanding Talent Engineering program which presents the overall direction and key measures for the corporate talent management system. This has four main aspects: strengthening a team of leaders, optimizing employees' team structures, improving comprehensive incentive mechanisms, and promoting ability and quality (China Mobile Limited Sustainability Report 2016). Thus, China Mobile understands the critical relevance of talented human resources in realizing its growth strategy and to achieve its objectives it promotes practices to attract, develop and retain the most talented employees.

China Mobile puts a lot of effort into training and promotion of its talent. The company sees the knowledge and skills of all employees as the basis of its constant innovation and growth. It provides employees with diverse and in-depth training through offering them opportunities for learning and promotion. Employee training programs are reconsidered and updated yearly which, on the one hand, provides employees with well-tailored training courses that help them to develop their careers and, on the other hand, supports China Mobile's growth strategy implementation. Apart from professional training, employees are also offered diverse training about life skills, which helps them to develop interests and hobbies that are valuable for both life and work.

To realize its training and promotion system, China Mobile University set up a platform of co-construction and sharing for employee training, which contains group training resources, a process training management and assessment system, and a professional method system of training design and implementation (China Mobile Limited Sustainability Report 2016). The online study platform of China Mobile University has introduced innovative study models by integrating multiple means of study:

personal computers, mobile phones, WeChat, live-broadcasting and massive open online courses (MOOC). The platform provides employees with training courses and learning materials on corporate and business strategies, corporate culture communication, work skills certification and employee development. More than 395,000 people used the platform to study various courses in 2016, clocking up a total of 17.56 million study hours (China Mobile Limited Sustainability Report 2016). In 2014, China Mobile University was awarded an "ATD – Excellence in Practice Award" and "China's Best Enterprise University", the next year it received the "2015 Engine Award – China Benchmarked Enterprise University" and the "2015 Innovation Award in China's E-learning Industry" (China Mobile Limited Sustainability Report 2016). In 2016, China Mobile University was awarded the "Award of Excellent Corporate University" in the Award of 2016 China's Talent Development, the "Best Corporate University and Best Learning Project" in the Ranking List of 2016 China's Best Corporate Universities, the gold award in the first session of CSTD Corporate Learning Design Contest, the "Award of Outstanding Implementation of China's E-Learning Industry" and the "Award of Learning and Development of Cases with the Greatest Value" (China Mobile Limited Sustainability Report 2016). These awards undoubtedly confirm that the company's efforts in the area of employee development are valuable, advanced and highly efficient.

To stimulate business and technical development, China Mobile puts a strong emphasis on talent attraction, selection mechanisms and motivation incentives through the Millions of Talents Plan, One Thousand Talents Plan and the special government allowance recommendation. The company conducts research and develops a professional skills certification system, which includes relatively standardized mechanisms and procedures aimed at development, maintenance and implementation of the skills model database certification examination.

China Mobile has been constantly innovating its appraisal system according to best international practices, tying it to company performance, and thus motivating employees to be more efficient. The company has formulated a guide for the implementation of a quantitative performance-based remuneration system. By the end of 2013, the quantitative performance-based remuneration system covered all the sales and call-center employees, corporate account managers and telesales managers (China Mobile Limited Annual Report 2013). China Mobile launched a pilot project for front-line network employees to adequately stimulate their commitment and enhance their sales capabilities and service quality (China Mobile Limited Annual Report 2013); it has also been promoting the transformation of the remuneration incentive mechanism with a "flexible job structure and up-and-down job movements" (China Mobile Limited Annual Report 2015).

China Mobile uses various approaches for the recruitment of new employees. In 2015, it launched a pilot unified written test for recruitment attracting 33 organizations in more than 1000 test centers with students participating more than 40,000 times (China Mobile Limited Annual Report 2015). To attract talent and promote its employer brand, the company regularly organizes presentations and on-site recruitment sessions targeting thousands of people.

Similar to some other large Chinese companies, China Mobile introduced and broadened its performance management system to cover the daily work of the different levels of management; first of all, through adoption of the balanced scorecard approach. This assumes the construction of a top-to-bottom KPI indicator system, whereby the results of performance evaluations are closely linked to compensation and rewards so as to enhance the motivational effect of performance evaluations and stimulate employee initiative and activism, thereby ensuring employee enthusiasm and assertiveness, and the realization of China Mobile's strategic objectives. To align employees' interests with company performance and motivate employees to increase efficiency and shareholder value, China Mobile implemented and enhanced its Share Option Scheme for senior and middle managers, as well as core employees.

Similar to Geely, China Mobile has succeeded in combining effective practices for talent attraction, selection, development and retention with traditional Chinese values, which has created a working environment where employees can feel part of a bigger family, and are also motivated for higher individual contributions to achieve better organizational performance.

Fosun Group: Talent Development

Fosun Group, founded in 1992 (Fosun 2017), is an example of a success story. It has evolved from a small entrepreneurial firm to a leading investment group following a development model which includes four core businesses: insurance, industrial operations, investments, and asset management. Following the philosophy of value investment, Fosun aims at "combining China's growth momentum with global resources" (Fosun 2017). To do so, Fosun extensively invests in sectors that could significantly benefit from China's growth. They include consumption upgrade, financial services, resources and energy, manufacturing upgrade and others. In its business, Fosun maintains a strong base in China and invests in the country's growth fundamentals, which are stimulated by the restructuring of China's economy toward higher domestic demand. At the same time, Fosun tries to reinforce its position both inside and outside the domestic market as a Chinese expert with global capacity.

Fosun has built its capabilities and grown rapidly, developing a value chain based on three principles: identification and capturing investment opportunities from China's growth, improvement of management and the value of investees, and the establishment of a multichannel financing system to access quality capital. Along with a stable economic development, Fosun is also oriented to the development of its staff, partners and communities, and contributing to society in return. Fosun also supports improvements in the country's natural environment and the rejuvenation of the Chinese economy and culture (Fosun Group 2016).

Fosun's investment business includes three major parts: strategic investment, private equity and venture capital investment, and secondary market investment. Its wealth management business is mainly focused on asset management, banking and other financial business. Fosun has recently made successful investment in several projects with the aim of creating a new type of financial industry based on up-to-date internet technologies, including cloud computing, through building a multidimensional ecosystem. Due to the specificity of Fosun's business models in terms of human capital, such approaches need highly skilled and talented people who can deliver on these ambitious corporate goals. Moreover, there is a significant difference between the insurance and investment business in terms of the way talent is usually treated. Though the insurance industry has long-term customers, insurance professionals do not usually stay long with a company, so the relevance of talent management practices might not be a priority. In contrast, the investment business usually takes a long-term view of talent management; in particular, top talent individuals are often made partners in order to retain them for the long-term. Realizing this, Fosun actively supports and encourages its divisions to ensure that the brightest talent stays with the company (Ang 2014).

Fosun is also involved in industrial operations which include five key segments: health, happiness, steel, property development and sales, and resources. Such unrelated diversification provides benefits but increases costs. The complexity of the corporate portfolio requires very well-thought through approaches to its management, which increases the need for well-qualified and highly motivated personnel.

Fosun actively promotes and develops its social responsibility through protection of the environment, use of valuable resources, adoption of more environmentally friendly designs and technologies, and enhancement of environmental protection among its employees, business partners and customers. The policy of "Self-improvement, Teamwork, Performance and Contribution to Society" reflects Fosun's corporate values which are specifically aimed at implementation of the company's strategy for sustainable development. Through the implementation of a systematic, scientific and regulated management system, Fosun tries to establish a business model which will function in all sectors of society to build healthy natural and business ecosystems (Fosun 2015).

The type of business Fosun is involved in largely determines the company's attitude toward its employees as its most valuable asset. Fosun has aimed to become the best employer and the best platform for employees to realize their goals. It strongly protects employee interests through constant improvement of incentive schemes, care and services. Many efforts are directed toward personal development, cultivation of outstanding talent with an international mindset, and offering professional and systematic training and career development planning. Fosun also strengthens employee loyalty and commitment through improvement, innovation and a comprehensive and diversified benefits system. Fosun cares not only about its employees, but also about their families, for instance, through the all-round care program, "Children of Fosun employees". Thus, guided by the "self-improvement, teamwork, performance and contribution to society" principles, Fosun differentiates between various categories of employees and provides them with a bespoke treatment. It enhances caring for expatriate employees and their families, and develops specific models for junior and senior employees; it also identifies its core employees, outstanding employees and young employees with high potential and affords them opportunities for development (Fosun 2015).

To facilitate internal communication and interaction between management and employees, Fosun has introduced an intranet and a personnel service hotline mobile application "A La Ding" through which it delivers information about updates on remuneration and human resource policies. Moreover, a self-developed application "Fosun Pay" allows internal financial transactions (e.g. it could be used to organize virtual fairs). Fosun's employees can also get assistance in obtaining various certificates and permits, for example, from full-time service staff, which frees their time for learning and development. Fosun's employees are stimulated to use English in internal interactions and processes in line with the company's internationalization strategy and integration of expatriates. Such a corporate policy creates the grounds for productive knowledge and expertise sharing among local and overseas talented employees. To strengthen these processes and to accelerate expat integration into Fosun's corporate culture, the company has introduced induction courses and the "Partner" program.

Fosun's recruitment policy is aimed at attracting three types of talent: management talent, investment talent and financial talent (Join Fosun 2017). Fosun sees talented employees as being the basis of its competitive strengths and, thus, provides them with a wide set of opportunities for self-realization and development. The achievement of tasks through team work and building of an elite culture are considered to be favorable conditions for personal growth both for individual and company benefit.

Fosun constantly improves its talent development system, which includes a multifaceted selection of best practices. Employee training is aimed at obtaining a common understanding of Fosun's corporate culture and values. The training sessions and development workshops are organized and implemented by external consulting companies and universities or colleges, which use various techniques and sources for the training materials. A unified mechanism of promotion, guidance, communication and co-ordination allows the cultivation, development and retention of talent and the attraction of new talented personnel. Considering the accelerated speed of Fosun's internationalization into diverse foreign markets, it encourages the exchange of talent between domestic and overseas units focusing on cross-cultural management issues.

To co-align core elements of the corporate strategy with available human resources, Fosun has established a four-tier, pyramid-shaped, talent training system, which contains a Leadership Development Program for the general management level, a Management Excellence Program at the director level, a Young leader's program for all other managers and a Fo-star Program for graduates. Such an approach provides different learning paths for various categories of employees ensuring their rapid growth and development. For example, the Fo-star Program is a "1+1", two-year, talent fostering program, which supports talented graduates from top universities worldwide (e.g. from the Massachusetts Institute of Technology) who were recruited by the group. The Fo-star Program offers several training and development modules during the first year that range from training in financial modeling and valuation, to military training and more advanced training on leadership and team management (Fosun Group 2017 Campus Recruitment 2017). It helps new employees to better understand the corporate environment. Fosun sees this program as the foundation of its talent-echelon pyramid (Fosun Annual Report 2015). This program aims to reinforce Fosun's competitive position as a global company.

Fosun provides opportunities for internal learning and expertise exchange to develop talent. Its think-tank contains a large number of cases related to typical working situations and exceptional cases of excellent performance by the most talented employees, which allows free access to best practice. This stimulates the active professional training and sharing of investment experience through internal knowledge transfer and exchange. Moreover, such an approach helps to strengthen existing competences and develop new ones by utilizing the accumulated and shared experience at all management levels.

Professional talent training goes beyond just theoretical learning to become familiar with cases from the past. The company organizes a wide range of professional and specialized training focused on investment, insurance, finance, risk control and human resources; through these employees are encouraged to learn from best practice.

Another initiative introduced by Fosun includes the establishment of a lecture hall where employees can gain basic knowledge and skills to improve their efficiency and effectiveness at work. Fosun introduced a mobile learning platform, which offers various training courses in the form of "micro-lectures". The range of courses is constantly widened and updated while many courses are provided in the form of games to increase participant engagement.

To stimulate interfirm co-operation and knowledge sharing further, Fosun regularly organizes lunch-time sharing sessions where employees from different management levels discuss key issues associated with group activities and share their views on corporate strategies, investment perspectives and best practices. For example, in 2015 Fosun held 33 lunch-time sessions attended by more than 2300 employees (Fosun Annual Report 2015).

Fosun's activities in talent development are not limited to its internal environment. The company supports a wide range of projects organized by various organizations in China and abroad. For instance, Fosun provides support to the Youth Innovation Competition on Global Governance and Global Teenager Community among others. Such initiatives not only create a positive image of the company, but additionally allow it to form a pool of talent for recruitment.

Conclusion

This chapter presents the changes that have been taking place in the Chinese business environment in terms of managing human resources. Outlining the talent management practices of three leading Chinese companies—Geely, China Mobile and Fosun—we illustrate how a modern talent management system is integrated, adapted and co-aligned with traditional approaches to managing people in the Chinese culture.

Despite the differences in talent management approaches, there are a number of general strategies for companies implementing talent management in China. Most Chinese companies attend to their employees, considering them as a part of a large "family". Many companies have stopped pursuing a cheap labor strategy and are developing sophisticated attraction and retention policies and approaches for employing and keeping talented specialists. Such changes can be explained by a large staff turnover, which in some companies exceeds 40%. In addition, companies try to support not only their employees, but also members of their families, thus establishing trust and commitment relationships, which in turn encourage moral obligations in employees. Most Chinese companies are also active in team building, organizing seminars on personal and career growth, away-days, lecturing, and so on. Their leadership strives to ensure that every employee as an important part of the company team.

Many Chinese employees, in order to stay with a company for a long time, expect to be treated fairly in a transparent promotion system that supports them in career development and with rewards for outstanding performance. Employees change jobs more often if they do not see career prospects or when they have a more favorable job offer; that is why many Chinese companies have various contests and programs stimulating employees to develop themselves and obtain financial gain as well as moral satisfaction.

Chinese firms share a common understanding that talented people are much more effective in educating themselves. Therefore as Geely has created Beijing Geely University, and China Mobile has founded China Mobile University, many companies either interact with Chinese universities or create their own educational institutions and advanced training courses. One of the most common strategies is to attract talent in the early stages of education or training. All Chinese universities hold job fairs at least once a year where companies have the opportunity to introduce themselves and communicate with the most talented and promising students. A distinctive feature of large Chinese companies is their active interaction with government bodies, as well as participation in government programs.

Most Chinese talent management practices have their roots in the Confucian philosophy and in China's history and culture. The priority of gaining collective benefits at the expense of individual ones, the aptitude to be guided rather than to lead the team, the avoidance of both public reprimand and praise is typical in Chinese society. This creates a culture where talented Chinese employees painstakingly work for the benefit of the company and the country. The examples of Geely, China Mobile and Fosun confirm that this is possible. Moreover, instead of trying to dismiss specific attributes and build a Western-style corporation, Chinese firms adapt innovative practices and integrate them in traditional management approaches in order to create supportive conditions for employees to develop and exploit their talents.

The complex approaches to talent attraction and selection, as well as the systematic organization of educational and training programs offered by Geely, China Mobile and Fosun to their employees, have created a solid foundation for building and sustaining these firms' competitive advantages not only in the Chinese market but also overseas, which is especially important considering the international scope of their operations.

References

Alon, Ilan, Marc Fetscherin, and Philipp Gugler. 2012. *Chinese International Investments*. Houndmills, Basingstoke, Hampshire: Palgrave Macmillan.

Ang, Benjamin. 2014. Fosun: The Investment Edge. *Asia Insurance Review*. http://www3.asiainsurancereview.com/Magazine/ReadMagazineArticle?aid=35586. Accessed 21 July 2017.

Apple. 2013. China Mobile & Apple Bring iPhone to China Mobile's 4G & 3G Networks on January 17, 2014. https://www.apple.com/newsroom/2013/12/22China-Mobile-Apple-Bring-iPhone-to-China-Mobiles-4G-3G-Networks-on-January-17-2014/. Accessed 17 July 2017.

Beijing Geely University. 2017. http://www.bgu.edu.cn/. Accessed 17 July 2017.

Björkman, Ingmar, and Yuan Lu. 1999. The Management of Human Resources in Chinese–Western Joint Ventures. *Journal of World Business* 34 (3): 306–324.

China Mobile Limited Annual Report. 2006. http://www.chinamobileltd.com/en/ir/reports/ar2006.pdf. Accessed 17 July 2017.

China Mobile Limited Corporate Social Responsibility Report. 2006. http://www.chinamobileltd.com/en/ir/reports/ar2006/sd2006.pdf. Accessed 19 July 2017.

China Mobile Limited Sustainability Report. 2016. http://www.chinamobileltd. com/en/ir/reports/ar2016/sd2016.pdf. Accessed 21 July 2017.

China Mobile: Annual Report 2013. 2013. http://www.chinamobileltd.com/ en/ir/reports/ar2013.pdf. Accessed 21 July 2017.

China Mobile: Annual Report 2015. 2015. http://www.chinamobileltd.com/ en/ir/reports/ar2015.pdf. Accessed 21 July 2017.

Christian, Andrew. 2012. Geely, Volvo Signed a Technology Transfer Deal. https://www.4wheelsnews.com/auto/geely-volvo-signed-a-technology-transfer-deal-20677.html. Accessed 26 June 2017.

Connell, Julia, and Pauline Stanton. 2014. Skills and the Role of HRM: Towards a Research Agenda for the Asia Pacific Region. *Asia Pacific Journal of Human Resources* 52: 4–22.

Cooke, Fang L. 2012. *Human Resource Management in China: New Trends and Practices*. London: Routledge.

Cooke, Fang L., Debi S. Saini, and Jue Wang. 2014. Talent Management in China and India: A Comparison of Management Perceptions and Human Resource Practices. *Journal of World Business* 49 (2): 225–235.

eBeijing. 2017. Beijing Geely University. http://www.ebeijing.gov.cn/feature_2/ TourismOpenDay/Changping/t1290833.htm. Accessed 17 July 2017.

Fosun. 2017. http://ir.fosun.com/phoenix.zhtml?c=194273&p=irol-IRHome. Accessed 21 July 2017.

Fosun Annual Report. 2015. http://infopub.sgx.com/FileOpen/1%20Eng%20 EW656.ashx?App=Announcement&FileID=401681. Accessed 21 July 2017.

Fosun Group. 2016. https://www.fosun.com/wp-content/themes/fuxing/document/report-2016-s-en.pdf. Accessed 21 July 2017.

Fosun Group 2017 Campus Recruitment. 2017. http://asiancareerfair.mit.edu/ job/2016/9/19/fosun-group-2017-campus-recruitment. Accessed 21 July 2017.

FT 500. 2015. https://www.ft.com/ft500. Accessed 17 July 2017.

Geely. 2017. http://global.geely.com/. Accessed 26 June 2017.

Geely Announcement. 2015. Announcement of Interim Results for the Six Months Ended 30 June 2015. http://www.geelyauto.com.hk/core/files/ announcement/en/LTN20150819253.pdf. Accessed 17 July 2017.

Geely Annual Report 2016. 2016. http://www.geelyauto.com.hk/core/files/ financial/en/2016-02.pdf.

Geely Linkein Profile. 2017. https://www.linkedin.com/company/geely/ careers?trk=top_nav_careers. Accessed 17 July 2017.

GlobalCarBrands. 2015. https://www.globalcarsbrands.com/geely-logo-history-and-models/. Accessed 13 July 2017.

GSM Arena. 2017. https://www.gsmarena.com/glossary.php3?term=td-scdma. Accessed 17 July 2017.

Iles, Paul, Xin Chuai, and David Preece. 2010. Talent Management and Human Resource Management in Multinational Companies in Beijing: Definitions, Differences and Drivers. *Journal of World Business* 45 (2): 179–189.

Join Fosun. 2017. https://www.fosun.com/language/en/fxjob/1.html. Accessed 21 July 2017.

Jürgens, Ulrich, and Martin Krzywdzinski. 2013. Breaking Off from Local Bounds: Human Resource Management Practices of National Players in the BRIC. *International Journal of Automotive Technology and Management* 13 (2): 114–133.

Latukha, Marina. 2016. *Talent Management in Emerging Market Firms: Global Strategy and Local Challenges*. London: Palgrave Macmillan.

Li, Shenxue, and Hugh Scullion. 2006. Bridging the Distance: Managing Cross-Border Knowledge Holders. *Asia Pacific Journal of Management* 23 (1): 71–92.

Morningstar. 2011. http://quicktake.morningstar.com/err/abde/chl.pdf. Accessed 19 July 2017.

NetDimensions. 2013. Geely Partners with NetDimensions to Build a Top-class Learning and Talent Management Solution for China's Automobile Industry. http://www.netdimensions.com/company/press-room/view-news/geely-partners-with-netdimensions-to-build-a-top-class. Accessed 30 June 2017.

Ng, Ying C., and Noel Y.M. Ciu. 2004. Training and Enterprise Performance in Transition: Evidence from China. *The International Journal of Human Resource Management* 15 (4–5): 878–894.

Panibratov, Andrei. 2017. *International Strategy of Emerging Market Firms: Absorbing Global Knowledge and Building Competitive Advantage*. New York: Routledge.

Reuters. 2009. China's Geely to Pay Up to $40 Mln in DSI Purchase. https://www.reuters.com/article/geely/chinas-geely-to-pay-up-to-40-mln-in-dsi-purchase-idUSHKG6622220090328. Accessed 26 June 2017.

Rowley, Chris, and John Benson. 2002. Convergence and Divergence in Asian Human Resource Management. *California Management Review* 44 (2): 90–109.

Statista. 2017. https://www.statista.com/statistics/232705/number-of-employees-at-china-mobile/. Accessed 19 July 2017.

The Global 2000. 2017. https://www.forbes.com/global2000. Accessed 17 July 2017.

Top 10 Domestic Car Manufacturers in China. 2016. http://www.chinabangla.net/top-10-domestic-car-manufacturers-in-china/. Accessed 13 June 2017.

Tung, Rosalie L. 2007. The Human Resource Challenge to Outward Foreign Direct Investment Aspirations from Emerging Economies: The Case of China. *International Journal of Human Resource Management* 18 (5): 868–889.

Vorhauser-Smith, Sylvia. 2012. *Into China: Talent Management Essentials in a Land of Paradox*. Melbourne: Pageup People Research.

Wang, Lieke. 2011. A Case Study of the Acquisition of Swedish Volvo by Chinese Geely. Master thesis, Blekinge Tekniska Högskola. https://www.diva-portal.org/smash/get/diva2:829635/FULLTEXT01.pdf.

Warner, Malcolm. 2009. 'Making Sense' of Human Resource Management in China: Setting the Scene. *The International Journal of Human Resource Management* 20 (11): 2169–2184.

Xue, Yi. 2014. Talent Management Practices of Selected Human Resource Professionals in Middle to Large-sized Manufacturing MNC in China. PhD dissertation, The Pennsylvania State University. https://etda.libraries.psu.edu/files/final_submissions/10045. Accessed 13 July 2017.

Zhu, Cherrie J., Mingqiong Zhang, and Jie Shen. 2012. Paternalistic and Transactional Human Resource Management: The Nature and Transformation of Human Resource "Management in Contemporary China". *The International Journal of Human Resource Management* 23 (19): 3964–3982.

4

India: Growth Embedded in Tradition

Anna Veselova and Liudmila Veselova

India is an emerging economy that has become integrated in the global environment in two ways. On the one hand, many Western companies invest in it by outsourcing their support activities such as call centers, and, on the other hand, Indian companies have invested in developed and other emerging and developing economies through mergers and acquisitions. Due to its large population, India is one of the word's leaders by volume of a rather diverse labor force. A half of Indian workers are involved in agriculture, while others have predominant specializations in computer technology, healthcare and other categories. There are still significant differences between the country's urban and rural regions in

---

A. Veselova (✉)
Graduate School of Management, St. Petersburg State University,
St. Petersburg, Russia
e-mail: a.s.veselova@gsom.pu.ru

L. Veselova
School of International Relations, St. Petersburg State University,
St. Petersburg, Russia

© The Author(s) 2018
M. Latukha (ed.), *Talent Management in Global Organizations*,
Palgrave Studies of Internationalization in Emerging Markets,
https://doi.org/10.1007/978-3-319-76418-4_4

41

terms of education, infrastructure and healthcare, which accounts for different distributions and characteristics of the labor force (Latukha 2016).

The liberalization of the Indian economy, its restructuring and its economic transition brought about fierce competition between domestic and foreign business players. The inflow of foreign multinationals not only caused changes in revenue and market share distribution, but it significantly influenced the way organizations functioned (Bhatnagar 2007). The need for advanced management approaches and qualified personnel became evident. Despite close co-operation and intensive interaction with foreign partners, Indian companies still have management systems that have been formed under the influence of traditional Indian culture and values. Indian multiculturalism causes additional challenges for managerial mindsets in terms of family bonding and mutuality of obligations (Chatterjee 2007). Another important feature of Indian traditional society is the caste system which strongly influences a company's organizational architecture and management practice (HRM in India 2017). In the traditional Indian caste system, Brahmins (priests and teachers) were at the top, while Kshatriya (rulers and warriors), Vaishya (merchants and managers) and Shwdra (artisans and workers) were on lower levels. Until very recently, belonging to a particular caste was a determinant of position and promotion, but more so when employed by a company. Recruitment and career development were dependent on caste origin (Venkata Ratnam and Chandra 1996).

Strengthened global linkages and market liberalization forced a substantial transformation of attitudes toward human resource (HR) policies and practices (Gopalan and Rivera 1997). Along with an increasing number of university graduates, the number of working positions that could be taken by newcomers stayed the same, which worsened the unemployment situation. This has been coupled with concerns about the retention of knowledge workers (Bhatnagar 2007). To confront these issues, an increasing number of foreign and domestic firms have been implementing formal talent management systems (Bhatnagar and Budhwar 2009). Many companies have been enthusiastic about adopting talent management practices, especially those associated with foreign multinationals.

The working environment in India can be characterized as a "family culture", which assumes that it is more company-oriented rather than person-oriented; however, some companies feature a hybrid orientation when both collectivist and individualistic values are of equal importance. Due to the strong cultural influence, many Indian employees lack initiative and feel much more comfortable when being guided (Sparrow and Budhwar 1997). This definitely affects the way they are treated by senior management. In contrast, Indian managers have a rather paternalistic approach to leadership and their corporate status spreads over other social spheres (Sparrow and Budhwar 1997). Indian employers emphasize individual and department goals to measure key performance areas and thus determine which employees should be trained first. However, it has taken a long time to co-align the social and financial objectives of companies in order to develop personal skills and boost wider professional development. Many Indian companies do not have explicitly formulated approaches to performance measurement and still follow vague procedures for employee evaluation. Thus, paternalistic manager-subordinate relationships affect the individual ratings of employees due to the fact that managers tend to overrate poor performers who they like (Amba-Rao et al. 2000).

Talent motivation and rewarding practices have undergone a progressive transformation. If before liberalization individual pay was not correlated with individual performance, after this, performance-based pay was first introduced for top management levels, and only after this was the application of performance-based compensation widened to include all managers and key employees (Budhwar 2003). Some leading Indian companies have applied performance-based remuneration; however, they do it mostly on a group basis rather than on an individual basis. In contrast to Chinese companies, who feel a real need for fresh talent as they are losing many of their best employees, Indian companies do not have such a problem and favor internal recruiting (Latukha 2016).

In this chapter, we discuss talent management practices and challenges in Indian companies. We elaborate on what the good or best talent management strategy is and what else is important for firms from India when managing talented employees in comparison with other countries in the Asia-Pacific region.

Infosys: Promotion Perspectives

Infosys Ltd. is a large Indian multinational corporation that provides business consulting, information technology (IT) and outsourcing services. According to its 2017 revenue, Infosys ranked as the third largest Indian IT services company (Revolvy 2017). It provides end-to-end business solutions for business performance improvement for customers operating in various industries from all over the world. Infosys offers IT, engineering, consulting and business process outsourcing (BPO) services, products and platforms. The company's end-to-end business solutions include business IT services (application development and maintenance, independent validation services, infrastructure management, engineering services comprising product engineering and life-cycle solutions and business process management), consulting and systems integration services (consulting, enterprise solutions, systems integration and advanced technologies) (Forbes 2017a), and product and business platforms and solutions to accelerate intellectual property-led innovation (e.g. Finacle, Infosys Nia, Infosys Information Platform, Edge Verve, Panaya and Skava) (Infosys 2017a).

Today, Infosys is a global company serving customers in more than 50 countries and supplying them with the most progressive and innovative technologies (SAP Hybris 2017). Infosys helps its customers generate more value through their transformation and renovation in line with changes in the global environment. Providing strategic consulting, operational leadership, and the co-creation of breakthrough solutions, such as mobility, sustainability, big data and cloud computing, Infosys contributes to strengthening its customers' competitiveness. To achieve the company's strategic objectives and build a sustainable corporation with relevance for customers and investors, Infosys prioritizes the principles of "new" and "renew" for all its businesses, in other words developing solutions and service offerings, clients and employees' engagement processes and operational processes (Infosys Limited 2015). This approach is reflected in its major strategic focus. First of all, Infosys aims to provide differentiated solutions and service offerings to improve its customers' productivity, obtain better accuracy and reduce overall costs with the use of automation and artificial intelligence. Infosys has already developed and introduced such advanced differentiated platforms as Edge suite, FinacleTM and Infosys information platform, and is continuing to invest in emerging mobile and digital technologies and big data analytics. Moreover, Infosys implements an expansion strategy by initiating strategic alliances and acquisitions which target leading technology software providers. In this way, Infosys masters existing and augments new expertise, penetrates new markets or strengthens positions in existing ones, and accelerates the execution of its corporate strategies. Infosys emphasizes building trustworthy and impactful relationships with its clients. Apart from focusing on key products and services, Infosys has created a corporate culture which spurs delivery of innovative products and services to its customers. To create innovation supportive structures, ecosystems and economic models, Infosys applies design thinking methods to develop solutions through bridging its knowledge of particular industries and the latest advances of emerging technologies. Infosys has already invested millions of dollars to gain access to the innovation networks of start-ups and educational institutions and, consequently, to directly benefit from new thinking and business models that the company could adopt.

While providing up-to-date solutions to its customers, Infosys constantly monitors and optimizes its operational processes in order to increase agility and reduce costs. Infosys continually re-evaluates critical cross-functional processes, benchmarking them with best practices, and refining them to co-align with corporate strategies and goals in the utilization of resources, distribution of employees around the globe, as well as in other areas. Thus the company understands the relevance of acquiring and retaining high-performing and talented employees to secure long-term competitiveness.

Infosys has a hybrid talent definition and treats talent in a rather universalistic and individual-based (industry-specific) way with the aim of creating a pool of future leaders. Considering its employees to be the most valuable company asset, Infosys has introduced the Fast Track Program, designed exclusively to identify high performers and to provide them with challenging opportunities to grow within the organization. This program has boosted the morale of the company and consequently improved productivity (The Hindu Business Line 2014). Infosys creates an entrepreneurial environment to empower talent by introducing programs which recognize and reward performance, provide opportunities for constant acquisition and development of knowledge and skills, and prioritize openness, integrity and respect for its employees (Infosys Limited 2015).

One of the company's key strategic focuses is the attraction and retention of international, diverse, motivated and high-performing employees. Infosys recruitment is targeted at engineering departments of top Indian universities, as well as campuses in the United States, the UK, Australia and China. To find the best talent committed and able to strengthen its brand, Infosys has implemented a rigorous multi-level selection process including written tests and interviews (Infosys Limited 2015). The company strives to keep the title of "employer of choice" by attracting high-performers who can support its competitive position in the global technology services industry.

To gain access to new talent, Infosys has launched several programs with academic institutions in an attempt to build a partnership model that will enhance the competences of a pool of highly capable talent, especially in the IT area. For example, Infosys Spark is a one-day exploratory program, oriented to high school and college students from different age groups in urban and suburban areas, which allows assessment of students' readiness for work in the IT industry, as well as their aspirations (Campus Connect 2017). The flagship industry-academia partnership program, Campus Connect, has launched electives to help engineering colleges develop new curricula (Globe 2017). Another initiative is Aspirations 2020, a platform helping students from engineering colleges prepare themselves to become smart professionals (Aspirations 2020 2017). This initiative includes a three-stage contest testing and training students in teamwork skills and competences in programming.

According to one of Infosys' top HR managers, the three key factors that have enabled Infosys to attract, develop and retain the best talent are a clear focus on succession planning and leadership, a unique career architecture and a closely aligned training and development program (Inside HR 2014). Talent management is separated from traditional HR functions and mostly considered as "a shared partnership between the business and the executives, with HR as a facilitator" (Inside HR 2014).

The company appointed a global Head for Talent Fulfillment, which allowed the entire process—starting from recruitment to enablement and fulfillment (including training and mobility)—to be consolidated under one single function, which stimulates agility and speed of decision execution (Mishra 2014).

Leadership and succession planning is implemented, first of all, by the Infosys Leadership Institute (ILI) which is tasked with the identification of high-potential performers who are capable of taking "destination jobs", such as chief financial officer (Inside HR 2014). Its goal is to assist potential leaders in developing and executing their personal development plans through initiatives such as "leading value creation" (Infosys 2017b). ILI is focused on the preparation and development of leaders for current and future leadership positions. It provides a wide range of development programs, such as classroom training, individual coaching sessions, experience sharing, and leaders' teaching sessions ("Leaders Teach") to managers from both Infosys headquarters and subsidiaries (Infosys Limited 2015). Some particular programs are developed and delivered in partnership with top universities, for example the Global Leadership Program developed by Stanford Graduate School of Business (Globe 2017).

Infosys has also taken the lead in the development of "Infoscions" through training. Its training center in Mysuru is the world's largest corporate university (Revolvy 2017). The company's Education, Training & Assessment Plan focuses on talent development, with a number of continuous education programs covering technology, business and process issues, to keep the competences of experienced employees up-to-date and relevant for its fast-changing operational requirements (Infosys 2017b). In addition, Infosys has made significant investment in hardware and software assets to boost infrastructure capabilities and to create a unique learning experience for its employees. Infosys introduced an integrated learning platform covering teaching, hands-on experience and assessments of in-class training. Moreover, this was supplemented by mobile app-based learning to increase participation and self-directed learning (Infosys Limited 2015).

Infosys is an Indian firm with a strong commitment to open appraisal systems gathering 360-degree feedback (Infosys Limited 2015), which serves as a basis for performance appraisal and innovation, and support and training of poorly performing employees. A series of measures have been initiated to empower employees through trust and accountability. Infosys has overhauled its performance management system to bring in more objectivity, created an internal marketplace for employees to work on challenging assignments and strengthened its focus on providing a transparent and safe working environment. The firm is guided by its value system (C-LIFE), which motivates attitudes and actions and includes client value, leadership by example, integrity and transparency, fairness and excellence (Infosys 2017c).

The company trains its employees to think like designers by using rationality and creativity to design software, processes and strategies within an iterative process of trying, testing and improving upon new ideas until they serve a clear purpose. To be closer to their customers and fully understand their needs, Infosys implements the five-step approach, oriented at looking around and learning from others, doing something over and beyond the scope of a project, doing something better than before, articulating the value of innovation in a way that matters to users, and sharing that knowledge with others (Infosys 2017d). Each idea is articulated, considered and evaluated on its potential, viability, feasibility, desirability and clarity. Hence, employees have a higher motivation to create and innovate and this will impact on their appraisals.

In terms of mobility, Infosys enables multiple job choices for talent within the company. The "Learn, Practice, Apply" framework provides information on positions and lists developmental opportunities. The stated goal is to enhance employee expertise in the current position and to ensure an employee's capacity to perform in another role (higher or lateral) through up-skilling or cross-skilling. As a consequence, time spent in a job position is divided into several phases, for example at the Pathfinder NEXT stage, an employee can work on internal projects and assignments with access to technology, business domains and other service lines. The other project, SmartStaffing, provides access to a market portal which allows employees who are not working on any project to contact delivery managers directly and apply for any vacant projects (Sengupta 2012).

The dynamism of the IT industry forces the company to stay innovative. To reach its goals, the company has to work hard to attract and develop its talent. Understanding the crucial role of human capital for its survival and prosperity, Infosys heavily invests to create favorable conditions for its employees.

Oil and Natural Gas Corporation Limited (ONGC): Path to Excellence

Oil and Natural Gas Corporation Limited (ONGC) is India's largest multinational oil and gas exploration and production company founded in 1956 and headquartered in Dehradun, Uttarakhand, India (IBEF 2017). It is engaged in the exploration and production of oil, natural gas and liquefied petroleum gas. The company also focuses on related business areas like the processing of crude oil and natural gas, oil field services, transportation of oil and natural gas, and production of value added products (IBEF 2017).

ONGC has the best infrastructure and state-of-the-art seismic data acquisition, processing and interpretation facilities. It also uses one of the top 10 virtual reality interpretation facilities in addition to having one of the biggest enterprise resource planning (ERP) systems in Asia. With the use of the world's best business practices for modernization, expansion and integration, ONGC has managed to create alliances with corporations such as Transocean, Schlumberger, Halliburton, Baker Hughes, IPR, Petrobras, Norsk, ENI and Shell. ONGC operates the longest pipeline in India which accounts for more than 26,600 kilometers, including sub-sea pipelines (ONGC 2017a).

With the aim of being a global leader in the energy business, ONGC is dedicated to leveraging competitive advantage in research and development (R&D) and technology with its employees' competences (ONGC 2017b). The focus on innovative development and people brings the issue of talent management to the core of ONGC's organizational culture, based on strong intellectual property, information, knowledge, skills and experience (Perspective Plan 2030 2013).

ONGC possesses a wide range of in-house service capabilities in all areas of exploration and production of oil and gas, as well as some other related oil-field services, which determines the need for highly specialized and competent staff. It employs over 18,000 technically competent, experienced scientists, engineers and specialist professionals, most of who are graduates from the best Indian and foreign universities (ONGC 2017c). Apart from specialists in geology, geophysics, geochemistry and engineering, there are highly qualified experts in finance, human resource management and IT (ONGC 2017c).

ONGC sees its talent management role in the adoption and continuous innovation of its talent management practices to support employee engagement, empowerment and enthusiasm. The company was awarded for its HRM practices with the "Best Employer" award, "Voice of Employee" award in 2013, "Most Attractive Employer in the Energy Sector", "Human Resource Management Excellence Award" and a number of others (Indiamart 2017a). These acknowledgments reflect a well-thought-through HR policy. It prioritizes the culture of integrity, belongingness, teamwork, accountability and innovation. To strengthen its competitive advantage, ONCG attracts and nurtures, engages and retains the most talented candidates on the Indian job market. The firm places a strong emphasis on continuous enhancement of employee competences. It believes that a comfortable and joyous work environment stimulates higher individual performance and has an overall positive impact on organizational performance. Conducting regular benchmarking checks against global talent management practices, ONGC ensures high standards through upgrading its talent management approaches. Measuring and auditing talent performance allows further improvements in talent management. ONGC conducts several business games every year. They have two objectives: to improve the business capabilities of company's executives in a competitive scenario under simulated business constraints; and to test their abilities through business quizzes, business simulations and case-study presentations (ONGC Annual Report 2016–17 2017).

Talent parameters are also improved through individual mentoring and coaching to nurture and groom fresh talent new to the company, and an engagement survey is used to monitor loyalty and dedication. To stimulate excellent performance, ONGC constantly reconsiders welfare benefits to employees and their families; in particular, it provides medical care, education, housing, and social security (ONGC 2017a). The company actively promotes a work-life balance and integrates employees' families into the organizational environment. It educates its employees in terms of corporate social responsibility (CSR) and sustainability.

ONGC's talent management policies focus on talent acquisition and retention, training and development, compensation management and social security. As for talent attraction and recruitment, the company hires the best available talent in various disciplines through a rigorous selection process. ONGC advertises any vacancies in the newspapers and online. Only the applications specific to the advertisements and received during the stipulated time limit are considered. Applications that are without reference to specific notifications are neither considered nor replied to. ONGC follows an openness policy when full information about the position, including the salary, is publicly available. In addition, ONGC makes regular visits to the campuses of leading educational institutions and headhunts critical talent that meets its need.

In terms of training and development, an integral part of ONGC's employee-centered policies is its thrust on knowledge upgrading and development. The firm partners with global human resource consulting firms to create a pool of accredited mentors who can support its employees. ONGC has also implemented a number of initiatives to promote leadership programs within the company. For example, the development program "EXPONENT" aims to train future leaders for individual effectiveness and team-building. ONGC Academy is a corporate university in technical and management sciences and develops petroleum industry-related skills. The ONGC Academy is a major agency responsible for developing the human resources of ONGC. Previously known as the Institute of Management Development (IMD), ONGC Academy, along with seven other training institutes, plays a key role in keeping the knowledge and competences of the workforce up-to-date.

As for employee retention, the company takes care of each and every employee. ONGC has in-built systems of recognition and rewards which are implemented systematically and updated periodically. There is a complex system of measures for employee compensation and welfare, which is modified regularly in response to changing requirements. To enhance productivity, ONGC has introduced a productivity bonus scheme, job and quarterly incentives, reserve establishment honorarium, a roll out of succession planning models, and provided group incentives for cohesive team work, among others (ONGC 2017c). The company's remuneration package is considered to be one of the best among all Indian companies. It includes basic pay, a variable allowance, 47% of basic pay as a cafeteria allowance, a house rent allowance, a conveyance maintenance reimbursement, a contributory provident fund with unparalleled medical facilities for employees and their dependants, gratuities, a self-contributory post-retirement scheme, a composite social security scheme and soft loans (ONGC 2017d).

Motivation plays an important role in talent development. The company has incorporated several schemes to keep its employees motivated such as a reward and recognition scheme, a grievance handling scheme and a suggestion scheme. Significant labor turnover that is expected in the Indian oil and gas sector will lead to a shrinking pool of talent with expertise in the area, which in turn may create a knowledge gap between new employees and experienced industry leaders. As a number of highly qualified staff is facing retirement, staff retention has become a key concern for the company. Talent retention, coupled with talent attraction, is a major issue; yet, financial incentives like performance-based remuneration have not been developed. As a consequence, competence mapping is a priority due to the great number of highly specialized jobs. Thus, it is a key task for ONGC to develop a pool of talent to secure the procurement of skilled workers.

ONGC's talent management policy has always given preference to a large and multi-disciplined workforce. It also acknowledges the significance of good industrial relations and tries to cultivate them. By enabling employees to participate in management, ONGC develops their engagement and dedication. ONGC's employees are provided with an opportunity to be involved in informative, consultative, associative and administrative forums which stimulate interactive participation and foster an innovative culture (ONGC 2017c).

Promoting respect and dignity as key corporate values, ONGC teaches its employees to be conscious about their responsibility to society. For this purpose, it has developed guidelines for socio-economic development programs, which address education, healthcare and family welfare, community development, promotion of sports and culture, calamity relief, development of infrastructural facilities and the socially and economically weaker sections of society (ONGC 2017c).

To conclude, the adoption of talent management practices by ONGC has ensured that it stays at the forefront of recruitment and retention of talent, has created a positive image of the company as an employer and has improved its overall performance. In contrast to Infosys, which focuses on employee development, ONGC emphasizes talent employment and retention. Such an approach could be partly explained by industry specificity, which is mostly associated with traditional technologies and incremental, innovative transformations. In such conditions, the most optimal talent management strategy is to keep existing, highly competent employees. Though there is a constant inflow of newcomers, they mostly replace those who leave the company owing to natural turnover rather than those who are less efficient. This creates a less competitive, but more comfortable for employees, working environment, increasing their loyalty and dedication to the company.

Larsen & Toubro (L&T): First-Comer in Talent Management

Larsen & Toubro (L&T) is a multinational conglomerate with headquarters in Mumbai, India. It was founded in Bombay (Mumbai) in 1938 by two Danish engineers, Henning Holck-Larsen and Søren Kristian Toubro (Shreyas Technologies 2017). The company is engaged in core, high-impact sectors of the economy and its integrated capabilities span the entire spectrum of "design to deliver" (Indiamart 2017b). L&T is a diversified conglomerate operating in investment, construction, engineering and manufacturing sectors with additional interests in electricity, automation and IT, among others. In particular, L&T operates in the engineering and construction of buildings and factories, transportation infrastructure, heavy civil infrastructure, power transmission and distribution, and water and renewable energy projects. It develops turnkey solutions for coal-based and gas-based thermal power plants, including power generation equipment with associated systems. L&T's metallurgical activities include manufacturing and supply of critical equipment and systems to core sectors such as fertilizers, refinery, petro-chemical, chemical, oil and gas, thermal and nuclear power, aerospace and defense. It also manufactures rubber processing machinery and cast-ings, industrial valves, construction equipment and industrial products. Moreover, L&T is also active in information technologies and integrated engineering services, retail and corporate finance, housing finance, infra-structure finance, general insurance, asset management of mutual fund schemes and related advisory services (Forbes 2017b). Such diversifica-tion requires well-thought-through complex solutions in all functional areas of the company's activities, including talent management. L&T's activities define the strategies and approaches used by the company to attract and treat its employees.

L&T employs a team of more than 50,000 young professionals who work both in India and abroad (Larsen & Toubro 2017a). It is quite impres-sive that 50% of L&T's employees are aged below 30 and the company constantly attracts graduates with engineering backgrounds (Larsen & Toubro 2017a). L&G tries to create an environment in which experience and professionalism could be combined with a culture of trust and care. The company stimulates its employees to train their skills and develop their tal-ents through various leadership opportunities, as they are believed to ensure the development of L&T's competitive advantage and its stable growth. To explore and empower employees' potential, the company formulates chal-lenging tasks and assignments for its talent (Larsen & Toubro 2017a). The well-articulated and caring talent management policy of L&T makes the company an attractive employer, which is confirmed by the award from a Randstad survey for being one of "India's Top 10 Most Attractive Employers". L&T is the only engineering, construction and manufacturing company in India that entered this list. Moreover, L&G is in the top fifth of "Best Companies to Work For" (Larsen & Toubro 2013).

Considering its continuous innovative development, L&T has a par-ticular focus on talented employees, and it defines talent more on a specialist and individual basis, first of all, paying attention to diplomas and engineers' profiles. Employee assessment is performed on a regular basis in order to identify best performers and enroll them in a seven-step leadership development process. Talent management policies and prac-tices are designed to enable employees to realize their full potential and are centered around creation of an environment that attracts, nurtures and rewards talent. The company is forming a unique ecosystem through the attraction and retention of engineering talent who are provided with the opportunities to build their careers within L&G and benefit from a long cycle of professional development. L&T attracts talent not only from Indian educational institutions, but from all over the world (Larsen & Toubro Annual Report 2014–2015 2015). L&T provides a structured, seven-stage, leadership development program, conducted in collaboration with the world's top management institutes. This supports building of a robust talent pipeline at all levels (Larsen & Toubro Annual Report 2014–2015 2015). L&T is especially attractive for young candidates as it values their intellectual capital and offers a mix of opportunities, responsibilities, growth and purpose.

L&T sees the constitution of talent pools as one of its main objectives: for example with the Power Projects Professional Program in its power business, the company aims to supply project managers with the latest knowledge in their area, form a reserve of experts and increase the overall skill inventory for the implementation of mega projects. The firm's integrated talent management framework model enhances employee capabilities and nurtures both professional and behavioral competences (Larsen & Toubro 2017b). A comfortable working culture motivates L&T's employees to think creatively and beyond the conventional borders, to innovate and improve their individual and organizational performance.

Talent acquisition is a prime concern for all L&T's businesses, especially considering the company's growing involvement in international projects. L&T visits more than 100 university campuses looking for talented and promising engineers and offering them opportunities for building their careers in the company (Larsen & Toubro 2017c). The selection process is rigorous and is not limited to written tests and formal interviews. To meet selection criteria and join the company, candidates should match L&T's value system, have a strong theoretical base with profound knowledge in the area, and have the skills to convert theoretical knowledge into practice. Moreover, commitment and a passion for excellence are also among the selection criteria. All newcomers, when joining L&T's team, go through an induction program, a kind of "finishing school", which consists of technical projects and product simulations, and modules on various engineering and soft skills. The program is a good mix of technical and behavioral training combined with fun-filled activities such as games, contests and cultural events (Larsen & Toubro 2017c). The program not only provides employees with firm-specific knowledge, but also helps them integrate better and faster into the corporate environment.

Employees are supported in developing leadership skills by a wide range of activities from Mentor-Buddy systems to well-defined leadership development programs. L&G does a lot to align its talent management practices with global standards, constantly innovating and institutionalizing them. L&T stimulates its employees to grow and develop their talent by fostering a strong learning culture (Larsen & Toubro 2017d). It has a focus on several important areas, among which are knowledge and skills extension, leadership development, corporate citizenship fortification, and action-oriented training. To support continuous life-long learning, L&T implements a structured developmental program, realized both by company specialists and by partner universities. To deliver up-to-date knowledge to its employees, it has initiated regular e-publications, exhibitions and guest lectures.

In-house training is mainly delivered by the Leadership Development Academy, which offers excellent facilities and infrastructure to facilitate knowledge acquisition and dissemination within the company (Leadership Development Academy 2017). Considering project management as one of the company's strongest competences, L&T established the L&T Institute of Project Management that creates conditions for aligning knowledge and work experience and for applying experiential learning to real projects (Larsen & Toubro 2017d). Beyond in-house training, employees can be sent abroad to take courses on MBA programs offered by top universities (Larsen & Toubro Annual Report 2014–2015 2015).

Furthermore, L&T has developed and successfully introduced a robust learning management system (Any Time Learning, ATL) to provide various learning opportunities for its employees outside India. A comprehensive e-learning portal, ATL offers multiple online programs and courses which are available 24/7. It also provides access to online databases, references, management videos, e-books and journals (Larsen & Toubro 2017d).

A five-step leadership development process is specifically designed for high-skilled managers. The company's Center of Excellence for improvement initiatives promotes a structured approach to the creation of a coaching culture. It offers programs for the development and training of coaches and focuses on specialized programs such as value engineering, six sigma, total quality management, gemba, kaizen and so on (Larsen & Toubro 2017d).

Regarding talent motivation and reward practices, there are many annual and event-based programs such as long service awards, employee awards, sales awards and technology awards which stimulate better work performance. L&T cares a lot about statutory and regulatory norms regarding personnel treatment in terms of payment of wages and benefits to its employees. Remuneration for directors, key management personnel and key employees is based on their performance. In India, L&T has become a pioneer in developing performance management via open assessment systems.

L&T believes diversity and equal opportunities are the key driving forces for the creation of a motivating work environment which could attract new talent. The company has introduced new structures, processes and routines to enables its employees to integrate better in society. It prioritizes non-discrimination on the basis of caste, religion or political affiliation, gender, nationality, age, sexual orientation and disability. In this respect, it significantly differs from the vast majority of other Indian companies.

To conclude, L&T is a pioneer in the development of talent management practices and leadership development in India. Talent retention is also important for the company. It has an increasing need for talented employees due to the intensive development of technology, innovation and internationalization.

Conclusion

In this chapter, we consider how talent management processes in India are adapting to the new realities of the global business environment. Transformation of the traditional company culture in India started later than in China. A number of R&D centers, both autonomous and affiliated with large Indian companies, have emerged to support and/or lead in domestic talent development processes. Through the analysis of three cases of successful Indian companies (i.e. Infosys, ONGC and L&T), we identify those talent management practices which are critical for building a competitive advantage in the face of greater global competition.

It is worth noting that tradition still has a big impact on doing business in India. Unlike in China, where a talented young employee can join a team of top managers, in India, apart from a strict hierarchy, the caste system still prevails. This complicates talent management implementation. Protocol plays an important role, which is expressed in the tradition that each employee performs a specific task corresponding to his/her position. This is why it is difficult to promote talent development and strengthen the ability of people to have a wider vision and work "outside the box". In India, as in China and Korea, family ties play an important role, which has an impact on business relations. This is even more visible due to the fact that, in general, there are two types of companies: a family business, in which traditions are prioritized, and modern companies, which are gradually integrating best Western approaches, including talent management practices.

Similar to Chinese companies that also put huge effort into proper selection, development and motivation of personnel, some Indian companies have made significant investments in the creation of their own educational infrastructure. Another important aspect associated with employee training and development is the co-operation and partnership between big firms and world-class universities to upgrade the knowledge base. Regardless of the economic sector in which the company operates, management teams are aware that there is no chance of domestic and international market success without substantial investment in human capital to be able to address the need for innovation and performance improvement.

References

Amba-Rao, Sita C., Joseph A. Petrick, Jatinder N.D. Guta, and Thomas J. Von der Embse. 2000. Comparative Performance Appraisal Practices and Management Values among Foreign and Domestic Firms in India. *International Journal of Human Resource Management* 11 (1): 60–89.

Aspirations 2020. 2017. Aspirations2020 Programming Contest. campusconnect.infosys.com/aspirations/staticpages/ap/programmingcontest.aspx. Accessed 12 Aug 2017.

Bhatnagar, Jyotsna. 2007. Talent Management Strategy of Employee Engagement in Indian ITES Employees: Key to Retention. *Employee Relations* 29 (6): 640–663.

Bhatnagar, Jyotsna, and Pawan Budhwar. 2009. *The Changing Face of People Management in India*. London: Routledge.

Budhwar, Pawan. 2003. Employment Relations in India. *Employee Relations* 25 (2): 132–148.

Campus Connect. 2017. Spark. campusconnect.infosys.com/spark/Home.aspx. Accessed 12 Aug 2017.

Chatterjee, Samir R. 2007. Human Resource Management in India: 'Where from' and 'Where to?'. *Research and Practice in Human Resource Management* 15 (2): 92–103.

Forbes. 2017a. Top Multinational Performance Ranking 2017. www.forbes.com/companies/infosys/. Accessed 12 Aug 2017.

———. 2017b. Global 2000: World's Best Employers 2017 Ranking. www.forbes.com/companies/larsen-toubro/. Accessed 20 Aug 2017.

Globe. 2017. Infosys Ltd. www.globecapital.com/company-information/directors-report/Infosys/2806. Accessed 12 Aug 2017.

Gopalan, Suresh, and Joan B. Rivera. 1997. Gaining a Perspective on Indian Value Orientations: Implications for Expatriate Managers. *International Journal of Organizational Analysis* 5 (2): 156–179.

HRM in India. 2017. www.whatishumanresource.com/hrm-in-india. Accessed 8 Aug 2017.

IBEF. 2017. Oil and Natural Gas Corporation Ltd (ONGC). www.ibef.org/industry/oil-gas-india/showcase/oil-and-natural-gas-corporation-ltd. Accessed 20 Aug 2017.

Indiamart. 2017a. ONGC Energy Centre. https://www.indiamart.com/proddetail/ongc-energy-centre-7007499462.html. Accessed 20 Aug 2017.

———. 2017b. Larsen & Toubro. www.indiamart.com/company/4074897/aboutus.html. Accessed 20 Aug 2017.

Infosys. 2017a. Products and Platforms. www.infosys.com/products-and-platforms/. Accessed 12 Aug 2017.

———. 2017b. Careers. www.infosys.com/careers/. Accessed 12 Aug 2017.

———. 2017c. Our Culture. www.infosys.com/careers/culture/our-values/. Accessed 12 Aug 2017.

———. 2017d. The Infosys Approach. www.infosys.com/careers/culture/our-approach/. Accessed 12 Aug 2017.

Infosys Limited. 2015. https://www.infosys.com/investors/reports-filings/annual-report/form20f/Documents/form20F-2015.pdf. Accessed 12 Aug 2017.

Inside HR. 2014. Infosys' 3 Keys to Talent Management. www.insidehr.com.au/infosys-3-keys-to-talent-management/. Accessed 12 Aug 2017.

Larsen & Toubro. 2013. L&T in Top 5 'Best Companies to Work For'. www.larsentoubro.com/media/27686/businesstoday18072013.pdf. Accessed 20 Aug 2017.

———. 2017a. Overview. www.larsentoubro.com/corporate/careers/overview/. Accessed 20 Aug 2017.

———. 2017b. Employee Engagement. www.larsentoubro.com/corporate/sustainability/employee-engagement/. Accessed 20 Aug 2017.

———. 2017c. Campus Recruitment. www.larsentoubro.com/corporate/careers/campus-recruitment/. Accessed 20 Aug 2017.

———. 2017d. Learning & Development. www.larsentoubro.com/corporate/careers/learning-development/. Accessed 20 Aug 2017.

Larsen & Toubro Annual Report 2014–2015. 2015. investors.larsentoubro.com/upload/AnnualRep/FY2015AnnualRepL&T%20AR%202015_LRS.pdf. Accessed 20 Aug 2017.

Latukha, Marina. 2016. *Talent Management in Emerging Market Firms: Global Strategy and Local Challenges*. London: Palgrave Macmillan.

Leadership Development Academy. 2017. www.lnt-lda.com/about.php. Accessed 20 Aug 2017.

Mishra, Bibhu R. 2014. Infosys Broadens Scope of Talent Management. www.business-standard.com/article/companies/infosys-broadens-scope-of-talent-management-114011100672_1.html. Accessed 12 Aug 2017.

ONGC. 2017a. Corporate Profile. www.ongcindia.com/wps/wcm/connect/ongcindia/Home/company/corporate-profile. Accessed 20 Aug 2017.

———. 2017b. Vision & Mission. www.ongcindia.com/wps/wcm/connect/ongcindia/Home/company/vision-mission. Accessed 20 Aug 2017.

———. 2017c. Human Resource. http://www.ongcindia.com/wps/wcm/connect/ongcindia/Home/company/interface/human-resource. Accessed 20 Aug 2017.

———. 2017d. Recruitment Policy. hwww.ongcindia.com/wps/wcm/connect/ongcindia/Home/Careers/recruitment-policy/#crprofile. Accessed 20 Aug 2017.

ONGC Annual Report 2016–17. 2017. http://www.ongcindia.com/wps/wcm/PDF/AnnualReport/AR201617.pdf. Accessed 12 Jan 2018.

Perspective Plan 2030. 2013. www.ongcindia.com/wps/wcm/connect/7f74ae71-9f59-4a49-8e62-496066eb81cc/PP2030_VendorsMeet+July+2013.pdf?MOD=AJPERES&CACHEID=7f74ae71-9f59-4a49-8e62-496066eb81cc. Accessed 20 Aug 2017.

Revolvy. 2017. Infosys. https://www.revolvy.com/main/index.php?s=Infosys. Accessed 12 Aug 2017.

SAP Hybris. 2017. Infosys Limited. www.hybris.com/en/partners/details/infosyslimited. Accessed 12 Aug 2017.

Sengupta, Devina. 2012. Infosys: Measures that the Company Is Taking to Keep Up Its Bench Morale. economictimes.indiatimes.com/articleshow/14848510.cms?utm_source=contentofinterest&utm_medium=text&utm_campaign=cppst. Accessed 12 Aug 2017.

Shreyas Technologies. 2017. Larsen & Toubro Limited. shreyastech.com/web/company/larsen-toubro-limited/. Accessed 20 Aug 2017.

Sparrow, Paul R., and Pawan Budhwar. 1997. Competition and Change: Mapping the Indian HRM Recipe against World-wide Patterns. *Journal of World Business* 32 (3): 224–242.

The Hindu Business Line. 2014. Infosys to Begin Fast-Track Career Programme for High Performers Soon. www.thehindubusinessline.com/companies/infosys-to-begin-fasttrack-career-programme-for-high-performers-soon/article6114775.ece. Accessed 12 Aug 2017.

Venkata Ratnam, C.S., and V. Chandra. 1996. Sources of Diversity and the Challenge before Human Resource Management in India. *International Journal of Manpower* 17 (4/5): 76–96.

5

Korea: Culture and Reality

Anna Veselova and Liudmila Veselova

South Korea is one of the leading economic powers in Asia, the sixth largest exporter and twelfth largest economy in the world (U.S. News 2017). In a short period of time, the country has transformed itself from one of the poorest countries in the world to a more developed and high-income country, often referred to as one of the Asian Tiger economies. This phenomenon is called the "economic miracle", or the Miracle on the Han River (Revolvy 2017a). South Korean economic growth in the period 1960–1990s was to a large extent driven by huge industrial conglomerates, known as chaebols, which were often owned by people, families or clans who had close relationships to government. At the same time, the South Korean economy became dualistic with a sophisticated

---

A. Veselova (✉)
Graduate School of Management, St. Petersburg State University,
St. Petersburg, Russia
e-mail: a.s.veselova@gsom.pu.ru

L. Veselova
School of International Relations, St. Petersburg State University,
St. Petersburg, Russia

© The Author(s) 2018
M. Latukha (ed.), *Talent Management in Global Organizations*,
Palgrave Studies of Internationalization in Emerging Markets,
https://doi.org/10.1007/978-3-319-76418-4_5

export-oriented manufacturing sector of chaebols and a more backward service sector of small and medium-sized enterprises (SMEs) with low productivity. In the 2000s, South Korea experienced a slowdown, first of all, due to the world economic crisis of 2008 which caused a decrease in demand that was detrimental to export-oriented chaebols. Moreover, a recent slowdown in the Chinese economy has also affected South Korean manufacturers due to the fact that about a quarter of exports is directed to China (FT 2017). Thus, a combination of external and internal factors have determined the recent economic development of South Korea, which is now less dynamic than it was before the 2008 crisis. Nevertheless, South Korea still shows much more impressive trends than other countries in the Asia-Pacific region.

Starting from 2013, the government has been implementing a "Three-year Plan for Economic Innovation" which aims to improve labor productivity and spur innovation in the SME sector to overcome the constraints of the dual economy. The announced objective of the program is to achieve people's happiness and prepare for unification, and one of the nine focuses is an increase in female and youth employment (Ministry of Strategy and Finance 2017). In general, the South Korean labor market looks quite dynamic: both the economically active population and the number of employed people are constantly growing. Nevertheless, it faces a few challenges among which is a strong market segmentation reflected in unequal access to well-paid jobs for different groups of the workforce, a huge productivity gap between large firms and SMEs, and a high share of workers employed by very small firms. According to the OECD Employment Outlook, South Korea performs relatively poorly on several aspects of job quality and labor market inclusiveness. The most pronounced weakness of the Korean labor market is the gender-labor income gap, which is the highest among the OECD countries (OECD 2017). The specificity of the Korean labor market largely defines talent management approaches and practices used by Korean companies.

Similar to China, talent management in Korea was historically based on Confucian values which cherish order, hierarchy and collectivism. However, the specificity of Korea lies in the fact that the hierarchy in this country plays even more important role than in China. In Korea, the age and working experience of an employee is very important, which explains why leading positions in companies are usually taken by senior employees and it is much harder for a young talented employee to gain a higher position. Regarding human resource (HR) management, Korea still remains much more conservative than China. For example, very often in Korean companies subordinates cannot leave the workplace before their bosses leave theirs. That is why Koreans are considered one of the most hard-working and respectful nations, with respect shown to position, superiority, age and knowledge.

There has always been a high respect for older people in Korea. Even at work, young people have to consider and respect the elder workers' decisions, who in their turn feel responsible for new generations. As a result, group goals are perceived more as "family" goals and prevail over the individual ones (Choi 2004). The specific Korean management style has been developing over decades and is traditionally characterized as paternalistic with centralized decision-making and strong leadership. However, its uniqueness lies in the possibility of combining a hierarchical order of vertical communication with a harmony embedded in the internal environment. On the one hand, criticism of superiors' policy and questioning them are considered absolutely inappropriate, which makes most Western talent management approaches unsuitable for Korean companies, but, on the other hand, employees usually feel secure and safe because of life-time employment, non-competitive, trustful relationships between colleagues and a warm atmosphere within the collective body. Such a friendly working environment is stimulated by various activities such as the organization of holiday celebrations to build trust and loyalty. Employees are encouraged to work intensively and with commitment to exceeded the pre-set goals. A strict ethics code is a strong regulator of employee behavior.

Many Korean companies prefer to hire graduates directly from college, and develop and promote them within the company. Moreover, in their recruitment approaches, they give preference to generalists rather than to narrow specialists as they are thought to be easier to incorporate into the existing corporate culture through intensive indoctrination. In addition, a commonly used practice includes recruitment through family ties, when family members or close friends of a high-positioned employee pass through a less-complicated selection process and obtain a faster career promotion. Remuneration is usually based on seniority, but not on performance or competence; and group performance is given more attention than individual results. For this reason, Korean corporate culture has often been viewed as a hierarchy with the elements of a clan (Miles 2008).

While Korean businesses used to operate mainly within the country, this model was quite appropriate and effective. A company's competitiveness was based on imitation and manufacturing capabilities, and co-operation, harmony and diligence were sufficient enough for companies to survive. However, as soon as Korean companies started to penetrate foreign markets, the need to incorporate new talent management models and approaches became obvious (Bae et al. 2011). In the 1990s, many Korean companies adopted and adapted "new" practices of estimating employee individual competences and making decisions about compensation and promotion based on these estimates. Such changes significantly limited the career prospects for those who had not developed wanted skills. Moreover, in some cases mass graduate recruitment was replaced with irregular selection in accordance with demand. Some companies launched selective promotion with elements of leapfrogging, as well as programs of intensive employee training and development (Bae and Lawler 2000). This increased the horizontal mobility of the workforce as the most professional and talented people had the opportunity to consider changing their employer.

The gradual development of these trends lasted for about a decade until 1997 when the Asian economic crisis hit South Korean corporations, bringing some of them to bankruptcy. As a result, large firms started restructuring their human resource policies and more actively developing talent management systems through a tailored and adapted transfer of talent management practices from their subsidiaries located in foreign markets. However, due to the fact that transferred practices were often perceived as unnatural and artificial, they could hardly form a coherent system, but ended up with fragmented processes. Nevertheless, the policy of life employment in many companies was eroded with early-retirement programs. Companies started to promote and remunerate employees using performance indicators moving away slightly from a seniority-based to an efficiency-based approach (Lee and Kim 2006). In terms of incentive intensity, Korean companies switched toward multi-rater evaluation, absolute appraisal and feedback processes. In addition, recruitment and internal development of recent graduates was supplemented with attracting experienced specialists, which significantly increased workforce mobility and overall quality.

Furthermore, Korean companies started to introduce differentiated human resource policies toward particular groups of employees: for example, special treatment was provided to highly valuable employees, or "top talent", which led to the development of a wide range of talent attraction and retention practices. At the same time, new policies of replacement and outplacement were applied to poorly performing employees. Moreover, transactional and outsourcing strategies were implemented for contingent workers, which resulted in a shift to contract-based, short-term relations, thus increasing the proportion of "temporary" and decreased job security workers, accounting for higher labor turnover and lower employee job commitment (Rowley and Bae 2004). However, to reduce the negative consequences of these changes, many Korean companies have adapted differentiated practices of higher job security and development for permanent employees and more flexibility for temporary ones. These companies try to combine tenure track and life-employment for regular employees with offering less benefits to contract-based employees, being able to lay them off more easily. Training programs have become mainly focused on highly skilled employees. They aim to develop creativity, the capability of absorbing new knowledge and technologies and software skills. To attract experienced specialists, Korean companies have initiated active and pronounced advertising of vacant positions, thus switching to active recruitment. The inflow of new employees has also been stimulated through wide-ranging support of young talent by means of various scholarships and opportunities for internships (Tung et al. 2013).

To sum up, the recent stage of talent management development in Korean companies could be characterized as a transition one in which companies are still searching for a balance between the traditional Korean management system based on strong cultural values, which are aligned with the cultural and social norms of society, and modern efficiency-based strategies, which put pressure on creating a more differentiated talent management with practices leading to greater decentralization of management.

Hyundai Motors: Talent Attraction and Retention

Hyundai Motors is a South Korean transnational car manufacturing company that was established by Chung Ju-Yung in 1967 as a subsidiary of Hyundai Engineering & Construction (Revolvy 2017b). The company started by assembling cars and trucks for Ford Motor Company. In 1975, it produced its first car, the Hyundai Cortina, which was developed in partnership with Ford Motor Company. Within the next two years, they had become the thirteenth largest automaker in the world with a 2% market share in the world auto retail market (SuccessStory 2017a). To build its own car, Hyundai hired five of the best car engineers from Britain who designed the first car, the Hyundai Pony. It soon became the number one selling car in South Korea because of its small size and value-for-money pricing. Hyundai Pony entered the Canadian market within nine months and became the top-selling car there; and within 10 years, its production exceeded a million cars (SuccessStory 2017a).

Hyundai restructured itself by investing heavily in quality, design, research and manufacturing. As a result, it came up with the first proprietary gasoline engine with its own transmission including the four-cylinder Alpha. It started giving a 10-year or 10,000-mile warranty for all Hyundai cars sold in the United States. This improved the image and prompted more and more customers to choose a Hyundai car over other brands, which stimulated its international expansion to other countries and continents (Australia, New Zealand, Egypt and Japan, among others). By 2000, it had manufacturing plants in India, China, Pakistan, Turkey and the Czech Republic (Villegas 2017). In 2004, the company had US$56 billion in revenue with sales of more than 2.5 million units. By 2011, Hyundai had sold more than 4 million cars which made it the fourth largest car maker in the world behind General Motors, Volkswagen and Toyota. In 2012, Hyundai sold 4.5 million vehicles worldwide and together with its subsidiary Kia, its total sales exceeded 7 million units (Choy 2012). Since 2013, Hyundai has produced more than 3 million units every year in its plants spread across the globe (Villegas 2017). Now, it has more than US$80 billion in revenue and nearly 70,000 employees (Forbes 2017). Having had a cautious start in the automobile industry, Hyundai has become one of the most trusted four-wheel brands in the world. Hyundai's success has been a result of its continuous focus on expansion and customer satisfaction (Hyundai 2017a). Quality was announced as the main objective of Hyundai in the 1990s when the company decided to change its strategy from being the most affordable car to being a top-quality car. To achieve this, the company had to formally and strictly define most of its procedures. Hyundai has had a hierarchical culture, which is demonstrated by its declared values ensuring a sustainable future through a balanced promotion of the rights of its stakeholders, including customers, employees and partners (Hyundai 2017b).

To achieve its corporate goals, Hyundai has implemented the full range of management approaches and tools in various functional areas, including talent management. Considering the fast-changing environment and technology-driven industry in which Hyundai operates, it pays special attention to recruitment processes driven by the understanding of how essential it is to hire knowledgeable and creative people who aspire to constant development and innovation. Keeping this as a priority, Hyundai believes that the future is for young people to develop, so is focused on hiring graduates right after they finish university. To do this, the company has launched a special program, the Research Scholarship System, which aims to select 200 excellent students who are getting their PhD, master's or bachelor's degree from top-ranking universities all over the world, on an annual basis. They support these students with yearly scholarships, considering them as their potential future employees. Those students who participate in the selection process should meet a set of basic requirements, among which is the completion of basic university courses and elementary or mid-level education relating to automobiles. The selection procedure assumes a multi-step approach starting with an online application, document examination, aptitude and so-called "personality inventory" tests, interviews and, finally, a medical check-up (Hyundai Motor Group 2017). Hyundai has also established a tradition of holding the Global Top Talent Forum, which annually gathers the best students from world-renowned universities, such as Oxford, Cambridge and

MIT. Thus, the company strives for winning the "war for talent", which is a battle for young talented specialists who will contribute to the company's future development by bringing new ideas and knowledge, and staying with it for a long time.

The recruitment approaches in Hyundai are very similar to traditional Western practices. The expectations for candidates in managerial positions and for factory workers differ, as well as the respective recruitment processes. The age limit for applicants for managerial positions is 30 years, and higher education is required. The applicant goes through a detailed application document inspection with a particular focus on education and personal background. Applicants are tested on their analytical and verbal skills and on their English language skills. Successful applicants for management positions end up with a face-to-face group interview with top-management and HR specialists. The age limit for factory workers is slightly higher, set at 35 years, and the education level should be high school as a minimum. Factory workers are expected to possess general knowledge of the industry and some particular job-related skills (Lansbury et al. 2006). The selection process usually ends up with an individual interview with a human resource manager and head of department where the applicant is going to work. One more indicator that is relevant for any position is employee loyalty, which is assessed on the number of previous workplaces. If in the past a person had changed jobs several times, then it is assumed that in future this tendency will continue; therefore, this candidate is considered unreliable and is often rejected (Koh 2014).

When considering graduates, the company uses a technique of blind interviews in order to exclude any biased judgements. The qualitative assessment during the interviews is mainly focused on forethought of answers, thrift, positive attitude and collectivism. Regardless of the particular position, an applicant has to pass an obligatory medical check. Selection processes vary slightly between subsidiaries and significantly differ for permanent and temporary employees. Usually, for temporary workers, who are regularly hired in accordance with a sub-contractor, the recruitment process is simplified, because they are supposed to work only for a short period of time when the pressure of work is high and there is no time for a lengthy selection process (Lansbury et al. 2006). To summarize,

Hyundai's recruitment processes are based on a high-quality education, profound experience in the industry and loyalty.

Despite its quite advanced system of talent management, Hyundai does not have a complex employee motivation system. In fact, the company does not provide any sort of monetary appraisal for outstanding performance, its compensation system almost exclusively consists of fixed salaries. The system of performance appraisal for production workers existed until 1987 when Hyundai's management was forced to abolish it due to pressure from trade unions, and later attempts to reintroduce an individual incentive system as a part of the performance management system restructuring was not fully realized again due to employee dissatisfaction. Nevertheless, by 1997 the performance appraisal system had been partly applied to separate groups of workers, though it did not impact their wages (Park et al. 1997). Nowadays, performance appraisal in Hyundai is dependent on position level: for example, regarding the non-executive groups, several behavioral criteria are applied, including discipline, attitudes to work, co-operation, punctuality and attendance. However, the system is supposed to enhance competition between workers to achieve better performance, but it often causes conflict between managerial groups and workers, which disrupts the culture of internal harmony.

Hyundai has a two-level system for executive and non-executive employee promotion and training. On the first level, the training process is organized through Academies established in different countries. These Academies are, essentially, training facilities for national technical teams, which provide access to learning modules on sales, service, warranty and parts operations. Through these processes of professional development, employees are guided, assessed and encouraged to improve their skills and be promoted to the rank of Hyundai Master Technician. Apart from Academies, which are limited in number, Hyundai also organizes Go-to training programs for staff in provincial areas. There is also a Global Learning Center, which provides an online introduction to the core values of the company to the newly employed (Hyundai 2017c).

At the top of the promotion and training system is Hyundai University that is managed by the Chief Learning Officer. The university serves as a human resource development (HRD) center, which realizes a variety of functions. Firstly, it defines "HRD fundamentals" which are particular core competences required in different job positions. It also develops the company's corporate culture and philosophy. Secondly, the university is a major training center for selected high-performing employees with training programs on corporate culture indoctrination, leadership development, introduction to regional contexts, professional development, and cultural events. Thirdly, the university is in charge of making assessments and finding solutions to most HR issues, including control and co-ordination of all oversees HRD departments of Hyundai (Hyundai Motor Group 2017).

While the system itself is well-organized, another dimension of career development—company-wise requirements for a successful promotion—has been a constant source of issues. The authoritarian corporate culture has enabled superior quality and rapid expansion, but it has also caused misunderstandings and opposition from employees in overseas subsidiaries (Hübner 2014). The problem is that seniority and loyalty has often been valued more than talent. This issue has negatively affected the efficiency of the company's talent retention programs and much employee loyalty overseas.

To sum up, Hyundai, being among the leaders in the Korean business environment and an attractive employer to Korean employees, is still on the way to its transformation from traditional, local, talent-led management practices to more open and international ones. At present, Hyundai is sequentially introducing new talent approaches that are adapted to its corporate culture. It has succeeded in attracting local and foreign talent and subsequently developed these employees through in-house training. However, it has not yet managed to overcome some major challenges deeply rooted in the traditional Korean business culture and associated with strict hierarchy and paternalism. One, of course could question to what extent traditional values should be challenged by new business practices driven by efficiency and effectiveness, or perhaps the latter be creatively integrated into the fundamental values of a national culture.

Samsung: Best Practices and a Cultural Fit

Samsung is a South Korean multinational conglomerate headquartered in Samsung Town, Seoul. The company comprises numerous subsidiaries and affiliates united under the Samsung brand. Samsung was founded in 1938 by Lee Byung-chul as a trading company (SuccessStory 2017b). By the end of the 1960s, the company had diversified into food processing, textiles, insurance, securities and retail. Then, Samsung entered the electronics industry in the late 1960s and the construction and shipbuilding industries in the mid-1970s; these areas mainly drove its subsequent growth. Following its founder's death, Samsung was separated into four business groups, one of which was Samsung Group. Since that time Samsung increasingly globalized its activities related to electronics, producing mobile phones and semiconductors which has become its most important source of income (SuccessStory 2017b).

Samsung has several subsidiaries and a diversified business portfolio: Samsung Electronics, Samsung Heavy Industries (shipbuilder), Samsung Engineering and Samsung C&T (construction & trading); Samsung Life Insurance, Samsung Everland (the oldest theme park in South Korea) and Cheil Worldwide (an advertising agency). Since the 1990s, the company's strategy has been to provide further consolidation of its activities with a view to strengthen its global market presence. Samsung started its consolidation in order to merge its complimentary units and increase its efficiency. Success followed rapidly and, in 1993, Samsung was named the world's largest manufacturer of memory chips. In 1995, Samsung narrowed its focus to liquid-crystal display (LCD) production and soon became the world's largest producer of flat-screen TV sets. By 2010, the LCD business turned out to be very competitive, and to achieve its next level of growth, Samsung strategically entered the smartphone market by leveraging its innovation and management capabilities (R&R Research 2017).

Currently, the company and the market in which it operates are undergoing changes, which may entail further changes in Samsung's strategy. Samsung is revisiting its rigid hierarchal corporate structure and culture to confront innovation challenges, weak demand and increasing competition

(Kim 2016). It is expected that the smartphone business, like any other business in the long term, will also be disrupted by newer technologies. Having sensed this, Samsung is already moving into other promising industries, which will be a source of future growth for the company. Samsung has built significant capabilities in many businesses and its current strategy is to invest in clean energy, healthcare and biotechnology for business growth.

As for its corporate culture, it is more about hierarchy and market. Samsung adheres to the principles of Korean social and business culture and, as a result, it has quite a rigid corporate culture, entailing traits such as a family-centered business model, loyalty and strong relationships, centralism, respect for seniority, and authority. The hierarchy and discipline is quite strict within the company with limited employee flexibility and freedom of actions.

However, nowadays Samsung is taking steps to create a more flexible and creative culture in order to become more entrepreneurial (Brokaw 2016). It seems this is quite a difficult task for a company that employs over 300,000 people (Burnell 2017). Samsung tries to reduce uncertainty by minimizing external environmental contingencies and ensuring organizational stability. The vertically and horizontally differentiated organizational structure of Samsung Electronics implies a large degree of power distance, which may obstruct innovation. However, lately Samsung has tended to cut down on the levels of staff hierarchy, reduce overtime and encourage its employees to spend weekends with their families or in pursuing professional education opportunities (Brokaw 2016). A good example of Samsung's attempt to reduce the hierarchical control is its establishment of the Creative Lab (or C-Lab), which advocates holacracy (i.e. a specific way of organizing and managing teams). C-Lab's structure is not governed by a hierarchical system, instead each team has a leader and project members. The absence of a rigid structure enables everyone to participate in the creative process and to contribute to the success of the projects.

In 2015, Samsung developed its own Code of Conduct as a global corporate citizen that is expected to be adhered to by its stakeholders. The Code includes five underlying principles: complying with laws and ethical standards; maintaining a bright corporate culture; being respected by customers, shareholders and employees; taking care of the environment and safety; and being socially responsible. Any discrimination on the grounds of age, sex, race, sexual orientation and disability is prohibited in the company. These principles are clearly expressed in the slogan "we use talented people and technologies in order to create perfect products and services for the global society to utilize them". Samsung believes that talent is key to the future success of the company, stating "our future lies in nurturing global talent, which leads to innovation and creativity in our products and services" (Samsung Asset Management 2017).

Lee Byung-chul, the head of Samsung, understood that traditional Korean talent management approaches may limit the company's development, so he decided to change Samsung's recruitment and human resource management policy by borrowing elements and mechanisms from Western management practice. Through adapting and implanting appropriate Western methods of structuring the working process and a purposeful restructuring of the company's organizational structure he aimed to increase its flexibility. The restructuring has been carried out quite carefully, and Lee Byung-chul was trying different ways of strategy implementation, so if employees were dissatisfied with some innovations, the company either temporarily suspended the experiment, made some updates and relaunched it, or completely stopped it without any further reconsideration. So, using this approach the company has created a hybrid management system combining traditional Korean talent management practices and Western approaches. Thus, it has assumed a dual approach to employee recruitment, both on the basis of competition from outside the company and "internal" employee promotion. It has combined annual hiring processes for low-grade positions and Western methods of recruitment for experienced applicants. It has also allowed the co-existence of seniority-based and achievement-based approaches in defining salaries and promotions. Moreover, Samsung has implemented an annual managers' rotation to find the most appropriate position for every employee. This has made the image of Samsung as an employer a bit ambiguous for Korean applicants and the company is often associated with "overwork". In order to dispel these fears and prejudice, Samsung annually carries out special seminars where Samsung representatives from the HR department answer questions from students and other potential applicants about working in the company with the aim to overcome the stereotypical perception of Samsung as being a corporate monster.

Samsung invests in the development and training of its employees, considering this as a key to the company's success. Annually, the company provides different programs in the development of leadership skills, and carries out coaching sessions in marketing and IT. Samsung has a three-level training system, which consists of assisting employees in obtaining a sense of belonging to Samsung, "bringing-up" future leaders through leadership programs, and "bringing-up" industry leading experts through professional programs. The main aim of such a system is to develop employee competences and to foster talent development.

Samsung's Global Scholarship Program searches for talented people ambitious to develop their careers, with a focus on business and leadership skills development. The program was created in order to facilitate the development of selected employees who may become future leaders in Samsung Electronics' offices in other countries, the so-called "Future Global Leaders".

Furthermore, the company annually carries out a specific initiative which consists of two parts: a program for engineers (the MS Program) and a program for managers (the MBA Program). Seoul National University and Massachusetts Institute of Technology are the two corresponding partners in these programs. The MBA Program is the first program in South Korea realized in English. At the end of the program, all participants have an opportunity to work for Samsung for two years and their labor contracts can be prolonged in cases of mutual interest and agreement.

Apart from this, the company annually carries out an Expertise Development Process (EDP) assessment for all employees and focuses on self-directed learning by allowing personnel to set their own annual training plan in accordance with the results of their assessment. Samsung also carries out STaR (Samsung Talent Review) Sessions in association with its EDP. The STaR Sessions are a talent nurturing process helping employees to design a unique individual career path and create a common vision with their supervisor. Employees can apply for different human resource development programs, such as an MBA, academic training, regional expert class or job expert course through this process. STaR Sessions are mutually beneficial to both employees and the company itself: they give employees a greater opportunity in their developmental process to experience a variety of creative programs, while also allowing the company to create a pool of talented candidates to infuse employee learning and thus serve its strategic organizational needs.

Samsung provides a simple philosophy about its performance appraisal approach: where there is high performance, there is reward. Therefore, Samsung uses a traditional "Western" system of performance appraisal, the system of target versus achievement. Based on the principle of "performance-based compensation", the company ensures fairness, competitiveness and objectivity in its rewarding schemes. The company carries out annual performance evaluation of its personnel against the achievement of pre-set goals. The obtained data are used for rewarding, promoting and developing leaders. Salaries have to take into account evaluation results. Moreover, if an employee is not satisfied with the results of the evaluation, he or she may be re-evaluated if the objection and claim for re-evaluation is considered to be well-grounded (Samsung Electronics 2009). The company distinguishes and selects its best employees showing outstanding results by means of its reward system. The Samsung Reward of Honor was established not only for rewarding talented and hard-working employees, but also for playing the role of a "spreader" of the spirit of success within the company.

The company also enables its employees to change jobs internally using its Job Posting Program, giving its employees the opportunity to develop their careers within the company. The Job Posting Program can be used by employees at any time when there are job openings in the company. In 2001, Samsung launched the Career Consulting Centre (CCC) in order to help retirees find a new career path and to support current employees in their career development (Samsung Electronics 2016) through providing practical assistance and advice.

Stress management is in place and based on proper time management and a work-life balance policy in the company. In order to maximize performance and eliminate unnecessary overtime, Samsung has established a flexible work schedule to improve the work-life balance. Under these conditions, employees arrive at their work between 6.00 a.m. and 1.00 p.m. and have eight working hours per day. The flexible timetable helps not only to create a good and predictable working atmosphere, but also decreases stress levels among employees that in turn leads to improved performance and creativity.

Similar to Hyundai, Samsung is undergoing substantial changes, which are reflected in its talent management strategy. Through the use of a hybrid management system, combining traditional Korean managerial practices and Western approaches, the company has managed to organize itself to ensure its sustainable competitive advantage both in the home and international markets. In contrast to Hyundai, Samsung has created a strong system of appraisal, which stimulates its employees to perform better, along with a diverse and effective system of corporate education, personal and professional development, and promotion. Such an approach has formed a solid basis for the company's future growth. Some features of the traditional Korean management style that underline a specific Asian cultural foundation are deeply engrained in Samsung's management system.

SsangYong: Fast Growth Needs Talent

SsangYong Motor Company is located in Pyeongtaek-si and is one of the largest and most respected Korean automobile manufacturers with 4773 employees (Craft 2017). In 2011, the company became a subsidiary of the Indian multinational automobile manufacturing corporation Mahindra & Mahindra Limited. The company operates in South America, Europe, the Middle East, Asia and Africa. It has a vast portfolio of automotive brands including Chairman W, XLV, Actyonsports, Korando, Kyron, Rodius, Actyon, Rexton W, and Tivoli. Moreover, SsangYong also produces automobile spare parts. SsangYong sells its cars and spare parts through 1652 sales outlets in over 115 countries (MyAutoWorld 2017). In brief, the company operates worldwide, offers a wide range of automobiles including sports utility vehicles, pickup trucks, vans, luxury cars, industrial trucks, passenger buses and four-wheel drive vehicles. It also manufactures automobile accessories, including gasoline and diesel engines for its sports utility vehicles and passenger cars, as well as providing after-sale services. The company has four factories all over the world:

the biggest one is located in South Korea and produces a complete range of products; others are located in Russia, Ukraine and Kazakhstan and produce cars specifically for these and neighboring markets. In this way, the firm not only reduces costs, but also provides jobs in these countries. In addition, the company possesses one factory that manufactures engines, Changwon Engine Plant, which is a high-tech manufacturing facility with a central control assembly line. The major competitors of SsangYong are well-established Korean companies such as Hwashin, Hyundai and Kia Motors.

SsangYong's corporate philosophy is based on the following four pillars: customer safety and happiness; social contribution; customer-centered and innovative products and services; and sustainable and solid growth. SsangYong presents itself as the company that provides differentiated products and customer-satisfying services through innovations such as technological innovation, customer innovation that goes beyond customer needs and expectations, and service innovation that drives customer choices.

As for labor-management relations, SsangYong adheres to the moto "Stand Upright, Stand Together, Stand Again!" (SsangYong 2016) and uses it as a core principle to maintain harmony between management and employees. The company supports good relations through a Oneness and Harmony between Labor and Management Activities program that includes different experiences, spontaneous interaction, and meetings to share information about and plans for the company with all employees. The firm does its best to establish good communication between management and employees that ensures horizontal and vertical information flows. It should be emphasized that SsangYong has set the benchmark for Good Labor-Management Relations in the Korean automotive industry. Initiatives such as the Ethical Partnership of Labor-Management Practice Agreement and the Social Agreement between employees, management, the public and politicians for Good Labor-Management Relations have provided win-win schemes for the trade union and company.

Being an example of a company with a truly Korean internal environment, SsangYong follows the development of talent management approaches and practices, which are common in the majority of large Korean companies. Thus, while in previous years being strictly bound to its Korean organizational culture, currently SsangYong strives to effectively harmonize different management approaches as more and more foreign interventions have been experienced during the past ten years, subsequent to changes in the company's competitive environment. Now the company is under the ownership and control of an Indian firm and is expanding in the US market. After the merger and acquisition of SsangYong and Mahindra & Mahindra (M&M), the new management team introduced the so-called "revival plan" for improving the company's performance. Along with clear, goal-setting systems to measure company performance, variable remuneration and a new product strategy, the labor-management relations system has become a major factor in SsangYong's successful renewal.

Annual salary is predominantly based on the level of employee career development and technical expertise and is defined in the initial recruitment procedure—an interview with the manager of the department where the employee is going to work. Afterwards, salary might be annually adjusted based on the results from the employee performance evaluation. M&M has introduced a new performance management system at SsangYong which is now yielding results. It is based on regular interviews and evaluations, which are conducted twice a year. These results are reflected only in the following year's annual salary adjustment and serve as a means for raising employee motivation.

SsangYong has also established a couple of special acknowledgment awards for the best employees based on certain criteria. A Long Service Award is granted to an employee whose years of service go over a certain length of time. A Distinguished Service Award is given to an employee whose annual appraisal results and contribution to the company's performance are considered above those of others. Laureates are provided with a prescribed prize and an incentive, normally additional vacation days and financial bonuses.

A pool of new, foreign, top managers has joined the company tasked with changing the company's policy. With reference to internal HR policies, they decided to emphasize building the career paths of the employees based on Korean cultural subtleties. SsangYong opened its Regional Training Centers (RTCs) in Central and South America and is planning to open more centers in the Middle East and Europe. This was done to reinforce the global service capability and get the maximum benefit possible from coaching employees in the unfamiliar environment of foreign cultures, thus deepening the integration process with non-Korean management approaches.

Probably the most well-known public scandal around SsangYong was the notorious case of a labor strike in one of the company's plants in 2009. At that time, SsangYong announced a plan for the layoff of about 2026 workers (Kim 2015). As a result, in May 2009 the SsangYong company chapter of the Korean Metal Workers Union (KMWU) went on strike and about 800 workers occupied the plant (Cook 2009). This case played a dual role in future labor-management relationships by diminishing the SsangYong brand, on the one hand, and by giving an incentive for improvement, on the other hand. The strike went on with the supply of water, electricity and gas deliberately cut off by SsangYong's management who was trying to discourage the strike. Although about 600 workers resisted until the end, the occupation was finally suppressed and the company's union president was forced to agree to the layoff plans which saved only half the workplaces. Afterwards, 96 union activists were sentenced to jail. As for the case resolution, after six years of dispute between the new Indian management and the union, the parties came to an agreement to incrementally rehire a group of workers dismissed in 2009 and normalize relationships, as M&M had promised a year after the strike (Park and Noh 2016).

Conclusion

In this chapter we looked at the transformational processes of talent management practice associated with the integration of Korean companies into the global business environment. Traditional management approaches that are similar to those in China have been challenged and slowly infused with more individual, performance-based, talent management approaches. Providing a detailed description of the major talent management practices in Hyundai Motors, Samsung and SsangYong, we aim to highlight the importance of the evolutionary enhancement of existing culturally rooted talent management practices, carefully adapted to local norms and Western practices in order to create competitive advantages over the long term.

Korean talent management is strongly influenced by Confucian values associated with an indisputable collective vision and trustful harmonious relations between colleagues. On the other hand, Korean managerial practices are also characterized by a powerful paternalistic approach with strong leadership caring for its employees, centralized decision-making and clear subordination. However, the analysis of the cases presented in this chapter shows that the key to success is the capability of organizations to carefully integrate the traditional hierarchical order of vertical communication with an internal environment based on harmony and commitment. Samsung managed to create an environment associated with trust and harmony where each employee is encourage to feel like a member of the company family, which makes them eager to contribute to the company's innovation and development, while Hyundai and SsangYong are still looking for unique ways to find the right balance between traditional, familiar approaches and requirements and the expectations of international markets.

References

Bae, Johngseok, and John J. Lawler. 2000. Organizational and HRM Strategies in Korea: Impact on Firm Performance in an Emerging Economy. *Academy of Management Journal* 43 (3): 502–517.

Bae, Johngseok, Shyh-Jer Chen, and Chris Rowley. 2011. From a Paternalistic Model Towards What? HRM Trends in Korea and Taiwan. *Personnel Review* 40 (6): 700–722.

Brokaw, Alex. 2016. Samsung Wants to Reform Its Culture to Be More Like a Startup. https://www.theverge.com/2016/3/24/11297616/samsung-corporate-culture-shift-startup-design-goals. Accessed 15 Aug 2017.

Burnell, Max. 2017. 5 Stunning Stats About Samsung. http://money.cnn.com/video/technology/2017/08/25/samsung-surprising-facts-mxb-lon-orig.cnnmoney/index.html. Accessed 15 Aug 2017.

Choi, Jong-Tae. 2004. Transformation of Korean HRM Based on Confucian Values. *Seoul Journal of Business* 10 (1): 1–26.

Choy, Danny. 2012. Hyundai Hunts Big Three in Global Sales Race. http://www.autoguide.com/auto-news/2012/01/hyundai-hunts-big-three-in-global-sales-race.html. Accessed 15 Aug 2017.

Cook, Terry. 2009. Korean Unions End SsangYong Occupation on Company Terms. http://www.wsws.org/en/articles/2009/08/skor-a07.html. Accessed 15 Aug 2017.

Craft. 2017. https://craft.co/ssangyong-motor-company. Accessed 15 Aug 2017.

Forbes. 2017. https://www.forbes.com/companies/hyundai-motor/.

FT. 2017. https://www.ft.com/content/129efeac-1745-11e6-b8d5-4c1fcd-be169f. Accessed 15 Aug 2017.

Hübner, Carsten. 2014. Unfair Play! Labour Relations at Hyundai: A Critical Review. http://www.industriall-union.org/sites/default/files/uploads/documents/hyundai_-_unfair_play_-_industriall_42014_-_engl.pdf. Accessed 15 Aug 2017.

Hyundai. 2017a. https://www.hyundai.com/worldwide/en/about-hyundai/corporate/information/history/2013-2017.

———. 2017b. https://www.hyundai.com/worldwide/en/about-hyundai/ir/corporate-information/corporate-governance-charter/preface. Accessed 15 Aug 2017.

———. 2017c. Teaching the Art of Customer Service. http://www.hyundai.com.au/hyundai-info/careers/hyundai-academy.

Hyundai Motor Group. 2017. Human Resource Development. http://www.hyundaimotorgroup.com/Careers/Human-Resource-Development.hub. Accessed 15 Aug 2017.

Kim, Min-kyung. 2015. Six Years After Layoffs, Ssangyong Workers Keep Passing Away. *The Hankyoreh*. http://english.hani.co.kr/arti/english_edition/e_national/689678.html. Accessed 15 Aug 2017.

Kim, Yoo-chul. 2016. Hierarchical System to Be Reformed with Leadership Shift. http://www.koreatimes.co.kr/www/news/tech/2016/09/133_207977.html. Accessed 15 Aug 2017.

Koh, Angela. 2014. Korean Companies' Selection Criteria for Expat Professionals. http://english.careercare.co.kr/home/news_room/global_news_view/108437/? Accessed 15 Aug 2017.

Lansbury, Russell D., Seung-Ho Kwon, and Chunk-Sok Suh. 2006. Globalization and Employment Relations in the Korean Auto Industry: The Case of the Hyundai Motor Company in Korea, Canada and India. *Asia Pacific Business Review* 12 (2): 131–147.

Lee, Eun-Suk, and Seongsu Kim. 2006. Best Practices and Performance-Based HR System in Korea. *Seoul Journal of Business* 12 (1): 3–17.

Miles, Lilian. 2008. The Significance of Cultural Norms in the Evolution of Korean HRM Practices. *International Journal of Law and Management* 50 (1): 33–46.

Ministry of Strategy and Finance. 2017. 3-Year Plan for Economic Innovation. http://english.mosf.go.kr/popup/14_PolicyFocusBanner_20140401/popup.html. Accessed 15 Aug 2017.

MyAutoWorld. 2017. http://myautoworld.com/brand/ssangyong. Accessed 15 Aug 2017.

OECD. 2017. Employment Outlook 2017. How Does Korea Compare. https://www.oecd.org/korea/Employment-Outlook-Korea-EN.pdf. Accessed 15 Aug 2017.

Park, Hyun-jung, and Hyun-woong Noh. 2016. Ssangyong Announces Plan Allowing Dismissed Employees to Return to Work. http://english.hani.co.kr/arti/english_edition/e_business/724403.html. Accessed 15 Aug 2017.

Park, Young-bum, Byoung Lee, and Seog-Hun Woo. 1997. Employment Relations in the Korean Automotive Industry: Issues and Policy Implications. *Economic and Labour Relations Review* 8 (2). http://www.freepatentsonline.com/article/Economic-Labour-Relations-Review/237940798.html.

R&R Research. 2017. Evolving Business Strategy of Samsung. http://revenuesandprofits.com/evolving-business-strategy-of-samsung/. Accessed 15 Aug 2017.

Revolvy. 2017a. https://www.revolvy.com/main/index.php?s=Miracle%20on%20the%20Han%20River. Accessed 15 Aug 2017.

———. 2017b. https://www.revolvy.com/main/index.php?s=Hyundai%20Universe&item_type=topic. Accessed 15 Aug 2017.

Rowley, Chris, and Johngseok Bae. 2004. Human Resource Management in South Korea After the Asian Financial Crisis: Emerging Patterns from the Labyrinth. *International Studies of Management & Organization* 34 (1): 52–82.

Samsung Asset Management. 2017. Code of Conduct. http://www.eng.samsungfund.com/renewal/about/conduct_1.jsp. Accessed 15 Aug 2017.

Samsung Electronics. 2009. Sustainability Report 2008–2009. http://www.samsung.com/common/aboutsamsung/download/companyreports/2009_SustainabilityReport_Eng.pdf. Accessed 15 Aug 2017.

———. 2016. Sustainability Report 2016. http://images.samsung.com/is/content/samsung/p5/uk/aboutsamsung/SAMSUNG_SUSTAINABILITY_REPORT_2016_ENG-PEOPLE.pdf. Accessed 15 Aug 2017.

SsangYong. 2016. http://www.smotor.com/en/med_cen/brochure/__icsFiles/afieldfile/2016/04/01/2016_SYMC_Brochure_EN.pdf. Accessed 15 Aug 2017.

SuccessStory. 2017a. https://successstory.com/companies/hyundai-motor-company. Accessed 15 Aug 2017.

———. 2017b. https://successstory.com/companies/samsung-group. Accessed 15 Aug 2017.

Tung, Rosalie L., Yongsun Paik, and Johngseok Bae. 2013. Korean Human Resource Management in the Global Context. *The International Journal of Human Resource Management* 24 (5): 905–921.

U.S. News. 2017. https://www.usnews.com/news/best-countries/south-korea. Accessed 15 Aug 2017.

Villegas, Faviola. 2017. Case Study: Hyundai and Kia in Mexico. http://www.academia.edu/16413595/Case_Study_Hyundai_and_Kia_in_Mexico. Accessed 15 Aug 2017.

Part II

Talent Management in Central and Eastern Europe

6

Talent Management in Central and Eastern Europe: Similarities and Differences

Victoria Tikhonova, József Poór, János Fehér, and Valeria Dvornikova

Central and Eastern Europe (CEE) was introduced as a regional term by the Organization for Economic Cooperation and Development (OECD) with reference to the group of former socialist countries comprising Albania, Bulgaria, Croatia, the Czech Republic, Hungary, Poland, Romania, the Slovak Republic, Slovenia and the three Baltic states of Estonia, Latvia and Lithuania (OECD 2017). Researchers note that the CEE is characterized by a growing economic heterogeneity and a fast-changing socio-cultural

V. Tikhonova (✉) • V. Dvornikova
Graduate School of Management, St. Petersburg State University,
St. Petersburg, Russia
e-mail: tikhonova@gsom.pu.ru; st014475@student.spbu.ru

J. Poór
Szent István University, Gödöllő, Hungary
e-mail: poorjf@t-online.hu

J. Fehér
Károli Gáspár University of the Reformed Church in Hungary,
Budapest, Hungary
e-mail: feherdr@t-online.hu

© The Author(s) 2018
M. Latukha (ed.), *Talent Management in Global Organizations*,
Palgrave Studies of Internationalization in Emerging Markets,
https://doi.org/10.1007/978-3-319-76418-4_6

context, accelerated by privatization, restructuring, increased foreign direct investment, emerging individualism and deepening social divisions (Morley et al. 2010) that have dramatically affected organizational survival, strategy and environment.

The systemic shift from centrally planned to market-led economies in the 1990s brought dramatic changes to the CEE countries. A massive distortion in labor markets replaced previously dominant full employment, causing company collapse, neglect and ruin, accompanied by a huge rise of unemployment and labor emigration (Borgulya and Hahn 2008). Harris and Moran (1996) wrote in their book: "After decades under rigid communist control, East Germany, Poland, Czechoslovakia, Hungary, the disintegrating Yugoslavia, Romania, Bulgaria and Albania, as well as the CIS itself … are left with exhausted labor reserves and high unemployment, ill-prepared and unproductive workers, out-of-date machinery and plants. In addition to the severe shortage of food and consumer goods, these nations are devastated by a frightful legacy of environmental pollution, ecological and economic ruin, as well as a collapsing infrastructure" (as cited in Borgulya and Hahn 2008).

In the CEE group of countries, the three Baltic states regained their independence in 1990. As a part of the USSR, these countries were the most reform-oriented. At the end of the 1980s, when reforms began in the other CEE countries, the Lithuanian economy was already an example to follow. The Baltic countries introduced strict financial policies, and Estonia, being ahead of Latvia and Lithuania, applied a liberal policy in the area of budgetary restrictions. The CEE countries used different approaches to the privatization of state-owned companies, with Estonia being the most successful in this process (Liptak 2012).

CEE countries have had several common features: heavy-handed bureaucracies, inefficient business environments, the major role of personal relations in organizational culture, a low level of development of formal organizational skills, and a lack of strategic human resource expertise (Morley et al. 2010). Due to the differences in the political and economic system, management techniques and philosophy differed in the former socialist CEE countries from Western-European ones. Despite the fact that these countries started a process of transformation, there are still differences in management practices and mindsets, and especially, in the overall culturally embedded people's beliefs and behavior. Since CEE companies' managers were trained under socialist conditions and ideology, a change in mindset and implementation of Western management practices have become a necessary prerequisite for improving company performance on the basis of new efficiency and effectiveness norms, improved productivity and concern for human talent in management practice (Pieper 1992). The CEE transition process has created huge challenges to the development of the human resource function in organizations, as traditionally managed local companies have had a personnel function based on keeping a record of employee working conditions, hours, tasks, employment, retirement and qualification improvement, rather than adopting a more active targeted approach to talent recruitment, motivation, rewarding and retention (Poor et al. 2012). CEE countries started the process of internalization late and this was mainly driven by privatized or restructured companies and newly emerging small and medium-sized (SME) private enterprises that were trying to engage in global market competition. After the collapse of the COMECON system and the opening up of national economies to foreign investment, the number of multinational companies operating in the CEE markets has grown drastically to fill the gaps created by the previously supply-deficit economies. These foreign investments, dominated by Western multinational corporations and later on by Western SMEs, acted as the main driver of innovation in the region (Horwitz 2011). The labor markets of CEE countries were not able to meet the needs of international companies in terms of market-oriented management skills, talent management, finance and controlling knowledge, and so on (Poor et al. 2012). Since the 1990s, the role of talent management in managerial thinking has increased along with its importance in contributing to the competitive advantage of companies (Morley et al. 2010; Horwitz 2011).

In the process of integration into the global environment, CEE companies have started to pay much greater attention to the acquisition and adaptation of existing human resource and talent management practices of leading European and US firms, especially in the talent attraction and retention areas. The CEE region is of particular interest due to the fact that regardless of its relative geographical proximity to the developed European economies and the overall internal similarity, the performance

92   V. Tikhonova et al.

and size of companies from these countries differs significantly (Schwartz and McCann 2007). This poses interesting questions and raises discussion about the specifics of the human resource and talent management approaches not only linked to CEE-developed countries relationships, but also to CEE countries' internal diversity based on their different cultural and behavioral norms and roots.

In the following chapters, we describe the idiosyncrasies of the transition process in three countries from the CEE region (Hungary, Poland and the Czech Republic), which are situated close to each other and thus have many things in common concerning the transition process. We focus our analysis on investigating the possible influence of the country-specific environment and labor market development on talent management practices in the example companies. The chosen companies are from different industries: oil and gas, airplane, brewing, information technology, pharmaceuticals, and automobile. This provides a multiple overview of talent management practices such as talent attraction, evaluation, training and development, rewarding, and so on, and illustrates the practices applied by these companies in the process of managing people to better understand the phenomenon of talent management in the current CEE context. This analysis helps us understand the similarities and differences in approaches to talent management in these countries.

References

Borgulya, A., and J. Hahn. 2008. Work Related Values and Attitudes in Central and Eastern Europe. *Journal for East European Management Studies* 13 (3): 216–238.

Harris, P., and R. Moran. 1996. *Managing Cultural Differences*. 4th ed. Houston/London: Gulf Publishing Company.

Horwitz, Frank. 2011. Future HRM Challenges in Eastern and Central Europe. *Human Resource Management Journal* 21: 432–443.

Liptak, K. 2012. Analyzing the Labour Market Situation in the Central and Eastern European Countries -Improvement or Decline? *Club of Economics in Miskolc (Theory, Methodology, Practice)* 8 (1): 33–40.

Morley, M., C. Brewster, and I. Buciuniene. 2010. The Reality of Human Resource Management in Central and Eastern Europe. *Baltic Journal of Management* 5 (2): 145–155.

OECD. 2017. Glossary of Statistical Terms. https://stats.oecd.org/glossary/detail.asp?ID=303. Accessed Oct 2017.

Pieper, R. 1992. Socialist HRM: An Analysis of HRM Theory and Practice in the Former Socialist Countries in Eastern Europe. *Thunderbird International Business Review* 34 (6): 499–516. http://onlinelibrary.wiley.com/doi/10.1002/tie.5060340604/abstract. Accessed Oct 2017.

Poor, J., F. Farkas, and A. Engle. 2012. *Human Resource Management Issues and Challenges in Foreign Owned Companies: Central and Eastern Europe*, Research Monograph. János Selye University Komárno. http://www.ceeirt-hrm.eu/publication/EN/HR_at_Foreign_Owned_Firms_in_Eastern_Europe_2012.pdf. Accessed Aug 2017.

Schwartz, G., and L. McCann. 2007. Overlapping Effects: Path Dependence and Path Generation in Management and Organization in Russia. *Human Relations* 60 (10): 1525–1549.

7

Poland: How to Become a Leader

Victoria Tikhonova

Poland is the largest economy in Central Europe and the sixth largest in the European Union (EU). In 2015, Poland ranked twenty-fifth in the Ease-of-Doing-Business indicator (World Bank 2017), which makes the country attractive for foreign direct investment and generic business growth. In 1989, Poland started on a path of political and economic transformation from a communistic system (centrally planned) to a democratic (free-market) one that had to be implemented by a shift in the political system and in the economy. The responsibility for restructuring the Polish economy was led by Professor Leszek Balcerowicz, who became Polish Minister of Finance in 1997 (Forbes 2014). The most significant changes he introduced were a new taxation policy, a new banking law, a new law for foreign investors and privatization of state-owned companies. However, the rapid changes were not popular among many Poles (Polskie Radio 2014a), as the country was facing another big economic

V. Tikhonova (✉)
Graduate School of Management, St. Petersburg State University,
St. Petersburg, Russia
e-mail: tikhonova@gsom.pu.ru

© The Author(s) 2018
M. Latukha (ed.), *Talent Management in Global Organizations*,
Palgrave Studies of Internationalization in Emerging Markets,
https://doi.org/10.1007/978-3-319-76418-4_7

problem, which could not be easily resolved quickly. The prices of commodities were no longer under government control, which led to a sharp drop in the value of money and caused hyperinflation (Polskie Radio 2014a). Polish households were losing their savings and that made their economic situation even worse (Statistics Poland 2017). People were leaving for Western Europe to apply their knowledge and entrepreneurial skills. Until 2001, the Polish economy had undergone crucial changes that resulted in stabilizing the inflation rate (Statistics Poland 2017).

Another significant step in the economic transformation was the privatization of inefficient Polish state-owned companies in order to avoid generating government debt (Statistics Poland 2017). In the past, the main purpose of the government was to provide everyone with a job even if it was not required by the competitive environment as market competition between companies was not welcome (Statistics Poland 2017). Additionally, a poor manufacturing infrastructure and high level of corruption made it impossible for the Polish labor market to develop effectively. The process of closing down thousands of Polish enterprises led to high unemployment in 2002 (20% of the whole country's labor power was unemployed) (Statistics Poland 2017). One of the ways to deal with the labor market challenges was the country's openness to foreign investment, which continued to grow until 2007 (NBP 2008). Foreign capital created new opportunities for people seeking a new job within the country (NBP 2008).

The Polish economic and political transformation was supported by the country's accession to the EU in 2004. This helped to boost the economic development level with investments coming mostly from Western Europe and the United States. Cohesion funds from the EU played an important role in boosting infrastructure investments and giving the economy an additional impulse for further growth (Polskie Radio 2014b). Poland was the only country in the EU to avoid the recession during the global financial crisis of 2008 and this turned it into the fastest-growing economy in the EU. The country's main economic strengths are rooted in the careful and well thought through policies of its National Bank, relatively stable inflation, dynamic exports, foreign direct investments and the emergence of numerous micro- and small enterprises, which comprise about 96% of all enterprises operating in Poland

(European Commission 2016). This is also supported by growing domestic demand resulting in the increase of private consumption (European Commission 2016).

The Polish labor market has overcome the difficulties it experienced at the beginning of the 1990s and in the early 2000s (Statistics Poland 2017). There was a sharp decline in real wages, leading to an increase in poverty and inequality in society that was previously considered as a more egalitarian one (Skuza et al. 2013). Between 1989 and 1992, 710,000 new small enterprises were established, mostly driven by surviving entrepreneurship that led to an increase in the number of people employed in the private sector by 2001. A rapid growth in foreign investment has also led to an increase in the number of foreign businesses providing new job opportunities in Poland (Skuza et al. 2013).

The unemployment rate in Poland has been decreasing systematically to the lowest level ever after the end of the communist era in the country (Statistics Poland 2017). The decrease in the unemployment rate is not only a reflection of better economic conditions. After EU accession, more than 3 million Poles migrated to Western European countries to work: this represents almost 10% of the whole Polish labor force (RP 2015). In the UK there are almost a million Polish economic migrants (RP 2015). Many researchers suggest that this represents a "brain-drain" as many migrants are well-educated and recognized specialists, who had gained their know-how in Poland and left the country to seek better pay. These specialists, who left the country, are cost-free to Western European economies mostly in terms of their education and skills, and to date, they contribute to the growth of other, mostly European, economies (RP 2015).

In order to fulfill the need for qualified employees, Polish enterprises hire migrants from Belarus and Ukraine, who are willing to work for relatively low salaries and perform well. Poland used to be considered as a low-cost country in terms of its labor costs, providing highly educated and very efficient workers at the same time (Polskie Radio 2014c). It was the main reason why the country attracted so many foreign companies to invest there. According to data collected in 2014, foreign firms employ one-third of the Polish domestic labor force and pay on average 60%

higher salaries compared to Polish-owned companies (Polskie Radio 2014c).

Another important feature of the Polish labor market is its demographic structure. People over 60 years of age comprise a large part of the Polish population (CIA 2017). This may result in a need to attract more workers from abroad to the Polish labor market. The labor force participation rate in the country is as follows: 67% of the working-age population participates in the workforce; 61% of Polish women work and this is a low percentage in comparison to the average European level of 68%; women aged 25 to 54 have the lowest labor participation due to the lack of childcare services (McKinsey & Company 2015).

Poland has become the center of the SSC (shared services centers) industry in Central Europe. International information technology (IT) firms, banks and business service providers locate their offices, for internal and external business processes, in Poland. A high level of education, improving co-operation between foreign companies and universities, developing infrastructure and still relatively low labor costs are the key success factors for this industry in Poland. It is believed that the country may become the world capital of shared services in the near future (PulsHR 2016).

Polish society can be described as hierarchical, individualist, masculine, short-term oriented, with a strong tendency for uncertainty avoidance (OnetBiznes 2016). Poland is a country with one of the highest scores, when it comes to gender equality in the workplace. According to recent research, 48% of jobs in management positions are performed by women (OnetBiznes 2016), although salary inequality between men and women still exists. Polish women have 7.7% lower salaries on average than men in the same positions (Egospodarka 2016). Polish society is characterized by religious homogeneity, that is why some practices within companies are considered to be acceptable if not desirable in Poland, for example, the Christmas Eve meeting for employees in working hours or a dedicated Catholic mass for the employees of particular companies in some industries (Egospodarka 2016).

The Polish nation is famous for its great hospitality toward foreigners (Paih 2013). Foreign employees in companies located in Poland do appreciate this national characteristic. International teams are easily formed in Polish companies. This quality is even considered to be one of the strengths of the Polish business environment. Since the number of Ukrainian immigrants has increased rapidly, human resource departments not only have to know how to recruit and hire them, but also have to prepare current employees for co-operation with migrants (Paih 2013). Polish hospitality helps human resource departments make this process much easier.

Human resource and talent management practices in Polish companies are changing year by year. Human resource departments used to deal with administrative issues only and were not involved in solving human resource challenges (Ryan 2006). Their main function was limited to personnel record keeping: to list competences and to collect personal data about and employee's family. Such practices did not require those in HR departments to have specific qualifications and the expectations of their performance were also quite poor.

When international companies started to relocate their operations to Poland, they introduced their talent management systems, but many of them faced two major challenges (Ryan 2006). Old human resource management practices had to be reorganized and all employees had to go through a number of training sessions. Some of them could not get along with new standards and left their positions. Some companies had to think of cutting costs and increasing profitability. Low salaries and the absence of bonus and incentive systems were a result of cutting costs (Ryan 2006). Top management in Polish companies understood the essence of human resources: it helps companies to maintain their leadership positions in the long term, and increase operational performance and profitability. Hence companies needed to develop thorough human resource management and talent management policies.

With the development of the Polish economy, the importance of talent management has been growing (Ryan 2006). The increasing competition for talent in Poland is the result of the transition to a market-led economy. Foreign companies are forcing HR departments in domestic organizations to follow innovative practices in attracting, managing and retaining scarce talent. The increasing share of retired people is also one of the challenges for talent management in Poland (Skuza et al. 2013). The talent management landscape in the country represents a process of continuous adoption of best practice common for businesses in developed countries. In the period 2000–2010, Polish companies have been introducing sophisticated human resource management practices and policies applied by foreign corporations doing business in Poland (Ryan 2006). The major impediment for this development was a lack of local professional human resource managers, and the absence of modern human resource management education in Polish universities (Ryan 2006). Companies' efforts were directed toward instilling a positive attitude toward human resource management in the top management of Polish companies (Ryan 2006). By the end of 2010, Polish companies turned from reducing human resource costs to the introduction of human resource management IT systems and outsourcing (Ryan 2006). Many companies started to face challenges of staff internalization, which also posed a challenge for human resource managers. Finally, companies turned their attention toward the development of work productivity and supporting a better work-life balance for their employees. These concerns indicated a move toward treating employees as valuable assets, and not as operational units.

Cultural changes in the work and performance of Polish managers has led to an almost entire convergence of human resource management practices in Polish firms with those of Western business (Ryan 2006). Most managers now reflect individualistic behavior, but at the same time they are more sensitive toward gender and cultural differences. Likewise, a new generation of Polish managers is more open to new contacts and supports experiential learning between different layers of the organizational hierarchy (Ryan 2006). Researchers emphasize one unique role of human resource management in Poland: it acts as spokesperson for employees, which helps to mediate relationships between employees and employer (Ryan 2006). This is embedded in Polish legal complexity, which makes it hard for both companies and employees to fully understand their rights and responsibilities (Ryan 2006).

Leadership skills are one of those skills that still require a lot of attention. Human resource departments are looking for leaders who can manage organizational change and present appropriate soft skills, being able to communicate with all employees. It is getting more and more difficult for companies to hire future potential leaders and to retain them within the organization. For this reason, Polish enterprises have to introduce dedicated mentoring programs and additional benefits for those employees with the highest potential (Deloitte 2016). The digitalization of human resource management is becoming more important as foreign market competitors have already started implementing digitalized tools for improving knowledge management and communication within companies. The example of Orange Polska suggests that a full digitalization of human resource processes is already possible. The company has already digitalized 95% of its human resource processes (Orange Polska 2017). We continue this discussion with the analysis of three Polish companies, namely ORLEN, LOT and Tyskie to show their experience in talent management.

ORLEN: Integrated Talent Management System

Polski Koncern Naftowy Orlen SA (ORLEN) is the parent of an international oil and energy group, the largest company in Central and Eastern Europe and the only Polish company included in the Fortune 500 list of the largest companies in the world (ORLEN Group Integrated Report 2016). It is strategically located on the key pipeline network and has access to the crude oil terminals in Poland and Lithuania. The specialization of the company is the manufacturing, distribution, wholesale and retail of refined petrochemical products. Its main activities can be divided into three parts: refining, retail and petrochemical. ORLEN's product portfolio includes fuel and petrochemical products, and oil derivatives (petrol, heating oil, aviation fuel and plastic). It also produces and distributes electricity and thermal energy (FT 2016). The company has one of the most advanced and largest production systems in the region. The British financial magazine *Euromoney* published rankings that show ORLEN as being the best managed oil company, the most valuable Polish brand and the best employer. The company also got a reward as the "World's Most Ethical Company" (ORLEN 2017a). In 2016, due to its robust financial performance, the company topped the list of most valuable companies on the Warsaw stock exchange (ORLEN 2017b).

ORLEN is represented in Poland by a network of 2700 service stations in the premium (ORLEN brand) and economy (BLISKA brand) segments, thus being an undisputed leader of the fuel market in Central Europe (ORLEN 2017c). ORLEN is the major stakeholder of Unipetrol, a Czech oil refiner, and is responsible for strategic management in crude processing, petrochemical production and distribution of fuels within the company. ORLEN Lietuva is a wholly owned subsidiary of ORLEN (ORLEN 2017d). In Germany, ORLEN owns 581 filling stations under the economy segment brand Star (ORLEN 2017d). It also operates in Estonia and Slovakia. Moreover, the company expanded to Canada in 2015. The Canadian market offers good access to drilling services, qualified personnel, a stable tax regime and a business-friendly regulatory environment (ORLEN 2017e).

The company has a strong market position; this increases its bargaining power and helps to maintain its brand profile. The Company's Investment Program of 2015 was focused on the construction of new services stations and motorway service areas, the reconstructing of existing sites and rebranding BLISKA stations into ORLEN. Food services and new shop formats were developed (ORLEN 2017c). However, ORLEN has to compete in a highly competitive market to keep its market share and operating margins. Main competitors of the company are BP, Exxon Mobil, OMV and Statoil.

The company aims to transform itself into an energy conglomerate by consistently developing hydrocarbon exploration and production and power segments (ORLEN 2017a). In defining its strategy, ORLEN has focused on its main goal: meeting customer needs and expectations by maintaining a position of quality leader on the Polish and international markets. Customers are provided with the highest-quality, environmentally friendly products. ORLEN pays much attention to pollution control, environmental protection along with protection of the life and health of its employees by providing them with safe and hygienic conditions at work (ORLEN 2017f).

ORLEN's strategy for the period 2017–2021 states that value creation, people and financial strength remain the key pillars of the company's growth. The company focuses on enhancing its market position, becoming more customer oriented, strengthening the role of its petrochemical business and developing upstream projects (ORLEN 2017b).

The company itself and all its divisions are characterized by highly motivated personnel and a strong management team (ORLEN 2017a). The company values its employees, customers and stakeholders. It is committed to sustainable development and pays much attention to the internal and external environment (ORLEN 2017a). ORLEN is going to strengthen its human capital in terms of commitment to the highest standards of employee safety, zero tolerance of accidents, and raising staff qualifications (ORLEN 2017b). Security ensures not only a peaceful work environment, but is also reflected in the financial performance of the company (ORLEN 2017g). Finally, a strong focus on innovation with value-creating potential is another important element of the strategy (ORLEN Group Integrated Report 2016).

Talent management in ORLEN has three key principles: competent, committed and motivated staff; simple and effective management practices and processes; and building a cost-effective organization (ORLEN 2017b). ORLEN claims that its recruitment policy focuses on attracting highly skilled, qualified workers whose knowledge and skills, together with the experience of existing staff, would sustain the continuity and highest quality of the company's business processes, and whose values and attitudes are convergent with ORLEN's ethical values and codes of conduct (ORLEN 2017b). A mobility policy was implemented to support the internal recruitment process and staff retention within the company.

ORLEN's value-based corporate culture is evolving in response to the needs of the changing business environment. ORLEN has realized that in order to respond to challenges and be successful in implementing its strategy, much emphasis should be placed on the management culture and corporate culture within the company. The company is running a comprehensive corporate social responsibility CSR) strategy (based on the "Core Values and Standards of Conduct") to meet the needs of internal and external stakeholders. Furthermore, ORLEN is a CSR leader in Poland and was recently declared the most valuable Polish brand for the fourth consecutive year by the *Rzeczpospolita Daily*. In its CSR strategy,

ORLEN mentions three main strategic areas: building lasting relationships between its employees and the organization based on diversity, a sense of security, development opportunities, and social and professional roles; a close environment, where the main goal is to develop a social conscience and responsibility in partners and customers by sharing best practices and implementing the highest CSR standards; a distinct environment, based on promoting innovation, high standards in business ethics and environmental protection (ORLEN Group Integrated Report 2016).

In order to reinforce the "Core Values and Standards of Conduct" and promote desirable behavior among personnel, and to motivate employees to look for new ideas and innovative solutions, talent management programs and projects based on core values were implemented (ORLEN Group Integrated Report 2016). The staff are provided with opportunities to participate in various activities (for instance, ORLEN Olympics, the annual sports games for employees) to enhance their sense of affiliation with the company. The main goal in this area is to build communities outside the workplace and help employees' personal interests develop (ORLEN 2017h).

The Employee Volunteering Program, based on employee initiatives, is the project that enhances corporate culture. The "ORLEN Passion" project assists employees with specific interests and hobbies. The company also conducts an "Open Doors Day" for families of employees, and has traditional year-end meetings of the Management Board with employees (ORLEN Group Integrated Report 2016). The company is also engaged in a number of social sponsorship projects, as development of social capital is one of its main trends (ORLEN Group Integrated Report 2016).

ORLEN also works closely with the academic community to inspire students and graduates to take part in the activities of the company. It has participated in job fairs at technology universities and helped students and graduates gain hands-on job experience by organizing internship and work placement programs. ORLEN has also carried out educational projects in the form of workshops for students (ORLEN 2017b).

ORLEN pays attention to the training of its employees. There is an Adaptation Program, which allows new employees to become familiar with ORLEN's operations and its organizational culture. Apart from introductory meeting and workshops with experts, under the Adaptation Program employees also take part in two online learning programs, one covering ORLEN's history and current organizational issues, while the other is focused on the values of the company and its code of conduct (ORLEN Eco 2017). ORLEN's activities in professional development and training are concentrated both on enhancing employee qualifications to meet business goals and on developing a desired corporate culture that supports the implementation of the company's strategy and increases employee engagement (ORLEN 2015). In 2015, the company launched a program called the Leader Zone, which is a leadership development program conducted in the form of workshops for managers to improve their skills in team management, development of team potential, team engagement and innovation, as well as strengthening managers' authority (Terenowo 2014).

In 2016, ORLEN employees could attend postgraduate and MBA courses, industry conferences, and seminars in Poland and abroad. They could also learn foreign languages as part of ORLEN Language Academy and summer English courses. In order to promote a safety culture on the roads, the company launched the Safe Driving Academy in 2016 (ORLEN Group Integrated Report 2016). The structure of the workforce shows that most employees at ORLEN are working under full-time permanent contracts. Only a small proportion of workers have part-time contracts (ORLEN 2015). Despite the type of contract, employees are provided with benefits, such as co-financing of holidays or hospital treatment, childcare, holidays for children and teenagers, school starter kits, non-repayable allowances, and housing loans.

The company's activities described above suggest that employees are the company's main resource in achieving its business goals and financial performance. There are several challenges in the development of human resource practices that the company has to face. These include the influence of Polish authorities on the top management of the company (as ORLEN is a state-owned company) and the lack of a large pool of specialists in the Polish labor market (it is a challenge for ORLEN to maintain its talent management policy in order to keep its position as the best employer in Poland) (Employer Branding 2016).

LOT: Meeting Passengers, Partners and Employees

LOT Polish Airlines is one of the CEE legacy carriers, founded in 1929 as a state-owned corporation (the government owns 99.8% of shares) (ATO 2017) and still connects the CEE to the rest of the world. LOT is considered to be the third oldest airline company in Europe and the sixth in the world (LOT 2017a). The company's headquarters are located in Warsaw.

The history of the company can be divided into the following main periods. The pre-war period was characterized by fast growth. In 1929, the company launched its operations and in 1930, LOT Polish Airlines becomes a member of the International Air Transport Association (IATA) (LOT 2017a). During the Second World War period most of LOT's fleet was either destroyed or evacuated to Romania. Since 1945, the company restarted its operations by receiving Soviet-built airplanes and renewing both domestic and international flights (LOT 2017a). The first training programs for flight attendants were initiated then (previously the flight attendant's function was implemented by mechanics). In 1988, the company decided to purchase American aircraft and LOT became the first carrier in the CEE to fly American airplanes. New flight routes were established to Singapore and North America. In the third period, the company was restructured in 1992 to adapt its operations to the conditions of Poland's new market economy (LOT 2017a). In 1997, LOT established a sister company EuroLOT to be in charge of domestic flights. In 1998, LOT recorded the highest number of charter flights in its history. In 2000, due to the transformation of Warsaw's airport into a hub, the city became an attractive location for local and transit traffic. In 2012, LOT became the most sought after airline for flights between Western and Eastern Europe (LOT 2017a).

However, from 2008 to 2014 the company experienced financial difficulties due to liquidity problems—the sources of funding used until then were exhausted (European Commission 2014). In 2012, LOT was on the edge of bankruptcy and in order to avoid this, the company was forced to ask for urgent aid from the European Commission. The

Commission approved a rescue loan upon the commitment of Poland to develop a restructuring plan capable of ensuring the long-term viability of the firm. This operation prevented any further state support over the next 10 years and also imposed restrictions on the airline's activities in the course of the restructuring plan, that forced LOT to drop a number of routes (European Commission 2014).

To date, LOT is constantly improving its market position, stabilizing its finances and growing rapidly. Since 2016, after introducing the program, 33 new flight routes were launched (ATO 2017). The company develops its operations within the framework of a profitable growth strategy LOT-2020. Every year LOT carries more than 5 million passengers, providing them with most efficient and comfortable journeys from Warsaw to more than 60 destinations worldwide (LOT 2017b). It is the only airline in the region that offers long-haul flights directly to New York, Chicago, Toronto and Beijing. Since 2016, LOT has also considered its expansion into the Asian markets: LOT connects Europe with Tokyo, Seoul and Bangkok (LOT 2017b). The company also offers direct charter flights to Cuba, Costa Rica, Mexico, Sri Lanka, Thailand, South Africa and Vietnam (LOT 2017c).

The further strategic development of the company lies in the expansion of long-haul flights as the most profitable part of the company's business; developing Warsaw as a connecting hub; competing with other East European carriers; boosting its effectiveness; and building a committed team (LOT 2017c). In order to strengthen the company's position and consolidate the fragmented market of Central and Eastern Europe, LOT has co-operated with the Estonian airline Nordica (Nordica 2016), involving a joint commercial platform and ticket sales system along with sharing of airline codes (Nordica 2016). This co-operation, on the one hand, will provide passengers travelling from Tallinn with more flight possibilities and transfer options and, on the other hand, LOT will gain access to a modern fleet that will enable higher operational flexibility and cost efficiency.

All in all, the company is actively watching the market to optimize the network on a seasonal basis and to provide interesting destinations that offer opportunities for profitable growth. LOT is a responsible and committed company. It positions itself as a united team of professionals who are always open to innovations and development. The company values its passengers, takes care of their comfort by regularly updating its flight schedule in order to offer transfers in Warsaw that are as short as possible (LOT 2017d).

LOT provides a stable working environment for its employees with opportunities for their personal growth and career promotion. The airline cares about the environment by using modern fleet, the most advanced technologies, as well as constantly improving energy efficiency. LOT has received numerous prestigious awards, including the best employer award. It is one of only few companies to be singled out by Polish students as a target for their career development. The company organizes a "Sky's the limit internship", where interns are allowed to experience working in the company (LOT 2017e). A modern flying school, LOT Flight Academy, which was been founded under the LOT brand, prepares students to obtain all major licenses in aviation and helps them to pursue their passion (LOT Flight Academy 2017). The company is actively involved in social charity programs, for example Breast Cancer Awareness (the promotion of cancer prevention and pro-health attitudes), that indicates LOT's awareness of the importance of safety and health. In order to pursue a social responsibility strategy at LOT, the company promotes a passion of flying among children by creating a special educational program, which allows them to learn the most interesting and important aspects of aviation. This program is dedicated to children aged between 5 and 12 years (LOT 2017f).

In the process of staff selection, LOT pays great attention to a candidate's competences, motivation, achievements and involvement. It is crucial for LOT to select ambitious and goal-oriented people, who demonstrate initiative and are not afraid of challenges. LOT Crew specializes in the multi-stage recruitment of cabin crew and ground staff. LOT Cabin Crew, together with LOT Team, is a member of the LOT Group. The main goal is to conduct recruitment processes, which allow teams to formed of the best candidates—employees willing to co-operate across areas, and who value and care about passenger comfort. Communication skills are highly valued at LOT as they are important in building a well-defined and mature corporate culture (LOT 2017f).

The training program for pilots and flight attendants in LOT complies with international standards. With regard to other professional fields, the company does not provide any formal training. In most cases, young workers are engaged in a variety of tasks without prior training and familiarization. However, each department has inspiring, active and experienced staff who work as mentors for newcomers.

Being an international company, LOT brings together people from all over Poland and the world and provides opportunities to attend intensive Polish language courses, which are held in the main office in Warsaw (LOT 2017d). The corporate culture gives employees confidence that they are working for one of the best companies in Poland with a team of professionals (LOT 2017f).

Talent management in LOT is developed to fit the strategy of the company and to correspond to the regulations of Polish Labor Law. Despite the relics of a communist past, LOT has invested significantly in the transformation of its human resource management function and has shifted it from a bureaucratic supportive function to a value-adding strategic activity. In the process of its development, the company tries to move from a hierarchical organizational structure toward a flexible one, where free exchange of ideas around the organization is appreciated and room for initiative on lower levels is provided.

The issue of employee retention is crucial for the company as professional pilots, representing a scarce human resource, have strong employee power and can easily leave for a better salary at another airline company. The company is working on improving its appraisal system in order to correspond to international standards in terms of employee salaries that differ from the developed world's average salaries.

Tyskie: Focus on Talent Training and Development

Tyskie, a well-known Polish brand of beer, is a part of Kompania Piwowarska group. The brand name is determined by the location of the brewery, which is situated in the Upper Silesia town of Tychy. The

Brewery in Tychy (Princely Brewery Tychy) is one of the oldest breweries in Europe, and has existed since 1629—beer has been produced here for nearly 400 years (Kompania Piwowarska 2017).

Kompania Piwowarska, the Polish brewery group, was founded in 1999 in Poznan, but since 2009 is fully owned by SABMiller (Kompania Piwowarska 2017). The company, which controls 45% of the Polish beer market, owns three factories and three beer brands, the names of which correspond to the location of the breweries: Brand Lech, brewed by Lech Broaware Wielkopolski, Poznan (with 10% of the Polish beer market); Brand Dojlidy, brewed by Browar Dojilidy, Bialystok (with 15% of the Polish beer market); and Brand Tyskie, brewed by Tyskie Browary Książęce, Tychy (with 20% of the Polish beer market) (Kompania Piwowarska 2017).

Despite the fact that the company has been both privately owned and a state-owned company, the brand maintains its traditions. This indicates its stability. Taking the leadership position in such a large and fairly competitive beer beverage market in Poland (the market is as developed as in the Czech Republic), makes the company a desired employer (Kompania Piwowarska 2017). Tyskie's parent company is famous for its wide range of beers, which caters to the needs of all consumers, including the most sophisticated. The same can also be said about the Tyskie brand. The company uses an innovative approach to everything connected with its brand, for example, the design of the beer bottles is widely known for a beautiful white label with a gold border, which depicts the royal crown to commemorate John III Sobieski, the King of Poland. This is quite a symbolic sign, as the year of the King's birthday coincides with the foundation of the brewery in Tychy, in 1629 (Brewing Awards 2017). One of the company's strengths is to create a culture of beer drinking and promote it to the masses. The company's mission is to disseminate knowledge about how beer should taste, at what temperature it should be drunk and with what meal it should accompany. In order to maintain its strategy of disseminating a beer culture, Kompania Piwowarska opened the Brewing Museum in Tyskie in 2004, which is an important destination for beer fans in Poland. Adhering to the chosen strategy, the company constantly uses the most modern approaches in marketing and advertising and does not forget to take care of customers, partners and suppliers, so that they are all be familiar with new products and updates in the company.

Piwowarska is a socially responsible company. It is involved in actions to fight AIDS and HIV, and created distribution centers for returning empty cans and bottles. Tyskie was awarded a Gold Medal and Grand Prix at the Brewing Industry International Awards (Brewing Awards 2017). The second award Tyskie won in 2005, the Grand Prix, was at a global beer fair hosted by Drink Tec in Munich. The third one, in 2011, a Silver Medal, was won at the Brewing Industry International Awards and then a Gold Medal at Monde Selection in Brussels. In 2012 Tyskie was awarded with the highest, three-star Superior Taste Award by the International Taste & Quality Institute.

For Tyskie, its employees are its greatest asset. The company describes its relationships with employees as long-term oriented, providing investment in workers' development, which correlates with its corporate strategy. The company provides effective talent management, since this is one of the basic processes which allows it to develop the established corporate strategy and reach the company's growth objectives (ABInBev 2016). For Tyskie, talent management means gathering information about employee strengths and areas of development and planning ways for personal development. As a part of its talent management system, Tyskie holds discussions with employees about their development, talent review sessions and succession planning based on personal development plans (PDP) (ABInBev 2016).

Tyskie has a number of training programs for employees. In order to maintain the performance of strategic corporate objectives, the company establishes special training courses for managerial staff to develop key leadership competences for various groups of managers (ABInBev 2016). Its first time manager program targets newly appointed managers to introduce them to their roles in the company, and familiarize them with leadership behavior and management standards (ABInBev 2016). The manager communication program is for managerial staff who need to improve their interpersonal skills to help them cope with day-to-day management. During the workshop, they learn how to provide feedback, filter the incoming information and eliminate factors that negatively affect company performance Managers are also trained in how to build employee motivation and commitment. Employee involvement by coaching gives managers the required practical coaching skills. The project management training program focuses on developing skills in project management, as this allows managers to operate effectively in a matrix structure, giving opportunities to gain competences in approaching project management, from developing objectives and schedules to managing teams, communication and risks.

Some programs at Tyskie were also created for sales employees. The sales excellence agenda aims to implement the company's sales standards for workers. It also trains employees in basic sales skills such as customer service and sales techniques. The sales academy aims to present sales department employees with the broad business context of the company's operation. The participants in this program are familiarized with the company's brands, develop knowledge about standards of behavior, and learn about the beer market in Poland, its segmentation and competition. This course ends with workshops in which employees have to demonstrate their ability to use the gained knowledge. A client communication course completes the training program for trainees. After that course, trainees are able to identify the types of target audience, to learn how to persuade customers and to deal with different sales processes through any trade channels. In order to succeed, skills in efficient negotiation are learnt. The sales manager academy develops line managers and their particular skills such as analyzing data and making decisions, negotiating and establishing relationships with customers.

The Gem training program is based on the continuous improvement of operational processes. The training consists of several sections called GEMs (fundamental practices): work arrangement and standardization, visualization and methods for achievement measurement, teamwork, continuous improvement and preventing losses, health and environment safety, manufacturing flexibility, quality and property management. Employees also study the fundamental processes of beer production (raw materials, brew house, fermentation, cellars, filtering and packaging and main quality requirements) and are engaged in the exchange of knowledge between workers and experts where the main purpose is to provide broader specialized information and to refresh knowledge.

The company follows strong specific procedures in order to effectively attract, retain and develop people. Tyskie recruits people with diverse talents to fulfill current and future needs. The key part of its talent management is performance management as it guarantees a high-performance and commitment culture. The performance management system at Tyskie includes required competences and approaches, which motivate employees and evaluate their productivity. Such a system enables the best results in achieving the company's goals. At the same, each employee is involved in personal development and performance improvement. Performance management feedback is given to employees and based on this, different evaluations are made by managers. If progress in performance is made, an employee is rewarded. Simultaneously, managers improve their efficiency and skills because they face responsibilities and have to collaborate between departments.

In addition to the strict internal company control system and strict requirements of workers, there is a Code of Ethics, which was adopted by the company (ABInBev 2016). Such values as honesty, responsibility to employees and mutual respect are the main principles, which regulate workplace relations. Moreover, a good environment among workers is established and maintained, so employees feel part of the company and appreciate their work there. They can compile reports about unethical behavior; such engagement plays a crucial role in the development of an organizational culture. A permanent Ethics Committee controls and supervises the working environment. It promotes and increases workers' awareness of what they can do in a conflict situation or in situations when their rights are violated. In addition, all reports about ethical policy and other issues are available to any worker. Another incentive the company provides is contests and appreciation programs for employees. As for the Du˝e Piwo (Large Beer) program, every employee can recommend another employee or a group of employees for a best practice award. Tyskie provides a special benefits sports packages, subsidizing holidays for children, home improvement loans on preferential terms, a unique healthcare package, beer allowance, subsidized dining at canteens, life and accident insurance. To ensure effective communication, the company has an innovative communication platform the Małe Piwo (www. malepiwo.net), which is the employees' social network. This platform has a variety of facilities to exchange information quickly between employees and management. Also it provides equal rights and can be accessed not only from work, but also from home. Moreover, twice a year the company invites employees to the management board meeting in a series of road show events, which are designed to present the company's results. This meeting gives an opportunity to every worker to ask questions and to be engaged in a dialogue with directors. *Âwiat Piwa*, an internal publication, has been appearing every month since 1999. It provides information about the company's development, its branches and environment.

Tyskie established its own talent management processes aimed at gaining a competitive advantage specifically by introducing a well-developed training and development system. Tyskie's has focused on communication and responding to employee needs by setting an appropriate motivation system, which it considers effective and helps the company to compete in domestic and international markets.

*   *   *

This chapter sheds light on some of the specifics of talent management practices in three Polish companies by telling the story of how the country-specific and firm-specific environment plays a major role in developing and retaining qualified specialists in the country. In the 1990s, the Polish economy suffered the consequences of a dramatic transition that negatively affected millions of people in its labor market over the short- and medium-term. Foreign direct investment, generic business growth, liberalization and privatization have helped the country overcome the negative influence of the transition period and opened up new opportunities for business development and bringing on new talented employees. ORLEN, LOT and Tyskie represent three companies willing to innovate. They hold a leading position in their industry and develop training programs for their employees.

All three companies are or have been state-owned (note: Tyskie was acquired by INBev), meaning that the Polish government not only owned the firms, but set requirements and provided support for their development as key local job providers. In the process of transition toward a more knowledge-based economy and keeping their leadership position, these companies have tried to implement a flexible organizational model instead of a traditional one. They try to promote strong co-operation with universities in order to be able to attract young high-skilled workers, develop appraisal systems in terms of both financial and non-financial benefits for employees, and create safe working conditions.

In these cases, the reputation of the company is of highest value. ORLEN, Tyskie and LOT take care of their employees and customers, and concentrate on a highly educated labor force, innovation and efficiency gains to compete with foreign and domestic companies.

References

ABInBev. 2016. Overview from Our CEO. http://www.ab-inbev.com/betterworld/how-we-manage-sustainability/overview-from-our-ceo.html. Accessed Sept 2017.

ATO. 2017. Польский журавль http://www.ato.ru/content/polskiy-zhuravl. Accessed Sept 2017.

Brewing Awards. 2017. http://www.brewingawards.org/. Accessed Sept 2017.

CIA. 2017. Europe: Poland. https://www.cia.gov/library/publications/theworld-factbook/geos/pl.html. Accessed Oct 2017.

Deloitte. 2016. Trendy HR 2016: Polskie firmy poszukują liderów, którzy poradzą sobie z wyzwaniami nowoczesnego biznesu. https://www2.deloitte.com/pl/pl/pages/press-releases/articles/polskie-firmy-poszukuja-liderowktorzy-poradza-sobie-z-wyzwaniami-nowoczesnego-biznesu.html. Accessed Sept 2017.

Egospodarka. 2016. Wigilia w pracy. Impreza, bony świąteczne czy premia? http://www.egospodarka.pl/137535,Wigilia-w-pracy-Impreza-bony-swiateczne-czy-premia,1,39,1.html. Accessed Apr 2017.

Employer Branding. 2016. Top Employers nagrodzeni. http://employerbranding.pl/top-employers-nagrodzeni/. Accessed Aug 2017.

European Commission. 2014. State Aid: Commission Approves Restructuring Aid for LOT Polish Airlines. http://europa.eu/rapid/press-release_IP-14-883_et.htm. Accessed Aug 2017.

———. 2016. Poland-Robust Growth Amid Expansionary Fiscal Policy. https://ec.europa.eu/info/sites/info/files/ecfin_forecast_autumn_2016_pl_en_0.pdf. Accessed June 2017.

Forbes. 2014. 25 lat "planu Balcerowicza". https://www.forbes.pl/wiadomosci/25-lat-planu-balcerowicza/0n4vwcp. Accessed July 2017.

FT. 2016. Polski Koncern Naftowy Orlen SA. https://markets.ft.com/data/equities/tearsheet/profile?s=PKN:WSE. Accessed Aug 2017.

Kompania Piwowarska. 2017. History. http://en.kp.pl/about-us/history. Accessed Sept 2017.

LOT. 2017a. History. http://corporate.lot.com/pl/en/history. Accessed Sept 2017.

———. 2017b. About Us. http://corporate.lot.com/pl/en/about-us. Accessed Sept 2017.

———. 2017c. Connections. http://corporate.lot.com/pl/en/connections. Accessed Sept 2017.

———. 2017d. Warsaw-hub. http://corporate.lot.com/pl/en/warsaw-hub. Accessed Sept 2017.

———. 2017e. Internship. http://corporate.lot.com/pl/en/internship. Accessed Aug 2017.

———. 2017f. What's New. http://corporate.lot.com/pl/en/. Accessed Sept 2017.

LOT Flight Academy. 2017. Why LFA. https://lotflightacademy.pl/en/dlaczego-lfa_en. Accessed Sept 2017.

McKinsey & Company. 2015. Poland 2025: Europe's New Growth Engine. https://www.mckinsey.com/~/media/mckinsey/business%20functions/economic%20studies%20temp/our%20insights/how%20poland%20can%20become%20a%20european%20growth%20engine/poland%202025_full_report.ashx. Accessed Aug 2017.

NBP. 2008. Wpływ globalizacji na polską gospodarkę. https://www.nbp.pl/publikacje/materialy_i_studia/ms230.pdf. Accessed May 2017.

Nordica. 2016. Nordica and LOT Polish Airlines to Launch Strategic Cooperation. https://www.nordica.ee/en/about-the-company/press-center/nordica-and-lot-polish-airlines-to-launch-strategic-cooperation/. Accessed Aug 2017.

Onet Biznes. 2016. Jak zmiejszyć lukę płacową między kobietami a mężczyznami? http://biznes.onet.pl/praca/zarobki/roznice-w-wynagrodzeniach-kobiet-i-mezczyzn/ysf36e. Accessed July 2017.

Orange Polska. 2017. OPL.WA – Orange Polska SA Strategy Presentation. http://www.orange-ir.pl/sites/default/files/OPL-WAR_Transcript_2017-09-04_0.pdf. Accessed Oct 2017.

ORLEN. 2015. Responsible Employer. https://raportzintegrowany2015.orlen. pl/en/responsible-company/responsible-employer.html. Accessed Aug 2017
———. 2017a. PKN ORLEN. http://www.orlen.pl/EN/Company/Pages/ default.aspx. Accessed Aug 2017.
———. 2017b. Strategy. http://www.orlen.pl/EN/Company/Pages/Strategy. aspx. Accessed Aug 2017.
———. 2017c. ORLEN in Poland http://www.orlen.pl/EN/Company/ ORLENInEurope/Pages/OrlenInPoland.aspx. Accessed Aug 2017.
———. 2017d. ORLEN in Germany. http://www.orlen.pl/EN/Company/ ORLENInEurope/Pages/ORLENInGermany.aspx. Accessed Aug 2017.
———. 2017e. ORLEN Upstream. http://www.orlen.pl/EN/Company/ Upstream/Pages/default.aspx. Accessed Aug 2017.
———. 2017f. ORLEN Management Systems. http://www.orlen.pl/EN/ Company/LicenseAndCertificate/Pages/default.aspx. Accessed Aug 2017.
———. 2017g. HSE. http://www.orlen.pl/EN/CSR/Pracownicy/Pages/HSE. aspx. Accessed August 2017.
———. 2017h. ORLEN for Employees. http://www.orlen.pl/EN/CSR/ Pracownicy/Pages/ORLENForEmployees.aspx. Accessed Aug 2017.
ORLEN Eko. 2017. Company. http://www.orleneko.pl/EN/Company/Pages/ default.aspx. Accessed Aug 2017.
ORLEN Group Integrated Report. 2016. https://raportzintegrowany2016. orlen.pl/pub/ORLEN_Raport_EN.pdf. Accessed Aug 2017.
PAIH. 2013. HR SWOT of Poland. http://www.paih.gov.pl/files/?id_ plik=20787. Accessed May 2017.
Polskie Radio. 2014a. Mija 25 lat od "planu Balcerowicza". Problemem była hiperinflacja i brak budżetu i mechanizm tzw. Popiwku. http://www.polski-eradio.pl/42/273/Artykul/1319563,Mija-25-lat-od-planu-Balcerowicza-Problemembyla-hiperinflacja-i-brak-budzetu-i-mechanizm-tzw-popiwku. Accessed May 2017.
———. 2014b. 10 lat w Unii opłacalne: za każdą wpłaconą złotówkę dostaliśmy z UE trzy złote. http://www.polskieradio.pl/42/273/Artykul/1113944,10-lat-w-Uniioplacalne-za-kazda-wplacona-zlotowke-dostalismy-z-UE-trzy-zlote. Accessed Apr 2017.
———. 2014c. Inwestycje: już co trzeci Polak pracuje w firmie z udziałem zagranicznego kapitału. https://www.polskieradio.pl/42/3306/Artykul/11 20448,Inwestycjejuz-co-trzeci-Polak-pracuje-w-firmie-z-udzialem-zagranicznego-kapitalu. Accessed July 2017.

PulsHR. 2016. Centra usług BPO/SSC w Polsce. Gdzie najwięcej pracy? http://www.pulshr.pl/bpo/centra-uslug-bpo-ssc-w-polsce-gdzie-najwiecej-pracy,35572.html. Accessed Sept 2017.

RP. 2015. Polacy pierwszymi imigrantami w UE. http://www.rp.pl/artykul/1248881-Polacy-pierwszymi-imigrantami-w-UE.html#ap-1. Accessed June 2017.

Ryan, L. V. 2006. Current Ethical Issues in Polish HRM. *Journal of Business Ethics* 66: 273–290.

Skuza, A., H. Scullion, and A. McDonnell. 2013. An Analysis of the Talent Management Challenges in a Post-Communist Country: The Case of Poland. *The International Journal of Human Resource Management* 24 (3): 453–470.

Statistics Poland. 2017. https://stat.gov.pl/en/. Accessed June 2017.

Terenowo. 2014. Nabór do ORLEN Team! Rusza Akademia Młodych talentów. http://www.terenowo.pl/newsy/2649-nabor-do-orlen-team-rusza-akademia-modych-talentow.html. Accessed Aug 2017.

The World Bank. 2017. Doing Business Report. http://www.doingbusiness.org/rankings. Accessed Sept 2017.

8

Czech Republic: Making Differences Important

Victoria Tikhonova and Valeria Dvornikova

The Czech Republic is one of the most industrialized countries in Central and Eastern Europe (CEE) (BBC 2018). Being a part of Czechoslovakia until 1993, the Czech Republic has a robust democratic tradition, a highly developed economy and a rich cultural heritage (BBC 2018). It is in the top 50 countries in terms of gross domestic product (GDP), the thirty-fourth economy in the world in terms of GDP per capita, the ninth biggest exporter in Europe and the thirty-third largest export economy in the world (CIA 2017).

It emerged from over 40 years of Communist rule in 1990, and was the first former Eastern Bloc state to acquire the status of a developed economy (BBC 2018). The Czech Republic is a prosperous market economy that has one of the highest GDP growth rates (2.5% in 2016) and lowest unemployment rates (5.6% in 2016) in the European Union (EU), but it depends heavily on exports that makes economic growth

V. Tikhonova (✉) • V. Dvornikova
Graduate School of Management, St. Petersburg State University,
St. Petersburg, Russia
e-mail: tikhonova@gsom.pu.ru; st014475@student.spbu.ru

© The Author(s) 2018
M. Latukha (ed.), *Talent Management in Global Organizations*,
Palgrave Studies of Internationalization in Emerging Markets,
https://doi.org/10.1007/978-3-319-76418-4_8

vulnerable to contractions in external demand (CIA 2017). The country's export comprises 80% of GDP and largely consists of automobiles, the single largest industry. The Czech Republic entered the EU in 2004 (CIA 2017). The country's main export partners are Germany, Slovakia and Poland, while its main import partners are Germany, Poland and China (European Union 2016).

The government that came to power in 2014 undertook several reforms in an effort to reduce corruption, attract investment and improve social welfare programs, which could help increase revenue and improve living conditions for the Czech people. The government introduced an online tax reporting system in December 2016 in order to reduce tax evasion and increase revenue. It also plans to remove labor market rigidities to improve the business climate, bring procurement procedures in line with EU best practice and boost wages. The country's low unemployment rate has led to a steady increase in salaries and the government is facing pressure from businesses to allow greater migration of qualified workers from Ukraine and neighboring Central European countries (CIA 2017).

Despite the progress made, the government faces challenges with the rapidly aging population, a shortage of skilled workers, a lagging education system, funding an unsustainable pension and health care system, and diversifying away from manufacturing toward a knowledge and service-based economy (CIA 2017). Since the 1990s, personnel work in the Czech Republic has faced significant changes mainly because of the increased importance of knowledge and innovation in achieving a long-term competitive advantage. These changes have demanded the development and adoption of new human resource management practices from Western companies. This mainly resulted in higher requirements regarding the quality of human resource management in companies.

One of the major concerns of human resource management in the Czech Republic is lack of experienced, strategic human resource expertise. Recent research by Stacho et al. (2013) on human resource management in Slovakia and the Czech Republic found that companies have started to realize that human resource strategy is an important part of the overall organizational strategy and a human resource management representative should therefore have a position in the middle or top manage-

Czech Republic: Making Differences Important 121

ment of firms. Yet, only in 53% of Czech organizations do human resource managers have a position in top management (Stacho et al. 2013).

In the recruitment process, Czech organizations prefer to hire the person responsible for human resource management primarily from internal employees (Stacho et al. 2013). This fact is also mentioned by Skoludova and Brodsky (2015). Most often employee mobility occurs vertically (when an employee is relocated to another position either above or below the current one). The most widespread recruitment methods are interviews, application forms and references. Assessments, psychological tests and interview panels are rarely used. The dominant method is a one-to-one interview (Skoludova and Brodsky 2015). The education and development of employees is usually outsourced, especially in smaller organizations that do not have enough qualified trainers and educational centers (Stacho et al. 2013).

The major reason for conducting performance appraisal in Czech companies is performance improvement. It is also used for the pay assessment of employees both in terms of salary and bonuses. Employees are most often evaluated by their direct manager, using a combination of quantitative and qualitative evaluation. The most common types of performance evaluation are done twice a year and monthly. Evaluation tools such as 360-degree feedback and assessment centers are rarely used (Skoludova and Brodsky 2015). According to a study by Lanik et al. (2009) the major motivation for Czech employees are compensation for effort, competitiveness, status, self-control, flexibility and eagerness to learn. Engagement and preference for performing difficult tasks are less motivating (Lanik et al. 2009). It is important for companies not only to make the best decision during the recruitment process, but also to be able to retain employees. However, a small proportion of companies focus on work and social adaptation processes (Skoludova and Brodsky 2015). A strict hierarchy is characteristic for Czech companies, which means that the role of each employee is strictly defined and the authority of the superior level is undisputed, which can be an obstacle for talent development (Dubravska and Solankova 2015).

According to Hofstede's 6D model of national culture, the Czech Republic is a hierarchical society. Within the organization, hierarchy is seen as reflecting inequalities, promoting centralization and telling subordinates what they have to do. The Czech Republic is also characterized by individualism where social frameworks are paramount and individuals only take care of themselves and their families. Thus, hiring and promotional decisions for employees are based on merit only. Society is driven by competition (masculine society), equity and performance (Hofstede Insights 2017). We continue with the analysis of three Czech companies, namely Škoda, Unipetrol and CEZ.

Škoda: Following the Leader

Škoda, one of the oldest automobile manufacturers, is based in Mladá Boleslav (the Czech Republic). It was founded by the mechanic Vatslav Laurin and bookseller Václav Klement in 1895. Within 10 years, they were manufacturing bicycles under their own design but, by 1905, the company went on to produce cars (Škoda 2017a). The first car made by Laurin & Klement became highly successful and provided a stable position on the flourishing international car market. Thus, the company was ready to expand its production. Production of civilian vehicles shrank during the period of the German occupation from 1939 to 1945 and, after the Second World War in 1946, the company was renamed AZNP and became a national monopolist in the production of passenger cars (Škoda 2017a). After the political changes in 1989, the Czechoslovakian government and the management of Škoda began searching for an influential international partner, with experience and financial resources, to ensure the company's competitiveness in the long term. Thus, the joint venture between Škoda and Volkswagen was set up on April 16, 1991 under the name of Škoda, automobilová a.s., which became the fourth brand in the Volkswagen Group (Škoda 2017a).

In 1991, Škoda started its expansion to other countries, opening sales offices and back-offices and defined its priorities in international markets in an attempt to upgrade the image of company (Škoda 2017b). Following the same goal, 14 years later in 2015, Škoda started its expansion in India, Ukraine and China, trying to get a bigger market share and produce a product suitable for everyone, despite its geographical position.

Today Škoda Auto's mission is to anticipate consumer needs and provide safe, quality, reliable and innovative automotive products and services around the world. Škoda Auto represents three basic values: intelligence (the company continuously looks for technical solutions and new ways it can meet customer needs), attractiveness (the company develops automobiles that are aesthetically and technically of high standards and are always attractive to offer to customers, not only in terms of design or technical parameters, but also in the diversity of offered services), and dedication (the company is following its founders' steps, enthusiastically working on the further development of its vehicles and identifying with the product) (Škoda 2017b).

As Škoda Auto is a part of Volkswagen Group (VW), it does not develop its own strategy, but holds to the strategy developed by VW. Therefore, the business strategy of Škoda until 2025 is called "Together" and stands for a way of thinking, an approach that has become vital for the Volkswagen Group to move forward (VW 2017a). Together, all VW brands, including Škoda, keep on satisfying their customers with tailor-made mobility solutions and meeting the diverse consumer needs with a portfolio of strong brands.

The new group strategy comprises of a range of far-reaching strategic decisions and specific initiatives, essentially aimed at safeguarding the long-term future of the firm and generating profitable growth. To achieve this, the "Together – Strategy 2025" future program is built on four key building blocks: transform the core business, build a mobility solutions business, secure funding and strengthen innovation power (VW 2017a). With the "Together – Strategy 2025" Škoda aims to excite its customers with fascinating vehicles and innovative mobility solutions, to be a technology leader and a role model when it comes to the environment, safety and integrity (VW 2017b). In order to achieve this, the company needs competent talent who wants to work for it.

Since the company has become a part of the Volkswagen Group, its strategy comprises many levels. The controlling entity is the parent company of the group. Activities of the controlling entity include the development of vehicles and aggregates, the production and sale of passenger and commercial cars, trucks, buses and motorcycles, as well businesses covering spare parts, large-bore diesel engines, special gear units and turbo machinery (Škoda 2015). Hence, Škoda does not have strategic independence.

The organizational culture of the company is based on its Code of Conduct. Each manager is responsible for employees and must operate strictly in accordance with the Code of Conduct. By providing regular information and guidelines about employee rights and responsibilities, managers support employee behavior that complies with the Code of Conduct. Managers should place confidence in their employees, stipulate goal-oriented behavior and allow employees to have personal responsibility and freedom of action as much as possible. Moreover, as a major aspect of managers' responsibility, they must prevent unacceptable conduct. Trustful and great participation is reflected in common and open sharing of data and support. Managers and employees inform each other about important relevant facts and businesses matters for the simplification and transparency of decision-making processes. Since Škoda Auto joined the Volkswagen Group, it has adopted the organizational culture established in by the group.

Additionally, Škoda has four dimensions that represent the culture of the company: "Lakshya"—the company is focused on results in the disciplined way; "We care"—the company is sensitive to and reliable for stakeholders; "Dil se"—the company puts its head and heart in whatever it does; and "Hum Saath Saath Hai"—the company is a unit cell, it values the team it has that forms Škoda's talent management approach (Škoda 2017c).

Škoda Auto has an impressive amount of official documents, which determine its talent management policy and attitude to workers, putting its employees among its most important stakeholders. Škoda's main objective in human resource management is maintaining the status of the most attractive employer that can hire talented people globally. Obviously, its existing talent management practices should reflect the aforementioned statement.

The recruitment process in Škoda begins with a definition of the necessary quota for future workers, followed by creation of job descriptions, and then applications and CV analysis, written exams/online tests for candidates, and finally interviews. The quantity of interviews and necessity of such evaluations varies from country to country and from vacancy to vacancy. Škoda is eager to work with young employees or graduates and provide them with the necessary education and training (Škoda 2017c). Also, each employee is provided with induction training (Škoda 2017c).

An innovative project, the "High Performance Organization", aims to strengthen the company's future competitiveness and support employees in key strategic areas (Automobilwoche 2015). As a result of this project, the company's talent management system was significantly reformed and improved. The company accomplished the following steps: the corporate organizational structure was simplified in order to optimize internal information flows and speed up the decision-making process; career paths for specialists, managers and project managers became clearer and more specific; interdepartmental objectives aimed at the horizontal development of employees were implemented; and bureaucracy was "permanently" reduced with the arrival of a "Smart IT Support" system that enabled the company to reduce the number of indirect staff involved in excessive bureaucratic routines (VW 2016). The "High Performance Organization" was a shining example of the successful implementation of change management: moving from the senior level to operational employees. The system of motivation in Škoda Auto comprises a diversity of benefits apart from financial compensation. Although pay within the company is good, it contributes to the common welfare of employees (VW 2016). As the company strengthen its brand and remained competitive on the labor market, it devised a diverse range of additional benefits: an extra week of holiday and a program that stimulates employees to travel more, which includes a travel insurance package or a contribution to recreation; contributions from the company related to special (or important) occasions in the employee's life, for example a wedding (the company provides a wedding car) or addition to an employee's family (financial contribution). Meals are also provided by the company, including snacks, six-dish meals with a reduced price; and the company helps to provide employees with its core product by offering discounts on car purchase and rentals as well as special insurance premiums and service; plus accommodation (the company gives accommodation or subsidizes an employee in when acquiring or reconstructing property), additional internal career opportunities (such as flexible internships abroad and development programs), and access to Škoda's private medical centers that incorporate a wide range of rehabilitation, reconditioning and preventive health programs. Škoda offers extensive professional and personal training in the Škoda Academy corporate university, which is the first and the only company-owned university in the Czech Republic. Stimulating technical awareness in the employees, the company gives financial and technical support, such as cellphone plan compensation and support for hardware and software purchases. Also, Škoda has a wide range of minor benefits such as days off, pension savings plans and nursery compensation (VW 2016).

The aforementioned benefits indicate that Škoda takes care of its employees and strongly adheres to its commitment to maintain high employment standards. Nevertheless, while a prosperous situation may exist in the home market this does not mean that the standards in foreign subsidiaries are the same. As soon as we consider peripheral countries like India, where the market is actually forcing companies to discard high corporate standards and use the cheap workforce to the fullest, the commitment immediately becomes invalid.

The performance appraisal at Škoda follows the guidelines of the Volkswagen Group according to the agreement of 2013. The guidelines refer to the annual appraisal system, that combines performance appraisal with development planning for all employees (VW 2016). As was set out in the Volkswagen Group remuneration system, each employee of every company in the group receives payments in accordance with his or her performance (VW 2016). Such performance assessment is done annually, where the workers of a company have a meeting with line managers. The main goal of the meetings is to recognize an employee's shortfalls or successes, and provide any training or bonus according to an employee's performance, finally developing a career development plan. The best workers get the opportunity of corresponding training and further may be promoted both vertically and horizontally (Škoda also provides an opportunity to work in co-partners' brands within the Volkswagen Group) (VW 2016).

Škoda sees its employees and teamwork as a major asset. Therefore, it invests in teambuilding and employee development. Škoda provides such opportunities for employee development as language courses, training for the individual development of employee skills and e-learning courses, the Apprentice Car project (where students build a car prototype), health training (in Škoda Policlinic, aimed at reducing the negative impact of work practices and prevent illnesses), and assessment of employee potential (VW 2016).

Škoda has training centers located in the Czech Republic and in other countries. Training centers annually help a large number of employees with skills improvement. The Czech automaker has a wide network of training centers for local industries. Plants in the Czech Republic and in India have a so-called "vocational training center" (VW 2016) and the Škoda Training Center opened at the main plant in Mladá Boleslav (VW 2016).

The Škoda Academy educational center was designed to offer educational courses to develop employee knowledge and competences (VW 2016). The Academy's programs are designed to improve technical and interdisciplinary skills. The Academy itself develops programs taking into account the strategy of Volkswagen Group's Academy. In addition, the Academy participates in the technical education of students and talent development. The main goal of the Academy is to unite social and technical skills, to share experiences and to prepare students for practice. The Škoda Academy offers adult training to develop technical specialists in innovative approaches by offering 14 courses in IT mechatronics, logistics, auto mechanics, electrical engineering and tooling, including a special course for disabled apprentices, and develops employee assessment (VW 2016).

Škoda Auto has its own corporate university, unique for the Czech Republic, located in Mlada Boleslav, close to one of the biggest Škoda factories. The university plays not only a corporate role, but it is open to any university candidate. It offers bachelor and master degree programs to school graduates who might consider developing their career in Škoda. The number of students is about 1000 including part-time students who are Škoda's employees. Thus, the university is an example of related diversification in order to achieve synergies. Consequently, all training and development programs at Škoda are derived from or related to the corporate university. It provides a bachelor program in management and economics which is divided into three specializations (Universities CZ

2017): business management and production; business management and sales; and corporate finance management. The university also provides a master's program. The bachelor degree program includes one semester of mandatory internship in an industry enterprise, usually in Škoda Auto; furthermore, the best students are placed in foreign subsidiaries of the Volkswagen Group (Cedefop 2016). The follow-on master's degree program is offered in Czech or English and there is a high degree of interaction between lecturers and students during seminars and exercises (Cedefop 2016).

Škoda Auto organizes an annual trainee program (Tschechien AHK 2017). The principles of the program are also shared by the regular recruitment practice, even in foreign subsidiaries. Škoda is widely promoting its annual trainee program aimed at high-potential candidates. The program is flexible enough to provide potential employees with access to the tasks in a wide range of departments while still being standardized. Trainees are involved in a horizontal development process by various rotations outside the target department. The trainee program has strict requirements including a completed master's degree, English language at advanced level and work or study experience abroad or work experience during studies (Tschechien AHK 2017). The assessment center is used for developing and carrying out staff assessments. Generally, the trainee program consists of the following stages: production experience, job rotation in a target department, job rotation outside the target department, a foreign internship, work experience in a dealer network and then a career beginning. To sum up, the trainee program has the goal of attracting graduates and giving them a diverse work experience as well as to develop them.

Škoda participates in a joint expatriate program with the German-Czech Chamber of Industry and Commerce and the Volkswagen Group (Tschechien AHK 2017). The Volkswagen Partner Support Program is aimed at helping expatriates who work in the Volkswagen Group to have a comfortable international assignment. This program helps to adapt and integrate expatriates into the new working environment.

The Volkswagen Partner Support Program has three aspects: career and profession, studies and professional training, and cultural and honorary engagement (Tschechien AHK 2017). The career and profession block includes basic information on the profession, studies and professional training advice on all questions related to the establishment of Czech business ventures, including legal and tax provisions, a customized job search, access to various networking events, and a Czech labor law overview. Studies and professional training are about advice and identification of further education possibilities, including advanced studies and vocational (re)training, language courses and further individual courses. Cultural engagement includes cultural awareness training, cultural background and benefits study, improvement of intercultural communication, and promotion of social engagement and exploration. The Volkswagen Group also provides its expats with a special brochure, which contains all the important information about international assignments.

Despite the fact that Škoda is a part of the VW Group and follows its strategy and approaches to talent management, the company has developed and initiated new practices and directions in talent management.

Unipetrol: Driven by Business

Unipetrol is a group consisting of refinery and petrochemical companies that process crude oil, produce plastics and operate filling stations in the Czech Republic. The Unipetrol Group is one of the key participants in CEE markets (Unipetrol 2011). Unipetrol was established in 1995 with the privatization of the Czech petrochemical industry. Before the privatization process, there were several independent state enterprises; these companies were consolidated to form a conglomerate that could compete with massive multinationals. Unipetrol was not totally privatized as 63% of its shares were still owned by the Czech state (Unipetrol 2011). The others were held by private proprietors, mainly investment funds and small shareholders. The privatization was completed in 2005, when the Czech state sold 62.99% of Unipetrol shares to the Polish company ORLEN, a major player in the CEE (Unipetrol 2011).

The company's objective is to ensure a long-term and constant growth of value for its shareholders. Therefore, it is focused on four strategic segments: processing of crude oil and wholesale of refinery products; petrochemical production; and retail of motor fuels and energy independence

(Unipetrol 2011). The company's management points out that the key profit source for Unipetrol is the petrochemical segment. Unipetrol's strategy is focused on improving its efficiency and operational excellence across the main business segments in order to ensure long-term growth (Unipetrol 2013).

The activities of Unipetrol are diverse: it operates in the production and sale of refined oil, chemical and petrochemical products, polymers, fertilizers and specialized chemicals (Unipetrol 2011). Thus, Unipetrol consists of several companies: Unipetrol RPA deals with refinery, petrochemical and agrochemical products; Paramo produces asphalts, lubricating and fuel oils, fuels and other refinery products; Benzina is the largest operator of filling stations in the Czech Republic; Unipetrol Doprava is a specialized shipper of chemical, petrochemical and all related products; and Česká rafinérská (Unipetrol is its major shareholder holding 52.22%) is the main processor of crude oil and producer of refinery products in the Czech Republic (Unipetrol 2016).

Unipetrol is a joint-stock company (Unipetrol 2016). It is managed by the Board of Directors, which consists of seven senior managers and executives from companies which belong to the Unipetrol Group (Unipetrol 2017a). The overall structure may be defined as functional as executives occupy their positions according to the responsibilities of the departments they lead.

Unipetrol's mission is to process natural resources (oil) for fueling the future. The company has strict ethical principles, which aim to: ensure long-term growth for its shareholders, provide the best possible products and services to customers, and develop best solutions for management and motivation (Unipetrol 2015). Unipetrol shares corporate values which are responsibility (the enterprise is liable to its stakeholders, respects them and the natural environment), progress (the company is innovation-driven led by employees' high expertise), people (personnel is considered as one of the key resources), energy (it is people's commitment that ensures success), and dependability (the company's products and services are safe) (Unipetrol 2015).

Unipetrol's organizational culture is determined by the specifics of its area of business and its business strategy. A company operating in the field needs well-developed standards, clear procedures, well-defined structure with clear lines of authority and decision-making, and strong control to ensure stability and growth. The talent management strategy and practices correspond to that. In the recruitment process, Unipetrol actively uses assessment centers to explore the vocational potential of prospective employees (Unipetrol 2017b). The center designs the selection of the most appropriate candidates by evaluating their competences and abilities. Based on the obtained information, projected career paths are created, and starting points for training and development activities are planned. As the recruitment policy of Unipetrol focuses on attracting highly qualified specialists, the company closely co-operates with educational institutions at different levels. Unipetrol has established a long-term partnership with the Institute of Chemical Technology in Prague in order to attract talent to the chemical industry. The company supports the popularization of chemistry by giving regular lectures and presentations as well as providing funds to support the research of talented students. Unipetrol has also constructed a unique research and education center, called UniCRE, to combine the efforts of company researchers and talented students. The center delivers a special teaching and research program (Unipetrol 2017b).

Through these activities, the company attracts new prospective employees to participate in the Trainee Program (for graduates eligible for higher positions), in Student Apprenticeships (for current students) and in the Junior Program (for graduates) (ORLEN 2007). They enable the company to carry out an accurate assessment of the competences of any applicants who want to work in the company. The Adaptation Program helps new employees to familiarize themselves with Unipetrol's operations and its organizational culture (ORLEN 2007). Apart from an introductory meeting and workshops with experts, under the Adaptation Program employees also take part in e-learning programs covering Unipetrol's history, current organizational and employee issues, as well as its core values and standards of conduct.

The training of Unipetrol's talent is focused primarily on maintaining the qualifications of the production personnel and further professional development. Employees receive mandatory training, and attend professional or vocational seminars and foreign language courses.

Unipetrol provides its employees with various benefits, such as co-financing of employee holidays or spa treatments, childcare, holidays for children and teenagers, school starter kits, financial support for families with low incomes, recreation and sports activities, cultural and educational activities, non-repayable allowances, repayable housing loans, and Christmas gifts for employees' children (Unipetrol 2017b).

As a company implementing modern-day solutions aimed at keeping the balance between work and family life, Unipetrol instigated out the Family-Friendly Employer project, offering benefits, including an additional two days off to care for a child under three years old, one additional hour for breastfeeding, quick access to a pediatrician, comprehensive medical care during pregnancy, baby feeding rooms and sending company updates to female employees on maternity and parental/childcare leave (Unipetrol 2017b). The company provides extensive preventive medical care going beyond the scope of occupational medicine, including consultations with specialists, outpatient treatment, diagnostic tests, rehabilitation, vaccinations and preventive healthcare programs (Unipetrol 2017b).

The company has embraced "The Core Values and Standards of Conduct", addressing ethical issues related to human rights, diversity, equal opportunities and corruption prevention (Unipetrol 2017a). The goal is to build good relations and mutual trust within the organization. The uniqueness of the system is that any employee has a number of options on how to deliver feedback or information, varying in terms of channels and the organizational level on which information will be delivered.

In talent management implementation, Unipetrol acts as a business partner, change agent, administrative expert and employee advocate (KB Manage 2017) addressing the following issues: remuneration and bonus systems, improvement of working time organization, reorganization processes, and competence and employee-engagement development. The company faces challenges that are typical in the Czech economy. One of the main challenges is an aging staff. Unipetrol's employment structure shows that employees aged between 40 and 50 account for 36% of personnel, while those aged between 50 and 60 make up 29% (Unipetrol 2015). In the modern, rapidly changing world, this ratio weakens the strategic position of the company. To be able to generate ideas and innovations in the future, Unipetrol needs to attract new talent and in recognition of this fact began to address this issue in the early 2000s. It now co-operates with Czech educational institutions such as the University of Chemistry and Technology and the Institute of Chemical Technology. The company has established strategic partnerships with these institutions, which include a joint university center, scholarship programs, and competitions such as case championships for students and scholars (Unipetrol 2015).

As Unipetrol is now owned and controlled by ORLEN, it has aligned its approaches and strategies with the parent's corporate objectives and strategies. This involves a strong co-operation with universities in order to grow, select and attract new talent, supporting employees' loyalty by promoting ORLEN's strategy in the Czech Republic, and providing employees with the necessary training and benefits to help the company to develop its position of a leader in its domestic market.

CEZ: To Get the Best

CEZ is a Czech company generating, distributing and trading electricity, gas and heat across Central and Southeast Europe. The company is based in Prague, the Czech Republic, and currently employs around 26,000 people (CEZ Group 2017a). CEZ is a joint-stock company since 69.8% of its shares are owned by the Czech Republic's Ministry of Finance (CEZ Group 2017a). The major products and services include power production and trading, distribution and sale, mining and other business activities which are spread across Central and Southeast Europe (CEZ Group 2017a).

CEZ was founded by the National Property Fund of the Czech Republic after the collapse of the state-owned Czech Power Networks in 1992 (CEZ Group 2017a). After formation, the company was partially privatized, and its utilities were totally privatized. Up until 1998, CEZ had made vast investments into desulfurization of its power plants. In 2002, a merger between CEZ and the regional distributors was approved by the Czech government (CEZ Group 2017a). The merger significantly contributed to the maintenance of the company's leading position in Central Europe. In 2010, CEZ started to supply around 90 customers in the Czech Republic with natural gas and a new program, "New Vision", began a process of internal performance review and upgrading of the CEZ Group (CEZ Group 2017a). In 2013, CEZ Korporatnisluzby was formed with responsibility for accounting, asset management and human resources. Later that year, an agreement with the European Commission was signed on the divestment of several CEZ power plants (CEZ Group 2017a). CEZ's Chvaletice power plant was sold to Litvinovskauhelna (CEZ Group 2017a). A contract was signed with the heating company TauronCieplo in order to ensure that the supply of heat to end users continued. In 2015, the company, on behalf of its fully owned investment company Inven Capital, started investing in innovative energy advancements and cutting-edge storage systems (CEZ Group 2017a).

The company is engaged in power production and trading, distribution and sales, mining and other business activities. The company's key products and services include coal, electricity, heat, natural gas, electricity generation and distribution, electricity sales to end customers, natural gas sales to end customers, heat generation and distribution, gas trading, coal mining and coal exports (CEZ Group 2017b). The main principles of the organizational culture are as follows: the safe creation of value, taking responsibility for results, strong team-playing, development of potential, growing beyond its borders, seeking new solutions, and fair play (CEZ Group 2017c). The principles are shared with all employees and require their practical implementation.

The company strives to create, maintain and support its corporate ethics and culture by imposing strict ethical standards. One of the integral components of CEZ's corporate culture is a long-term support for education, culture, sports and community life via execution of corporate sponsorship (CEZ Group 2017c). CEZ is also known for its high corporate social responsibility standards and active sponsorship. The company has its own foundation, the Nadace Foundation, contributing to the development and implementation of public-benefit projects.

CEZ's safety policy is implemented through emphasizing protection of life and people's health over other interests. To diminish any kind of demoralizing risk, the company regularly evaluates risks, prevents or eliminates them, or decreases them to an acceptable level. Notably, creating value safely is one of the seven principles of CEZ's corporate culture.

Since 2015, the labor market has been characterized by a continuously decreasing number of job seekers and an increasing number of vacancies (CEZ Group 2017c). In spite of this situation, CEZ managed to fill advertised vacancies as required. Work with young people is based on a partner network with high schools, technical colleges and universities. In addition to nuclear, energy and distribution extracurricular programs and the Summer University, an Innovation Marathon is organized for college and university students (CEZ Group 2017c). In spite of all these activities, CEZ's position in the employer attractiveness rankings, which are based on college and university students' votes and published regularly, deteriorated in 2015 (CEZ Group 2017c).

CEZ has launched the two-year CEZ Potentials Program (CEZ Group 2017c), which is intended for university graduates. After passing the selection procedure, program participants are appointed to specific job positions in CEZ companies. Over a period of 12 months, they undergo a specially designed program involving the development of soft skills, workshops, coaching, tours of CEZ operations and motivational meetings with top management.

The strategic talent recruitment activities support technical education. The "I Know Why" contest, held among middle-school and high-school students, is intended to motivate young people to shoot videos of physical experiments (CEZ Group 2017d).

CEZ and its integrated subsidiaries are highly technology-oriented companies that place high demands not only on employees' professional qualifications but also on their physical and psychological fitness for their jobs. However, CEZ has made it possible to employ people with disabilities in selected positions, giving them an opportunity to integrate into society and improve their quality of life (CEZ Group 2017e). CEZ was one of the first organizations to sign the Memorandum on the Promotion of Equal Opportunities in the Labor Market and Active Application of Gender Balance Principles (CEZ Group 2017e).

The main objective of motivational programs and benefits at CEZ is to ensure employee motivation and retention in order to help achieve the company's strategic goals while efficiently managing personnel costs and optimally allocating them to individuals. The remuneration system and wage policy are designed to facilitate internal fairness and external competitiveness. CEZ employees are paid wages that are in line with CEZ's long-term financial performance and position in the labor market. Base wages are differentiated according to the complexity, responsibility and difficulty of the work performed. Variable wage components ensure a bond with corporate and individual goals as well as behavior in accordance with corporate principles (CEZ Group 2017f). They motivate employees to take personal responsibility for results as well as to reach strategic goals.

CEZ has a shortened, 37.5-hour working week, one additional week of paid vacation is provided beyond the statutory minimum, and employees get paid leave beyond that required by law (CEZ Group 2017f). CEZ provides employees with a broad portfolio of benefits, such as personal accounts intended especially for recreation, contributions to supplemental pension insurance, life insurance, employee meal plans, contributions during the first three days of sick leave, health care, special bonuses for employee jubilees and on retirement, the Mobility Support program (intended for key employees changing their place of work within CEZ) and one-time only social aid in extraordinary cases (CEZ Group 2017f). In addition to the benefits arising from collective agreements, the employer negotiates discounts on selected companies' goods and services for its employees. CEZ strives to offer its employees benefits that are advantageous, while offering a wide variety of benefits to encourage and allow as many employees as possible to take advantage of them. Although the company incurs considerable expense to provide these benefits, employees often see them as an entitlement or a natural part of employment relations rather than an additional expression of the employer's care and appreciation.

In order to fulfill the corporate culture action plan and strategic goals of the Performance and Enterprise Program, the Management Growth Program for directors and managers was launched along with the People Development Forum, a joint platform for CEZ's top management to discuss development and career opportunities for program participants) (CEZ Group 2017g).

In talent development, CEZ focuses on building up expertise and soft skills tailored to departments and specific target groups. It also supports qualification improvement, especially at technology-oriented secondary schools, colleges and universities. CEZ is focusing on the development of its key employees, specifically promoting their performance, entrepreneurship and motivation in the period of changes and instability. Key employees can choose from a wide portfolio of development programs, in which they can use their personal development plans with the support of an external coach. CEZ also develops strategic management and defines six managerial competences based on CEZ's current strategic needs, which are mandatory for each manager (CEZ Group 2017g). CEZ management expects that the new managerial competences will make company management more efficient, improve the performance of directors and their teams, and create the conditions for dynamic growth and faster adoption of changes. The management development program involves continuous, repeated activities that aim to achieve an optimum level of managerial performance (CEZ Group 2017g).

When providing training to its employees, CEZ also uses an e-learning platform. The portfolio of e-learning courses keeps growing, currently including more than 100 courses in such areas as mandatory training and development programs, and expert courses tailored to CEZ's specific needs (CEZ Group 2017g). As a result, its training needs are fulfilled with greater efficiency.

CEZ pays special attention to training for nuclear plant personnel. Managers from generating unit control rooms regularly take part in "Play Safe" courses, focusing on teamwork and safe and efficient decision-making. A project named Electronic Job Descriptions for Enhanced Safety was launched in 2013 with the aim of allowing managers to cross-link activities undertaken by their subordinates with qualification selection, placing an increased emphasis on "safety requirements" (CEZ Group 2017g).

The top management supports career management, including job rotations, succession, and development of managerial competences to support the company's strategic initiatives. This step has a positive effect on CEZ's corporate culture. Participants in the management development program work for a year on their own development action plans

(CEZ Group 2017g). While the main responsibility for achieving development goals is held by program participants, they receive support from their managers and all available development tools from the talent management system. The progress in managerial competences is measured using 360-degree professional feedback (CEZ Group 2017g).

CEZ uses a wide variety of communication tools to keep its employees informed, such as the *CEZ NEWS* magazine, intranet sites, including the audiovisual CEZ TV, direct newsletters with keynote information, SMSs or audio messages, notices on bulletin boards, or elements of internal marketing (CEZ Group 2017h). Employee involvement and engagement are strengthened by workshops, meetings with the management of divisions, subsidiaries and power plants, professional employee meetings, meetings across subsidiaries, or skip level meetings that were newly introduced at the nuclear power plants and were recognized as best practice by the international OSART mission (CEZ Group 2017h).

Employees can file their complaints and comments regarding employment relations to the head of human resources (CEZ Group 2017h). Concrete complaints are handled by the Social Relations Department (CEZ Group 2017h), which makes sure the complaint is examined and a response is sent to the employee. Employees can also file their complaints and comments through relevant labor unions according to the collective agreement. Suggestions and observations are submitted by means of the "Orange Mailbox". This is mostly electronic communication using intranet forms. Employees submit their questions as well as opinions with the aid of a table of topics (CEZ Group 2017h).

One of the important ways to obtain feedback from all employees is via the corporate and safety culture survey, organized by CEZ every three years. Based on the feedback, CEZ not only promotes changes in corporate culture, but also motivates employees to express what should be improved and what should be sustained in the company. Employees can check and amend the interpretation of the results and help propose solutions and appropriate measures at task workshops. The outcomes are action plans in which employees can participate personally, with management's support.

CEZ's strategy, to some extent, can be compared with that of the other Czech companies, described above. In the process of moving toward a knowledge economy, the company tries to attract, develop and retain the most valuable resource—its employees—by creating safe and comfortable working conditions, developing training programs and improving appraisal systems. Similar to Unipetrol, CEZ tries to co-operate intensively with schools, colleges and universities to grow its future employees.

*   *   *

As a former post-socialistic country, the Czech Republic is still in the process of transition toward a knowledge-based economy. Analysis of talent management practices in Czech companies suggests that the country-specific environment and social relationships influence the development of human resource management within organizations.

The positive trend that is clearly seen in companies' activities is that they are becoming more agile and customer-oriented in organizational behavior. For this reason, many companies are changing their organizational design from a traditional, functional one toward a flexible one. One of the challenges faced is nurturing the leaders who can take these companies forward and strengthen their competitive advantage in the longer term. In this case, companies have to face two major challenges: attraction of qualified, talented employees and their retention. To overcome the first obstacle, the above presented companies promote intensive collaboration with schools and universities. (In terms of employee retention, motivation systems were launched in the companies and apart from financial compensation, benefits for employees include development programs, flexible internships abroad, co-financing of employee holidays, and childcare, among others. The companies pay much attention to the safety of working conditions. Realizing the growing role of innovation for long-term competitiveness and economic performance, CEZ, Škoda and Unipetrol have implemented e-learning platforms for easier knowledge transfer within the company.

References

Automobilwoche. 2015. High Performance Organization: Škoda schlägt Fitnesspfad ein. https://www.automobilwoche.de/article/20150324/HEFTARCHIV/150329978/high-performance-organization-skoda-schlaegt-fitnesspfad-ein. Accessed Aug 2017.

BBC. 2018. Czech Republic Country Profile. http://www.bbc.com/news/world-europe-17220018. Accessed Jan 2018.

Cedefop. 2016. Skill Shortages in Europe: Which Occupations Are in Demand – and Why. http://www.cedefop.europa.eu/en/news-and-press/news/skill-shortages-europe-which-occupations-are-demand-and-why. Accessed Aug 2017.

CEZ Group. 2017a. Introducing Czech Power Company CEZ. https://www.cez.cz/en/cez-group/cez.html. Accessed Sept 2017.

———. 2017b. Processing Companies. https://www.cez.cz/en/cez-group/cez-group/subsidiaries/processing-companies.html. Accessed Sept 2017.

———. 2017c. Education Program. https://www.cez.cz/edee/content/micrositesutf/odpovednost2011/en/socialni-odpovednost/korporatni-identita/vztahy-s-verejnosti/vzdelavaci-program.html. Accessed Sept 2017.

———. 2017d. Support for Technical Education. https://www.cez.cz/edee/content/micrositesutf/odpovednost2013/en/socialni-odpovednost/podpora-technickeho-vzdelavani.html. Accessed Sept 2017.

———. 2017e. Diversity, Equal Employment Opportunity. https://www.cez.cz/edee/content/micrositesutf/odpovednost2013/en/socialni-odpovednost/zamestnanci/diverzita.html. Accessed Sept 2017.

———. 2017f. Motivational Programs and Benefits. https://www.cez.cz/edee/content/micrositesutf/odpovednost2013/en/socialni-odpovednost/zamestnanci/motivacni-programy-a-benefity.html. Accessed Sept 2017.

———. 2017g. Learning and Development. https://www.cez.cz/edee/content/micrositesutf/odpovednost2013/en/socialni-odpovednost/zamestnanci/vzdelavani-a-rozvoj.html. Accessed Sept 2017.

———. 2017h. Employee Turnover and Outplacement. https://www.cez.cz/edee/content/micrositesutf/odpovednost2013/en/socialni-odpovednost/zamestnanci/fluktuace-a-pece-o-odchazejici-zamestnance.html. Accessed Sept 2017.

CIA. 2017. Europe:Czechia. https://www.cia.gov/library/publications/resources/the-world-factbook/geos/ez.html. Accessed July 2017.

Dubravska, M., and E. Solankova. 2015. Recent Trends in Human Resources Management in Selected Industry in Slovakia and the Czech Republic. *Procedia Economics and Finance* 26: 1014–1019.

European Union. 2016. Czech Republic. https://europa.eu/european-union/about-eu/countries/member-countries/czechrepublic_en. Accessed Aug 2017.

Hofstede Insights. 2017. What about Czech Republic? https://www.hofstede-insights.com/country-comparison/czech-republic/. Accessed July 2017.

KB Manage. 2017. Ulrich Model. https://www.kbmanage.com/concept/ulrich-model. Accessed Sept 2017.

Lanik M., G. Thornton, and S. Hoskovcova 2009. A Flat World? A Comparative Study of Achievement Motivation in the Czech Republic and the United States. https://www.researchgate.net/publication/286867662_A_flat_world_A_comparative_study_of_achievement_motivation_in_the_Czech_Republic_and_the_United_States. Accessed June 2017.

ORLEN. 2007. Annual Report. http://raportroczny.orlen.pl/report_en_employees_2007. Accessed Aug 2017.

Škoda. 2015. Annual Report. https://cdn.skoda-storyboard.com/2016/05/skoda-annual-report-2015.pdf. Accessed Aug 2017.

———. 2017a. The History of Škoda – Over 100 Years of Getting People from A to B. http://www.skoda.co.uk/skoda-history. Accessed Aug 2017.

———. 2017b. Corporate Governance in Škoda Auto. http://www.skoda-auto.com/en/company/compliance/corporate-governance/. Accessed Aug 2017.

———. 2017c. Škoda Career. https://www.skoda-career.com/about-us. Accessed Aug 2017.

Skoludova, J., and Z. Brodsky. 2015. Current Trends of Selected Aspects of Human Resource Management in the Czech Republic. *Procedia Economics and Finance* 26: 603–660.

Stacho, Z., H. Urbancova, and K. Stachova. 2013. *Organisational Arrangement of Human Resources Management in Organisations Operating in Slovakia and Czech Republic.* Acta universitatis Agriculturae et Silviculturae Mendelianae Brunensis. https://acta.mendelu.cz/media/pdf/actaun_2013061072787.pdf. Accessed July 2017.

Tschechien AHK. 2017. Volkswagen Partner Support Program Czech Republic. http://tschechien.ahk.de/fileadmin/ahk_tschechien/Dienstleistungen/Partner_Support_Programm/Flyer_VW_Partner_Support_Program_English.pdf. Accessed Aug 2017.

Unipetrol. 2011. Unipetrol Group Profile. http://www.unipetrol.cz/en/AboutUs/Documents/profil_spolecnosti_11_2011.pdf. Accessed Aug 2017.

———. 2013. Unipetrol Strategy for 2013–2017. http://www.unipetrol.cz/en/Media/PressReleases/Pages/Unipetrol-Strategy-for-2013-2017.aspx. Accessed Aug 2017.

———. 2015. Annual Report. http://www.unipetrol.cz/cs/VztahySInvestory/vyrocni-zpravy/Documents/2015%20ANNUAL%20REPORT/Unipetrol_Annual_Report_2015.pdf. Accessed Aug 2017.

———. 2016. Articles of Association. http://www.unipetrol.cz/en/AboutUs/Documents/UNI_Stanovy%202016%20EN%20CLEAN_08072016.pdf. Accessed Aug 2017.

———. 2017a. History. http://www.unipetrol.cz/en/AboutUs/Pages/History.aspx. Accessed Aug 2017.

———. 2017b. Responsible Care Program. http://www.unipetrol.cz/en/CSR/Pages/Environment.aspx. Accessed Aug 2017.

Universities CZ. 2017. Skoda Auto University. http://www.universities.cz/czech-universities/private-universities/skoda-auto-university-. Accessed Aug 2017.

VW. 2016. The Brand from Central Europe. http://sustainabilityreport2016.volkswagenag.com/brands/skoda.html. Accessed Aug 2017.

———. 2017a. Strategy 2025. https://www.volkswagenag.com/en/InvestorRelations/strategy/Strategy_2025.html. Accessed Aug 2017.

———. 2017b. Our Strategy – For Tomorrow's Growth. https://www.volkswagenag.com/en/group/strategy.html. Accessed Aug 2017.

9

Hungary: Creating New Opportunities for Talent

József Poór, János Fehér, and Victoria Tikhonova

Hungary is a parliamentary republic in Central Europe. Hungary joined the European Union (EU) in 2004 and has been a part of the Schengen Area since 2007. Hungary is a member of the United Nations, NATO, the World Trade Organization, the World Bank, the AIIB, the Council of Europe and Visegrád Group (RSM 2017). Considering the natural decrease in population, gross domestic product (GDP) per capita is growing annually (2013–2015) by 3.1% on average (Hungary is ranked 70

J. Poór (✉)
Szent István University, Gödöllő, Hungary
e-mail: poorjf@t-online.hu

J. Fehér
Károli Gáspár University of the Reformed Church in Hungary,
Budapest, Hungary
e-mail: feherdr@t-online.hu

V. Tikhonova
Graduate School of Management, St. Petersburg State University,
St. Petersburg, Russia
e-mail: tikhonova@gsom.pu.ru

© The Author(s) 2018
M. Latukha (ed.), *Talent Management in Global Organizations*,
Palgrave Studies of Internationalization in Emerging Markets,
https://doi.org/10.1007/978-3-319-76418-4_9

out of 229 countries in the "Doing Business" ranking) (RSM 2017). Both births and deaths per 1000 inhabitants are growing with the death rate exceeding the birth rate (13.4 versus 9.3 per 1000), leading to a natural decrease of population of around 40,000 annually. Expected life duration is 75.9 years as of 2015 and is increasing from year to year. Hungary has one of the world's lowest infant mortality rates (ranked 177 out of 225 countries) and high health and education expenditures (7.4% and 4.6% of GDP accordingly) (CIA 2017).

The unemployment rate in Hungary has been constantly decreasing since 2012 (CIA 2017). The Hungarian labor market is considered to be one of the most advanced in Central and Eastern Europe (CEE). It has flexible conditions for signing fixed-term contracts, quite a low ratio of minimum wage to value added by worker (0.3), average premiums for night shifts (15% of hourly pay) and for overtime work (50%). Also, there is no politically tolerated gender discrimination, and the average annual paid leave is 21.3 days. There is a full wage for maternity leave; employees have five fully paid days of sick leave per year and unemployment protection after one year of employment (The World Bank 2017).

Along with fair labor market regulations, there are quite acceptable conditions for doing business in Hungary. According to the "Doing Business" rating, there are no problems for entrepreneurs in trading across borders, acquiring credit, registering property or having the power to enforce contracts (The World Bank Group 2014). Hungary's Human Development Index (an average measure of basic human development achievements in a country) value for 2015 is 0.836—which puts the country high in the human development category—positioning it at 43 out of 188 countries and territories (UNDP 2016). Between 1990 and 2015, Hungary's Human Development Index value increased by 18.9%. Between 1990 and 2015, the life expectancy at birth increased by 6.0 years, years of schooling increased by 3.3 years and gross national income per capita increased by about 46.3% between 1990 and 2015 (UNDP 2016).

The country's organizational culture changed a lot owing to the transformation of the economy from being centrally planned to free market-led. Hungary was under the influence of the Soviet Union for 45 years until 1989. After that, the country had a transition from socialism to Western-style democracy. The complicated transition process had a set of

Hungary: Creating New Opportunities for Talent **145**

basic elements, of which several should be mentioned with respect to human resources at the macro-economic level: the New Labor Law, implemented in 1992, covering all aspects of employment; an end to the egalitarian pay structure; the end of workers' permanent job contracts; and a restructuring of the social welfare system (Budai 2011).

During the transition, Hungary had a relatively flexible labor market. In 1968 after the reforms, the state could affect the wages paid by companies and employers could choose the level of employment. As administrative rules did not limit the change of jobs, there was a high level of labor turnover. Liberalization continued till 1989: wage regulation collapsed and institutions supporting free enterprise were established. The situation changed with the collapse of the Soviet system and Hungary had access to the EU with new regulations being developed (Liptak 2012).

In the 1990s, in parallel with the economic and social changes, organizational development also experienced a change. Multinational companies entered the turbulent and under-supplied market quickly, and consequently, concentration of capital increased, leading to changes in the Hungarian organizational culture. More companies resorted to change processes. The need for training and education increased and this led to a focus on talent management (Budai 2011).

CRANET research (2016) of 272 public and private organizations (companies and institutions) with a total headcount of 337,433 (which is more than 8% of all people currently employed in Hungary) provides us with data about the overall picture. About half of the companies (52%) are in the small and medium enterprise bracket (employing from one to 249 people), while the remaining 48% are "larger" companies which employ more than 250 people. The workforce consists mainly (47%) of professional employees (non-managerial), followed by a similar proportion (41%) of office and/or manual workers and then by executives/managers (12%). In the public sector, the proportion of professional staff (54%) is much higher than in the private sector (43%). The proportion of clerical/manual workers and of managers is 8% and 3% lower than in the private sector.

The economic transformation brought significant changes in the role of the human resource management (HRM) function in most companies and institutions where this area has become strategically significant. In

146   J. Poór et al.

80% of the surveyed organizations there is an independent human resources (HR) department. In the private sector, the proportion is slightly lower (79%) than in the public sector (84%). In the participating organizations there are, on average, 63 employees for each HRM employee. In the private sector one HR employee arranges the affairs of an average of 55 people, while in the public sector the number is higher (70). Regarding HR outsourcing, in the private sector, training/development, recruitment and payroll are often entrusted to external service providers (50–57%), while in the public sector, 35–43% of organizations use external service providers.

As for the level of organizational influence on human resource management, the research suggests that managers can make decisions at their own discretion and without consulting with human resources on increasing or laying off staff (49%), and on pay and benefits (46%), and decisions related to recruitment and selection are made by 41% of managers after consultations with the HR department. Most pronounced is the decision-making role of the HR department in labor relations, training and development. In 36% of organizations the training and development decisions are made by HR department staff, after consultation with managers.

Regarding Hungarian recruitment and selection practices, a high proportion of companies (66–68%) use internal recruitment methods in the case of managers and professional staff. In the recruitment of professional staff and clerical/manual workers, advertisements are placed on the company's website, oral information is provided and 'word of mouth' support by the employees is crucial. Recruitment agencies are mostly used to head-hunt managers and professional employees in the private sector. Labor centers are mainly used to recruit clerical/manual workers. The least frequently used recruitment resources are social media and employment centers.

Based on the responses, it is clear that a performance appraisal system (PAS) is quite a widespread HR practice, since more than 66% of the organizations in all job categories use one. The role of performance appraisal in each sector is most prominent in the case of professional employees (private 74%, public 83%). The difference between the sectors in terms of application practice in the public sector regarding managers and professional employees exceeds 13%, and this is 9% the private sector. The respondent organizations mostly determine salary and bonus levels (77%) and career movement and development opportunities (66%) on the basis of the performance appraisal. A PAS is used in the public sector more frequently, although the results are less widely applied than in the private sector (Budai 2011).

As for the employees' work- and performance-related behavior, the average annual turnover rate for all organizations is 8%. The organizations reported an annual average of 10 days of absence/sick leave per employee. In this area, however, there is a huge gap between the data referring to workers in the private and public sectors. In contrast to the private sector, where there is an average of three days of absence/sick leave, for every worker, in the public sector it is 16 days.

Regarding training and development activities, the analysis concludes that a systematic needs assessment of personnel training and development is typical of half of the interviewed organizations. According to respondents from the public sector, a higher proportion of their organizations prepare systematic needs assessments (55%) than in the private sector (47%). According to the organizations, the number of days spent annually in formal training is the highest among managers and professional staff, with values close to each other (7.68 and 7.62 days/year). In the private sector, it is the executives who enjoy most training, with an average of 7.30 days per year, while in the public sector it is the clerical/manual employees who have the most training (10.06 days per year). In both sectors, the clerical/manual staff have the fewest training days; in the private sector under four days per year on average.

Regarding the compensation system, the basic salary/wage is determined at individual and corporate level. In this area, the least important role is played by regional collective bargaining. It is notable that in 50% of the organizations there are no trade unions at all. In the private sector, such organizations predominate (66%), while in the public sector the figure is much lower at only 20%. In the private sector, determining the basic salary of managers mostly occurs at the individual level (62%). Basic wages for professional staff and clerical/manual employees are mainly the result of company-level decisions and individual bargaining. According to the responses received from the public sector, salaries are primarily determined by national collective bargaining (37–39%), but, especially for managers, determination is also possible at the individual level.

The most common financial incentives, besides basic salary, are bonuses based on individual goals and non-monetary incentives. Bonuses based on organizational goals play an important role in motivating managers. In 42% of the organizations, the amount of benefits received by managers depends on this. Employee share and stock option programs, as well as profit sharing, are quite rare and mostly apply only to management. In the private sector, there is more emphasis on employee incentives which are linked to organizational and team goals, although individual performance-related pay is also a solution applied in the public sector.

The most widespread methods used in career management are taking part in team projects, on-the-job training, knowledge expansion project work and specific work tasks. Formal career plans and succession plans have lower importance than before. Mentoring and e-learning are becoming more and more a tool of career management in a growing number of organizations. At present, the least-used method is the development center.

The research provides data about development and career support action programs for special groups of employees. Only a small proportion of organizations have action programs to help the disadvantaged in the labor market (2–4%), and these programs mostly focus on young workers (20–24%). Recruitment, training and career development programs are addressed least to workers belonging to ethnic minority groups and the over-50s. In the public sector 4 to 5% more organizations have developed programs for ethnic minorities than in the private sphere, although 3 to 12% fewer organizations have training, recruitment, and career development programs for women (Budai 2011).

Gedeon Richter: Going Beyond Expectations

The Chemical Works of Gedeon Richter plc (Gedeon Richter) is a European innovation-driven specialty pharmaceutical company with products distributed in more than 100 countries worldwide (Gedeon Richter 2016). Its headquarters are situated in Budapest, Hungary. Gedeon Richter employs around 11,000 people worldwide (Gedeon

Richter 2016). The company is present in more than 38 countries with five manufacturing facilities, 29 representative offices and 38 sales subsidiaries or wholesale companies (Gedeon Richter 2016). Gedeon Richter, Hungarian pharmacist, founded the company in 1901 and the firm was restructured as a limited company called the Gedeon Richter Chemical Works in 1923 (Gedeon Richter 2017a). Before the Second World War, the company was constantly growing, yet it lost important markets in Western Europe in the post-war period. This prompted the company to conduct research to formulate original drugs, and eventually, the company invented its own process to manufacture vitamin B12, which gained great success in the market (Gedeon Richter 2017a).

The key markets for Gedeon Richter are Russia and other Commonwealth of Independent States (CIS) countries as they account for 36% of sales revenue (Gedeon Richter 2016). The company made a great effort to become an important player in Western Europe and have it as the second important region in terms of sales revenues. Gedeon Richter is also seeking official approval to market certain products in China and Latin America (Gedeon Richter 2017b). That position, together with North American partnership agreements and the many decades of presence in Central and Eastern Europe and the CIS region, have resulted in Gedeon Richter becoming a global pharmaceutical company specializing in gynecological products (Gedeon Richter 2017b).

Vertically integrated, the company is engaged in research, development, manufacturing and marketing of more than 200 pharmaceutical products. These include original, generic and licensed products, which provide effective treatment in almost every therapeutic area. Gedeon Richter focuses on the development and manufacturing of gynecological, cardiovascular and central nervous system products. Gedeon Richter also produces a wide range of products that are available in pharmacies without prescription (OTC, "over-the-counter") (Gedeon Richter 2017c).

The corporate culture of Gedeon Richter reflects its position as a multinational pharmaceutical company. Its key principles are enduring values, stability, ethics, a livable workplace, innovation, commitment, performance orientation and teamwork, and maintenance of trust and reliability with customers as the pharmaceutical industry reflects health and well-being (Gedeon Richter 2017d).

According to Aon Hewitt's "Most Desired Employers" study (Gedeon Richter 2015), Gedeon Richter was the most desirable workplace in the pharmaceutical industry in 2013 (Gedeon Richter 2015). The company was also selected as the most desirable workplace in the pharmaceutical and chemical industry sector, winning the "Randstad Award" in 2014 and 2015 (Gedeon Richter 2015). Such recognition confirms that Gedeon Richter's values are very much appreciated by employees in Hungary (Gedeon Richter 2015). Gedeon Richter is also famous for a high average number of years spent in employment at the company (nearly 14), which is highest in Hungary (Gedeon Richter 2017d).

It is crucial for the company to attract the best and brightest employees in order to maintain a competitive advantage on a global scale. The recruitment process at Gedeon Richter is competitive and transparent, aimed at highlighting the candidate's professional skills, experiences, career goals and attitudes. At the first stage of selection, the applications received by the company are pre-screened (Gedeon Richter 2017e). After that, applications are evaluated, and the candidates who make it to the next round are invited to a job interview conducted by the line manager and the human resource manager responsible for making the selection (Gedeon Richter 2017e). For some positions, there is also an additional stage of the selection process that includes a competence-based psychological test and other rounds of testing to establish candidate's professional ability. The company goes beyond selecting employees with the best technical knowledge of the pharmaceutical and medical industry as they are intent on choosing candidates who share the same system of values and beliefs of the organization. In other words, Gedeon Richter is focused on finding the right person for the company. This is clearly displayed by the behavioral interview technique and psychological tests conducted in the interview process (Gedeon Richter 2017e). The process may also include an interview with a senior manager for some positions. Finally, the best candidate is offered an employment contract. As the last step of the selection process, all the applicants who participated in the job interviews are given feedback. Gedeon Richter also goes the extra mile by providing each candidate that participated in the selection process with feedback (Gedeon Richter 2017e). That underlines tits commitment to not just its employees but to prospective ones as well. This feedback

Hungary: Creating New Opportunities for Talent   **151**

enable candidates to improve upon their shortcomings and apply elsewhere or to another position at Gedeon Richter (Gedeon Richter 2017e).

In the process of recruiting new personnel Gedeon Richter seeks team-oriented, outstanding, dedicated people, who are motivated to make a sustainable contribution to the company and have the ability to develop professionally in pharmaceutical manufacturing, research and development, sales and marketing (Jobisland 2015). The company is considered to be a very good place to start a career as it is open to hiring recent graduates and is, therefore, committed to training young talent providing coaching, language and leadership programs. There is also a Welcome Program for young employees aimed at giving an insight to the organization, its activities, corporate culture and values (Gedeon Richter 2015). Additionally, all new employees at Gedeon Richter must attend an orientation program hosted by the organization. This orientation program comprises of both lecture-style presentations and "hands-on" experiential visits to factories and laboratories (Gedeon Richter 2015). The orientation is aimed at equipping new employees with a comprehensive understanding of Gedeon Richter's business activities, business history and corporate culture (Gedeon Richter 2015).

Training does not just include a new employees' welcome or graduate program, but also continuous programs to develop existing employees. Gedeon Richter also conducts management training programs to assist middle- and senior-level managers. These training programs are primarily concerned with identifying potential in existing employees, building skillsets and advancing career progression (Gedeon Richter 2015). Due to Gedeon Richter's standardized business operations, training is very well structured and executed among global operations (Gedeon Richter 2015). All employees must attend and participate in safety, quality assurance, environmental protection and pharmacovigilance training programs. That maintains company standards regardless of the host country the company operates in (Gedeon Richter 2015). In order to further enhance performance, Gedeon Richter also encourages employees in developing capabilities through various learning programs implemented by the company. The company offers training programs pertaining to the development of both technical (IT skills) and soft skills (coaching, foreign language courses, etc.) to all employees (Gedeon Richter 2015). In order to build the best possible skilled workforce, the organization also offers scientific and professional education and post-graduate training. University education is an important factor for the organization as it encourages and supports employees in attaining post-graduate degrees. All of these initiatives enhance employees' development and, as a result, their performance (Gedeon Richter 2015).

Performance is a large part of the work culture at Gedeon Richter as employees are constantly being given feedback on their performance that enables them to discuss individual goals and career advancement with their superiors. This planning process makes sure, that employees set business and behavioral goals within the organization and helps to identify specific training for career development (Gedeon Richter 2015).

At Gedeon Richter employee's compensation is progressive and performance-based. In addition, employees can also earn special allowances by superior performance and the accomplishment of business targets (Gedeon Richter 2015). Another incentive program that Gedeon Richter executes is annually awarding treasury shares to its high-performing employees (Gedeon Richter 2015). Since the company's success has always depended on the competitiveness of its products, innovation is a very important part of every area of the company's business. Gedeon Richter promotes creative thinking among employees in order to uphold the creative environment of the workplace. The company established a special RITA Award to encourage and acknowledge creative thinking and innovation on a daily level in 2010 (Gedeon Richter 2017d).

Gedeon Richter invests a multitude of resources and capital into its human resources division globally in order to refine the recruitment process that ensures that only the best of employees are selected to work for this multinational corporation. The company is intent on maintaining a balance of strong values with high-performance levels when recruiting and selecting prospective and talented employees. Although Gedeon Richter emphasizes a work-intensive environment intent on challenging employees, the company greatly cares about its staff members (Gedeon Richter 2015). Company's employee incentive programs are an additional incentive for employees to invest in long-term employment with the company. Gedeon Richter's full-time employees are offered health, dental, vision insurance, flexible spending accounts, life and accidental death and dismemberment insurance, supplemental and dependant life insurance, disability benefits, paid time off, an employee assistance program, healthy lifestyle reimbursement and educational assistance (Gedeon Richter 2015). Many global locations are also equipped with state of the art recreational facilities (e.g. swimming pools, gyms, sports grounds) and the company has built holiday facilities, to be used by employees and their families (Gedeon Richter 2015). Another initiative aimed at enhancing the health of employees at Gedeon Richter is the screening for different illnesses conducted annually. The company also goes above and beyond standard benefits by enabling employees to use their vacation time in the healthiest manner (Gedeon Richter 2015). Gedeon Richter aids the families of employees through the implementation of nursery schools, which are maintained at a high standard and ensure parents are provided with a safe and educational environment for their children in a cost-effective manner. Lastly, due to the fact that Gedeon Richter aims to sustain and retain employees on a long-term basis, benefits are provided to young employees upon joining the organization. Some of these benefits include long-term insurance facilities, low-interest and interest-free company loans, travel contributions and housing opportunities. Therefore, all services provided to employees by the company serve as motivators. These compensatory tools enable Gedeon Richter to stand out as a top employer as they go beyond the standard expectations when it comes to taking care of the workforce (Gedeon Richter 2015).

It is also worth mentioning that the company designed and introduced its own occupational health and safety management system (OHSMS), since over 5000 employees have to regularly work in contact with dangerous chemicals and are exposed to significant health risks (Gedeon Richter 2017f). In order to keep the risks under control, the company devotes much attention to training and continuous training. The goal of the company is to provide safety working conditions that ensure all of the employees return home healthy after each working day (Gedeon Richter 2017f).

Gedeon Richter takes great care about the personal and professional development of its employees, their health and well-being, as well as the working conditions and competitive compensation. Company's talent management strategy is focused on long-term employment and investing significant resources into young specialists for their development into loyal employees. To achieve this, Gedeon Richter provides workers with various training and learning opportunities, extensive social packages and prospects for their development.

MOL: Opportunities for Development

MOL Group (MOL) is an international oil and gas company with headquartered in Budapest, Hungary. The company is active in all oil and gas industry areas: exploration and production, refining, distribution and marketing, petrochemicals, power generation and trading. Moreover, it has operations in over 40 countries worldwide with nearly 2000 service stations in 11 countries (mainly in Central and Eastern Europe) under seven brands (MOL Group 2017a). Additionally, the company's most significant regions of operations are Central and Eastern Europe, Southern Europe, the North Sea, the Middle East and Russia with the number of employees exceeding 26,000 (MOL Group 2017a).

MOL was established on October 1, 1991 (MOL Group 2017b). In 1995 MOL adopted a privatization strategy in order to respond to international market challenges and start a regional consolidation of the oil and gas industry. The company purchased a 25% stake in Croatia's national oil company INA in 2003 (MOL Group 2017b). In 2006 MOL launched a joint exploration project in the Zaláta area designed to secure new volumes of natural gas (MOL Group 2017b). MOL activities in mergers and acquisitions (M&As) include the acquisition of Shell Romania, the purchase of a fuel storage facility in Korneuburg, the acquisition of the Roth filling stations chain in Austria, the purchase of Italiana Energia e Servizi S.P.A. (the owner of the Mantua refinery and a chain of 165 retail stations) in Italy, strategic co-operation with the Czech power utility CEZ and the purchase of Russian Surgutneftegas' shares (the Hungarian stake is 21.2% of the shares within Surgutneftegas) (MOL Group 2017b).

MOL offers a wide range of products and services. The company's portfolio includes, among other things, gasoline, diesel, heating oil, aviation fuel, lubricants, bitumen, sulfur and liquefied petroleum gas (LPG) products. Furthermore, MOL's retail network is composed of nearly 2000 service stations in 11 countries, predominantly located in the supply radius of the company's refineries, which maximizes synergies between refining, marketing and retail (MOL Group 2017c). All business operations can be divided into two main areas: upstream and downstream. Considering the upstream area, MOL has over 75 years of experience in exploration and production and its diverse portfolio includes oil and gas exploration assets. Moreover, it has a well-established presence and thriving partnerships in the CIS region, Middle East, Africa and Pakistan. In 2014, MOL also entered the United Kingdom and later Norway in order to increase its reserves and enhance its offshore experience (MOL Group 2017c). It is important to notice that MOL has been committed to doing business responsibly and sustainably, supporting communities and striving to meet the best possible health and safety and security standards wherever it is present. Considering MOL's downstream activities, the company operates four refineries and two petrochemical plants, and provides support to different business activities that are part of an integrated value chain (MOL Group 2017c). This value chain turns crude oil into a range of refined products, which are moved and marketed for household, industrial and transport use. In addition, it produces and sells petrochemicals worldwide and holds a leading position in the petrochemical sector in the Central and Eastern Europe region (MOL Group 2017c).

MOL's vision is to be "the energy of positive change" (MOL Group 2017c). This statement means that the company cares about content development taking into account the evaluation and feedback of customers, as this is the direction of "positive change". MOL's first ethos is desire to win. This is the most important aspiration that any company should have, because it is the desire to achieve goals, get the maximum profit and change positively. Secondly, besides achieving business results, behaving in line with MOL's values and leadership excellence are equally important. A highly valued and important management skill is to create a positive and collaborative team spirit and working environment, along with acting with sensitivity. The core of sensitivity refers to understanding that every individual, and more specifically, every customer, however different, is equal. This means that the company should respect them and satisfy their demand. The third ethos is unyielding integrity which is delivering on commitments, safeness and fairness in action. Integrity includes always serving talented employees by providing them with safety and truthfulness. MOL has established a standard of fairness, commitment and safety during operational processes (MOL Group 2014).

MOL recognizes its employees and related talent management practices as one of the keys to the company's success. That is why talent management is targeted at the development of employees on a constant basis and contribution to the sustainable success of the company (MOL Group 2017d).

MOL actively attracts young talent. The main programs for graduates and young professionals are Growww, Uppp, and Freshhh (MOL Group 2017e). These programs focus on marketing the company among youth, as well as creating a pool of potential talented employees. The Growww Graduate Program is a one-year program that offers a unique opportunity to start an international career within the company without any work experience and learn about the oil and gas industry globally (MOL Group 2017e). The Uppp Student Competition is a new, exploration and production-dedicated, international, talent acquisition program which was launched to students and graduates in the fields of geoscience and petroleum engineering (MOL Group 2017f). The Freshhh Student Competition is an online international student competition, where teams of students have to take over the management of an integrated oil corporation (MOL Group 2017f). The top teams from the Freshhh competition have an opportunity to take part in the Live Final event, and the best students can be potential joiners of MOL Group's Growww Graduate Program or preferable candidates for its open-start positions (MOL Group 2017f).

Another practice aimed at attaining high-profile workers is strategic partnerships with many universities and so-called PIMS Academies (MOL Group 2017c). This allows MOL to overcome some of the challenges (e.g. an increasing skill gap as a result of a large number of retiring experienced workers) by securing a sufficient amount of candidates in the talent pool and building up a supply of talented employees for the future. Experienced professionals are hired after a standardized process, which includes an application, interviews and assessments (MOL Group 2017g).

Hungary: Creating New Opportunities for Talent   157

MOL's values considering its employees' career and talent development are success and growth, courage and decisiveness, teamwork and partnership, expertise and responsibility. MOL's employees need to have enough skills to move ahead, act without fear, overcome frontiers, face challenges and provide more intelligent solutions in one team (MOL Group 2017g). Providing such development for employees is the important part of the company's talent management system.

MOL provides its employees with two main career development paths—leadership and expert. If an employee is identified as a leader (using a performance and career management system) and expresses strong motivation and willingness to pursue a leadership career path, he or she is continuously assessed and developed to be ready to take over a potential managerial role when the opportunity arises. In order to empower the opportunity, individual development plans and activities are defined and set up to ensure a smooth transition to the new position (MOL Group 2017h). Furthermore, the company developed and launched two global leadership programs, Lead and Intensity (MOL Group 2017h). Lead focuses on three groups of leaders: emerging (future leaders that are at the beginning of their path), growing (existing employees expanding their managerial skills) and advanced (top management getting ready to reach its ultimate form of expertise). This program is enabled by various collaborations (i.e. with 20 Thunderbird Global Schools of Management located in the United States) (MOL Group 2017h). Intensity is widely available to any person in a leadership position. Not only does it allow managers to take various electives in order to improve their skills, but also creates a unified system for corporate leaders of all levels that allows them to communicate more effectively by speaking a common language and working more productively since they are familiar with models that their colleagues use (MOL Group 2017h).

The second path, which is opened to excellent performers who are keen on developing their professional expertise involves ever-more constant improvement of key knowledge and skills and the opportunity to increase one's qualifications (MOL Group 2017i). One of the opportunities available to experts is UpppEdu which employs a horizontal rotation practice, allowing employees to develop multidepartment functionality and professional expertise (MOL Group 2017i). More experienced professionals become part of the Technical Career Ladder which presents growth and promotion opportunities in a clear and transparent way (MOL Group 2017i). Finally, all workers are granted access to the Internal Academy platform, a knowledge resource within the company. Official data, provided by MOL, indicate that during the course of three years (2013–2016), the company managed to increase training coverage from 69.8% in 2013 to 88.5% in 2016 (MOL Group 2017i). In 2016, 21,178 employees (out of 23,936 in total) were subject to some kind of training, which on average took around 34 hours, as opposed to only 24 hours in 2015, and this became a significant result achieved in just a year (MOL Group 2017i). MOL puts emphasis on the constant development of the qualification and skills of its employees.

Another important pillar of MOL's talent management is managing the composition and broadness of its workforce. To address this function, MOL employs various equality-diversity management techniques. The process starts during the recruitment process when the company uses fair and equal hiring. This means that people from different backgrounds, cultures and perspectives get the same opportunities and are not discriminated against. The firm also promotes fair employment conditions for current employees. MOL stands for fair employee relations and seeks to support workers' unions and associations, namely European Works Councils, which inform workers about the current state of affairs and any important changes to come (MOL Group 2017i). Some 94.9% of employees of MOL are represented by some trade union (MOL Group 2017i).

Although equality is a valuable asset, managerial teams do not forget about another major key to the success of their company, which is diversity. Working in a huge company, operating across borders, means working with colleagues from different cultures, of different ages and expertise, and that is a challenge to be tackled by promoting diversity. MOL's official position states that by diversifying its workforce the company is trying to internationalize itself, make sure that high-quality knowledge is transferred between generations, and promote innovation (MOL Group 2017j). The Women Leadership Network program is aimed at strengthening the company's female leaders' communication, collaboration and professional network, and is one of the practical talent management solutions that the company employs (MOL Group 2017j). Another solution for increasing diversity is MOL's diversity employee value proposition which was created in 2015 to support the attraction and retention of young talent. These measures allow the company to fulfill its diversity strategy by providing knowledge transfer between generations and developing employees internationally without distinction and discrimination. A comprehensive framework that provides the tools to identify and address systemic barriers in order to build a diverse and inclusive workforce is in the process of development. This, moreover, suggests the means to integrate diversity and include values and practices into existing corporate processes, and enable progress and results to be measured departmentally and corporately (MOL Group 2017j).

Recognizing the importance of the reward and performance assessment, MOL has developed and introduced a "Total Remuneration" approach (MOL Group 2017k). This approach structures all key compensation elements (such as incentives and benefits and annual basic salary) using a world-renowned HAY chart technique (a point-based job evaluation system) that provides the company with a clear and transparent and, therefore, fair payment assessment method (MOL Group 2017k). Furthermore, MOL revises and updates salaries with regards to internal factors (individual performance indicators) and external markets (competitors' salary levels) regularly in order to stay competitive. An addition to the "Total Remuneration" approach, a benefits scheme exists, which is composed of a variety of initiatives aimed at protecting employees (MOL Group 2017k). It includes social care, health and wellness services, and financial well-being along with creating and stimulating a safe workplace environment. An example of this scheme would be life and accident insurance, to which MOL employees are entitled to use in case of accidental events (MOL Group 2017k). MOL's remuneration schemes reinforce the merit-based culture and encourage high achievement via short-term and long-term incentives. Great results are based on outstanding performance which yields significantly higher returns to MOL. Therefore, MOL provides incentives for employees to deliver on the company's strategy and rewards them for the achievement of strategic and individual goals (MOL Group 2017k). MOL is heavily involved in the development of its employees and underlines that employees are its highly valued resource without whom it is impossible to provide outstanding results and stay in the market.

Prezi: Talent Management for Innovations

Prezi Inc. is a large information technology (IT) company with its headquarters in Budapest, Hungary. It was launched in 2009 (Prezi 2017a) and its largest foreign office is in California, San Francisco. Prezi produces cross-platform software that allows over 75 million users to create a unique cloud-based presentation with a record of more than 260 million presentations since 2009 (Prezi 2017a). Prezi's mission is to promote the spread of good ideas (Prezi 2017a). The company history began when two Hungarians first developed the idea of a cloud-based cross-platform presentation. Adam Somlai-Fische (an artist) and Peter Halacsy (an IT-specialist) started work on Prezi as presentation software for architecture companies (Techcrunch 2009). By 2008, the Swedish-Hungarian entrepreneur Peter Arvai joined their team of Fische & Halscsy and, in 2009, they presented Prezi to the public (Techcrunch 2009). In 2009, the start-up attracted funding from American and European funds, such as TED and Sunstone Capital (Techcrunch 2009). Both funds invest money in promising software, mobile and internet companies and Prezi has the advantage of having the co-founder of Twitter, Jack Dorsey, among its advisers and mentors (Techcrunch 2009). Prezi software is regularly used in TED and LeWeb conferences. Even though the company is a recent start-up, Prezi donated $100 million in software licenses to educational organizations in 2014 (VB 2016).

Prezi's business strategy represents its current mission and values. There are five values that the company stands for which are making the world better, a stand-up attitude, a get-it-done approach, an innovative approach and elegance (Prezi 2017a). Making the world better is part of Prezi's belief that better communication is a vital condition for creating a brighter future. Making great software is one of the ways to provide better communication and a stand-up attitude, because a conformance to the status quo is against company values. New ideas and honest criticism are welcome along with a get-it-done approach allowing Prezi and its workers to claim to deliver on their promises. An innovative approach underlines that Prezi is always ready to learn new things and make innovative decisions. Elegance highlights that Prezi's innovative products are not only of high quality, but they are accomplished in an elegant manner. Prezi wants people to literally enjoy using its software.

Talent management at Prezi starts with the company's mission, aiming to reinvent how people share knowledge, tell stories and inspire their audiences to act (Prezi 2017a). Moreover, one of the current strategic objectives of Prezi is to maintain and accelerate its growth. Hence, the company keeps to its policy of raising new capital. Although Prezi has positive cash flows, the company reinvests its money in order to maintain its rate of growth (Forbes 2016).

Prezi needs to adapt to a highly competitive and ever-changing environment while maintaining its flexibility and keeping the spirit of entrepreneurship. Hence, Prezi's organizational structure has a linear form, because it is vertically and horizontally concentrated, simple and dynamic, and keeps the spirit of entrepreneurship within the company. Having expanded from an IT start-up it is subject to organic processes and with a flat structure this contributes to flexibility in working processes, employees are given freedom to make decisions and the management of the company is easily accessible for ideas sharing. Team leaders do not have their own offices but instead sit among their co-workers, and the CEO is also easy to approach as he works with others and is open to discussion of company issues (Prezi 2017a). The company is very concerned about the product it offers to its consumers (corporate or individual) and pays a lot of attention to customer support and product upgrading that are reflected in Prezi' talent management system focusing on innovation development and customer orientation. Talent management practices at Prezi have some important directions, such as talent development by diverse training, improvement programs and healthy working conditions, and talent attraction based on testing for specific roles, interviews and an onsite assessment period (1–5 days depending on role and level) (Prezi 2017b).

Prezi offers a variety of social benefits to its employees starting from a comfortable working office environment, good-quality food and lunches at restaurants, working out in the sports gym, a bike repair service and use of the Prezi library—all for free. The company gives employees opportunity to travel and stay healthy with full healthcare coverage, the possibility of playing games (including board games) and to feel adventurous. Prezi encourages its talent to participate in conferences and ongoing professional development, allows flexible vacations that are really attractive for employees with families, an even-more enhanced healthcare package and additional perks such as disability insurance, pet insurance and so on (Prezi 2017b). The company also provides all workers with their preferred conditions, depending on their work and lifestyles. For some people it offers a work-from-home approach and creates private rooms that people can book to eliminate disruption or noise during intensive work periods (Changing minds 2016). The main idea within the company is to create an inclusive environment for all personalities.

Prezi's CEO has created an environment within the company that adds satisfaction, happiness and motivation to each working day. Prezi's offices contain both private and open environments, so employees can find a quiet corner to work in silence or to share with their colleagues their energy and inspiration. Prezi is in charge of its employees' needs so advocates that the best way is to listen to them and understand their requirements in order to make the company successful.

Prezi emphasizes that talent development fully depends on professional performance (Entrepreneur 2017). The company is targeted at recruiting talented people all over the world but appreciates everyone's ideas. Prezi strives to improve itself, its employees and the world. It tries to promote learning from mistakes, acquiring new knowledge and skills, doing things that were never done before, and using empathy as a guide to producing quality work (Prezi 2017c). As the company is operating in the IT sector, the main instruments of talent management are targeted at stimulating and forming the innovation process. That is why the development of creativity and innovativeness are considered to be the main opportunities that the company provides its employees with.

* * *

The three Hungarian companies, analyzed above, represent a good example of multinational organizations producing innovative products and taking leading market positions. Gedeon Richter selects candidates with the best technical knowledge of the pharmaceutical and medical industry and tries to continuously develop employee knowledge at different management levels, assisting those who want to get a post-graduate degree. MOL's talent management practices focus on attracting employees through programs organized for graduates and young professionals, by marketing the company and creating a pool of potential talented workers. Prezi tries to attract talented individuals who will add more value to the company in terms of imagination and creativity.

In order to retain talented people within the organization, safety and comfortable working conditions as well as financial and non-financial motivation systems are created. Gedeon Richter's talent management strategy is focused on long-term employment and investing significant resources into young specialists for their development into loyal employees. MOL also offers a lot of benefits to its employees. Prezi creates an environment within the company that adds satisfaction, happiness and motivation for each employee. Alignment of talent management practices in terms of attraction, on-the-job support and retention of professional workers helps these companies to retain their positions as attractive employers in their respective industry or services sector.

References

Budai, T. 2011. The Significance and History of Organization Development-in Hungary & International Relations. *Eurasian Journal of Business and Economics* 4 (8): 87–99.

Changing minds. 2016. The Competing Values Framework. http://changing-minds.org/explanations/culture/competing_values.htm. Accessed Sept 2017.

CIA. 2017. Europe: Hungary. https://www.cia.gov/library/publications/resources/the-world-factbook/geos/hu.html. Accessed July 2017.

Entrepreneur. 2017. How 5 Companies Found the Perfect Company Culture within their Business. https://www.entrepreneur.com/article/304655. Accessed Nov 2017.

Forbes. 2016. How Prezi's Peter Arvai Plans to Beat Power Point. https://www.forbes.com/sites/forbestreptalks/2016/06/07/how-prezis-peter-arvai-plans-to-beat-powerpoint/#564ef1906126. Accessed Sept 2017.

Gedeon Richter. 2015. Annual Report. https://www.richter.hu/en-US/investors/company-reports/Company%20report/Richter-Gedeon-Annual-Report-2015.pdf. Accessed July 2017.

———. 2016. Corporate Brochure. http://www.richter.hu/en-US/about-us/Documents/RGcorporatebrochure2016.pdf. Accessed July 2017.

———. 2017a. Our History. http://www.richter.hu/en-US/about-us/Pages/corporate-history.aspx. Accessed July 2017.

———. 2017b. Corporate Strategy. http://www.richter.hu/en-US/about-us/Pages/corporate-strategy.aspx. Accessed July 2017.

———. 2017c. Quality Self-Medication-Gedeon Richter Brands Without Prescription. http://www.richter.hu/en-US/our-activity/otc-products/Pages/Our-products.aspx. Accessed July 2017.

———. 2017d. Richter as Employer. http://www.richter.hu/en-US/career/Pages/Richter-as-employer.aspx. Accessed July 2017.

———. 2017e. Selection Process. http://www.richter.hu/en-US/career/Pages/Selection-process.aspx. Accessed July 2017.

———. 2017f. Safety and Health at Work. https://www.richter.hu/en-US/corporate-responsibility/Pages/Safety-and-health-at-work.aspx. Accessed July 2017.

Jobisland. 2015. Gedeon Richter Plc. https://www.jobisland.com/jobs/company/5033/. Accessed July 2017.

Liptak, K. 2012. Analyzing the Labour Market Situation in the Central and Eastern European Countries -Improvement or Decline? *Club of Economics in Miskolc (Theory, Methodology, Practice)* 8 (1): 33–40.

MOL Group. 2014. Health, Safety and Environment Management System. https://molgroup.info/images/molgroup/pdf/sustainability/sustainability_and_mol/HSE_management_system/HSE%20_Management_System.pdf. Accessed Aug 2017.

———. 2017a. MOL Group at a Glance. https://molgroup.info/en/about-mol-group/mol-group-at-a-glance. Accessed Aug 2017.

———. 2017b. Our History. https://molgroup.info/en/about-mol-group/our-history. Accessed Aug 2017.

———. 2017c. Our Business Model. https://molgroup.info/en/about-mol-group/company-overview/our-business-model. Accessed July 2017.

———. 2017d. Human Capital. https://molgroup.info/en/sustainability/human-capital. Accessed Aug 2017.

Hungary: Creating New Opportunities for Talent 165

———. 2017e. Growww Graduate Programme. https://molgroupcareers.info/en/students-and-graduates/growww-graduate-programme. Accessed Aug 2017.

———. 2017f. Uppp Student Competition. https://molgroupcareers.info/en/students-and-graduates/uppp-student-competition. Accessed Aug 2017.

———. 2017g. Career and development. https://molgroupcareers.info/en/working-at-mol-group/our-employees/career-and-development. Accessed Aug 2017.

———. 2017h. Leadership Development. https://molgroupcareers.info/en/working-at-mol-group/our-employees/career-and-development/leadership-development. Accessed Aug 2017.

———. 2017i. Technical/Professional Development. https://molgroupcareers.info/en/working-at-mol-group/our-employees/career-and-development/technical-professional-development. Accessed Aug 2017.

———. 2017j. Diversity and Inclusion. https://molgroupcareers.info/en/working-at-mol-group/our-employees/diversity-and-inclusion. Accessed Aug 2017.

———. 2017k. Rewarding Employees. https://molgroupcareers.info/en/working-at-mol-group/our-employees/rewarding-employees. Accessed Aug 2017.

Prezi. 2017a. Visualizing Great Things. https://prezi.com/about/. Accessed Sept 2017.

———. 2017b. F.A.Q. https://prezi.com/jobs/faq. Accessed Sept 2017.

———. 2017c. Our Values at Work. https://prezi.com/our-values/. Accessed Sept 2017.

RSM. 2017. Doing Business in Hungary. http://doingbusinessinhungary.com/general-information#overview. Accessed July 2017.

Techcrunch. 2009. Prezi Gains VC Funding and Jack Dorsey as an Advisor. https://techcrunch.com/2009/07/20/prezi-gains-vc-funding-and-jack-dorsey-as-an-advisor/. Accessed Sept 2017.

The World Bank. 2017. Labor Market Regulation. http://www.doingbusiness.org/data/exploretopics/labor-market-regulation. Accessed July 2017.

The World Bank Group. 2014. Back to Work. Growing with Jobs in Europe and Central Asia. www.worldbank.org/content/dam/Worldbank/Feature%20Story/ECA/BW_InfoGraphics_Chapter1%20final.pdf. Accessed July 2017.

UNDP. 2016. Human Development Report. Hungary. http://hdr.undp.org/sites/all/themes/hdr_theme/country-notes/HUN.pdf. Accessed July 2017.

VB. 2016. With 75M Users, Prezi Targets Businesses with New Collaboration and Analytics Tools for Presentations. https://venturebeat.com/2016/06/07/75m-users-on-prezi-targets-businesses-with-new-collaboration-and-analytics-tools-for-presentations/. Accessed Sept 2017.

Part III

The Commonwealth of Independent States: Soviet Heritage in Action

10

CIS: Soviet Heritage in Action

Louisa Selivanovskikh

The Commonwealth of Independent States (CIS) is a successor of the Soviet Union, and includes the majority of the former Soviet republics such as Russia, Belarus, Ukraine, Kazakhstan, Moldova, Armenia and Azerbaijan. The collapse of the socialist system in the 1990s led to massive layoffs as a result of market collapse and wild privatization of state-owned assets, which caused instability in the labor market (Poór et al. 2012). In that period, basic compensation practices were introduced, in other words a basic salary system that reflected the importance of a particular job to a company, leading to high differentiation of salaries between positions belonging to both different hierarchical levels and functions (Lewis and Heckman 2006). The changes in the company ownership structure (i.e. from state-owned to private or mixed), the volatility in the labor markets and economic unpredictability forced these countries to seek new business governance solutions, including the adoption of talent

---

L. Selivanovskikh (✉)
Graduate School of Management, St. Petersburg State University,
St. Petersburg, Russia
e-mail: l.selivanovskikh@gsom.pu.ru

© The Author(s) 2018
M. Latukha (ed.), *Talent Management in Global Organizations*,
Palgrave Studies of Internationalization in Emerging Markets,
https://doi.org/10.1007/978-3-319-76418-4_10

management practices to be applied at firm and country levels (Meardi 2006; Novitskaya and Brewster 2016). However, CIS countries had to consider the embedded cultural-cognitive characteristics and social norms when introducing new talent management practices and this aspect presents a challenge to local companies even today.

Though most scholars who study this region identify the heritage of the Soviet Union as the key factor that determines the specifics of local human resource and talent management systems (Vaiman and Holden 2011), their manifestation in the individual CIS countries remains under-explored in extant literature (Latukha 2015). The general belief is that CIS countries, to some extent, have inherited a number of "traditions" from the Soviet management system, the key characteristics of which are centralized leadership, hierarchical organizational structure, a high level of bureaucracy and the substantial role of collectivism in working relations (Vlachoutsicos and Lawrence 1990). Meanwhile, the human resource and talent management systems themselves are usually characterized by under-investment in human capital (Alas and Svetlik 2004), poor development of business education and, consequently, a shortage of managers that possess up-to-date managerial competences (Vaiman and Holden 2011). The unwillingness of managers to involve their subordinates in decision-making processes is still widespread. Managers still find it difficult to incorporate new thinking from younger employees and consider their innovation potential as a huge organizational asset. Often, there is disapproval of young specialists' proactivity, which is perceived as a threat to older managers' professional and personal status and authority (Skuza et al. 2015).

Before the collapse of the Soviet Union, most human resource management activities, including those related to talent management, were limited to personnel administration and record-keeping (May et al. 1998). Rather limited attention was paid to talent attraction as government authorities were highly involved in the recruitment and specialist allocation process (Leites 1985). Young specialists were allocated a position in a specific organization on completion of their university degree, which led to virtually full employment following the obtained degree. Some workers got their jobs through referrals from the labor department, leading to nepotism in organizations. Meanwhile, training and career development were planned and strictly controlled by the government (Minbaeva and Muratbekova-Touron 2011; Mockler et al. 1996; Novitskaya and Brewster 2016). Special attention was paid to increasing professional qualifications without taking into account the particular needs and desires of the workers. Meanwhile, the compensation system was characterized by low salary differentiation with a high emphasis on non-monetary benefits, for example giving employees free of charge or at a nominal cost holiday stays at spas, an opportunity to make use of vacation hostels, Young Pioneer camps, industry-sponsored hospitals and free housing (Gurkov and Zelenova 2011). In particular, performance appraisals were rather unpopular since employee rewards were tied to government-set objectives on company performance (Minbaeva et al. 2007; Novitskaya 2015). Workers were guaranteed a monthly wage regardless of productivity. However, those who achieved outstanding productivity and performance results were awarded motivational prizes.

Since the start of the transition to a market-led economic system, Western-like practices have been gaining popularity among CIS human resources professionals. With a growing number of foreign companies operating in these countries, using talent management practices to obtain and sustain competitive advantages is becoming more common. Thus, many Western firms are investing rapidly in companies in the CIS countries (Buckley 2017; Godlewski 2017). Despite these large investments, Western managers know relatively little about the specificity of managerial practices that are quite different from those in the West. Since the early 1990s, East European political reforms aimed at improving productivity have instead caused decreased output, reduced wage rates and more downsizing and layoffs. Privatization and price/wage deregulation have produced resistance to change among workers (Dixon et al. 2014; Novitskaya and Brewster 2016). Some prefer the old centralized economy characterized by job security, guaranteed pay and highly structured jobs. Others benefit from a system plagued by corruption, the black market and gray economy, and Party membership rewards. However, CIS countries continue the transition to a market economy with changes occurring in work values, employment practices and strategic human resource management. Compared to foreign companies, CIS managerial practices are immature and the talent management concept is still rather new and controversial.

With the following chapters we aim to present an analysis of talent management in Kazakhstan, Belarus and Ukraine. The first of the three countries, being the largest of the former Soviet republics strategically linking the fast-growing markets in the East and the West, has surprisingly not been a very popular setting for management research. Specifically, from a human resource management perspective the context has recently been considered only by a small group of scholars who aim to explore the nature of social integration mechanisms that moderate relationships between cultural distance and social integration following one Kazakhstani company, KazOil, for 10 years and identifying the differences in the levels of post-acquisition social integration based on two acquisitions by Hurricane and CNPC (organizations from Canada and China, respectively) (Minbaeva and Muratbekova-Touron 2011). As for Ukraine and Belarus, the number of studies is limited as well. In particular, some authors try to address the problem of Ukrainian firms experiencing managerial difficulties due to a lack of qualified managers by explaining the organizational improvement model developed based on a small advertising agency (Fuxman 2004),whereas other researchers compare current Belarusian labor management practices with those before 1989. These studies are obsolete in terms of current trends and dynamics in the labor market of each country (Danilovich and Croucher 2011), which is why we focus on the CIS context.

We analyze the country-specific environment that shapes the characteristics of talent management practices and discuss the issue of Westernization or/and localization of these practices in the CIS context. In particular, we demonstrate that organizations from Kazakhstan, Belarus and Ukraine share a common feature of talent management policies and practices, being more formalized and highly regulated, especially when compared to Western European and American countries and some other Central and Eastern European countries. We show that in Belorussia and Kazakhstani companies open performance appraisal systems are unpopular and performance-based remuneration mechanisms remain under-developed. Meanwhile, in Ukrainian companies, we see a persistence of elitist talent definitions and a pre-eminence of talent retention practices. Whereas in Belarusian and Ukrainian companies we observe a prevalence of universalist talent definitions, with organizations from

Kazakhstan focusing more on talent development practices and Belarusian firms concentrating on specific aspects of talent management (i.e. the attraction, development or retention of young specialists). We finally conclude with demonstrating that talent management is influenced by a number of factors, some of which are rather specific to each of Kazakhstan, Belorussia and Ukraine, but at the same time can be featured as common for the CIS context.

References

Alas, Ruth, and Ivan Svetlik. 2004. Estonia and Slovenia: Building Modern HRM Using a Dualist Approach. In *Human Resource Management in Europe: Evidence of Convergence?* ed. Chris Brewster, Wolfgang Mayrhofer, and Michael Morley, 353–384. Oxford: Elsevier Butterwort-Heinemann.

Buckley, Neil. 2017. Opportunities and Risks for Investors in Central and East Europe. *Financial Times*, May 8. www.ft.com/content/4248a712-07da-11e7-ac5a-903b21361b43. Accessed 1 Aug 2017.

Danilovich, Hanna, and Richard Croucher. 2011. Labour Management in Belarus: Transcendent Retrogression. *Journal of Communist Studies and Transition Politics* 27: 241–262.

Dixon, Sarah E.A., Marc Day, and Chris Brewster. 2014. Changing HRM Systems in Two Russian Oil Companies: Western Hegemony or Russian Spetsifika? *The International Journal of Human Resource Management* 25: 3134–3156.

Fuxman, Leonora. 2004. Emerging Trends in Ukrainian Management Styles and the Challenge of Managerial Talent Shortage. *International Journal of Commerce and Management* 14: 28–43.

Godlewski, Andrzej. 2017. German Companies Are Increasingly Investing in Russia. *Central European Financial Observer*, July 11. https://financialob-server.eu/cse-and-cis/german-companies-are-increasingly-investing-in-rus-sia/. Accessed 1 Aug 2017.

Gurkov, Igor, and Olga Zelenova. 2011. Human Resource Management in Russian Companies. *International Studies of Management & Organization* 41: 65–78.

Latukha, Marina. 2015. Talent Management in Russian Companies: Domestic Challenges and International Experience. *The International Journal of Human Resource Management* 26: 1051–1075.

Leites, Nathan. 1985. *Soviet Style in Management*. New York: Crane, Russak.

Lewis, Robert E., and Robert J. Heckman. 2006. Talent Management: A Critical Review. *Human Resource Management Review* 16: 139–154.

May, Ruth, Carol Bormann Young, and Donna Ledgerwood. 1998. Lessons from Russian Human Resource Management Experience. *European Management Journal* 16: 447–459.

Meardi, Guglielmo. 2006. Multinationals' Heaven? Uncovering and Understanding Worker Responses to Multinational Companies in Post-Communist Central Europe. *The International Journal of Human Resource Management* 17: 1366–1378.

Minbaeva, Dana, and Maral Muratbekova-Touron. 2011. Experience of Canadian and Chinese Acquisitions in Kazakhstan. *The International Journal of Human Resource Management* 22: 2946–2964.

Minbaeva, Dana, Kate Hutchings, and Bruce S. Thomson. 2007. Hybrid Human Resource Management in Post-Soviet Kazakhstan. *European Journal of International Management* 1: 350–371.

Mockler, Robert J., Chiang-Nan Chao, and Dorothy G. Dologite. 1996. A Comparative Study of Business Education Programs in China and Russia. *Journal of Teaching in International Business* 8: 19–39.

Novitskaya, Olga. 2015. The Impact of Host Country Effects on Transferring HRM Practices from Western Headquarters to Ukrainian Subsidiaries. *International Journal of Social, Behavioral, Educational, Economic, Business and Industrial Engineering* 9: 1477–1485.

Novitskaya, Olga, and Chris Brewster. 2016. The Impact of National Context Effects on HRM Practices in Russian Subsidiaries of Western MNCs. *Journal of East-West Business* 22: 1–27.

Poór, József, Ferenc Farkas, and Allen D. Engle, eds. 2012. *Human Resource Management Issues and Challenges in Foreign Owned Companies: Central and Eastern Europe*. Komárno: Janos Selye University.

Skuza, Agnieszka, Anthony McDonnell, and Hugh Scullion. 2015. Talent Management in the Emerging Markets. In *Handbook of Human Resource Management in the Emerging Markets*, ed. Frank M. Horwitz and Pawan Budhwar, 225–243. Cheltenham: Edward Elgar Publishing.

Vaiman, Vlad, and Nigel Holden. 2011. Talent Management's Perplexing Landscape in Central and Eastern Europe. In *Global Talent Management*, ed. Hugh Scullion and David Collings, 178–193. London: Routledge.

Vlachoutsicos, Charalambos, and Paul Lawrence. 1990. What We Don't Know About Soviet Management. *Harvard Business Review* 68: 50–63.

11

Kazakhstan: Leaving the Past Behind

Louisa Selivanovskikh

The Republic of Kazakhstan (hereafter referred to as Kazakhstan) is the largest in territory of the former Soviet republics, excluding Russia, is the ninth largest country in the world and has the strongest performing economy in Central Asia. It is the world's largest landlocked country equal to that of Western Europe, strategically linking the fast-growing markets of China and South Asia and those of Russia and Western Europe by road, rail and a port on the Caspian Sea (The World Bank 2017). It also shares borders with a number of smaller countries, such as Kyrgyzstan, Uzbekistan and Turkmenistan. This strategically advantageous location is one of the key success factors of Kazakhstan. Thus, the World Bank has provided a number of loans throughout the years in support of various projects that include agricultural development, environmental protection, health and general infrastructure and capacity building. The country has also received

L. Selivanovskikh (✉)
Graduate School of Management, St. Petersburg State University,
St. Petersburg, Russia
e-mail: l.selivanovskih@gsom.pu.ru

© The Author(s) 2018
M. Latukha (ed.), *Talent Management in Global Organizations*,
Palgrave Studies of Internationalization in Emerging Markets,
https://doi.org/10.1007/978-3-319-76418-4_11

175

billions of US dollars in sovereign and non-sovereign loans from the Asian Development Bank to finance upgrades to transport networks along the Central Asia Regional Economic Cooperation transport corridors and, as a result, strengthen regional trade and economic integration (Export.gov 2016).

In less than two decades after the collapse of the Soviet Union, the country has managed to change its status from lower-middle-income to upper-middle-income mainly due to its huge reserves of oil and natural gas. Meanwhile, due to the protracted slowdown in global oil prices, a decline in real wages, and weak domestic demand, gross domestic product (GDP) growth has decelerated after 2013 compared to that of the previous years, specifically, before the financial crisis of 2008–2009 (Sarsenov and Urazov 2017). Heavy reliance on the revenue from oil products and, as a result, fluctuating oil prices in the international arena have led the country to lose its ability to effectively plan financially leading to contracting GDP and budgetary deficits (WorldAtlas 2017). Consequently, the vulnerability of the economy to external shocks is considered the major source of risk (WorldAtlas 2017). A macro-economic adjustment is required to fit the new realities that would address various financial sector issues and foster the development of an export-oriented and productive private sector in order to transform the country economically toward sustainable growth (Sarsenov and Urazov 2017). Here, the long-term development challenge is to reduce the country's reliance on natural resource extraction, making the economy more diversified and competitive and increasing the significance of the private sector (The World Bank 2017). There is deeply rooted government corruption and an under-developed bank loan system, which block entrepreneurial spirit from flourishing.

The World Bank data show that throughout the past 60 years the population of Kazakhstan has increased, with a short period of decrease after the collapse of the Soviet Union. The population density is relatively low (The World Factbook 2017). Nearly half of the country's population is part of the labor force. According to the International Monetary Fund, the unemployment rates in Kazakhstan have declined rapidly since 2000 due to the country's robust economic growth (International Monetary Fund 2014). In particular, youth unemployment has substantially fallen

(Trading Economics 2017) after the government's targeted intervention (e.g. an expanded vocational and the training system has been implemented to create employment opportunities for youth) (Nesporova 2015). Another feature of the Kazakhstani labor market is gender equality—the current legislature supports female workers, thus reducing income inequality and boosting economic development (the Law of the Republic of Kazakhstan of November 16, 2012 No. 50-V ratifies the Convention on equal treatment and equal opportunities for working men and women). Nevertheless, since the onset of the global crisis the relationship between job creation and economic growth has weakened variously in different sectors of the economy, including manufacturing and agriculture. The country lacks effective mechanisms of labor market regulation, while social benefits are inadequate compared to more developed countries (e.g. due to the plunge in oil prices, salaries of workers were reduced) (Nesporova 2015). Moreover, long-term employment elasticity in Kazakhstan is relatively low, which is due to a capital intensive economy being dominated by the oil sector and an under-developed private sector (International Monetary Fund 2014). The International Monetary Fund lists several factors contributing to lower elasticity of employment to GDP, some of which are the over-sized public sector negatively affecting labor market efficiency, excess demand for workers with higher and vocational education and excess supply of workers with general secondary school education (International Monetary Fund 2014).

In order to ensure sustainable growth and become more dynamic and "anti-fragile", Kazakhstan needs to set an ambitious structural reform agenda that would highlight its competitive advantages: access to different natural resources, a large territory, a favorable geographic position (a "bridge" between West and East) and legal development. The key priority areas must include strengthening human capital and institutions and lowering the role of the state in a more diversified economy (International Monetary Fund 2014). Considering the fact that Kazakhstan, unlike Russia, has made smaller and more careful steps toward achieving its long-term objectives (e.g. when shifting from the Soviet command economy to a market one), the country's talent management landscape today is relatively more homogenous compared to that of the other Commonwealth of Independent States (CIS) countries.

There are some talent management issues that Kazakhstan has to deal with due to its Soviet heritage. Specifically, talent attraction and recruitment are a serious concern for Kazakhstani organizations (Davis 2012). Even though companies operating within the country's borders have tried to give up their outdated Soviet recruitment practices in favor of the more effective Western ones, they still employ a variety of practices that significantly differ from those implemented by Western European and American firms (Minbaeva et al. 2007). In particular, Kazakhstani companies try to attract and eventually hire those candidates who were recommended by friends, colleagues, family members or acquaintances (i.e. recruiting is realized on the basis of "word of mouth"). Moreover, companies tend to give promotion to current employees rather than hiring new workers for open positions, even though there is a pool of new recruits better suited and more qualified for the job. However, attracting and recruiting foreign specialists is difficult due to an inefficient use of state quotas for foreign workers and various bureaucratic procedures (Anderson and Hancilova 2011; Yessengeldin et al. 2015). Nevertheless, large Kazakhstani companies do have a rigorous recruitment process, but some of the stages in the selection process that should ensure fair hiring based on merit are considered to be redundant and omitted (Minbaeva and Maral Muratbekova-Touron 2013).

Talent development practices implemented by Kazakhstani organizations are similar to those of their Western counterparts. Nevertheless, the general motivation behind the realization of training and development activities differs for local and foreign firms. Most Kazakhstani companies, excluding small and medium size firms and multinational corporations, invest in development programs for their high-potential employees only because they have a legal obligation to do so (set by the government). Meanwhile, performance appraisal procedures are not as popular in Kazakhstan as in many European countries and in the United States because of socio-cultural issues (Minbaeva et al. 2007). For instance, the 360-degree technique is usually not practiced in Kazakhstani organizations (Minbaeva et al. 2007), which can be explained by relatively high power distance in society, in other words, when individuals conform to a hierarchy where everybody has a certain place. (Many Kazakhstani companies actually try to preserve a vertical organizational structure even when it does not benefit them.)

Clanism seriously affects talent management implementation in Kazakhstan (Minbaeva and Maral Muratbekova-Touron 2013), but its influence varies from one organization to another. In state-owned companies, for instance, the effect of clanism is strong, meaning an employee's success at an interview or further promotion depend on his or her social capital, while in private companies and international organizations this effect is rather moderate and even low (Minbaeva and Maral Muratbekova-Touron 2013). Nevertheless, due to the increased competition caused mostly by private and international firms entering the Kazakhstani market that aims to attract the best employees to gain a competitive advantage, more and more people without special connections get employed by state-owned organizations. To avoid nepotism and other pressures, human resources managers develop formalized recruitment processes that are strictly regulated. Meanwhile, though discrimination by age and gender is generally prohibited in Kazakhstan, many headhunting agencies set various constraints and barriers for certain groups of workers. In particular, a number of organizations prefer hiring younger candidates and recent graduates, offering them, at the same time, smaller salaries (Smirnova and Tatibekov 2013).

Young workers, having been exposed to Western ways of thinking and conducting business as a result of advanced globalization, demand changes in the employer-worker relationship, which additionally facilitates renovation of the working environment. Consequently, in terms of innovative managerial solutions Kazakhstan is indeed leaving the past behind and moving toward a more stable and positive future. To expand the topic further, we proceed with a review of specific Kazakhstani firms (specifically, KAZ Minerals, Kazzinc and Tengizchevroil) and their talent management systems. We show that despite the dynamic but steady economic growth of the country's economy, talent management practices are still in transition from those inherited from the Soviet era to the ones that currently exist in Western multinationals.

KAZ Minerals: Strategy in Action

Having a market capitalization of US$2.0 billion as of January 1, 2017 KAZ Minerals is currently known as one of Kazakhstan's highest-profile and fastest-growing companies listed on the Kazakhstan, London and

Hong-Kong stock exchanges (KAZ Minerals PLC 2017a). This UK-based copper company operates in the natural resources industry through five segments, the East region, Bozymchak, Aktogay, Bozshakol and Mining Projects, all engaged in mining and processing of copper and other metals and the development of metal deposits and processing facilities in Kazakhstan (*Financial Times* 2017). Over the past couple of years it has built a strong track record of operational performance: in 2016, for instance, the company completed the construction of two major Greenfield projects thus successfully delivering on its promise to become a high-growth, low-cost producer.

KAZ Minerals has had a long journey to reach today's success. Though the company's operations began at the Balkhash copper smelting complex in Kazakhstan in the 1930s, KAZ was officially established in 1992 after the collapse of the Soviet Union (KAZ Minerals PLC 2017b). An organization known as "Kazakhmys" for over 60 years becomes "Zhezgazgantsvetmet", an open joint-stock company fully owned by the Kazakhstan government. Such an ownership structure, however, does not last for long—within a decade the government's stake was reduced from 100% to zero through a series of privatizations. In October 2005 the company joined the wide range of international mining firms listed on the London Stock Exchange. In January 2010 it received funding from the China Development Bank Corporation for the first of two growth projects. A month later it sold 50% of its Ekibastuz GRES-1 power plant to the National Welfare Fund Samruk-Kazyna. In 2013 the company became a majority free-float company by offering certain shares to Eurasian Natural Resources Corporation (ENRC) shareholders.

The year 2014 became a landmark for the company. Firstly, it decided to focus on copper mining and approved the disposal of its 50% stake in the Ekibastuz GRES-1 power station. Later that year, independent stakeholders of this smaller and more-focused group commence a major restructuring which resulted in the disposal of a number of producing assets in Zhezkazgan and the Central regions of Kazakhstan. Some US$240 million was transferred as working capital to the Cuprum Holding, a company owned by a well-known businessman in Kazakhstan, Vladimir Kim, resulting in the formation of a new privately owned company, originally called Kazakhmys (Kayakiran 2014). Following completion of the restructuring, the remaining part of the group, consisting of mining and processing assets in the East region, Bozymchak (the new mine and concentrator in Kyrgyzstan) and the three Major Growth Projects (Bozshakol, Aktogay and Koksay), was officially renamed as KAZ Minerals PLC. In the following two years, KAZ started production of its two major growth projects in Aktogay and Bozshakol.

The company's mining operations are successfully managed due to having access to all of the necessary inputs, such as natural resources, power, water, transport, end markets, licenses, labor and finance. KAZ Minerals sells its products to customers in China or Europe, depending on available pricing, and the rewards are shared with its key partners and stakeholders: customers and suppliers, local communities, the government and people of the Republic of Kazakhstan, employees and lenders. Nevertheless, there are a lot of material risks that have to be addressed in a timely manner to prevent harm to people and the environment.

According to the company's annual report (KAZ Minerals PLC 2016), these risks include geological and technological challenges, natural phenomena (resulting in damaged or failed equipment and unplanned expenditure), political instability or social and economic changes in the countries in which it operates (again, negatively impacting its business, financial performance and license to operate). Moreover, world supply and demand for copper and investor sentiment (the company is heavily dependent on commodity prices for copper, gold, silver and zinc that can fluctuate significantly) are also significant factors, as are fluctuations in exchange rates and inflation (leading to increased costs), a high exposure to China (treatment and refining charges are dependent upon Chinese smelting capacity and the level of copper concentrate supply in the region), and health and safety incidents (resulting in production disruption, financial loss and reputational damage). In addition, failure to identify and manage the concerns of local communities and labor unions (affecting reputation and social license to operate), non-compliance with legislation and environmental laws (resulting in regulatory challenges, fines, litigation and ultimately the loss of operating license) play a part. And finally, the inability to attract and retain highly skilled personnel (resulting in higher operating costs to recruit required staff) is of concern. KAZ's business strategy is strongly supported internally. It encompasses delivering major growth projects, optimizing existing assets and taking advantage of further natural resource opportunities in Central Asia, by enabling the company to access capital, reduce operational costs, build relationships with regulators and local communities, and manage talent (KAZ Minerals PLC 2017c).

The overall goal of KAZ Minerals is to enhance social and economic development by running safe and efficient operations that meet regulatory requirements and international standards, contributing to the economy of Kazakhstan through taxes, employee remuneration and spending, and finally, improving health and safety performance, as a safe workplace is the minimum employees and contractors expect. In order to reach this goal the company annually reviews its corporate strategy. Currently, the Board has agreed on the following (KAZ Minerals PLC 2017c): developing as the leading resources company in Central Asia (the company's vision) by delivering value for shareholders and maintaining a strong social commitment to its employees, community and the environment (the company's objective). The company's strategy encompasses three main areas (KAZ Minerals PLC 2017c): delivering growth projects over the next two years, employing optimization programs aimed at improving efficiency of all assets and operations, and acquiring natural resources in the Central Asia region to maintain a long-term project pipeline.

KAZ Minerals sees its employees as one of its key stakeholder groups: it acknowledges the critical role a highly skilled workforce plays in sustainable competitive advantage. Therefore, it is highly committed to training and developing its workers, incentivizing them to stay with the business and ensuring safe working conditions, providing fair pay and benefits, an open dialogue with management and a workplace culture which respects equality and diversity at all levels of the organization (KAZ Minerals PLC 2017d). As of year-end 2016 KAZ Minerals employs approximately 13,000 workers (KAZ Minerals PLC 2016), the overwhelming majority of which are local residents, whereas the remaining minority are foreign nationals in Kazakhstan who are employed by the company to address short-term skill shortages and gain from particular areas of expertise. Therefore, its talent management practices are aimed at two groups of employees: international and local talent. As for overcoming gender issues, the company is proud to state that female senior managers have a high representation in what is a small but significant part of the workforce (KAZ Minerals PLC 2017e). We can observe a persistence of elitist talent definitions—although, formally, the company tries to focus on all of its employees when conducting talent management practices—as a selective group of high-performing and/or high-potential foreign talent is offered special treatment. KAZ Minerals is highly dependent on its ability to attract skilled personnel. Failure to do so could have a negative impact on operations or the successful implementation of growth projects and result in higher operating costs to recruit required staff. The remote location of some operations increases this challenge. The company, however, recognizes the high migration levels in the Kazakhstani labor market: work applications are submitted to the company from all over the country, which means that people are ready to work not only in the region of their permanent residence. The key pull factors are: (1) a competitive salary which is, according to KAZ Minerals' research on the mining industry (KAZ Minerals PLC 2017f), higher than the average wages in Kazakhstan; (2) the possibility of working on the newest equipment; (3) opportunities for career growth and development; (4) provided accommodation; and (5) relocation costs and various expenses are covered by the company.

Considering mining is a hazardous industry, involving heavy equipment and harmful chemicals, another important pull factor for the company is its safe and productive operating environment. Skilled managerial and specialist staff are offered safe working conditions, fair remuneration in line with market rates of pay and social benefits packages for themselves and their families (KAZ Minerals PLC 2016). The company actively promotes its safety culture based on risk awareness and its implemented policies and procedures designed to identify and monitor risks and minimize health and safety incidents (KAZ Minerals PLC 2017g). For instance, workers exposed to health risks are monitored by medical specialists; all employees regardless of their occupation are guaranteed medical examinations (when hired) and annual checkups to prevent, detect and treat occupational diseases.

All employees, regardless of their country of origin, are required to use the latest technology and be familiar with the best practices. The company aims to select the most qualified candidates, but for foreigners the working requirements are more stringent (hence the difference in position and wage). Due to these international specialists having the unique expertise and knowledge required for the implementation of complex projects, they are usually hired as managers. Specifically, the main responsibilities of these foreign experts, due to the experience they have gained by working for multinational mining corporations, include building up the technological process and ensuring the successful launch of new enterprises. Foreign specialists have a tremendous working experience, which they are ready to share with Kazakhstani employees. For companies operating in Kazakhstan, this experience is essential. Nevertheless, the company is highly invested in decreasing its dependence on labor from abroad. For the years to come, the human resources department sets its key task as creating a highly diverse, local talent pool. In order to attract local talent, various benefits are offered to Kazakhstani workers, especially to women in the workforce, who, according to KAZ Minerals' human resources department, are hard to attract to mining careers.

KAZ Minerals also pays huge attention to the development of its employees—in 2015 alone employees received on average 49 hours of training (KAZ Minerals PLC 2015a). All employees, regardless of their occupation, undergo special training and education, enabling them to build rewarding careers. Specifically, in the first two weeks all newly hired workers receive mandatory industrial safety training (with a focus on electrical and fire safety, labor protection, physical fitness and professional development) required by the regulator in Kazakhstan (40 hours per year for supervisory staff and 10 hours for operational staff). Afterwards, depending on position, they undergo specialized training that differs in length and content for different groups of employees: managers and engineers are offered personal development programs aimed at advancing professional skills, whereas the operating staff receive additional training on accident prevention and occupational safety as well as physical training and professional development. All employees become closely acquainted with the technological processes and the requirements for their jobs, while continuing training on special simulators. Additionally, after each stage of training the company evaluates individual performance to determine the level of knowledge employees have gained during training.

According to the company's official statement, KAZ Minerals' training programs allow employees to reach their full potential and ensure they enjoy a motivated workforce that helps to achieve the corporate goals. When KAZ Minerals was first hiring new workers on its Bozshakol growth project it provided a special three-month training program on the company's growth projects (KAZ Minerals PLC 2015b). Moreover, in the middle of 2015, the company introduced its mentoring program directed at the development of its operating staff (Kazminerals.info 2015). The purpose of the program is to provide newly hired employees with the essential knowledge necessary for them to develop practical skills and to facilitate their cultural adjustment. On June 20, 2016 there were 61 working mentors and 164 trained mentors in KAZ Minerals' subsidiary in the Eastern region (Meyer 2016). The mentoring program, however, is not introduced in all of the company's subsidiaries. Finally, KAZ Minerals sponsors its employees in developing their professional skills and qualifications, including sponsoring or subsidizing some of them through higher education (KAZ Minerals PLC 2016).

KAZ Minerals states that employees, like any other asset of an organization, require certain preventive and regular maintenance and in order to increase labor productivity, the human resources department set the following objectives (KAZ Minerals PLC 2015b): to improve the quality of human capital, to minimize staff turnover, and to adjust manufacturing business processes to current business needs. Meanwhile, in order to introduce fundamental qualitative changes in an asset of this sort, an organization has to make large investments in talent management, specifically in training and development. Due to Kazakhstani culture being more collectivistic compared to that of more developed countries, employees may react in an unpredictable way to Western-like talent retention practices. The power-distance scores are generally high with Kazakh people showing a strong respect for authority that could result in rather formal relations between employees and managers and potentially cause problems when establishing confidential communication in the company. In order to develop mutual trust in the organization and provide employees with a clear vision that they are all, regardless of position and occupation, part of a united company, company managers introduced a list of five KAZ Minerals' corporate values, which serve as a basis for its corporate culture (Kazminerals.info 2016): professional development, long-term efficiency, safety, teamwork and honesty.

Following the devaluation of the tenge in 2015, KAZ Minerals sought to mitigate the impact of a weaker local currency on its employees and their families. In particular, free medical and dental services as well as leisure benefits are provided for all employees and at less than half price for their families and retirees (KAZ Minerals PLC 2017f). Workers have an opportunity to spend their vacations in health centers and their children have access to summer camps. In addition, all employees are provided with three hot meals a day. With regard to transportation issues, the company acquires a railway ticket for workers to transfer them to their final destination. The company base is equipped with a gym and rest rooms; a library and a hall for table games are in production. As in most Kazakhstani companies involved in copper mining and smelting activities, operating staff and managers are assessed based on health, production efficiency and cost control and ecological safety, thus incentivizing safety and productivity at the workplace. Bonuses for divisional heads are also linked to health and safety performance, as well as compliance with government-set environmental targets and the amount of environmental fines incurred. Moreover, in accordance with local regulations, KAZ Minerals is obliged to make payments to employees and former employees for illness and disability sustained in the company's operations. The company contributes to defined contribution pension schemes in Kazakhstan, where this is a legal requirement.

KAZ Minerals has a rather complex yet relatively effective talent management system consisting of a variety of practices aimed mostly at developing qualified employees. The key challenges it encounters in order to develop and sustain its competitive advantages are mostly connected to the specifics of the industry it operates in. Therefore, the key, long-term, talent management objective is to ensure industrial safety and create a stable working environment, which means most talent decisions are aimed at reaching this goal. KAZ Minerals invests a considerable amount of its resources in developing certain skills of its workers, arranging a variety of safety programs and training on simulation machines, thus increasing their awareness of safety regulations to reduce future injuries and fatalities at the workplace and, as a result, create a positive image of company so that it can further attract talent.

Kazzinc: Orientation to the Future

Kazzinc, a subsidiary of Glencore International AG based in Ust-Kamenogorsk, is a leading, vertically integrated, polymetallic producer in Kazakhstan which accounts for a major share of zinc ore and zinc metal output along with considerable amount of copper, precious metals and lead. Most of the company's core operations are in the East Kazakhstan region (Kazzinc 2017a). The company's products are zinc metal, zinc-aluminum alloy, bismuth Bi1, lead bismuthate, gold, silver, copper in copper concentrate, copper blister, cadmium, indium, thallium, selenium, aluminum, mercury, antimony concentrate, zinc sulfate and sulfuric acid.

Kazzinc was established in 1997 through the merger of three majority state-owned Eastern Kazakhstan non-ferrous metal companies: Ust-Kamenogorsk Lead and Zinc Combinate, Leninogorsk Polymetallic Combinate and Zyryanovsk Lead Combinate, thus allowing it to pool the resources and systems of different independent economic entities to create a complete production cycle. Before the merger, these companies had not been able to maintain a cost-effective and balanced mine, concentrator and smelter operation due to lack of resources. With good financial support from Glencore, a world leader in the production and sale of metals, minerals and energy and agricultural products, Kazzinc consolidated the efforts of hundreds of teams and thousands of people and became a major company in the region (Uatkhanov 2016).

As of February 1, 1997 it has significantly increased production capacity and output becoming one of the world's five, lowest-cost zinc producers (Kazzinc 2017a). In different years Kazzinc was certified for its quality management systems—recent certification was under the ISO 50001 Energy Management standard—that successfully continue to operate with annual recertification. Additionally, for the second time since its incorporation, Kazzinc was declared a leader of the year in the support and development of small and medium scale businesses in Kazakhstan. Specifically, in 2012 Kazzinc created a special department to develop local content under the memorandum of co-operation signed by different parties, including the East Kazakhstan Regional Administration, and since 2013, the company has signed 63 memorandums with domestic producers (Uatkhanov 2016). Two years later, the East Kazakhstan regional administration and Kazzinc signed a document on the acquisition of goods, works and services from regional companies for US$175 million. At the 2017 International Astana Mining and Metallurgy Congress it was awarded the eighth Golden Hephaestus Prize (Kazzinc 2017b), a national award for breakthrough innovative solutions, research and development in the mining and metallurgical industry established by the Ministry of Investments and Development of the Republic of Kazakhstan. The nomination was Leader of the Year for Local Content.

According to the company's official statement (Kazzinc 2017c), the main long-term corporate objectives are as follows: (1) to minimize adverse health and environmental impacts by implementing best practices and introducing advanced technologies to mitigate the harmful effect on human health and prevent the occurrence of occupational injuries; (2) to increase geological resources and reserves through targeted greenfield and brownfield exploration; (3) to improve production and management techniques by implementing effective ways to improve performance and reduce production costs; (4) to expand the business locally and regionally through the merger and acquisition of new assets by using their quality, size, location and fair value as the key performance indicators aimed at achieving maximum acquisition capitalization; and (5) to fulfill its corporate social responsibility commitments in all regions. Top management believes that incremental progress and prudent use of natural resources with a minimum risk to the environment would help create sustainable value for shareholders, employees, partners and the community.

Kazzinc determines seven corporate values (Kazzinc 2017c), all of which reflect on the specifics of the Kazakhstani labor market, industry specifics and corporate strategy (described above via key corporate objectives): people, unity, development, efficiency, stability, fairness, and zero tolerance for corruption. Firstly, employees are considered to be the company's greatest asset and since mining is a hazardous industry, one would anticipate the safety, health and well-being of the people as being Kazzinc's first priority in the workplace. Secondly, Kazzinc promotes mutual respect and trust, an ability to listen and understand, non-indifference to co-workers' problems and dedication, since such features help people in achieving greater success at work by positively affecting knowledge transfer between different departments and creating stronger intra-organizational teams. As for efficiency and stability, the company strives to ensure production stability and efficiently maintains high-performance outcomes. A good indicator of success in this field is the fact that the company managed to survive the 2008–2009 financial crisis without losing its production and personnel. Finally, fair and transparent processes and solutions that are fully observant with the law are necessary elements of the management system. Attitude toward co-workers, proficiency and decency are appreciated to the same extent as high performance of employees, while any actions with a corruption element are strongly condemned.

According to official documentation, Kazzinc employs over 20,000 people across 500 different professions, of which more than a quarter has received higher education (Kazzinc 2017d). The organization clearly embraces a universalist definition of talent and focuses on all of its employees rather than a selective group of high performers and/or high potentials when conducting talent management practices. The following statement serves as proof: "Our people are the key for our success. Our teams consist of talented people with various experience, culture and knowledge" (Kazzinc 2017e). This is one of many examples where the company uses "talent" or "highly qualified personnel" interchangeably with "employees" and "workers" in its official statements. In fact, the sincere belief that well-skilled, mobile and motivated human capital is Kazzinc's key competitive advantage is one of the main reasons why senior management supports large investment in talent management practices. Specifically, continuous improvement and innovation are stipulated in the company's development strategy and policy (Uatkhanov 2016)—training, career development opportunities and an open environment for ideas and creativity are offered to all employees (Kazzinc 2017d).

As for attracting talent, Kazzinc has graduate programs and pre-hiring special tracks with partner universities. Based on information provided to popular recruitment agencies, the company is interested in students from foreign technical universities, who are in their final- and penultimate year of education studying geology, metallurgy, mining, and mining electromechanics (Kazzinc 2017f). The overall recruitment process is more or less transparent, and understandably, the employment of local people is prioritized. When filling higher-level positions, Kazzinc mostly relies on internal talent.

The key factors negatively affecting the company's ability to attract talent are low perception of workplace safety and environmental issues. Similar to other organizations operating in hazardous industries, Kazzinc continuously promotes the actions it takes in ensuring a safe and healthy working environment. In 2013, for instance, the company launched its comprehensive multi-phased project, SafeWork, aimed at preventing occupational injuries by changing the attitude of both its contracted and own personnel to safety aspects (Kazzinc 2017g). The project is based on long-term practices applied by similar operations in other countries that managed to establish the best occupational safety systems in the world. As for environmental protection, the company is highly concerned with energy saving issues, sulfur dioxide and solids emissions, arsenic and other wastes. It frequently reports on its efforts to neutralize the negative effects of its operations.

Corporate social responsibility is one of the key attracting factors of Kazzinc. The company plays an active role in the economic and social development of the towns and regions it operates in, contributing to education, health, sport and cultural projects. It facilitates infrastructure development and provides support to socially vulnerable groups (Uatkhanov 2016). In the East Kazakhstan region, specifically in Ridder and Zyryanovsk, Kazzinc has arranged shelters for children, provided assistance to orphanages and boarding schools, and implemented programs to assist orphans and disabled people. Together with the region's administration it has helped over 100 children to find new homes, and provided others with housing and decent professions.

Finally, in order to become an internationally competitive company and gain access to the global talent pool, Kazzinc makes large investments in science (Uatkhanov 2016). It actively co-operates with external research centers and laboratories based in countries such as Finland, Germany, and Russia to gain knowledge about new technologies.

As for talent development, employee training including professional training, retraining and advanced training are arranged by Kazzinc on a regular basis to ensure the required qualification level of its workers. To feed its talent needs, the company annually invests over US\$2 million in supporting training programs that are available to workers, leaders and managers of all levels and encompass environmental and occupational safety and health protection (Kazzinc 2017h). Moreover, for training and development purposes Kazzinc has established a corporate university comprising of nine departments: mining and geology, power engineering, mineral processing, metallurgy, automation and information technologies, personnel safety, environment, fixed assets maintenance, economics and management (Kazzinc 2017h). Any employee can upgrade his or her skills. In addition, the company has a distance learning system and several partnership agreements with leading higher education institutions in Kazakhstan and Russia, allowing, for instance, Kazzinc's managers to obtain a Business Administration master's degree. Nazarbayev University is one of these universities: senior specialists participate in the university's consulting commissions in related focus areas (Kazzinc 2017h). Finally, Kazzinc also focuses its attention on training its personnel to identify hazards and risks in the workplace, as part of its SafeWork implementation (Kazzinc 2017g). To improve training efficiency the company has built a pilot training center complying with the highest international industry standards.

According to the company's code of conduct (Kazzinc 2017e), convenient working conditions, a loyal team climate, opportunities for development, and just compensation are provided to all employees regardless of their race, nationality, religion, gender, age, sexual orientation, disability, ancestry, political or other opinion, or any other aspect. Kazzinc pays special attention to how young staff members are adapting and developing. It regularly assesses personnel competence and qualifications to identify talent, efficiency and potential, and provides relevant support and opportunities for their development.

As for talent motivation, the company has been developing its motivation system for nine years. Before the merger in 1997, each of the three metal companies—Ust-Kamenogorsk Lead and Zinc Combinate,

Leninogorsk Polymetallic Combinate and Zyryanovsk Lead Combinate—employed different systems of formation of tariff rates and salaries, which forced the newly established company to develop a new system based on the legislative acts of the Republic of Kazakhstan regarding labor and wages. Kazzinc conducted an anonymous survey of approximately 1000 employees to determine the importance of different motivation factors (based on Herzberg's theory of motivation in the workplace) and later, in 2005, the company launched Kazzinc's "Pyramid of motivation" based on Maslow's hierarchy of needs (Kolomytsev and Kanapianova 2007). Taking into account the particular business culture in Kazakhstan, the most significant achievement was virtually removing the "wage depriva-tion" factor from the Pyramid. Now, only in the case of a safety rules violation, can an employee lose the variable part of his or her salary. The "Pyramid of motivation" consists of the following steps (Kolomytsev and Kanapianova 2007): (1) creation of appropriate working conditions; (2) remuneration (monthly and quarterly payments, bonuses, single cash compensation, performance assessment system); (3) a social package; (4) non-financial encouragement and bonuses, creation of achievements rec-ognition; and (5) possibilities of self-realization.

Kazzinc pays considerable attention to shaping the corporate culture and developing the creative potential of its employees and their families. The company organizes a number of different corporate activities throughout the year, including New Year celebrations and sports events and the "Club of Cheerful and Sharp-witted" (a competition where employees can show off their dancing, singing and acting skills). The event of the year, however, is "Metallurgist Day", an all-city holiday with festivities and performances by Kazakhstani and foreign entertainment stars. On this day, employees who contributed greatly to the development of the company are awarded with Certificates of Appreciation from Kazzinc.

The talent management system at Kazzinc is well-developed, focusing more or less on all talent activities, including the attraction, development and retention of talent. Similar to other Kazakhstani organizations oper-ating in hazardous industries, like KAZ Minerals, Kazzinc's main concern is providing safe working conditions, considering that employee health and safety issues are among the most important problems in Kazakhstan.

Consequently, the key objectives of the talent management system at Kazzinc revolve around creating a healthy working environment.

Together with generally less competitive wages and lack of career development opportunities, compared to foreign internationalized corporations from developed markets, the company has to consider unconventional motivation techniques (e.g. the "Pyramid of motivation") that take into account people's current needs to overcome the economic barriers and specific cultural issues that currently exist in Kazakhstan. The company's efficiency is highly dependent on the level of motivation of its workers. In addition, there is the perennial problem of high power distance that exists in all of the post-Soviet countries, including Kazakhstan. In the context of a firm, this means employees and managers are at arm's length from each other which leads to potential problems in communication and interaction. Specifically, feedback systems that are usually implemented by leading organizations in the West for employee development purposes stop working the way they should, becoming less effective and rather formal. Nonetheless, the company invests a lot of its resources to address these negative factors by creating equal rights for all employees, carrying out activities (unrelated to work) to reduce the power distance, and continuously improving its learning and development as well as motivation systems.

Tengizchevroil: Creating Talent Value

Tengizchevroil is the largest Kazakhstani organization that produces and markets crude oil, liquid petroleum gas, dry gas and sulfur, exporting its products to Europe, the Americas, China, Russia, the Mediterranean countries, Central Asia and international markets. The company was formed by the Republic of Kazakhstan and American Chevron Oil Corporation on April 6, 1993. Currently, Chevron holds a 50% interest in Tengizchevroil (Chevron 2017), whereas ExxonMobil, KazMunayGas and LukArco hold 25, 20 and 5% respectively (Tengizchevroil 2017a). The President of the Republic of Kazakhstan, Nursultan Nazarbayev, and Head of Chevron, Kenneth Derr, signed an agreement on the establishment of a Kazakh-American joint venture to develop Tengiz, the world's deepest-producing supergiant oil field, in the Atyrau region of Kazakhstan (Tengizchevroil 2017b). Since then Tengizchevroil successfully launched a number of projects (Tengizchevroil 2017c), such as the implementation of a five-year social investment program (the Bonus Fund Atyrau Program) in 1993–1998. It also started Egilik social infrastructure projects in 1999 (including reconstruction of the central bridge over the Ural River in Atyrau as well as improvement of the oblast center), and the creation of Kazakhstan's Maritime Academy in 2013. Additionally, it launched an integrated Future Growth Project-Wellhead Pressure Management Project (FGP-WPMP) designed to increase the total daily production from the Tengiz reservoir and maximize the ultimate recovery of resources (the FGP-WPMP Final Investment Decision was announced in 2016) (Chevron 2017). Since the start of this program, Tengizchevroil has provided a number of interest-free loans to entrepreneurs and small businesses, like MontazhSpetsStroy JSC, a fully state-owned and -operated engineering, procurement and construction Kazakhstani company to upgrade their health, environment and safety practices to meet international standards (Chevron 2017). Now, according to the official annual and quarterly reviews, Tengizchevroil demonstrates excellent performance results in various areas, including crude production, sales, safety and environment, community outreach (supported projects planned to help improve the quality of health and education in the Atyrau region through the community investment program), workforce development, and so on.

Tengizchevroil's mission is to create superior value to all stakeholders, including the Republic of Kazakhstan, its employees, communities, business partners, customers and others, by becoming the safest, most efficient and profitable oil and gas enterprise in the world. Therefore, the company's strategy focuses on four key aspects (Tengizchevroil 2017d): differentiating performance via technology and functional excellence; developing reserves to grow profits and returns; delivering superior results through effective and efficient execution; and investing in people. In addition, as one of the most important objectives for Tengizchevroil is ensuring safety of its personnel and protecting the environment by preventing high-consequence events, the company has employed the Operational Excellence Management System (OEMC) as a part of its risk management program. OEMS consists of three parts (Tengizchevroil 2017d). The first is leadership accountability as leaders play an important role in helping the company achieve superior results. The second is the management system process. The third consists of operational excellence elements and expectations united into 13 elements (security of personnel and assets, facilities design and construction, safe operations, management of change, reliability and efficiency, third-party services, environmental stewardship, product stewardship, incident investigation, community and stakeholder engagement, emergency management, compliance assurance, and legislative and regulatory advocacy).

As for its corporate values, Tengizchevroil states that it conducts its business in a socially and environmentally responsible manner, taking very seriously corporate social responsibility, performing to the highest ethical standard, respecting the law and benefiting the local communities. These values are diversity and inclusion (i.e. celebrating the uniqueness of cultures and values of individual talents, experiences and ideas), high performance (i.e. striving for efficiency and continual improvement), integrity and trust, partnership (i.e. building productive and collaborative relationships with all stakeholders), and protecting people and the environment (Tengizchevroil 2017d). The last, as already mentioned above, is one of the most important objectives for the company.

In official reports and publications Tengizchevroil stresses that the company's major asset is its employees (Tengizchevroil 2013), who make the company's greatest achievements happen due to their high level of expertise, professionalism and dedication (Tengizchevroil 2016). Like Kazzinc, Tengizchevroil has a selective but inclusive definition of talent, meaning only those who possess the right attributes and skills or have high potential and promise are hired, while those who are already employed by the company have access to all relevant career and development opportunities offered by the talent management system.

The workforce includes people of various ages, experiences and qualifications who are being hired through both internal and external methods of recruitment. However, considering Kazakhstan's labor market, there is high demand for young talented professionals who are one of the least active job hunting groups. At the same time Tengizchevroil, as a growing company (and according to the trends in Kazakhstan recruitment), is interested in graduates and offers a wide range of career starting positions for them. Both young and more experienced employees are being approached through different external and internal recruiting channels. For external recruitment, several channels can be identified (Tengizchevroil 2017f): internet job boards (the company's job board on its official website) and job fairs, and major employment and networking events for hiring outstanding graduates for the company's engineering and analytical positions at the Atyrau and Tengiz locations. Job fairs take place at the premises of universities: they last several days and consist of aptitude tests and preliminary interviews. These career fairs help to attract young prominent professionals despite their general inactivity in searching for jobs.

Internal recruitment becomes possible due to the range of training and development programs held by the company that were brought to Kazakhstan by international companies. Western practices are implemented by the major owner of Tengizchevroil, Chevron, that facilitates effective training in the company which is generally not common among Kazakhstani employers. As a result of these intensive development programs, many talented employees are promoted to job positions with higher levels of responsibility. This, in its turn, substantially decreases the need for external recruitment. For instance, the most recent Tengizchevroil's report stated that due to these training projects 113 Kazakhstani specialists replaced foreign employees "in key managerial, supervisory and technical positions" during 2010–2014 (Tengizchevroil 2014). This shows that implementing training programs in Kazakhstani companies facilitates employment and further promotion of employees.

In addition, there is a trend to offer workplaces and career opportunities to Kazakhstani people first (and then to people from other regions) to support local communities. Most probably this stems from the significant shift in human resource management at a country scale from attracting foreigners with international experience to instead hiring local labor. The company is also known for its engagement in raising women's competitiveness on the job market including requalification and education of unemployed women in Astana and Almaty. This policy can be explained by Kazakhstan striving for and succeeding in gender equality.

As for long-term talent attraction practices, Tengizchevroil actively engages in corporate social responsibility. From 1993 to the first half of 2016, direct financial payments from the company to the Republic of Kazakhstan amounted to US$114 billion. These related to the salaries of Kazakh employees, the purchase of goods and services from domestic producers and suppliers, payments to state enterprises, and dividend payments (in the form of taxes and royalties as well), all transferred to the state budget (Tengrinews 2014). In addition, Tengizshevroil annually participates in and supports performances devoted to HIV/AIDS prevention at schools and colleges. The company has donated money to the water replacement and gasification projects in Kulsary and invested in the reconstruction of schools and kindergartens in the Aturay region. It has also renovated three parks during 2014–2015 and planted over 3000 trees.

Finally, similar to KAZ Minerals and Kazzinc, complying with all the safety requirements in the workplace is one of the company's priorities (achieved by means of a project called the Behavior Based Safety Program, implemented to create an injury-free work environment). Tengizchevroil strives to achieve industry-leading safety results in standard industrial safety measurements such as Days Away From Work and Total Recordable Incidents (Tengizchevroil 2017e). Achieving zero workplace injuries and fatalities is something potential employees, including talented workers, consider when searching and applying for an open position in such an unsafe industry, making industrial safety an important attracting factor. For instance, in 2016, Tengizchevroil employees and contractors worked 55 million hours without a single "Days Away From Work" incident, which was a personal record for the company. Thus, the politics of maintaining safety in the workplace creates a competitive advantage for Tengizchevroil as an employer, since safety issues are considered to be one of the main weaknesses of Kazakhstani companies in general.

To meet modern challenges, Tengizchevroil has put in place a strong experience-building training and workforce development plan that includes technical, computer, managerial, interpersonal, organizational and language training (spending about US$46 million over the past 10 years) (Tengizchevroil 2017g). Major activities in the field of talent development include the Leadership Program and a Temporary

International Assignment Program (Tengizchevroil 2014). The latter contributes to broadening personnel's knowledge through cross-functional, domestic and foreign work assignments. Presumably, these measures help to combine the need for an international working experience for employees and the hiring of local (i.e. Kazakhstani) people. In addition, different training and mentoring projects are implemented in order to improve the skills of technical staff. Tengizchevroil's expatriate workforce is below 13% (Tengizchevroil 2014), as Kazakhstani citizens hold the overwhelming majority of the company's positions. Kazakhstani managers and supervisors hold three-quarters of the firm's supervisor and manager positions (e.g. general manager of strategic planning, tax manager, plant superintendent, treasury manager, supply chain group category manager, comptroller and environmental supervisor). Moreover, Tengizchevroil financially supports and encourages its most prominent employees to acquire Master- and MBA-level degrees. The company annually sends over 200 people to foreign locations for training in their specific fields and provides international developmental work assignments for some talented workers. Along with all these educational programs, the company participates in joint ventures with foreign and local oil and gas suppliers, thus contributing to knowledge transfer and the acquaintance of local talent with the best practices in the industry (Tengizchevroil 2014).

There is a variety of opportunities for each talented worker to be fulfilled. First of all, Tengizchevroil has a policy of employees' career growth assistance. All of the educational programs that exist in the company are aimed at preparing a talented employee to take a higher job position with more responsibility. At the same time, new incentives are always encouraged by Tengizchevroil in order to make the company a better place to work in. In addition, every employee (talent and non-talent) can participate in the development of Tengizchevroil's social life by offering new ideas in the fields of entertainment, professional growth, sports activities and work and family balance.

Tengizchevroil pays great attention to talent retention and motivation. It offers one of the best employee benefits packages in Kazakhstan, covering housing, savings, support for employees' families and health benefits, including medical insurance for personnel and their families, special accommodation and recreation arrangements, interest-free mortgage loans and employees savings programs, sports programs, and so on. Tengizchevroil relies heavily on both monetary incentives and non-financial motivation, the combination of which facilitates the successful conversion of purely corporate goals to the personal goals of each and every employee, regardless of talent status. This is particularly relevant considering the strong migration patterns in Kazakhstan, which is why the company continuously develops its motivation system to ensure its employees will not leave the organization (and the country for that matter).

Tengizchevroil employees value their jobs for stability, competitive salaries and various opportunities for career growth through professional development within the company, which is crucial due to the recent market changes that left some Kazakhstani people without their pay and even their jobs. Therefore, a strong and effective benefits system is needed to reduce employee turnover in general and, as a result, retain the most talented. Tengizchevroil, indeed, pays attention to all these aspects, striving to become a desired employer for current and potential high performers. For instance, the company has a performance-based remuneration system, according to which salaries are paid based on merit. Employees are also awarded with letters of recognition during official ceremonies for their high quality of work, outstanding results and contribution to the progress of Tengizchevroil. However, as mentioned earlier, Kazakhstan is a country where appraisal systems are far from being effective due to specific socio-cultural factors. Moreover, in reality, compensation usually correlates weakly with actual performance in the Kazakhstani context, which indicates there is an opportunity for the company to develop a more meaningful and motivational reward and performance appraisal system.

Tengizchevroil strives to become a desirable employer, putting a lot of effort into attracting talented workers, developing them and creating a better working environment. However, the company faces a range of difficulties, the majority of which are connected to the environment the company operates in, that is Kazakhstan. Since the company's talent management objective is strongly connected to the corporate vision of becoming "the safest, most efficient and profitable oil and gas enterprise in the world" (Tengizchevroil 2017d), the main areas of concern are the rewards system, adaption of best management practices and cross-cultural management (considering foreign governance and the presence of different ethnic groups in Kazakhstan), industrial safety and talent recruitment. In particular, the reward system in Tengizchevroil that promotes high-quality performance does not seem to work successfully for all employees due to the general level of development of appraisal systems in Kazakhstan (as already witnessed in the KAZ Minerals and Kazzinc cases). Specifically, some workers organized a number of strikes, refusing to come to work unless their wages were increased (Tojken 2012). Such a situation is also a sign of drawbacks in internal communication as problems occurring within the organization are not solved promptly or are even ignored by managers, leading to public protests that negatively affect the company's reputation. Within this context, Tengizchevroil needs to take certain measures in order to lessen the power distance between employees and their supervisors and managers.

Tengizchevroil puts a lot of effort into increasing the share of the local population in its employee ranks; however, due to the country's ethnic diversity, it has to deal with conflicts that occur between workers of different cultural and/or ethnic backgrounds (Tumanov 2006). The main reason behind these conflicts is the general disagreement about what the "right" norms of behavior are in a workplace. Finally, similar to most Kazakhstani companies, Tengizchevroil has to regularly deal with clanism (common in this area) that can lead to biased recruitment and promotion (Minbaeva and Maral Muratbekova-Touron 2013).

Conclusion

Most of Kazakhstan's distinct talent management practices reflect its distinct cultural make-up and the country's historical legacy of the Soviet way of managing employees. However, the Western tradition is slowly seeping into Kazakhstan, resulting in a "hybrid" form of practices that shares the characteristics of both Western and local ways of thinking. This indicates that despite the dynamic economic growth of Kazakhstan, talent management is still in transition from Soviet era practices to ones current in foreign companies. The understanding of human resource management practices in Kazakhstani firms varies from administrative functions to using human resources strategically for a company's growth (i.e. focusing on talent management). Due the strong impact of its Soviet heritage on the different aspects of management and behavior of people, as well as certain cultural, economic and social factors in Kazakhstan and other CIS countries, there is generally a low variety of talent management practices. Specifically, as a highly formalized Soviet society which is perceived as a culture with a higher power distance between managers and subordinates and where social orientation prevails over task orientation, Kazakhstani companies employ talent management practices that show a high rate of formalization in recruiting and training policies. Talent management is developing due to the adoption of various talent management practices from Western companies, thus helping local companies become more competitive, boosting the development of the country's economic sectors (other than natural resources extraction and financial), and increasing Kazakhstan's attractiveness to foreign investors for further prosperity.

Compared to other CIS countries, such as Ukraine and Belarus, Kazakhstan has a rather mature and developed talent management system, which could be due to the fact that Kazakhstani organizations have been transforming their human resource management departments from post-Soviet toward the universalist approach at a quieter pace, allowing for sustainable organizational restructuring. It is worth noting, though, that in two of the reviewed cases—Tengizchevroil and Kazzinc—foreign companies from developed markets (specifically, from the United States and Switzerland) held a 50% or more interest, which could directly influence these companies' business operations. In particular, local companies most likely have direct access to valuable external knowledge (including access to larger talent pools with highly professional foreign experts); they receive more financial support which gives them additional freedom to implement unconventional managerial practices to achieve their corporate goals. So one can assume that in the case of Kazakhstan, ownership structures and countries of origin played an important role in the development of corporate talent management systems, talent attraction, development and retention practices. However, future research is required on the topic.

References

Anderson, Bridget, and Blanka Hancilova. 2011. Migrant Labour in Kazakhstan: A Cause for Concern? *Journal of Ethnic and Migration Studies* 37: 467–483.

Chevron. 2017. Tengiz Expansion. https://www.chevron.com/projects/tengiz-expansion. Accessed on 22 Aug 2017.

Davis, Paul J. 2012. HR Holds Back Economic Development in Kazakhstan: … and May Thwart Ambitions to Be a Top 50 Nation by 2020. *Human Resource Management International Digest* 20: 43–46.

Export.gov. 2016. Kazakhstan – Project Financing. Last Modified, December 9. https://www.export.gov/article?id=Kazakhstan-Project-Financing. Accessed on 1 Aug 2017.

Financial Times. 2017. Kaz Minerals PLC. Last modified January 23. https://markets.ft.com/data/equities/tearsheet/profile?s=KAZ:LSE. Accessed on 8 Aug 2017.

International Monetary Fund. Middle East and Central Asia Dept. 2014. Republic of Kazakhstan: Selected Issues. Country Report No. 14/243. https://www.imf.org/external/pubs/ft/scr/2014/cr14243.pdf. Accessed on 1 Aug 2017.

Kayakiran, Firat. 2014. Kazakhmys Completes Restructuring, Changes Name to KAZ Minerals. *Bloomberg L.P.*, October 31. https://www.bloomberg.com/news/articles/2014-10-31/kazakhmys-completes-restructuring-changes-name-to-kaz-minerals. Accessed on 8 Aug 2017.

KAZ Minerals PLC. 2015a. KAZ Minerals PLC Annual Report and Accounts 2015. http://www.kazminerals.com/media/2686/kaz-minerals-plc-annual-report-and-accounts-2015.pdf. Accessed on 8 Aug 2017.

———. 2015b. *KAZ Minerals Corporate Newspaper 1* (2). http://kazminerals.info/ru/media/newspaper/?page=2. Accessed on 8 Aug 2017.

———. 2016. KAZ Minerals PLC Annual Report and Accounts 2016. http://www.kazminerals.com/media/1725/ka149_book-small-cmyk-1.pdf// Accessed on 8 Aug 2017.

———. 2017a. About Us: At a Glance. http://www.kazminerals.com/about-us/at-a-glance/. Accessed on 8 Aug 2017.

———. 2017b. Group History. www.kazminerals.com/about-us/who-we-are/group-history/. Accessed on 8 Aug 2017.

———. 2017c. Our Strategy. www.kazminerals.com/about-us/our-strategy/. Accessed on 8 Aug 2017.

———. 2017d. Employees. www.kazminerals.com/corporate-responsibility/employees/. Accessed on 8 Aug 2017.

———. 2017e. Equality & Diversity. www.kazminerals.com/corporate-responsibility/employees/equality-diversity/. Accessed on 8 Aug 2017.

———. 2017f. Reward & Recognition www.kazminerals.com/careers/reward-recognition/. Accessed on 8 Aug 2017.

———. 2017g. Health & Safety. www.kazminerals.com/corporate-responsibility/health-safety/. Accessed on 8 Aug 2017.

Kazminerals.info. 2015. Mentors of the Kaz Minerals. Last modified July 30. http://kazminerals.info/ru/roots/projects/posts/nastavniki-kaz-minerals. Accessed on 8 Aug 2017.

———. 2016. Competition for Corporate Values: Results of 2016. Last modified July 30. http://kazminerals.info/ru/roots/projects/posts/nastavniki-kaz-minerals. Accessed on 8 Aug 2017.

Kazzinc. 2017a. About Us. www.kazzinc.com/en/About_us. Accessed on 15 Aug 2017.

———. 2017b. Awards. www.kazzinc.com/en/Awards/Industry_Leader. Accessed on 15 Aug 2017.

———. 2017c. Kazzinc Policy. www.kazzinc.com/en/Policy. Accessed on 15 Aug 2017.

———. 2017d. Human Resources. /www.kazzinc.com/en/Personnel. Accessed on 15 Aug 2017.

———. 2017e. Code of Conduct. www.kazzinc.com/files/code-of-conduct-en. pdf. Accessed on 15 Aug 2017.

———. 2017f. Internships Opportunities. www.kazzinc.com/en/Internship. Accessed on 15 Aug 2017.

———. 2017g. Safety. www.kazzinc.com/en/Safety. Accessed on 15 Aug 2017.

———. 2017h. Personnel Training. www.kazzinc.com/en/Personnel_training. Accessed on 15 Aug 2017.

Kolomytsev Andrei, V., and Galina A. Kanapianova. 2007. Introduction of Personnel Motivation System of JSC "Kazzinc". *Vestnik KAFU* 4:156. www.vestnik-kafu.info/journal/12/455/. Accessed on 15 Aug 2017.

Meyer, Tatiana. 2016. Mentors in the Business. Last modified June 30. http://kazminerals.info/ru/roots/news/posts/nastavniki-v-dele_. Accessed on 8 Aug 2017.

Minbaeva, Dana, and Maral Muratbekova-Touron. 2013. Clanism. *Management International Review* 53: 109–139.

Minbaeva, Dana, Kate Hutchings, and Bruce S. Thomson. 2007. Hybrid Human Resource Management in post-Soviet Kazakhstan. *European Journal of International Management* 1: 350–371.

Nesporova, Alena. 2015. Jobs and Skills for Youth: Review of Policies for Youth Employment of Kazakhstan. *International Labour Organization.* www.ilo.org/wcmsp5/groups/public/---europe/---ro-geneva/---sro-moscow/documents/publication/wcms_385997.pdf. Accessed on 1 Aug 2017.

Sarsenov, Ilyas, and Talimjan Urazov. 2017. Kazakhstan – The Economy Has Bottomed Out: What Is Next? *The World Bank Country Economic Update,* April 1. http://documents.worldbank.org/curated/en/585891494402103086/Kazakhstan-The-economy-has-bottomed-out-what-is-next-country-economic-update-Spring-2017. Accessed on 1 Aug 2017.

Smirnova, Yelena V., and Bolat L. Tatibekov. 2013. Older Experts Versus Young Enthusiasts: Whom Do Kazakhstani Employers Prefer? *Quality in Ageing and Older Adults* 14: 128–138.

Tengizchevroil. 2013. The Culture of Safety and Responsibility in Decision-Making. *TCO Newsletter* 11(197). www.tengizchevroil.com/docs/default-source/tco-newsletter/11-197_eng.pdf. Accessed on 22 Aug 2017.

———. 2014. Corporate Responsibility Report 2013–2014. www.tengizchevroil.com/docs/default-source/publications/crr-2014_eng_.pdf. Accessed on 22 Aug 2017.

———. 2016. 2016 Year in Review. www.tengizchevroil.com/about/overview/2016. Accessed on 22 Aug 2017.

———. 2017a. Company Overview. http://tengizchevroil.com/about/overview. Accessed on 22 Aug 2017.

———. 2017b. About TCO. http://tengizchevroil.com/about. Accessed on 22 Aug 2017.

———. 2017c. TCO Milestones. www.tengizchevroil.com/about/milestones. Accessed on 22 Aug 2017.

———. 2017d. The TCO Way. www.tengizchevroil.com/about/the-tco-way. Accessed on 22 Aug 2017.

———. 2017e. Working Safely. www.tengizchevroil.com/corporate-responsibility/working-safely. Accessed on 22 Aug 2017.

———. 2017f. Job Fairs. www.tengizchevroil.com/careers/jobfairs. Accessed on 22 Aug 2017.

———. 2017g. Career Development. www.tengizchevroil.com/careers/career-development. Accessed on 22 Aug 2017.

Tengrinews. 2014. TengizChevrOil Brings Payments to Kazakhstan to $15 Billion, February 25. https://en.tengrinews.kz/companies/TengizChevrOil-brings-payments-to-Kazakhstan-to-15-billion-26285/. Accessed on 22 Aug 2017.

The World Bank. 2017. *The World Bank in Kazakhstan*. Washington, DC: The World Bank Group. www.worldbank.org/en/country/kazakhstan/overview. Accessed on 1 Aug 2017.

The World Factbook. 2017. *Kazakhstan*. Washington, DC: Central Intelligence Agency. www.cia.gov/library/publications/the-world-factbook/geos/kz.html. Accessed on 1 Aug 2017.

Tojken, Sanija. 2012. Do Not Like It – Leave!. *Ak Zhajyk*, January 31. http://azh.kz/ru/news/view/8690. Accessed on 22 Aug 2017.

Trading Economics. 2017. Kazakhstan Youth Unemployment Rate. https://tradingeconomics.com/kazakhstan/youth-unemployment-rate. Accessed on 1 Aug 2017.

Tumanov, Konstantin. 2006. "Tengiz Massacre": Some Details of Mass Fights in Kazakhstan. *Fergana*, November 9. www.fergananews.com/articles/4710. Accessed on 22 Aug 2017.

Uatkhanov, Yerbolat. 2016. Kazzinc: Human Capital as Key Competitive Advantage. *The Astana Times*, July 12. http://astanatimes.com/2016/07/kazzinc-human-capital-as-key-competitive-advantage/. Accessed on 15 Aug 2017.

WorldAtlas. 2017. The Economy of Kazakhstan. Last Modified April 25. www.worldatlas.com/articles/the-economy-of-kazakhstan.html. Accessed on 1 Aug 2017.

Yessengeldin, Bauyrzhan, Diana Sitenko, and Aissulu Ramashova. 2015. Development of Human Potential in the Innovation Economy of Kazakhstan. *Public Policy and Administration* 14: 209–220.

12

Belarus: Moving Forward

Louisa Selivanovskikh

Belarus is an East European country, bordering Russia to the Northeast, Ukraine to the South, Poland to the West and Lithuania and Latvia to the Northwest. The country is a former Soviet republic that declared its independence on August 25, 1991 after the dissolution of the USSR. Now Belarus is a unitary semi-presidential republic that continues Soviet era economic and political traditions, such as state ownership of large sections of the economy—the government is continuing to increase its stake in a variety of businesses, while hardly selling off any of its state assets. There is strong governmental control over business and media. The country has durable ties with numerous former USSR countries, in particular, with the Russian Federation, which remains Belarus' major trade and political partner. Belarus is also a significant transit country for Russian goods. Additionally, the country leadership has taken a clear course of building a favorable business environment for domestic and foreign busi-

L. Selivanovskikh (✉)
Graduate School of Management, St. Petersburg State University,
St. Petersburg, Russia
e-mail: l.selivanovskikh@gsom.pu.ru

© The Author(s) 2018
M. Latukha (ed.), *Talent Management in Global Organizations*,
Palgrave Studies of Internationalization in Emerging Markets,
https://doi.org/10.1007/978-3-319-76418-4_12

nesses. According to the World Bank and International Finance Corporation report, "Conducting Business 2016" Belarus was ranked twelfth concerning the ease of registration of business entities (Business News 2015). The important areas of the country's economy are machine building (the automotive industry occupies the largest share in the machine-building complex, producing one-fourth of total production, specializing in the production of trucks, buses and special vehicles), metalworking, potash mining, as well as chemical and petrochemical industries. The main export countries are Russia, Ukraine and Germany (as key export destinations), followed by the Netherlands, the UK, Poland and Latvia.

In the Soviet post-war years, Belarus became one of the most prosperous parts of the ex-USSR. Following the collapse of the Soviet Union and the country's independence, the economic decline started. Belrus underwent a unique economic transformation, standing out from nearly all other ex-Soviet republics (Adarov et al. 2016). Most ex-USSR and post-communist countries had already gone through "conventional" market reforms by the mid-1990s, whereas Belarus remained "frozen", in contrast to the Central and Eastern European (CEE) economies as well as the Commonwealth of Independent States (CIS) countries and Ukraine. The country demonstrated high gross domestic product (GDP) growth, achieving a considerable degree of catch-up thanks to the internal cohesion and socially oriented reforms and policies, such as the "social contract" that provided the population with stability, order and low levels of income inequality (Adarov et al. 2016). To delay inevitable market reforms, Belarusian authorities, based on the formation of political alliances (and the long-lasting "loyalty rent") negotiated energy subsidies with the Russian Federation that provided gas and oil to Belarus at prices significantly below the world market prices (Adarov et al. 2016). Belarus processes fuel as well as oil- and gas-based chemicals and exports these products at international prices, which is the equivalent of an implicit cash transfer from Russia to Belarus. Meanwhile, inflation has been high and the business climate is considered unfavorable for foreign direct investment (The World Factbook 2017); the country's dependence on Russia for its energy supplies has also proven risky, as the Belarus economy would go into recession following a drastic drop in oil prices

(Sekhovich 2016). Meanwhile, the state sector absolutely dominates the economy in terms of proprietorship and employment (Adarov et al. 2016).

At the end of 2016, the population of Belarus was 9.5 million (The World Bank 2017). Nearly half of the population constitutes the labor force with the majority of workers employed in the service sector and the rest split between agriculture and industry. The inhabitants are evenly distributed throughout the territory of the country. Most of the people are Belarusians; the most populous minorities are Russians, Poles and Ukrainians among other nationalities (WorldAtlas 2015). The gender structure of the workforce is roughly equal (National Statistical Committee of the Republic of Belarus 2016).

The main government objectives are conserving the labor market at zero unemployment, raising individual disposable income and equalizing gender salaries (Adarov et al. 2016). The Ministry of Labor and Social Development, created in 2010, is responsible for the implementation of public policy, performing management functions in labor relations, labor protection, full employment, social security and demographic security, and co-ordinating the activities of this Ministry with other government institutions. A distinct policy instrument is implemented concerning wage scales to regulate all professions. Wages above recommended levels are associated with seniority and previous work experience. In election years, the government increased real wages by raising the respective professional scales. As these increases were implemented at a faster rate than productivity growth, they led to the over-heating of the economy in 2009–2010 and in 2012–2014 resulting in currency crises (Preiherman 2014; Kramer 2011; Bakunowicz 2015).

The managers of state-owned enterprises are not entirely autonomous in their decision-making, and must take political aspects into consideration instead of basing their verdicts entirely on economic indicators (Hellman et al. 2000). Additionally, executives at state-owned enterprises earn considerably less than their private counterparts. Thus, managers at state-owned firms do not have incentives to enhance performance or increase innovation. These managers are subject to an abundance of regulations and controls to ensure that they do not misuse their powers for personal gain. Even in private companies, all measures applied stifle productivity increase and economic growth, reduce performance and impact negatively on personal well-being, although they reduce economic inequality.

Migration to Belarus has a small impact on its labor market due to the impediments companies face in hiring foreign nationals. Belarus is not a particularly attractive destination for immigrating due to the lack of social protection and the recently introduced requirement to pay social security contributions (Adarov et al. 2016). Many Belarusians work temporarily in Russia because of the higher salaries there and greater employment opportunities. This is facilitated by the fact that both countries are part of the Eurasian Economic Union (Adarov et al. 2016). While workers usually send remittances home, the accompanying brain drain also hampers productivity and economic growth in Belarus.

The overwhelming majority of Belarusian organizations, as mentioned earlier, are state-owned, with state-appointed executives, payment based on seniority, and limited transparency of the administrative systems inherited from Soviet times. The system of "ideological control" in enterprises has grown much stronger over recent years, which presumably affected the talent management practices implemented by these organizations.

Belarus is the only European country where mandatory placement after graduation exists (Preiherman 2012). Nonetheless, local employers face various challenges when attracting high-quality workers due to the limited number of incentives they can offer (Carraher and Carraher 2006; Latukha 2016). Specifically, though organizations lean toward performance-based remuneration, there is a "ceiling" set by the government for both state-owned and private companies. Additionally, recruitment is mostly based on personal connections and networking, although human resource managers refute this statement (Latukha 2016). The traditional method of recruiting new employees via official job centers is mainly used for the hiring of low-skilled workers. The central government directly allocates university graduates to particular firms (Preiherman 2012). Personnel managers prefer hiring interns and prospective employees who have a certain, although limited, experience.

There is almost no remuneration gap between male and female workers. There is also high proportion of women in managerial positions

(Pastore and Verashchagina 2005). The above specifics have somewhat boosted productivity. Numerous Belarusian companies believe it is important to continue searching for and hiring female employees and managers to make their workforce more diverse (Pastore and Verashchagina 2005). The existing compensation system is similar to that of the Soviet times. The fact that a talented employee's salary and his or her performance are not aligned with payment rewards has far-reaching consequences for the motivation of talented workers and managers. Employers are significantly limited in the incentives they can provide to their talented employees and this is the case in private companies as well. Leeway exists in the form of additional compensation. Nevertheless, decision-makers evaluate high performance by determining who is compensated, how and when. Another interesting fact is that in the case of financial difficulties a company can compensate its employees with the products manufactured by the firm (according to Article 74 of the Labor Code of the Republic of Belarus). In such situations, employees are left with the choice of either accepting the offer or not being paid at all. Other non-monetary benefits (e.g. housing or daycare provision, social welfare, medical insurance, and the like) are provided on a limited scale by the state. Over the years, numerous firms have assumed these responsibilities. Now mostly the human resource departments of companies are responsible for providing non-monetary compensation (including even the organization of different social events aimed at resolving workplace conflicts) (Akulava et al. 2013; National Statistical Committee of the Republic of Belarus 2016). Therefore, employee turnover is particularly high among recent graduates who are allocated by the state to a specific enterprise. Once their mandatory allocation periods end, they tend to leave the firms due to the lack of career prospects, under-utilization of their skills and low compensation (the labor market has shown a low demand for professions, mostly young talented professionals) (Shraibman 2013). This highlights the importance of merit-based promotions rather than promotions based on personal connections. Highly skilled young graduates frequently lack such connections and are unable to move up the career ladder due to the fact that the positions they strive for are occupied by better-connected, often less-talented employees.

Talent development is entirely in the hands of enterprise management, with strict state supervision. The central government requires all companies to provide employment and professional training for first-time jobseekers under the age of 21, regardless of their skills and educational background (Article 280 of the Labor Code of the Republic of Belarus). In practice, however, firms tend to diverge from the Labor Code. For instance, due to the recent economic crisis companies had to reduce their costs, which negatively affected motivation, job security and productivity. Performance management practices are formal, mainly consisting of decision-making by mangers concerning the performance of their subordinates, and are embedded practices from Soviet times. Belarusian firms do not use performance-related pay, but employees are usually rewarded when completing complex assignments. To ensure intra-workforce co-operation and collaboration as well as employee commitments, great emphasis is placed on teamwork, the significance of which has somewhat diminished over recent years. Personnel managers try to keep up the collective spirit and develop the feeling of belonging to something important.

Therefore, the intervention of the state, reliance on personal connections and paucity of traditional management techniques raise numerous issues regarding talent management and organizational behavior in Belarusian companies. The country is widely recognized for gender equality, but it faces numerous issues concerning the attraction, development and retention of the best and brightest employees, which negatively affects firms' abilities to deal with uncertainty, properly implement change and respond to increased international competition in the labor market (National Statistical Committee of the Republic of Belarus 2016). Nevertheless, we can state that talent management in Belarus is noticeably improving (being the least developed compared to that in the other CIS countries). For instance, in 2015 the country's first human resource standard was developed based on an international human resource management standard. It describes all the functions of the human resource department grouped by topic (e.g. recruitment, adaptation, training and personnel development, motivation, corporate culture, evaluation, development and administration). It establishes ethical standards and developed key performance indicators for each type of activity and each level in a company's hierarchy (Lazareva 2015). Belarus annually holds the "HR-brand award of Belarus" event[1] that attracts hundreds of guests including business owners, chief executives, and human resource managers to provide the opportunity to learn about best practices and current trends in the human resource management and talent management fields, thus raising the level of managerial standards in the country.

What follows are three cases looking at large Belarusian firms, namely, BELAZ, Santa Bremor and Byelorussian Steel Works. These focus on their talent management systems, identifying the key trends and development perspectives in human resource and talent management. We show that Belarus, being economically and culturally connected to Russia, needs to find its own unique path in developing an effective management system.

BELAZ: Traditions in Action

BELAZ is a Zhodzina-based Belarusian manufacturer of mining dump trucks of heavy-duty and super-size load capacity, as well as other heavy vehicles used in the mining and construction industry. The company is an export-oriented enterprise. The majority of its products, mostly trucks, are sold primarily on the Russian and Ukrainian markets and to other CIS countries. The firm is among the seven leading giant companies for the production of mining equipment (BELAZ 2017a).

Throughout its history (see BELAZ 2017b) BELAZ has developed numerous versions of mining dump trucks with payload capacities up to 300 tonnes, and produced hundreds of thousands of units of mining dump trucks sold all over the world. The company began its production in 1948 when the first engineering buildings of "Torfmash" were constructed near the Zhodino railway station 50 kilometers away from Minsk, according to the Law on the Five Years' Plan for Restoration of the National Economy of the Belarusian Soviet Socialist Republic for 1946–1950. In 1951, the factory for building peat machines was transformed into a factory for soil-reclamation and road vehicles, Dormash,

---

[1] http://hrpremia.by.

which produced snowplows, flusher and auger vehicles, brush cutters and other equipment. Meanwhile, the enterprise was given its current name, Belarusian Autoworks, in 1958.

The enterprise proceeded successfully providing the former USSR with extra-large mining dump trucks, simultaneously winning quality prizes across the world. For the first time BELAZ's quality was recognized at an international exhibition in Leipzig in 1965. Then BELAZ-540 was awarded a gold medal. In subsequent years, BELAZ was internationally appraised in Europe, North and South America. The modern BELAZ-75710 was featured in the *Guinness Book of World Records* as the largest two-axle dump truck and the largest mining truck body (BELAZ 2017c). In 1978, Belarusian Autoworks stepped into the diversification stage introducing aircraft tugs to the market. Nowadays, apart from mining dump trucks, BELAZ's product lines include construction and road building equipment, vehicles for mine-servicing works, underground vehicles, vehicles for metallurgical works, special purpose vehicles and railway freight cars.

From the beginning of the twenty-first century Belarusian Autoworks in its new legal form PA BELAZ started merger activities acquiring Mogilev Autoworks, RUE Starodorozhski Mechanical Works, CJSC Mogilev Railway Car Building Plant, OJSC Kuzlitmash and OJSC Slutsk Lifting-And-Conveying Machines Plant. The consolidation process lasted 11 years and resulted in BELAZ-Holding in 2012. Plant and factories incorporated into the new holding company provide almost the whole production cycle starting from metalwork and spare parts and ending with final goods. The holding company's top management team comes from the principal operation streams of the company: engineering, industrial design, financial and economic issues, social and security issues, public relations and human resources.

Russia has always been the main consumer of BELAZ's production. Belarusian dump trucks occupy a significant portion of the Russian market (RBK 2015). This sustainable development is supported by the strong reputation built through many decades of collaboration and tight relationships with Russian customers. From a world point of view, the company holds a solid but modest share of the Russian market. Nowadays, BELAZ-Holding sets its goal of becoming more internationally competitive and therefore plans to expand globally. Rivalry is very strong, hence BELAZ is planning a system of measures to broaden its dealers' network worldwide and enhance the level of service quality in its international branches.

The holding company values the quality of its production: "Quality is a key indicator of the products' competitiveness and improvement of the company's economic status" (BELAZ 2017f). Quality is the core competitive advantage of the company on the global market. Local and international specialists verify quality standards regularly. The company invests the bulk of its resources in R&D to sustain quality levels and address the challenges of technological progress. One of the latest developments is the automation of heavy industries and their robotization, a trend that BELAZ has successfully followed.

BELAZ employs nearly 11,000 workers just in Belarus, and contributes over BYN1 trillion (Belarusian rubles in the pre-denomination period) annually to the country's GDP (Valex Consult 2015). Due to its size, the firm has a large number of strategic business units (SBUs) as well as numerous internationalized operations. BELAZ has the global challenge of uniting all the parts of the company into one whole, which will have the same organizational structure, working conditions and principles, and will follow the same values. It is important for the company to introduce and develop context-specific managerial practices aimed at attracting, developing and retaining the best employees to improve performance on the world market. Considering the specificity of the industry and the Belarusian management culture, the company employs a universalist approach toward talent management. The talent management strategy of BELAZ can be described as a combination of well-established Soviet practices, decent use of national pride motives, a rich international experience (especially in comparison to other companies in Belarus) and a family-like organizational culture where everybody stands together and united. However, the important role of talent management is not as recognized by the company compared to leading organizations in the West and from other CIS countries. The human resource specialists are seen as company employees responsible for hiring and firing of workers. Men mostly occupy senior managerial positions. The literature posits that a company's performance correlates positively with the increased percentage of women in management (e.g., Desvaux et al. 2017; Nielsen and Huse 2010; Wittenberg-Cox and Maitland 2008). Therefore, with this lack of gender equality in management BELAZ risks losing potential benefits from a larger female involvement in the firm's operations and decision-making processes.

The production of 450-tonnes cars requires an advanced level of technical skills and competences as well as the well-organized work of thousands of people. Therefore, BELAZ sets high requirements for new recruits. The company is mainly interested in hiring local talent for a number of reasons. Firstly, recruiting the foreign workforce is more expensive than recruiting locals. Secondly, due to the student allocation system in place, the costs for recruiting local talent are low. Most importantly, Belarusian companies have a predictable and stable flow of workers, even though they are sometimes forced to hire and work with low-skilled workers; and no further training is required for local workers due to the fact that they are familiar with the specifics and idiosyncrasies of the working environment (Bobrova 2015). However, when there are no local specialists available, the company does recruit foreign employees. Low-level job positions are offered to "self-grown" specialists, who join the company either with the help of career agencies, job centers or various career websites, such as Headhunter, JobSearch, and the like. At top-level positions, most managers are promoted either after working in the company for many years, or by using personal connections. Therefore, the general situation with talent attraction follows the talent management trends identified in the rest of the country.

To obtain high-quality recruits, BELAZ collaborates with Belarusian universities, actively encouraging young professionals to join the firm, inviting them to join its dynamic team. The key attracting factors are affordable housing, as BELAZ owns dormitories, and a fast career start. As many new recruits have to relocate and be separated from their friends and families, the company launched a special adaptation program for former students. During the first two weeks, new employees learn everything there is to know about the history of the company, its current performance, and the specifics of working in different departments (the company's management believes that these two weeks smooth the adaptation process) (BELAZ 2014). In order to increase its talent pool, BELAZ spends much of its resources on organizing various excursions (like the "BELAZ – Belarus brand" excursion) that demonstrate to young employees the way the company operates. Meetings and conferences for student graduates are organized. All of these activities aim at delivering relevant information to newcomers about the company (e.g. the Hall of Labor museum located close to the factory aims to introduce the rich history of the company to young specialists). Similar to other Belarusian companies, BELAZ pays salaries in US dollars due to the significant instability of the national currency, which is a good incentive for newcomers. Therefore, BELAZ is quite popular among new graduates.

Training sessions at BELAZ are mostly oriented at increasing the productivity of employees. Meanwhile, the company pays a lot of attention to various contests held by the government and organizes many such activities of its own. Winning any of these competitions is usually a great honor for both employee and employer. Moreover, during most of their time, employees work to improve their technical skills in order to achieve a higher qualifying category (BELAZ 2011). This does not change their occupational position but increases their salaries, allowing them to take on more interesting and complicated tasks. Another Soviet legacy is a developed mentorship system. This system is implemented in every department helping to reduce the amount of errors made by the new employees. In addition, all newly hired employees go through initial adaptation training and participate in the Adaptation Day—an event that helps to introduce new employees to the rich history of BELAZ, its mission and goals, culture and, of course, gives details about their social package and other non-monetary benefits.

There are numerous support and non-monetary remuneration systems implemented by the company in order to help its talent to find a work-family balance. Some of the key practices are employed only due to the strict requirements of Belarusian labor law. Nonetheless, BELAZ offers a lot more to its employees, thus motivating them to repeat their best results: extra days off for families with more than two children, bonuses for young families, up to three years of maternity care leave with additional support payments from BELAZ, etc. Recreation centers, camps and festivals for employees' children, annual gifts for retired workers—BELAZ takes real care of every aspect of its employees' lives. The company actively promotes a healthy lifestyle, holds many sports competitions at its facilities and sponsors the local football team, Torpedo-BELAZ. Sometimes, the younger generation sees these activities and events as a waste of their time and money.

To motivate young specialists to get a better understanding of their needs BELAZ has developed a corporate program "BELAZ Young People 2016–2020" (BELAZ 2017d). It promotes the company's human resource brand among the younger generation of workers and aims to change the firm's working conditions according to changes in the perceptions of its future employees. Nowadays, almost a third of the company's workforce is younger than 31 years of age and BELAZ tries to find ways to increase their involvement in company life. "Winner of youth award" (BELAZ 2017e) is the annual competition between young workers in classes such as "Sport and Health", "Production and Quality", "Young Manager", "Economics and Finance", and so on. Winners receive bonuses and are assigned a new qualification category, which increases their salary. Such events motivate young talent and empower them to realize their ideas that could potentially enhance company performance in the future.

In comparison to Russia, there are less foreign multinational corporations in Belarus due to current economic conditions, labor market idiosyncrasies and business environment specificities. This limited amount of international companies generally leads to Belarusian firms being less familiar with the most innovative managerial practices that could increase the ability of firms to effectively attract, develop and retain talent. This is the reason why the pace of development at BELAZ is low compared to that in organizations from other CIS countries. Therefore, if BELAZ keeps is practices unchanged regarding recruitment procedures, career development opportunities as well as retention mechanisms then it will evolve only slightly, as was the case in past decades. However, the company realizes the need for change. In fact, BELAZ is the first Belarusian company to introduce SAP Human Capital Management in order to automate human resource processes and generally catch up with modern approaches to conducting business.

Santa Bremor: To Attract the Best

Santa Bremor, a joint Belarusian-German venture, is not only the biggest food producer in Brest, Belarus, but also one of the largest, high-quality food product manufacturers not just in the Russian Federation, but also in Eastern Europe as a whole. Founded by Mikhail Moshensky in 1998, the firm has grown in two decades to one that employs more than 4000 employees (Santa Bremor 2017a). It yields more than 500 types of production (Santa Bremor 2017b), such as seafood products, herring, salmon, caviar, seafood, surimi and spreads. The firm sells these products in countries all over the world (Santa Bremor 2017c), including the United States, Canada, Israel, Lebanon, Georgia, Australia and New Zealand, as well as Germany, Luxemburg, Latvia, the Czech Republic, Bulgaria, Armenia, Cyprus and Canada. Its main offices are in Belarus, Moldova, Kazakhstan, Ukraine, Russia and Israel. The company operates its permanent sales offices in Moscow, Kiev and Kishinev and has an expanded distribution network in all Belarusian regions (Santa Bremor 2017c). It has established distribution centers in a number of Russian cities, such as St. Petersburg, Samara, Rostov, Yekaterinburg and Omsk, and in Ukrainian cities, such as Lvov, Kherson and Dnepropetrovsk. Due to the company's location on the Belarusian-Polish border (both, the head office and production facilities are located in Brest) the city has multiple advantages that set it aside in terms of handling freight traffic from Western Europe to the CIS countries and back.

At the very beginning, in 1993, the company was registered under the name "Santa Impex Brest" (Santa Bremor 2017b). Its primary business was the import and export of fish and other seafood from and to Belarus, specifically with regard to the wholesale and retail trade in addition to the transport and catering business. The company established the "Santa Bremor" five years later, with this subsidiary specializing in processing canned food, ice cream, salads and dumplings. In the following years, the company's rate of expansion started to rise exponentially. First, they built a fish processing plant, which opened in 2001 to increase their production significantly. Then they succeeded in opening a new facility in 2004, a plant that was built at a rapid pace (in nine months) to ensure they were able to meet the increasing demand for Santa Bremor's products. This new production plant allowed them to become more competitive in the market, lowering prices and increasing the production of surimi, salmon, caviar and other seafood.

In 2008, Santa Bremor began the construction of a new complex with a total area of 24,000 square meters for the production of herring fillet. This facility is equipped with the most advanced equipment from the Netherlands and Iceland, allowing the firm to produce ready-to-eat herring fillets more delicately and carefully. More important is the fact that this kind of optimized production reduced labor costs considerably due to increased automation. The fourth facility was constructed in 2010, greatly increasing the production capabilities of this highly popular company. Finally, the company expanded further in 2013, when it opened (with the participation of the Prime Minister of Belarus) a new factory for manufacturing frozen, half-finished products. This shows the extent to which Santa Bremor has grown, and just how important the firm is to the Belarusian economy.

The company is subject to macro-economic fluctuations, and must respond to any positive or negative changes accordingly. The recent sanctions on Russia by the European Union and the United States have brought about unforeseen consequences, especially concerning the food processing industry, i.e. the sector in which Santa Bremor is active. It transpired that there were more upsides than could be expected considering the economic situation in Russia, Belarus' main economic partner, as a whole. The sanctions were a great opportunity for Belarusian producers as export possibilities increased. Due to the Russian ban on Norwegian salmon, for instance, Santa Bremor increased its investment in fish processing to boost supply to catch up with the increased demand in Russia (Sekhovich 2016). Having said that, though, profits were slashed due to currency fluctuations. The Belarusian ruble has been depreciating over the past few years, and the currency was severely devalued in the middle of 2016.

Santa Bremor has seven functional parts: production, marketing, sales, logistics, economics and finance, IT and human resources. These units operate as staff with line managers helping to solve specific management problems. The basis of the linear-functional structure of Santa Bremor are sub-systems that are each responsible for their own specialization. Each sub-system has a hierarchy that permeates the entire organization from top to bottom. The results of any service management staff are estimated via indicators of the realization of their goals and objectives. This leads to the need for complex co-ordination between functional services in the preparation of an important document, reduces the efficiency of work and extend the terms of decision-making. Additionally, the company has a quality department, which introduces and operates quality and safety management systems, sanitary registration and the certification of raw materials and equipment, incoming control of raw stock and materials, and production supervision.

Operating in international markets, Santa Bremor employs thousands of workers—local, host-country and third-country nationals—and considers them to be the most valuable asset in the organization. The company aims at building business relations with employees, offering them: (1) interesting work in a dynamically developing entity; (2) the ability to gain world-class international experience; (3) professional and career development in a team of adherents; (4) free seminars and training programs; (5) a competitive salary and flexible system of bonuses; (5) a wide benefits package; and (6) corporate activities (Rabota.tut.by 2017).

Though Santa Bremor states that it is interested in experienced, high-performing workers, its human resource department is mostly concerned with enforcing its human resource policy and performing general personnel practices. They include employee recruitment, change management, retirement planning, basic employee training and development, contract management, damage control (representing the company in labor litigations and disputes), personnel compensation and motivation, performance management, conducting of interviews and surveys, provision of feedback, ensuring the security of personal information, and so on. When conducting talent management practices the company aims to target all of its workers, rather than a selective group of high performers, which suggests that the organization supports the ideas of equality in the workplace.

The company's key attracting factor is undoubtedly its leading position among processors of fish and seafood products in Europe. Since its establishment, Santa Bremor has become widely recognized not only in

Belarus, but also in the CIS, Baltic and European countries as the top employer that procures high-quality production conforming to international standards of quality. From the very beginning of its existence, the company has successfully dealt with various challenges, including a general low brand recognition and the resulting shortage of "big fish" in the firm's talent pool. Nowadays, Santa Bremor has significantly improved its talent attraction practices, including the selection and recruitment of high-potential employees—these practices are more effective and efficient, performed on a competitive basis. The company has stated: "What we always appreciate in others is motivation, creativity, high determination and responsibility" (Santa Bremor 2017a). However, it should be noted that its talent attraction is not as advanced compared to that of companies from other CIS countries. Main practices are more traditional, rather formal and standardized throughout the entire company, which reflects general trends in the development of Belarusian business culture and environment. Yet again, the company is well known in Belarus and the brand itself is a strong attracting factor. According to the results of a national survey in the category "Fish and seafood" the vast majority of interviewees voted for the Santa Bremor brand (Santa Bremor 2017d). This survey was conducted during the annual "Brand of the Year" contest, the main objective of which was to determine the actual perception of Belarusian brands by customers through a full-scale study launched in every region of Belarus.

Santa Bremor implements a system of continuous professional training as it is a necessary requirement for a company in modern economic conditions to continuously hone the professional skills of its workers. In particular, the organization offers advanced training courses, and thematic seminars held by the National Press center and the Belarusian Institute for Retraining and Professional Development. The company carries out its own personnel training programs that, depending on the employee's occupation and specialization, could last up to six months. This training and development system, thus, improves the quality of human capital, streamlines the process of the development of professional competences, develops an employee's ability to perform independently and efficiently his or her duties, and therefore achieving the high level of performance required by the company.

One of the most efficient ways of transferring knowledge and skills from more-experienced to less-experienced employees is mentoring. Santa Bremor introduced its mentorship program in 2009 to systematically influence the professional growth of employees and as a result ensure only the best specialists are working for company. Mentors are those individuals who are considered to have mastered certain professional activities. They take on additional responsibility to train newcomers and make their adaptation period shorter and the production process smoother. At the end of the mentorship program, the student-employee receives a state certificate and qualification rank after successfully passing the exam and completing the necessary graduate work. Santa Bremor regularly holds meetings to establish communication between mentors and discuss possible issues that could arise during training sessions as well collectively solve already existing problems (Santa Bremor 2017e).

Meanwhile, by keeping its employees motivated, making them feel proud about being part of the organization as well as creating a steady environment and cozy psychological working atmosphere, Santa Bremor improves its productivity, thus ensuring financial stability, long-term development and stable production. The company, in particular, focuses on improving working conditions and introducing new technology to its workers. For instance, after the construction of the fifth production facility, it imported new production lines and machines from the Netherlands. Additionally, to improve the quality of its products and services the company collects relevant data from its partners via an open dialogue system that connects Santa Bremor, other companies and society together. Finally, Santa Bremor aims at becoming a socially responsible organization by donating to those in need (e.g. a center for handicapped children) and investing in various sports activities and cultural events, and providing help and support to religious organizations.

The company faces a number of challenges, most of which arise from the Belarusian political system not being flexible enough to create a dynamic space for conducting business as well the general inertia of Belarusian organizations. The company is protected by state policies from real international competition. Thus, the pace of implementation and integration of innovative human resource management practices coming from the West (e.g., talent management practices used in European and

American organizations) or the East (e.g., the same talent management practices but adopted to the local context taking into account the political, economic and socio-cultural aspects of Russia) is slow, despite being a Belarusian-German venture.

Santa Bremor is on the path of developing clear human resource management policies to orient key managerial activities and procedures to achieve middle- and long-term (i.e. strategic) corporate objectives, rather than short-term goals of a functional nature. The responsibility for making decisions regarding personnel recruitment and selection, training and development, wage issues, labor relations and other important areas have begun to shift from line managers to specialized human resource units. This is a very positive trend, considering that line managers, having the dominant position in such matters, is generally a barrier to developing human resource management and, by extension, talent management in the company.

To prevent high employee turnover, Santa Bremor adopts more sophisticated non-monetary compensation systems instead of restructuring the human resource management system as a whole according to the actual demands of the labor market. Generally, the recruitment process and development practices are under-developed compared to that of other CIS countries, like Russia and even Kazakhstan. However, due to advanced globalization forces, talented employees can move more freely across national borders, meaning Santa Bremor will eventually make the necessary changes to meet the world standards in terms of talent attraction, development and retention as this would be a necessary condition for sustaining its competitive advantages.

Byelorussian Steel Works: Working Conditions for Talent

Byelorussian Steel Works (BSW) is a state-owned metallurgic company with headquarters in the town of Zhlobin. It is one of the country's top five largest enterprises and the flagship of the Belarusian metallurgical industry. The company consists of four technologically linked production facilities (steel melting production, rolling production, pipe production description, steel cord and wire production) (Byelorussian Steel Works 2017a). A number of infrastructure shops and administrative departments help in delivering its main volume of commercial products. They include concast and billets, shaped rolled products, reinforcing material for concrete structures, wire rod/bars in coils, seamless pipes, steel cord for tires, steel anchor and wavy fiber, microfiber and steel wire for various applications) (Byelorussian Steel Works 2014). The exports go to Europe and the CIS (consisting of about 82% of exports), as well as Australia, North and South America, the Middle East and Africa, as well as Southeast Asia. There are 107 destination countries worldwide for the company's exports (Byelorussian Steel Works 2017b). The production, with all its various facilities, is carried out on a single production site making it possible to form flexible production flows considering market conditions and maintaining stable sales volumes during long periods of time (Byelorussian Steel Works 2015).

The history of BSW begins in 1982 after the contract for the design and erection of the plant and all required infrastructural parts. The contract was signed on March 19, 1982 by the Austrian company Voestalpine AG and the Italian Danieli. The task for the plant's development was confirmed by the ex-USSR Ministry of Ferrous Metallurgy on November 19, 1982. The project was finalized with the participation of 30 companies from different European countries, including Germany, Italy, Sweden and Hungary representing the latest global achievements of science and technology at that time (Byelorussian Steel Works 2016). October 15, 1984 is considered to be the official foundation date. Nearly 20 years later BSW was reorganized into a stock company and at the end of August 2012 it became Byelorussian Metallurgical Company Holding, referring to all 22 mini-plants (steelmaking, engineering, agricultural productions, etc.) (Byelorussian Steel Works 2015). As the company is state-owned, the state, represented by the Ministry of Industry of Belarus, sets the annual targets and co-ordinates strategy for the plant's development. The plant, on its own, determines the approaches for achieving these targets and makes decisions of an operative nature.

BSW's efficiency of strategy and unity of its employees play an even more important role in the company's performance and business growth considering the instability of the Belarusian economy. To correspond to external changes, tendencies and risks, the plant carries out regular assessment of its activities and the effectiveness of achievement of all targets. It is constantly developed and modernized. The company is managed by the general director who acts in accordance with the national law and Articles of Association of the organization, and state representatives, and determines policy and objectives, distributing authority among the heads of the plant divisions. The corporate mission is stated to be the manufacturing of high-technology steel products to (1) increase income and (2) ensure environmental safety and employee health, the high welfare of its employees and the satisfaction of requirements and expectations of all parties involved (Byelorussian Steel Works 2017c). Hence, the corporate strategy is directed toward realizing this mission: the production of steel products of required quality, quantity and range as well as the development of corporative management standards to maintain and strengthen positions at the developed sectors of the market and a decrease of environmental impact owing to production activity. Executives believe that realizing this mission and strategy would foresee a timely response to continuous changes in external conditions and, as a result, the achievement of target indicators and forecasts of activity-related risks, like environment contamination, workplace injuries, occupational diseases, on-the-job accidents and so on (Byelorussian Steel Works 2017c).

BSW aims at becoming the best supplier of steel products satisfying the demands of all its customers in the steel market via the implementation of progressive, energy-efficient (yet environment-friendly) technologies and the continuous enhancement of the effectiveness of its management system as per international standards. Currently, the company identifies its key competitive advantages as follows (Byelorussian Steel Works 2015). Firstly, a high product quality level and, as a result, an excellent reputation among customers and high competitiveness of products. Secondly, a favorable geographic position (220 kilometers from the capital, Minsk). Thirdly, a strong position on international markets (e.g. one of the 10 global tire cord producers, the largest European producer of bead wire, a monopolist in the CIS market, and regional leader in hose wire production). Fourthly, regular investments in research and development activities (e.g. co-operation with the largest tire-producing concerns to gain access to unique knowledge and innovation solutions, and development of its own metallurgical research center and training center). Finally, high employee professionalism, which is a determining factor of the company's competitive ability.

Concerning the company's human resource and talent management practices, it is, first, important to state that BSW believes all of its employees, along with the environment, natural and other types of resources, partners, quality, knowledge and society, are of prime value. Second, the company builds up relationships based on social partnership and respect for mutual interests (hence, a relatively universalist talent management approach). The enterprise employs over 12,000 employees, 30% of whom account for the economically active population of the district (Byelorussian Steel Works 2015). According to company records, the age composition of employees with relevant knowledge and expertise is balanced (the average age of workforce is 39); meanwhile, the gender composition is strongly imbalanced, namely, 72.5% male and 27.5% female (Byelorussian Steel Works 2017d) due to often hazardous working conditions. BSW provides information on the educational background of its staff (aggregated data) with approximately a third having received higher education, a quarter has specialized secondary education and a few have obtained Candidate of Sciences and/or post-graduate degrees (Byelorussian Steel Works 2017d).

The strategic targets of the corporate policy for talent management stipulate the attraction of recruits ensuring transparency and fairness in selection and recruitment according to the professional skills and knowledge, and offering a competitive level of compensation packages. Moreover, supplementary health improvement opportunities are provided for all employees and their family members. The development of corporate social responsibility programs is on the agenda. The continuous development of the workforce is ongoing, including fair and unbiased assessment of work results, professional training, career development and promotion, and retention of talent. This last includes development of a corporate culture, ensuring a favorable moral and psychological climate in the working teams, the improvement of employee motivation systems, labor safety levels and social and living conditions at work, to supply the sub-divisions with employees with the required professional and qualification characteristics. All integrated strategic practices (i.e. those aimed at attracting, developing and retaining talented workers) conform to the legislation and legal norms of Belarus and involve all the units and business process participants. The ultimate human resource goal is the creation of a "prime choice company" based on honesty, dedication, a creative approach, optimism and the self-improvement of each worker (Byelorussian Steel Works 2015). At the same time, transparency and openness at BSW become the leading management principles.

BSW puts great emphasis on the recruitment and adaptation of responsible and hardworking specialists. Here, the image of a strong and continuously working organization that can provide social equality and an adequate standard of living for its employees and confidence in the future is what makes the enterprise attractive for employees and solves possible talent attraction issues for the prospective human resource provision. Additionally, considering the company's activities and operations, BSW actively promotes such basic principles as safe working conditions and a positive social-psychological climate in the working team. Finally, employment at BSW guarantees official registration, a decent salary, professional training, additional medical insurance and reduced price meals. Young professionals are also provided with housing.

BSW states that the most important condition for management succession, the enhancement of management effectiveness and efficiency, ensuring the stable development of the company, is discovering the individual potential of each employee and developing this in co-ordination with the strategic goals. In particular, methodical work with young talent (the organization of scientific and technical conferences and other projects, such as the "A strategic reserve of young employees" project aimed at establishing a multi-level personnel reserve of young workers prepared for managerial work in present conditions) is a special priority direction of the personnel policy (Byelorussian Steel Works 2016). In addition, the enterprise organizes rotation of specialists to decrease labor monotony and increase practical experience (required for career promotion) and stages human resource training programs to develop certain sets of competences. Specialists from the leading educational Belarusian establishments are engaged in the training process under bilateral contracts (Byelorussian Steel Works 2016). These programs stipulate education of the cadre reserve from the level of a supervisor to the top-manager level considering the specific characteristic of the work fulfilled. They allow employees to realize their professional ambitions, gain diverse experience and enhance their qualification degrees. BSW gives all its employees, irrespective of origin, age, gender, race, nationality and religion, the right to professional training at different stages of labor activity and considers education to be an investment in human capital. By carrying out its continuous professional education system, the company's training center meets a number of objectives. Some of them are the organization of experience and knowledge exchange, exclusion of the risk factor of untrained employees, and improvement of the forms and methods of training (for instance, providing employees with anytime-anywhere learning opportunities via the remote electronic system of module training "LearnBMZ" (Byelorussian Steel Works 2016)). As for efficiency management, the current evaluation system allows BSW to determine the compliance of each worker with the occupied position, and creates and maintains conditions for carrying out responsibilities more successfully. The assessment procedure is based on constructive dialogue between a worker and his or her supervisor.

Finally, the general talent retention strategy is directed toward satisfaction of employees' expectations ensuring their welfare and work-life balance to prevent staff turnover (Byelorussian Steel Works 2017c). BSW continuously improves its corporate culture, employees' moral responsibility and material liability for the quality of performed work. It creates optimal conditions for high-class work where all employees can demonstrate personal capabilities and initiative. In particular, it conducts various festive events for the purpose of moral stimulation. It holds, for instance, around 30 types of production competitions and contests on an individual and collective basis, including "Best in profession", "Best shop", "Professional Olympus", "Best innovator of the year", "Best young specialist", and so on (see Byelorussian Steel Works 2015). One of the main constituents of the corporate culture and an efficient way of enhancing workers' motivation is corporate awarding (all structural sub-divisions have "Halls of Fame" with pictures of the best workers). Management also organizes professional celebrations, sports and cultural events for the employees, their family members and the population of the region. These include sports and other competitions (e.g. volleyball, mini-football, fishing, hiking, bicycle rides and skiing), dancing and entertainment evenings, off-site seminars as well as special work groups in the Metallurgist Palace of Culture (Byelorussian Steel Works 2017e, 2017f). In the existing economic situation, such non-financial motivation schemes are very important. However, salary level remains one of the most precise indicators of social policy effectiveness as salary is the main factor for ensuring a certain standard of an employee's well-being. All categories of workers, though, receive similar benefits (e.g. women have the same salaries and tariff rates as men, if they occupy equal positions). The enterprise has a bonus scheme for labor stimulation. According to it, all employees share equal rights, have additional benefits aimed at their health and maternity protection (e.g. a parent of three or more children aged under 16 is given one extra day off in a week at her or his request which is paid for; pregnant women are given easier jobs to minimize the possible effects of hazardous labor). The accrued salary is in accordance with the established amount of the minimal salary in Belarus, while the tariff part of it is determined based on the monthly tariff rates established by the unified workers wage tariff system of Belarus and the collective agreement, in conformity with job evaluation in the organization (Byelorussian Steel Works 2015).

BSW has developed managerial policies and practices aimed at achieving its middle- and long-term strategic corporate objectives. Considering advanced globalization forces as well as the current economic situation in the country, BSW is doing quite well, promptly making necessary changes to its management systems in order to meet the international standards in terms of talent attraction, development and retention. BSW recognizes the significance of investing in its human capital to sustain and develop competitive advantages.

* * *

Due to the continuing Soviet-era economic and political traditions, resulting in the liability of outsidership (i.e. the consequences of having limited or no access to knowledge networks, which in this case means not being exposed to Western management practices, international standards, etc.), Belarus seems to be behind other CIS countries in terms of talent management development. Strong governmental control over business and, more specifically, state ownership has led to organizations being less integrated in talent management implementation, and human resource departments carrying out a functionalist role aimed at achieving short- and midterm corporate and personnel objectives. Because of various state policies and labor laws, Belarusian firms do not have to deal with severe competition outside the local market, which could provoke the lack of need to implement effective management practices. Human resource managers, for instance, might not be incentivized to develop and employ talent attraction practices when students after graduation are assigned to the organization anyway. There is a risk of this leading to higher employee turnover. Thus, mandatory allocation assumes that young, talented people do not really have a say in where they would work. There is low quality of the talent pool and under-developed human resource management policies, and lower involvement of human resource staff in the decision-making processes of the company: thus, senior management is still hesitant about investing additional resources into talent management. Belarusians do believe in the effectiveness of non-monetary compensation systems. At times of crisis, such systems usually serve as strong talent retention mechanisms that firms, such as BELAZ and Santa Bremor, use to ensure their employees continue working for the company. Belarusian organizations have a lot of promise and in order for them to obtain recognition internationally they have to restructure the entire human resource management system according to the actual demands of the labor market.

References

Adarov, Amat, Kateryna Bornukova, Rumen Dobrinsky, Peter Havlik, Gabor Hunya, Dzmitry Kruk, and Olga Pindyuk. 2016. *The Belarus Economy: The Challenges of Stalled Reforms*. wiiw Research Report No. 413, November. https://wiiw.ac.at/the-belarus-economy-the-challenges-of-stalled-reforms-p-4032.html. Accessed on 27 Aug 2017.

Akulava, Maryia, Robert Kirchner, and Gleb Shymanovich. 2013. *Recent Trends and Challenges in the Labour Market in Belarus.* German Economic Team Belarus, IPM Research Center, Policy Paper Series, Berlin/Minsk.

Bakunowicz, Tomasz. 2015. The Financial Crisis and the Changes in the Belarusian Government. *OSW Analyses,* January 14. https://www.osw.waw.pl/en/publikacje/analyses/2015-01-14/financial-crisis-and-changes-belarusian-government. Accessed on 27 Aug 2017.

BELAZ. 2011. Our Achievements. *BELAZ Press Centre,* April 18. http://belaz.by/press/news/2011/nashi_dostizhenija1/. Accessed on 3 Sept 2017.

———. 2014. Adaptation: A Training Course for Young Specialists Takes Place in BELAZ. *BELAZ Press Centre,* October 10. http://www.belaz.by/press/news/2014/adaptacija_v_oao_belaz_prohodi/. Accessed on 3 Sept 2017.

———. 2017a. Our Enterprise. http://www.belaz.by/en/about/. Accessed on 3 Sept 2017.

———. 2017b. History of the Enterprise. http://www.belaz.by/en/about/history/. Accessed on 3 Sept 2017.

———. 2017c. Awards. http://www.belaz.by/en/about/awards/. Accessed on 3 Sept 2017.

———. 2017d. Youth Policy in Action. *BELAZ Press Centre,* June 24. http://www.belaz.by/press/news/2017/molodezhnaja_politika_v_dejstv/. Accessed on 3 Sept 2017.

———. 2017e. Experience and Youth: The Creators of the First "BELAZ" Congratulated the Winners of the Youth Prize. *BELAZ Press Centre,* September 15. http://www.belaz.by/press/news/2017/opit_i_molodost_sozdateli_perv/. Accessed on 3 Sept 2017.

———. 2017f. Quality System. http://www.belaz.by/en/about/quality/. Accessed on 3 Sept 2017.

Bobrova, Anastasia G. 2015. The Labour Market in the Transforming Economy of Belarus. *Demoskop Weekly,* 649–650. http://www.demoscope.ru/weekly/2015/0649/analit04.php. Accessed on 3 Sept 2017.

Business News. 2015. Belarus Took 44th Place in Doing Business 2016 Thanks to Change in Methodology. Last modified October 29. https://doingbusinessby.com/belarus-took-44th-place-in-doing-business-2016-thanks-to-change-in-methodology. Accessed on 27 Aug 2017.

Byelorussian Steel Works. 2014. Product Catalogue. https://eng.belsteel.com/doc/cat_2014.pdf. Accessed on 17 Sept 2017.

———. 2015. Progress Report on Social Responsibility and Corporate Sustainability for 2015. https://www.unglobalcompact.org/system/attachments/cop_2017/352001/original/Progress_report_on_social_responsibility_and_corporate_sustainability_of_OJSC_BSW_management_company_of_BMC_holding_2015.pdf?1483964211. Accessed on 17 Sept 2017.

———. 2016. Corporate Social Report 2015. https://eng.belsteel.com/doc/social_otchet/sotsialnyiy_otchet_2015.pdf. Accessed on 17 Sept 2017.

———. 2017a. Structure of BMZ. https://eng.belsteel.com/about/about-bmz.php. Accessed on 17 Sept 2017.

———. 2017b. Export Geography. https://eng.belsteel.com/about/export-geography.php. Accessed on 17 Sept 2017.

———. 2017c. Corporative Policy. https://eng.belsteel.com/about/corporative-policy.php. Accessed on 17 Sept 2017.

———. 2017d. Staff. https://eng.belsteel.com/about/staff.php. Accessed on 17 Sept 2017.

———. 2017e. Culture. https://eng.belsteel.com/about/culture.php. Accessed on 17 Sept 2017.

———. 2017f. Sport and Recreation. https://eng.belsteel.com/about/sport-and-recreation.php. Accessed on 17 Sept 2017.

Carraher, Shawn M., and Sarah C. Carraher. 2006. Human Resource Issues Among SMEs in Eastern Europe: A 30 Month Study in Belarus, Poland, and Ukraine. *International Journal of Entrepreneurship* 10: 97–108.

Desvaux, Georges, Sandrine Devillard, Alix de Zelicourt, Cecile Kossoff, Eric Labaye, and Sandra Sancier-Sultan. 2017. Women Matter: Ten Years of Insights on Gender Diversity. *McKinsey Insights*. https://www.mckinsey.com/global-themes/gender-equality/women-matter-ten-years-of-insights-on-gender-diversity. Accessed on 3 Sept 2017.

Hellman, Joel S., Geraint Jones, Daniel Kaufmann, and Mark Schankerman. 2000. *Measuring Governance, Corruption, and State Capture: How Firms and Bureaucrats Shape the Business Environment in Transition Economies*. Public Policy Research Paper No. 2312. Washington, DC:World Bank.

Kramer, Andrew E. 2011. Belarus Economic Crisis Deepens as Currency Plunges. *The New York Times*, May 11. http://www.nytimes.com/2011/05/12/world/europe/12belarus.html. Accessed on 27 Aug 2017.

Largest Industrial Enterprises of Belarus. *Valex Consult*, January 14, 2015. http://valex.by/news/34-krupnejshie-promyshlennye-predpriyatiya-belarusi. Accessed on 3 Sept 2017.

Latukha, Marina. 2016. *Talent Management in Emerging Market Firms. Global Strategy and Local Challenges*. London: Palgrave Macmillan.

Lazareva, Tatyana. 2015. Personnel Management. The First HR-Standard Is Developed in Belarus. *Argumenty i Fakty*, June 23. http://www.aif.by/presscentr/articlpress/upravlenie_personalom_v_belarusi_razrabotan_pervyy_hr_standart. Accessed on 27 Aug 2017.

National Statistical Committee of the Republic of Belarus. 2016. Labour and Employment in the Republic of Belarus, 2016. http://www.belstat.gov.by/en/ofitsialnaya-statistika/publications/statistical-publications-data-books-bulletins/public_compilation/index_6404/. Accessed on 27 Aug 2017.

Nielsen, Sabina, and Morten Huse. 2010. The Contribution of Women on Boards of Directors: Going Beyond the Surface. *Corporate Governance: An International Review* 18: 136–148.

Pastore, Francesco, and Alina Verashchagina. 2005. The Gender Wage Gap in Belarus. *Transition Studies Review* 12: 497–511.

Preiherman, Yauheni. 2012. Mandatory Placement: A Soviet Remnant of Belarusian Higher Education. *BelarusDigest*, May 7. https://belarusdigest.com/story/mandatory-placement-a-soviet-remnant-of-belarusian-higher-education/. Accessed on 7 Aug 2017.

———. 2014. Lukashenka Reshuffles the Government Before the 2015 Elections. *BelarusDigest*, December 29. https://belarusdigest.com/story/lukashenka-reshuffles-the-government-before-the-2015-elections/. Accessed on 27 Aug 2017.

Rabota.tut.by. 2017. JV Santa Bremor Ltd. Last modified January 9. https://jobs.tut.by/employer/245547. Accessed on 10 Sept 2017.

RBK. 2015. The Russian Market of Dump Trucks. *RBK Group*, March 23. https://www.google.ru/search?client=opera&q=РБК&sourceid=opera&ie=UTF-8&oe=UTF-8&gfe_rd=cr&dcr=0&ei=e_1nWtzVCJCxX-ffgcAF. Accessed on 3 Sept 2017.

Santa Bremor. 2017a. Career. http://www.santa-bremor.com/careers/. Accessed on 10 Sept 2017.

———. 2017b. History. http://www.santa-bremor.com/company/history/. Accessed on 10 Sept 2017.

———. 2017c. Geography. http://www.santa-bremor.com/company/geo/. Accessed on 10 Sept 2017.

———. 2017d. Belarusians Named the Best Brands. *Santa Bremor Press*, January 30. http://www.santa-bremor.com/press/news/535.html. Accessed on 10 Sept 2017.

———. 2017e. Personnel Preparation: Meeting the Mentors. *Santa Bremor Press*, May 26. http://www.santa-bremor.com/press/news/525.html. Accessed on 10 Sept 2017.

Sekhovich, Vadim. 2016. Real Economy: A Period of Losses and Expectations. *Belarusian Yearbook* 1: 273–279. http://cyberleninka.ru/article/n/real-economy-a-period-of-losses-and-expectations. Accessed on 27 Aug 2017.

Shraibman, Artyom. 2013. Young Belarusians Choose Professions with Poor Employment Prospects. *BelarusDigest*, April 3. https://belarusdigest.com/story/young-belarusians-choose-professions-with-poor-employment-prospects/. Accessed on 27 Aug 2017.

The World Bank. 2017. *Belarus*. Washington, DC: The World Bank Group. http://data.worldbank.org/data-catalog/world-development-indicators. Accessed on 27 Aug 2017.

The World Factbook. 2017. *Belarus*. Washington, DC: Central Intelligence Agency, 2017. https://www.cia.gov/library/publications/the-world-factbook/geos/bo.html. Accessed on 27 Aug 2017.

Wittenberg-Cox, Avivah, and Alison Maitland. 2008. *Why Women Mean Business: Understanding the Emergence of Our Next Economic Revolution*. Chichester: John Wiley & Sons Ltd.

WorldAtlas. 2015. Belarus Facts. Last modified September 29. https://www.worldatlas.com/webimage/countrys/europe/belarus/byfacts.htm#page. Accessed on 27 Aug 2017.

13

Ukraine: Challenges for Further Development

Louisa Selivanovskikh

The Republic of Ukraine is a sovereign Eastern European state, bordered by Poland, Hungary and Slovakia to the West, Romania and Moldova in the Southwest, Belarus to the Northwest, and Russia in the East and Northeast. During the Soviet Era, the Republic was the most important economic component of the former Soviet Union, after Russia, producing about four times the output of the next-ranking republic (The World Factbook 2017). However, after achieving independence in 1991 with the dissolution of the ex-USSR, the country has encountered many socio-economic and political problems (Encyclopædia Britannica 2017; Sutela 2012). Since 1991, the Ukrainian economy has struggled to transform itself into a market-led economy. Attempts at economic reform have often been blocked by a combination of political inertia and interventions by politically connected business interests (The World Factbook 2017). The country's macro-economic environment has picked up since 2000, and its external position has improved, helped by the strong

L. Selivanovskikh (✉)
Graduate School of Management, St. Petersburg State University,
St. Petersburg, Russia
e-mail: l.selivanovskikh@gsom.pu.ru

© The Author(s) 2018
M. Latukha (ed.), *Talent Management in Global Organizations*,
Palgrave Studies of Internationalization in Emerging Markets,
https://doi.org/10.1007/978-3-319-76418-4_13

237

demand for exports to Russia. During the 2000–2007 period, the economy experienced growth, supported by strong domestic and foreign demand (The World Factbook 2017). Inflation, however, remained high due to the high prices of gas and food during that period. Then, growth stumbled, due to crumbling domestic demand and the global financial crisis. The Ukrainian economy witnessed an unprecedented contraction (Roubini 2009). Finally, the current political situation resulting from the prolonged Ukrainian crisis of 2013–2014, the military conflicts in different parts of the country (mostly in its Eastern regions), territorial disputes with Russia over Crimea, investment drain and so on has defined the course of the economy in recent years, making the economic environment extremely volatile (Iwański 2017). After the Euromaidan demonstrations, Ukraine cut all relations with Russia, which added to the economic recession. These events diminished by half the disposable income of the Ukrainian people (Credit Suisse Research Institute, Global Wealth Report 2015).

The backbone of the Ukrainian economy is its industrial production, which contributes the most to gross domestic product (GDP) and to the country's budget (Kolesnikov 2016). The sector representing natural resource production is the one that suffered the most in 2013, shrinking by 0.5%. By comparison, in 2011 it grew by 7.6% (Unian 2015). Additionally, many of the enterprises operating in specific industries are located in the Eastern part of Ukraine and now face many problems due the economic and geopolitical turbulence in the country, especially in its Eastern parts (Bonenberger 2017). All these led to instability in the Ukrainian financial markets, depreciation of the national currency and shortage of capital as well as rampaging inflation despite financial aid from the European Union (EU), the International Monetary Fund, the World Bank and numerous other organizations (Baker 2013). Consequently, numerous official ratings have stated that Ukraine is in recession. In 2015, Bloomberg called it one of the world's most depressed economies (Jamrisko et al. 2015). Nevertheless, Ukraine has a huge potential that is not completely exploited. On January 1, 2016, the Deep and Comprehensive Free Trade Area (DCFTA) trade agreement between the EU and Ukraine was effectuated. This agreement is expected to bring stability in and secure investments to the country (European Commission

2017). It foresees that Ukraine is going to be a part of the EU markets rather than of the Eurasian Economic Union (EAEU) consisting of Belarus, Kazakhstan and Russia.

The labor market comprises nearly a half of the Ukrainian population. In 2016, the population of the country was 45 million people with a labor force of 22.6 million (The World Bank 2017). Because of the crisis in the country, the net migration rate is negative, meaning that there are less immigrants than emigrants. The majority of the population is Ukrainian (The World Factbook 2017), with sizable minorities of Russians, Belarusians, Moldovans, Crimean Tatars, Bulgarians, Hungarians, Romanians and Poles. Concerning gender distribution, females dominate males.

The country's turbulence has significantly affected the labor market. After the state coup, the unemployment rate reached its highest level within the past decade (The Ministry of Finance 2018). This resulted from the massive layoffs that employers had to implement to avoid bankruptcy. During 2015, employers controlled the Ukrainian labor market. Jobseekers have faced excessive requirements, while people, afraid of losing their jobs, accepted the same salary levels with lengthy payment delays despite inflation reaching 43% and (Shkil 2015). People demonstrated little activity regarding job search, causing stagnation on the labor market (Shkil 2015).

The military conflict forced people to migrate from the Eastern part of Ukraine to other regions, which led to a dramatic increase in demand for work. Before the conflict escalated most displaced people were blue-collar workers, however during it more highly qualified people wanted to relocate. Due to the shortage of open positions, people had to apply for low-skilled jobs, usually referred to as brain waste (Mattoo et al. 2008), which increased professional degradation (Kovalchuk 2014). The situation is expected to improve due to positive dynamics in the national economy. Recent trends show that the labor market is recovering slowly and companies are becoming more preoccupied with the retention and motivation of young talent (Dvorskaya 2017). The latter includes different forms of monetary remuneration and retention techniques, such as additional bonuses and team-building activities (Ivanets 2016). Parliament adopted the new Labor Code in December 2015, which resembles the

EU labor law in some key aspects. For instance, anti-discrimination amendments were introduced banning discrimination on race, gender, sexual orientation and so on. Some of the introduced innovations aim at regulating labor relations during turbulent times. Thus, employees mobilized for military service retain their jobs, receiving their average pay for a one-year period. The new Labor Code is primarily concerned with providing social protection for employees. Taking into account the military conflict in the country, the authorities use the Labor Code as a tool to control unemployment rates.

According to the Global Competitiveness Index, Ukraine ranks low in labor market effectiveness. An inadequately educated and trained workforce and the poor work ethics of the national labor force are the most problematic factors (World Economic Forum 2017). Therefore, an effective talent management system can become a competitive advantage for Ukrainian firms.

Being quite similar to the countries of the Commonwealth of Independent States (CIS) and Central and Eastern Europe (CEE) in the early 1990s in terms of level of economic development, Ukraine did not follow the paths of these regions later on. While such countries as ex-Czechoslovakia, Hungary and Poland, received huge amounts of foreign direct investment from Western firms and adopted a West-European approach to managing people (Child and Czegledy 1996), Ukraine mostly resembled Russia rather than any other country. The post-Soviet practices applied to human resource (HR) management in Ukraine were formed in the 2000s, when employment relations were finally legitimized and new psychological contracts between workers and managers were settled. The latter implied behavior based on a large power distance, low degree of individualism, high uncertainty avoidance and a mixture of short-term and long-term orientation (Hofstede 1984). Personnel departments did not significantly differ in terms of structure and tasks in companies with various levels of competitiveness and development strategies (Gurkov and Zelenova 2009). The labor market faced an increasing shortage of highly qualified and skilled workforce (Fey et al. 1999), mostly due to the mass brain-drain phenomena and a drop in the quality of education (Khodakov 2012).

Though the Ukrainian mentality and work behavior are similar to those of the Russians, there are several features distinguishing employees of Ukrainian firms from Russian employees. The Ukrainian managers have noticed that local workers tend to complete tasks in a longer time than needed, which could result from the slower pace of life in the country. Moreover, employees seem to be satisfied with lower salary levels than Russian employees. At the same time, non-monetary motivation techniques tend to be neglected and under-developed (Talajlo 2010). Furthermore, the work-life balance is of extreme importance to Ukrainian people (International Labor Migration 2011). Business activities in Ukraine are not centered in any particular city. Consequently, doing business in the country requires a high level of mobility (Kupets 2012). Finally, tensions in Russia-Ukraine relationships in many ways determine the specifics of organizational behavior, from a decrease in motivation and increase of dissatisfaction that arise from open conflicts between employees of different nationalities (Borisov 2013).

Methods that local managers use for managing talented employees vary depending on the size of the company. For large companies, an autocratic leadership style is typical: managers tend to make decisions on their own without any consultation, setting tasks for employees in the form of indisputable orders (Lazorenko 2008). Managers of small and medium businesses, on the contrary, are mostly characterized by a democratic leadership style (Lazorenko 2008). Analysis of companies of different ownership structure show that private entities in Ukraine prove to have more resources for building efficient motivation programs; at the same time, workers of such companies are less protected with respect to employment preservation compared to those employed by state-owned company. In addition, a number of problems currently existing in Ukrainian organizations that influence human resource and talent management systems can be identified: a mismatch between organizational structure and a company's strategic goals and needs; outdated labor-regulating documentation; inefficient motivation systems; and under-developed control systems (Dorofeeva 2012). The prevalence of negative-based motivation techniques (e.g. threats, reprimands, penalties) over positive-based approaches is also highlighted (Talajlo 2010).

The Russia-Ukrainian conflict has affected talent retention practices as well. The war for talent resumed with renewed vigor due to the emerging career opportunities in the European labor market (Eurostat 2017; European Commission 2010). At the same time, domestic migration increased as well: many people and companies moved from turbulent areas to quieter and stable Ukrainian regions. Coupled with the economic downturn, this led to an unresolvable dilemma for companies located in the militarized areas: they had to somehow retain their key employees from moving to other regions at the same time securing their safety while reducing costs concerning HR-related expenses (Didenko 2014). Therefore, talent management is becoming more and more relevant to Ukrainian companies. In the Ukrainian context the concept is still rather new, and many companies are not yet successful in adopting key Western-like talent management practices, which is partially due to the fact that managerial practices are context specific; they usually do not work in environments that substantially differ from those where these practices were initially developed and successfully implemented.

In this chapter we provide a comprehensive view of talent management practices in the following Ukrainian companies: Azovstal, Clickky and Naftogaz. We discuss how talent management can be considered a source for a firm's success in the Ukrainian context.

Azovstal: A Focus on People

Azovstal is one of the largest Ukrainian steel manufacturers, based in Mariupol. Its industrial capacity allows the company to produce up to six million tonnes of cast iron and more than nine million tonnes of high-quality steel products annually, including flat products (e.g. slabs, heavy plate, steel plate used in heavy machinery, pipes production, automotive and mining industries, construction); rails (since 1952 Azovstal is the only producer of Ukrainian rails); grinding balls later used in mining for ore milling; products from slag that are components of cement, and abrasive materials, used in road construction (Azovstal 2017a). Azovstal is a subsidiary of the metallurgical division of the vertically integrated company Metinvest Holding LLC, ranked among the world's top steel producers.

As the leading subsidiary in terms of industrial capacity of the metallurgical division of Metinvest Holding LLC, Azovstal needs well-qualified managers and ironworkers. Considering that in Mariupol Metinvest is also represented by Ilyich Iron and Steel, the competition for young professionals is tough. However, in the long-term the enterprise may face a scarcity of young personnel, as recent trends in the Ukrainian labor market show that the industrial sector is very unattractive to young people. Additionally, the military operations in Eastern Ukraine posed another challenge for the enterprise: how to prevent massive layoffs?

The company was founded in 1930 according to the decision of the Presidium of Supreme Soviet of the National Economy in Mariupol, an ex-Ukrainian Soviet Socialist Republic (Mariupol was the closest destination for rich ore deposits discovered in Crimea). For construction purposes the government provided approximately three million rubles aiming to build the world's largest steel manufactory with production capacity of four million tonnes of cast iron per year (Semysev 2008). The company was initially provided with two blast-furnaces for iron processing and later, in 1935, the steel production line was put into operation. The enterprise demonstrated outstanding performance explained by the direct supply of raw materials and the latest equipment (a 250 tonne open-hearth furnace, the first in the former USSR was introduced in Azovstal (Azovstal 2017b). During Mariupol's occupation in the 1940s, production at the firm was suspended to prevent its acquisition by the German invaders. All workers and some of the equipment were relocated to the Urals for tank production, whereas the remaining blast-furnaces were incapacitated and left behind. The occupiers launched an industry restoration program and Azovstal's operational units were reactivated. In 1943, Azovstal was destroyed during the retreat of the German troops (Nesterenko 2015). Fortunately, the factory was completely restored in 10 years with new production lines and nearly 40 years later Azovstal receives international accreditations from industrial associations, which allows the enterprise to produce steel for shipbuilding and oil rigs.

Since 2006, Azovstal has been a part of Metinvest Holding LLC along with 10 other subsidiaries. Metinvest is a vertically integrated organization which allows it to control the entire production cycle from coal and iron-ore extraction to steel processing. The main benefits of the applied scheme are that Metinvest reduces exposure to commodity markets, as well as reducing costs by maximizing internal consumption of local raw materials thus providing greater sustainability. The holding consists of two main operational units: mining and metallurgy with Azovstal representing the latter. The production of the holding is very diverse and includes low- and higher-value-added products. Azovstal with its products fills the niches of steel production (crude steel), semi-finished (slag, pig iron) and finished products. To preserve its leading positions in the industry the company is focused on the following key points: modernization of production processes, implementation of energy efficient technologies and compliance with international standards. In addition, it aims at reducing its negative environmental impact by rational use of natural recourses.

As a strategic business unit of Metinvest Holding LLC the business strategy of Azovstal should follow the course of the parent company. Metinvest sets its main objective as becoming the leading integrated steel producer in Europe, performing sustainable growth and profit, despite the economic conditions. However, recent years have proved this strategy to be too optimistic. Due to the destabilization in Ukraine and decline in global prices for steel production, the output performance of Azovstal significantly decreased in comparison to previous years. It is clear that the proposed business strategy no longer corresponds with reality. Thus, Azovstal has designed its own strategy for the crisis period. The enterprise's new course can be described as a pause or no-change strategy. Management is primarily concerned with achieving stability: all capital-intensive projects have been cancelled. Nevertheless, layoffs have not been announced, which indicates that the company tries not to contribute to an already tough situation in Mariupol (Azovstal 2015a).

The organizational culture of Azovstal is characterized as hierarchical (Cameron and Quinn 2011) supported by the vertical integration of Metinvest Holding, which is one of the company's main competitive advantages, as it provides control over the whole production process. The enterprise structure is unified among all the subsidiaries, including Azovstal. In addition, improvement of production efficiency is Azovstal's top priority as modern technologies for efficient use of resources and equipment are constantly introduced to the production lines.

Metinvest is one of the largest employers in Ukraine, with more than 85,000 local and foreign employees at the end of 2016 (Metinvest 2016).

The holding is aware of the various challenges in attracting, developing and retaining talented young people and has built a fair and transparent talent management system, which includes a career promotion policy, open competitions for positions and job rotation principles (Metinvest 2016). However, for specific subsidiaries, like Azovstal, the implementation of such practices is sometimes impossible due to the aforementioned crisis.

Azovstal employs nearly 13,000 workers, the overwhelming majority of whom reside or used to reside in the Central and Eastern parts of the country (Azovstal 2017c). The primary talent management objective of Metinvest and its subsidiaries is to support all employees, regardless of their talent status (thus, a universalist approach toward talent definition), as well as their families during these challenging times, and help them reach their full potential by (1) ensuring social stability, (2) developing a professional training system, and (3) building a career management system (Metinvest 2016). The objective to ensure social stability as a direct response to the conflict in the Donetsk and Luhansk regions, which makes the social situation there very difficult with personnel outflow as the main consequence. There are no official figures about the number of people forced to migrate from the Eastern regions of Ukraine. According to the UN Refugee Agency, this number exceeds 514,000 (UNHCR 2014). The main issue is the destroyed infrastructure that forces people to seek better living conditions. At the same time, the entire Ukrainian economy has been stagnating since the beginning of the crisis: the hryvnia (UAH) has devalued, gas tariffs have increased and the consumer price index has gone up.

Despite the challenging economic and social conditions, Azovstal does its best to build sustainable employment policy that would allow the company to stay competitive on the world market. The recent measures taken by Azovstal are, simply, a response to the existing economic and political conditions rather than part of a long-term talent management agenda. From the very beginning of the crisis, Azovstal stated that it would reduce costs of human resources but without major layoffs. Later, in 2014, the enterprise hired nearly 200 young professionals and introduced shorter working hours for the administrative staff and non-working days for the mining and metallurgic divisions. In April 2015, Metinvest conducted a pay review, raising salaries for many of its employees (Azovstal 2015a). At the same time, the company implemented a number of cost-cutting programs due to low performance. In particular, many incentive mechanisms were temporarily discontinued (e.g. medical insurance of administrative personnel at production facilities became voluntary).

The new reality demanded changes in leadership styles to ensure corporate goals would be achieved. Metinvest created a new competency model based on the results of a comprehensive study conducted to identify the main leadership skills of its employees and determine key characteristics of "effective employees during crisis". These characteristics were efficiency, reliability, resourcefulness, authoritativeness, selflessness and kindness. The first five served as a basis for the competency model. In order to increase productivity, spare company resources and decrease operational costs, Azovstal launched a special system (implemented during the launch of the "lean production facility" program (5C) in 2011) (Azovstal 2012) for recognizing the good business ideas of its employees. The most innovative ideas with the highest-potential economic impact were realized later, bringing their idea-creators additional earnings. According to the official press release, during 2014–2015 the number of proposals increased by 60 times (Azovstal 2015b). In 2015 alone company employees submitted over 47,000 of proposals while the total sum of bonuses paid exceeded UAH2.3 million (Azovstal 2016a).

The mining and metallurgical industry is hazardous, so the human resource management department sets the objective of ensuring a safe working environment. In 2016, under the Workers' Amenities program, the group invested over UAH18 million to refurbish canteens, sanitary amenities and administrative buildings at Azovstal (Azovstal 2016b). With regard to these changes, the chief Executive Officer (CEO) of Azovstal stated: "There are basic things, which determine a lot. By creating descent conditions for work and leisure the enterprise tells its employees how much they are valued. This is an important part of motivation" (Azovstal 2016c).

Meanwhile, poor financial results forced the company to cancel some of its management and professional training programs. However, by reducing other operational costs the firm managed to spare some resources and invest money into new initiatives. Understanding the importance of professional training systems, Azovstal has implemented a system for auditing professional qualifications (some employees were reviewed to identify knowledge gaps) and for training instructors. It has also organized "professional schools" with various courses for its engineering and technical personnel, for instance, during the course on "The Theory of Inventive Problem Solving" employees were taught how to search for non-standard solutions to complex tasks (Azovstal 2015a).

Since 2006 Azovstal has been realizing a brand new educational project, "School–Higher education institution–Azovstal" at the Priazovskiy State Technical University aimed at finding talented young people and developing their abilities to transform them into highly qualified specialists (Azovstal 2017d). There are special classes in schools which have additional disciplines delivered by lecturers of the university. After graduation, these students enter the Priazovskiy State Technical University occupying state-funded places, where special disciplines, such as industrial psychology, quality management at iron and steel plants, production potential control, substantiation of business decisions and risk assessment, are taught to help young people see all the lines of activity at Azovstal from the inside, thus minimizing the adaptation period (similar to what is done in Belarusian companies). In addition, students do practical occupational training at Azovstal that involves meetings with leading specialists, summer internships as well as training for blue-collar occupations at the company's production and training center by obtaining the adequate qualification level. Upon graduating these students receive a certificate proving their qualification and serving as a recommendation for employment with Azovstal.

Another measure taken by the Azovstal to prepare the new generation of leaders for the new reality was the launch of a new career management system for executives. The main objective of this initiative was to integrate practices and processes already implemented by the organization (e.g. annual appraisals, talent pool expansion, training and development, career path development) into a unified system. For instance, 35 employees from the company's talent pool participated in the Strategic Leadership Development program (in partnership with INSEAD), completing three modules and working on eight different projects (Azovstal 2017c).

Azovstal is indeed a very prestigious place in the region to work at (together with Ilyich Iron and Steel Works of Mariupol). The salaries exceed the average and are paid on a regular basis, despite the crisis, which gives confidence in the future. The company has a clear talent management agenda; it recognizes the role talent management plays in an organization's success. However, there are a number of soft spots regarding talent procedures resulting from the fact that this large company is attempting to implement rather conventional and inflexible (here, long-term oriented) practices aimed at attracting, developing and retaining talent in the context of high uncertainty.

In conjunction with the large power distance, typical for Ukraine (Hofstede 1984), this leads to a significant obstruction to the knowledge flow within the company. The situation is worsened by the fact that this happens in both vertical and horizontal dimensions, which means that it is time-consuming to obtain information within one function from other hierarchy levels, as well as from other functions even if the hierarchy level is the same. This problem may lead to several undesirable consequences: (1) the lag in horizontal knowledge flow may increase the working cycle due to delays caused by untimely access to required information; (2) poor knowledge flow between different hierarchical levels obviously decreases the extent to which Azovstal is able to react to external challenges and thus undermines the company's flexibility, affecting its sustainability and calling into question Azovstal's future competitiveness and success; and (3) the inability of ordinary employees to access top managers easily results in a suppression of their capacity to innovate.

Although Mariupol is no longer under fire, the military conflict in East Ukraine is not completely resolved. Due to the situation in the region, people are forced to migrate to other parts of the country (or even relocate to other countries, such as Russia). The whole situation contributes to people's anxiety, and Eastern Ukrainian employers, including Azovstal, have faced low personnel performance and voluntary layoffs. While the state is the guarantor of the citizen's safety (although so far the Ukrainian government has failed to provide people with this basic need—the need for safety), the employer is the guarantor of stability.

In times of turbulence, the role of Mariupol employers and those in other cities of Eastern Ukraine has risen. Without them to provide people with jobs the region could collapse. Thus, Azovstal and other enterprises morally should support their employees; talent management and, more generally, human resource management practices should be aimed at forming the perception of stability, confidence and belief in a better future. Azovstal has already begun moving in this direction by announcing no dismissals, which demonstrated the employer's concern to provide its staff with decent working conditions and competitive salaries. The next step should probably be the formation of unity among employees on the basis of social commitment.

During the past years, the main objective of the company was to improve output by production process optimization and modernization. The key goal has been shifting toward the creation of a positive working environment that would help people to fight anxiety and thus preventing voluntary layoffs.

Finally, current trends on the Ukrainian labor market show that young people place industrial professions as one of the least prestigious professions, meanwhile according to HeadHunter, Ukraine industrial professions are among the top 10 occupations with good job opportunities (Headhunder 2015). This situation emphasizes that unfortunately all Ukrainian industrial enterprises will most likely face a scarcity of "fresh blood" (i.e. qualified young production workers). Azovstal is no exception as indeed it needs young specialists not only for managerial positions but for production lines as well.

Clickky: Looking for Global Talent

Headquartered in Odessa, Clickky is a leading mobile monetization and advertising platform with several offices located worldwide in Ukraine, the United States, India, China and Russia (Clickky 2017a). It is one of the biggest independent mobile marketing platforms in Eastern Europe and employs just under 100 employees working in its key offices. Its business field of activity is mobile advertising, a field that is growing rapidly in the current environment, bringing billions of US dollars to market leaders. Clickky's corporate strategy is focused on differentiation: for a price premium it provides unique services and products, including

Mobile Marketing Platform, Mobile Marketing Conference, and Mobile Stars School. Clickky daily generates over 30,000 advertising campaigns and has over five million monthly installs. Among its largest customers is the Chinese e-commerce company Alibaba. In 2017, Clickky made TOP-20 among advertising and marketing companies in the Inc.5000 Europe ranking (Inc. 2017). As at August 2016, Clickky made TOP-20 in the iOS non-gaming retention score posted by AppsFlyer (Clickky 2017a).

The history of the company (Clickky 2017a) began in 2010, when a Ukrainian businessman, Vadim Rogovskiy, launched a social app monetization network, Clickburner, in Odessa. In 2013, Clickburner turned into Clickky, a platform that aimed to unite mobile advertisers and publishers. The company opened its first offices outside of Ukraine, particularly, in Berlin and Moscow, in 2014; a year later it opened an office in the United States. The company announced a mutually beneficial partnership with Ad Japon, a global online advertising agency and advertising network company located in Japan. Ad Japon obtained access to Clickky's distribution and communication channels in Europe and North America, while Clickky, planning to open new offices in Asia, penetrated the Asian markets. In the following year, Clickky took off. In April 2015, iTech Capital, a Moscow-based venture fund, announced its two million dollar investment in Clickky, to support its global expansion and launch of new products. In May 2015, the company held the first Mobile Beach Conference on the shore of the Black Sea attracting over 300 participants. Later that year, Clickky launched a new automated mobile advertising platform that works through application programming interface (API)—Ad Exchange—a new technology solution that delivers fast and convenient exchange between developers, advertising networks, agencies and affiliates with the help of API. Now the company is deeply involved in its expansion in the American and Asian markets, as well as in the development of new technological solutions for the industry.

Clickky is mainly interested in young and highly talented people. The company is not large in headcount, even though it has several offices overseas, therefore all employees hired by the organization must possess a unique set of skills and competences that can directly and substantially affect performance in a positive way.

With its business expanding, Clickky needs to recruit more workers in the host countries. To inform the general public about the company's intension to hire new employees, Clickky usually employs socializing websites like Facebook, Vkontakte and LinkedIn as well as its own official website. In the process of filtering applicants, a person's social capital, general motivation, commitment, ambition, creativity and a number of other features demonstrating his or her working habits and ability to fulfill complex tasks are also taken into consideration by the employer. During the interview, technical and problem-solving skills as well as the interviewee's way of thinking are examined. The company's hiring process is very intensive due to staff turnover and constant opening of new vacancies. Clickky avoids hiring remote workers. Instead, it divides functional departments and country representatives between cities: for example, marketing specialists reside in Kiev, while developers work in Odessa (Clickky 2017a). After a CV screening process, successful candidates are invited for an interview with a human resource representative, the department manager and finally, the CEO. Applicants interested in technical positions also have to complete special assignments aimed at testing their level of qualification.

When recruiting talent for positions outside of Ukraine, Clickky focuses on the local talent pool since host-country talented workers are more familiar with the particulars of the external environment—they speak the national language and have a better understanding of the local culture (i.e. a smaller cultural and institutional distance) (Mäkelä et al. 2010). Such an approach can result in a lack of understanding between a foreign subsidiary and the parent company; it is difficult to convey the company's corporate culture to all of its international divisions. At the same time, for host-country employees is becomes difficult to gain experience outside their own country, which limits their growth and development.

The company's representatives admit that the job is highly intensive, requiring full commitment and involvement from the employee. As Clickky is rapidly growing and expanding into foreign markets, employees are sometimes required to work at holidays and weekends due to the time difference and cultural idiosyncrasies of the different countries the company operates in. The CEO reveals that many employees leave the company because of the intensive workload, which is why Clickky looks for highly motivated people, interested in the job and industry itself. The company does not provide additional fringe benefits or bonuses except for salary. This measure, of course, does not decrease the high employee turnover rate.

To reduce the risk of hiring people incapable of meeting the job requirements, the company has designed and launched a three-week training course (Mobile Starts School in Odessa) on digital marketing with the possibility of further employment for students who demonstrate good results.[1] Those individuals that cannot be physically present in Odessa can take the course online. Hence, the company aims to identify promising participants and further offer them full employment. Throughout many hours of training sessions, Clickky hopes to reduce uncertainty regarding the candidate's fit with the organization. In addition, the company offers a two-month paid internship for students (regardless of their background and specialization), the most successful of which get an offer after completing the program. The only requirements are motivation and English language proficiency. The latter is a necessary condition as the company's operations are internationalized. Language courses are of course provided to support those staff members that need to improve their language skills. Clickky also encourages professional development and regularly organizes and participates in conferences to raise brand recognition and attract international experts and professionals (Clickky 2017b).

The company uses its growth as an additional motivation factor for high-potential employees. All workers are provided with interesting tasks and a safe but informal and highly dynamic working environment; at the same time various team-building activities and other social events are organized (e.g. New Year's celebrations, sports tournaments). Top performers have the opportunity to represent the company at different international conferences to share their knowledge and experience with other professionals. Moreover, corporate culture is an integral part of the Clickky Family, the success of which is highly dependent on personal growth and team building. The key values are innovation (i.e. applying

---

[1] http://mobilestars.biz/.

innovative technologies to ensure progress and profit growth), happiness, efficiency (striving to be productive, complying with the set key performance indicators) and team (i.e. amplifying the company's potential by nurturing talent and continuously investing in human resources) (Clickky 2017a).

The company conducts twice per year performance reviews, the results of which are reported to top management and communicated back as feedback to each employee. Later, at the end of a fiscal year, compensation is revised based on these reviews. Thus, all workers have the chance to evaluate what their perspectives are of the company and understand their weaknesses for further improvement (as the average employee age is rather low, career development opportunities are crucial for young and inexperienced people). Finally, Clickky encourages its staff to commence their own projects within the framework of the corporate mission and objectives. Each employee can report ideas to the manager (all ideas are considered and the best are chosen) and get permission to spend the morning hours on the initiated project (Clickky 2017b). They would then have to systematically report on their progress, so that the results could be later evaluated. As with most IT companies, Clickky uses the customer relationship management system, Pipedrive, and task tracker, Worksection, to control the working process, to plan tasks, evaluate performance and organize multi-teams within the company.

Clickky's approach to talent management is unique in the sense that the company managed to integrate best practices adopted from leading organizations in the IT field and the strengths of the local management style. The analysis of Clickky demonstrates that it is in fact possible for Ukrainian companies "to overcome the crisis for further development". Even though the company is small (the workforce of Azovstal, for instance, is at least a hundred times larger, which has its own implications for the talent management strategy) and operates internationally (the company did not suffer from the Russian-Ukrainian conflict as much in comparison to local organizations), the general clarity in mission, corporate objectives and values as well as the strong belief that talented workers can make a difference are the key success factors. Driven by its faith in building a rapidly growing company with highly self-motivated employees, Clickky gives its workers a lot of freedom to make work-related decisions.

Since Ukraine's economic situation significantly affects the financial results of the company, Clickky, similar to other Ukrainian companies, encounters different issues connected to the extrinsic motivation of its employees that are acute not only from the financial point of view, but also from the personal point of view. It is important to mention that Clickky's corporate culture is very strong (with the words "dynamic" and "young" being part of the corporate values that the Clickky Family embraces) and serves as a mechanism for inner motivation.

Clickky has a set of standards to encourage intellectual competition between individuals and between groups. The company devises high expectations and lays pressure on employees with the aim of developing top talent: all workers are expected to and often work late into the night, because Clickky's transparency policy differentiates the high-achievers from the low-achievers.

Naftogaz: To Do No Matter What

Naftogaz is a gas and oil state-owned company that was founded in 1991 and is based in Kiev. It is the leading enterprise in Ukraine's fuel and energy complex (over 90% of the oil and gas in Ukraine is produced by the company's enterprises), and one of the largest Ukrainian companies, producing one-eighth of the country's GDP and accounting for one-tenth of state budget revenues. The company operates large complexes in Ukraine, Russia, Egypt and across Europe, and has a joint venture with the business group Al Jazirah Enterprise in the UAE. Naftogaz is a vertically integrated company engaged in the full cycle of operations, specifically in gas and oil field exploration and development, production and exploratory drilling, gas and oil transport and storage, supply of natural gas and LPG to consumers.

Naftogaz is a state-owned enterprise. The Ministry of Energy and the Ministry of Finance are represented on the Board and have a strong influence on decision-making. The firm operates in a strategic industry of high importance for GDP growth and country development, facing multiple issues during the past decade (the financial crisis of 2008–2009, the regime change in 2014, the ongoing disputes with Russia, regional instability in the Eastern regions of the country, etc.). A key challenge for the company was the issue of financial liquidity, in terms of payments to both Ukrainian and foreign creditors. At the beginning of 2014, Naftogaz accumulated multibillion debts, mostly in foreign currency, including outstanding invoices for imported gas and loans (Russia Today 2014). Specifically, the price for Naftogaz's imported gas was lower than its purchase price; thus, the company was in need of constant subsidies from the state budget and was accumulating debt. In order to address an acute liquidity crisis the company undertook a number of measures that aimed at reducing the deficit. Furthermore, as a result of numerous negotiations with Gazprom an agreement was reached to reduce the purchase price of gas. It was also ensured that the gas is imported from Europe at market price.

For years Naftogaz had a limited amount of opportunities to invest in production, whereas the need for imported gas remained consistently high. Recent developments in the country, such as further devaluation of the hryvnia and loss of gas resources in the Crimea and the Anti-Terrorist Operation zone, negatively affected the performance of the company. After years of operating losses the company reconsidered its inefficient and unsustainable business model. Specifically, senior management made a plan aimed at resolving the unprofitability problem in three ways, hoping that these steps would help the company not only to reach break-even point for the first time in many years, but also provide transfer payments to the state budget (Naftogaz 2014): firstly, by bringing the purchase price of imported gas to market levels; secondly, by increasing domestic production of gas; and lastly, by ensuring that all categories of consumers are supplied with gas at the market price.

Naftogaz stays hopeful, believing that the successful implementation of new corporate and state reforms would ensure its profitability. Its key values are: dedication to replace the old, corruption-prone, regulated environment with modern, competitive, market rules; responsibility for adding value for its customers and for society; striving to preserve the human, social, intellectual, manufacturing, natural and financial capital; and efficiency in achieving maximum results with minimal resources (Naftogaz 2017a). In addition, the company, aside from purely commercial objectives, plays an important social role and supplies natural gas to households, budget-funded institutions and utilities at prices set by the state.

Naftogaz is one of the largest employers in Ukraine with approximately 75,000 employees in 2016 (Naftogaz 2016). The vast majority of its employees are 35–50 years old, with male workers generally dominating female workers in headcount. Meanwhile, the personnel breakdown by skills demonstrates that while most employees are part of the technical staff and administration, nearly 28% are high-skilled professionals and specialists, all of whom have university degrees, while some have PhD degrees and other academic titles (Naftogaz 2016). Naftogaz's talent pool comprises skilled technical workers who are considered the core personnel, i.e. those with position knowledge and resources (and functional experts). Lastly the human resource management department was mainly focused on dealing with routine, especially recruiting new employees and providing remuneration. There were no human resource objectives (or talent objectives). Naftogaz, while restructuring some of its operations, clearly outlined its strategic mission concerning human capital (Naftogaz 2017b). First, to ensure a decent life for its employees and the whole society through sustainable growth of the firm's income, and to create opportunities for self-development and creative work (a major long-term aim). Second, to improve the ineffective management system, which is the post-Soviet approach legacy (a major mid-term aim). Third, to meet internal demand in human resources in order to continue the implementation of reforms (a major short-term aim).

Considering the fact that the state is the major shareholder in the company, talent attraction, development and retention decisions are made in accordance with the values of the dominant coalition that comprises state representatives and senior managers. Naftogaz uses traditional methods for attracting potential candidates, such as partnering with major recruiting agencies and posting relevant information on the company's webpage about open positions. Meanwhile the recruiting process is rather formal (i.e. human resource specialists assesses whether the candidate suits the criteria required for the company by screening his or her CV, interviewing, etc.). The company is very interested in becoming an internationally acknowledged organization from the perspective of equality, transparency and fairness in the workplace. The new human resource management strategy of Naftogaz tries to ensure that no potential and current employee experiences discrimination during the recruitment process (i.e. it positions itself as an equal opportunities employer) (Naftogaz 2016, 2017a). The main criteria are professional skills, background, motivation and international experience (Naftogaz 2016). As for the last, the company hires foreigners on a regular basis due to their knowledge of international best practices.

The company believes that investing in talent management practices would help close the skills gap of its workers as well as address the problem of talent scarcity in the Ukrainian labor market (Fuxman 2004; International Labor Migration 2014). In 2014, Naftogaz launched a new program for employee training and development (Naftogas 2015). Some of the program's elements include collaboration with universities, special internships and mentorship programs aimed at helping young specialists to quickly adapt to the corporate environment, and participation in and organization of academic conferences to interact with prospective students, academics and business representatives. Moreover, Naftogaz has established a corporate university (or rather something similar to a training center) where employees can improve their skills and professional qualifications, including foreign language proficiency (the company does operate internationally, after all) (Naftogas 2015; Grudzinskaya 2015). Additionally, Naftogaz is included in the list of clients of the training center "Speaker", which offers courses on business communication.[2]

Due to the turbulent political and economic environment resulting from the recent Ukrainian crisis, the employees of Naftogaz are mostly concerned with workplace safety and monetary remuneration as the two could ensure a minimum level of financial and social stability. Therefore, the top priority of both the human resource and talent motivation systems revolves around these aspects. Specifically, in order to become internationally competitive and decrease employee turnover, Naftogaz has begun offering "European" salaries that are above the Ukrainian average wage (Naftogaz 2016). Meanwhile, the social benefits package includes meal subsidies, tuition coverage, recreational programs for workers and their families, special support for pensioners, veterans and disabled

---

[2] http://www.training.com.ua/company/41.

employees and so on (Naftogaz 2014). Finally, the company employs a number of performance management practices and a standardized appraisal system for all workers to be rewarded fairly. However, it is worth mentioning that since most of these practices have been recently implemented, it is difficult to clearly determine their effectiveness in the Ukrainian context. Comparing Naftogaz to other Ukrainian companies and their performance would not provide us with a definite answer. But we can state that the company's general approach toward human resource and talent management has begun to bear fruit, despite many factors, like the size of the company (following lower flexibility and a higher level of organizational inertia), financial issues (wallowing in debt), instability of the market and so on, negatively affecting the company's operations, as described above.

To secure further development, Naftogaz has invested heavily in restructuring its operations and management system as the old ways of conducting business proved to be highly inefficient, unsustainable and costly. Specifically, before the events of 2014 the function of human resource management was cost-adding rather than value-adding. The system itself was rather inflexible regarding employee equality, industrial safety, transparent remuneration based on merit, and the like (the company does not even provide official data on its operations before 2014). Therefore, the dominant coalition made the decision to introduce Western-like managerial practices to speed up the company's "healing" process. Naftogaz is a state-owned enterprise, which means this coalition is also represented by state officials that get involved in the decision-making process, from time to time, to promote various state policies and realize the country's political agenda via the organization's operations, as mentioned before. Keeping in mind the ongoing conflict between Ukraine and Russia, the former has decided to look to the West and, as a result, Naftogaz underwent a series of significant changes for fewer than five years. These changes included creating a value-adding human resource management system with clearly set objectives, one of which was a long-term oriented talent management objective to ensure a decent life for society through sustainable income growth, and create opportunities for self-development and creative work (Naftogaz 2014). This objective reflects the current tendencies of the Ukrainian labor market—people want to have a stable stream of revenue, feel safe and have realizable career and development opportunities. However, there are gaps in the system due to the general impossibility of undergoing such complicated transition processes in a short period of time, considering the large size of this internationalized organization.

Some talent management practices are "highly recommended" by the state (Contact Ukraine 2018), thus limiting the ability of the company to make its own unbiased business decisions. In particular, organizational culture building as well as internal communication can be compromised due to the incompatibility of different groups of workers with varying political opinions. Talent recruitment, for instance, can be rigged due to the state's involvement in the selection and hiring processes, leaving Naftogaz with "B"-level employees. Moreover, one cannot outrun the past—Naftogaz employs a lot of people who gained their first working experience in the Soviet system. Such workers generally tend to lack the leadership skills required by modern multinationals. Naftogaz needs to acknowledge the important role of talent management (which is a rather new concept in the Ukrainian context) in developing and sustaining competitive advantages; however, the local environment and cultural idiosyncrasies also have to be considered.

To conclude, the talent management and human resource strategies of Naftogaz revolve around the same corporate objective of ensuring stability and safety. Since the oil and gas industry requires a certain set of skills and competences from workers in order for them to perform their duties effectively, the general approach to defining talent in Naftogaz is functionalist and selective. In addition, many of the adopted talent management practices are mature in a sense that they have passed the test of time in leading Western organizations; however, Naftogaz's human resource management system is still at the stage of rapid development. Meanwhile, the Soviet legacy still strongly affects the business environment in Ukraine, which results in many of Naftogaz's talent management practices being rather formal and ineffective, or following the same Soviet-like patterns.

* * *

In the time of crisis talent management in Ukrainian organizations is considered to be a necessary, socially responsible mechanism aimed at ensuring stability in the external and internal environment. Specifically, organizations with a clear talent management agenda are seen as guarantors of stability in the region since the state itself is unable to provide its citizens with the basic need of safety. This is what all of the three observed companies had in common. In addition, Azovstal, Clickky and Naftogaz share the same issue of the younger and older generations differently perceiving the value of talent management practices due to the former being exposed primarily to a Western management style and the latter to the Soviet authoritarian style. Nonetheless, Ukrainian organizations demonstrate the highest level of commitment when it comes to talent management implementation as they want to sever their ties with the Soviet past and become internationally recognized firms that adhere to international quality standards.

The key barrier, however, is the turbulent external environment which is slowing down the recovery of the entire region after the prolonged Ukrainian crisis of 2013–2014. Today Ukraine continues dealing with different political and economic issues. Therefore, it is very important that local firms do not to lose their competitive advantage.

References

Azovstal. 2012. "Lean Production Facility" Program Is Being Implemented at Azovstal Iron & Steel Works. *News and Press Releases*, January 18. https://azovstal.metinvestholding.com/en/press/news/show/1483?year=2012. Accessed 3 Oct 2017.

———. 2015a. General Directors of Mariupol Metallurgical Plants Told Metallurgists About the Anti-Crisis Plan and Dispelled Rumors. *News and Press Releases*, January 22. https://azovstal.metinvestholding.com/ru/press/news/show/6826. Accessed 3 Oct 2017.

———. 2015b. Azovstal Will Not Cut Down Expenses by Mean of Downsizing. *News and Press Releases*, March 26. https://azovstal.metinvestholding.com/ru/press/news/show/6889. Accessed 3 Oct 2017.

———. 2016a. Azovstal Saved More than 140 Millions UAH in 2015. *News and Press Releases*, January 29. https://azovstal.metinvestholding.com/ru/press/news/show/7180. Accessed 3 Oct 2017.

———. 2016b. Metinvest Increased Investment in Improvement of Workers' Amenities. *News and Press Releases*, August 17. https://azovstal.metinvestholding.com/en/press/news/show/7281. Accessed 3 Oct 2017.

———. 2016c. Steel Works in Mariupol Invested UAH 17 Million to Improve the Working Condition. *News and Press Releases*, February 9. https://azovstal.metinvestholding.com/en/press/news/show/7192. Accessed 3 Oct 2017.

———. 2017a. Products. https://azovstal.metinvestholding.com/ru/activity/products. Accessed 3 Oct 2017.

———. 2017b. History. https://azovstal.metinvestholding.com/ru/about/history. Accessed 3 Oct 2017.

———. 2017c. Azovstal Today. https://azovstal.metinvestholding.com/en/about/common. Accessed 3 Oct 2017.

———. 2017d. CSR Programmes. https://azovstal.metinvestholding.com/en/responsibility/local_communities/programs. Accessed 3 Oct 2017.

Baker, Luke. 2013. EU Talking to IMF, World Bank, Others About Ukraine Assistance. *Reuters*, December 11. https://www.reuters.com/article/us-eu-ukraine/eu-talking-to-imf-world-bank-others-about-ukraine-assistance-idUSBRE9BA0S120131211. Accessed 1 Oct 2017.

Bonenberger, Adrian. 2017. The War No One Notices in Ukraine. *The New York Times*, June 20. https://www.nytimes.com/2017/06/20/opinion/ukraine-russia.html. Accessed 1 Oct 2017.

Borisov, Konstantin. 2013. Peculiarities of Personnel Management in Ukraine and Kazakhstan. *Generalniy Director*, December 10. https://www.gd.ru/articles/3086-osobennosti-upravleniya-personalom-na-ukraine-i-v-kazahstane. Accessed 1 Oct 2017.

Cameron, Kim S., and Robert E. Quinn. 2011. *Diagnosing and Changing Organizational Culture: Based on the Competing Values Framework*. Reading: Addison-Wesley.

Child, John, and Andre P. Czegledy. 1996. Managerial Learning in the Transformation of Eastern Europe: Some Key Issues. *Organization Studies* 17: 167–179.

Clickky. 2017a. About Clickky. https://clickky.biz/about/. Accessed 10 Oct 2017.

———. 2017b. Careers. https://clickky.biz/about/careers/. Accessed 10 Oct 2017.

Contact Ukraine. 2018. Introduction to Employment Law of Ukraine. https://www.contactukraine.com/business-laws/ukraine-employment-law-guide. Accessed 17 Oct 2017.

Credit Suisse Research Institute. 2015. Global Wealth Report 2015. Zürich: Credit Suisse AG. https://publications.credit-suisse.com/tasks/render/

file/?fileID=F2425415-DCA7-80B8-EAD989AF9341D47E. Accessed 1 Oct 2017.

Didenko, Yuliya. 2014. War and European Integration: What Will Happen to the Labout Market in the Donetsk Region? *Novosti Donbassa*, December 25. http://novosti.dn.ua/article/5248-voyna-y-evroyntegracyya-chto-budet-s-rynkom-truda-doneckoy-oblasty. Accessed 1 Oct 2017.

Dorofeeva, Anna. 2012. Peculiarities of Organizational Behaviour of Personnel in Industrial Enterprises and Main Directions for Its Regulation. *Economy of Industry* 2–4: 59–60. http://dspace.nbuv.gov.ua/bitstream/handle/123456789/49454/ST45-34-_59-60.pdf?sequence=1. Accessed 1 Oct 2017.

Dvorskaya, Natalia. 2017. Ukrainian Labor Market – 2017: Top-6 Key Trends. *HR-Liga*, June 19. https://hrliga.com/index.php?module=news&op=view&id=16443. Accessed 1 Oct 2017.

Encyclopædia Britannica. 2017. Ukraine. *Encyclopædia Britannica, Inc.*, November 30. https://www.britannica.com/place/Ukraine/Independent-Ukraine. Accessed 1 Oct 2017.

European Commission. 2010. Europe 2020: A Strategy for Smart, Sustainable and Inclusive Growth. http://eur-lex.europa.eu/LexUriServ/LexUriServ.do?uri=COM:2010:2020:FIN:EN:PDF. Accessed 1 Oct 2017.

———. 2017. Ukraine. Last modified November 6. http://ec.europa.eu/trade/policy/countries-and-regions/countries/ukraine/. Accessed 1 Oct 2017.

Eurostat. 2017. Europe 2020 Indicators – Employment. http://ec.europa.eu/eurostat/statistics-explained/index.php/Europe_2020_indicators_-_employment. Accessed 24 Jan 2018.

Fey, Carl, Pontus Engström, and Ingmar Björkman. 1999. Effective Human Resource Management Practices for Foreign Firms in Russia. *Organizational Dynamics* 28: 69–80.

Fuxman, Leonora. 2004. Emerging Trends in Ukrainian Management Styles and the Challenge of Managerial Talent Shortage. *International Journal of Commerce and Management* 14: 28–43.

Grudzinskaya, Elena. 2015. In Ukraine, the Deficit of Talented Employees Negatively Affects the Work of the Company. *Golos.ua*, December 2. http://ru.golos.ua/suspilstvo/v_ukraine_defitsit_talantlivyih_sotrudnikov_negativno_vliyaet_na_rabotu_kompanii__ek_1. Accessed 24 Jan 2018.

Gurkov, Igor, and Olga Zelenova. 2009. Managing Human Resources in Russia. In *Managing Human Resources in Central and Eastern Europe*, ed. Michael J. Morley, Noreen Heraty, and Snejina Michailova, 279–312. Abingdon: Routledge.

Headhunder. 2015. Which Specialties Have a Future? Rating of the Most Promising Professions. *hh.ua*, November 25. https://hh.ua/article/17930. Accessed 24 Jan 2018.

Hofstede, Geert. 1984. Cultural Dimensions in Management and Planning. *Asia Pacific Journal of Management* 1: 81–99.

Inc. 2017. Inc. 5000 Europe 2017. Meet the Fastest-Growing Private Companies in Europe. https://www.inc.com/inc5000eu/list/2017/?cid=land5000eu17-list-full. Accessed 10 Oct 2017.

International Labour Migration. 2011. Measuring Decent Work in Ukraine. http://www.ilo.org/wcmsp5/groups/public/---dgreports/---integration/documents/publication/wcms_220118.pdf. Accessed 1 Oct 2017.

———. 2014. Ukraine Labour Migration Survey, June 18. http://www.ilo.org/wcmsp5/groups/public/---europe/---ro-geneva/---sro-budapest/documents/publication/wcms_247459.pdf. Accessed 17 Oct 2017.

Ivanets, Valentyna. 2016. The Labor Market of Ukraine: The Main Trends of the First Half of 2016. *EY* 9: 24–26. http://www.ey.com/Publication/vwLUAssets/ey-article-ivanets-sep-2016/$FILE/ey-article-ivanets-sep-2016.pdf. Accessed 1 Oct 2017.

Iwański, Tadeusz. 2017. The Stable Crisis. Ukraine's Economy Three Years After the Euromaidan. *OSW Commentary*, April 5. https://www.osw.waw.pl/en/publikacje/osw-commentary/2017-04-05/stable-crisis-ukraines-economy-three-years-after-euromaidan. Accessed 1 Oct 2017.

Jamrisko, Michelle, Catarina Saraiva, and Andre Tartar. 2015. The 15 Most Miserable Economies in the World. *Bloomberg*, March 2. https://www.bloomberg.com/news/articles/2015-03-02/the-15-most-miserable-economies-in-the-world. Accessed 1 Oct 2017.

Khodakov, Viktor E. 2012. *Higher Education: A View from Outside and Inside*. Herson: Higher Education.

Kolesnikov, Boris. 2016. Ukraine's Economy Is Based on Three Foundations. *Obozrevatel*, December 2. http://obozrevatel.com/blogs/19620-ekonomika-ukrainyi-stroitsya-na-treh-fundamentah.htm. Accessed 1 Oct 2017.

Kovalchuk, Anna. 2014. The Employer's Market Came to Ukraine. *Forbes Ukraine*, July 29. http://forbes.net.ua/business/1375829-v-ukrainu-prishel-rynok-rabotodatelya. Accessed 1 Oct 2017.

Kupets, Olga. 2012. *Characteristics and Determinants of Internal Labor Mobility in Ukraine (English)*. Washington, DC: World Bank. http://documents.worldbank.org/curated/en/224161468313770215/Characteristics-and-determinants-of-internal-labor-mobility-in-Ukraine. Accessed 1 Oct 2017.

Lazorenko, Larisa. 2008. *Peculiarities of Personnel Management in Commercial Organizations of Ukraine*. Presented at the International Research Conference dedicated to the anniversary of the Department of Economics and Management of Trade and Economics of Trade specialization, Varna, Bulgaria, October 10–11. http://ekmair.ukma.edu.ua/handle/123456789/718. Accessed 1 Oct 2017.

Mäkelä, Kristiina, Ingmar Björkman, and Mats Ehrnrooth. 2010. How Do MNCs Establish Their Talent Pools? Influences on Individuals' Likelihood of Being Labeled as Talent. *Journal of World Business* 45: 134–142.

Mattoo, Aaditya, Ileana Cristina Neagu, and Çağlar Özden. 2008. Brain Waste? Educated Immigrants in the US Labor Market. *Journal of Development Economics* 87: 255–269.

Metinvest. 2016. Annual Report 2016 (English Version). https://www.metinvestholding.com/ru/investors/reports. Accessed 3 Oct 2017.

Naftogas. 2015. Annual Report 2015. Personnel. http://annualreport2015.naftogaz.com/en/socialnaja-ta-ekologichna-vidpovidalnist/personal/. Accessed 17 Oct 2017.

Naftogaz. 2014. Naftogaz of Ukraine. Annual Report 2014. http://www.naftogaz.com/files/Zvity/Naftogaz_Annual_Report_2014_engl.pdf. Accessed 17 Oct 2017.

———. 2016. Naftogaz of Ukraine. Annual Report 2016. http://www.naftogaz.com/files/Zvity/Anual_report_eng_170608.pdf. Accessed 17 Oct 2017.

———. 2017a. Company. http://www.naftogaz.com/www/3/nakweben.nsf/0/3A25D65C2606A6C9C22570D800318869?OpenDocument. Accessed 17 Oct 2017.

———. 2017b. Code of Corporate Ethics. Last modified January 1. http://www.naftogaz.com/files/HR/Naftogaz-Code-Ethics-engl.pdf. Accessed 17 Oct 2017.

Nesterenko, Vadim. 2015. The German Occupants' Policy in the Sphere of Providing the Population with the First Need Things (on the Example of the Regions of the Military Zone in Ukraine in 1941–1943). *Rusin* 2: 134–147.

Roubini, Nouriel. 2009. A Global Breakdown of the Recession in 2009. *Forbes*, January 15. https://www.forbes.com/2009/01/14/global-recession-2009-oped-cx_nr_0115roubini.html#493fe0d3185f. Accessed 1 Oct 2017.

Russia Today. 2014. Ukraine's Multibillion-Dollar Gas Debt: Who Pays? Last Modified October 23. https://www.rt.com/business/198080-who-pay-ukraine-gas-debt/. Accessed 17 Oct 2017.

Semysev, Igor. 2008. Happy Anniversary, Workers of Azovstal! *PRiazovsky Rabochiy*, January 23. http://pr.ua/news.php?new=5824. Accessed 3 Oct 2017.

Shkil, Vitaliy. 2015. The Labour Market in Ukraine: "We'll Call You Back". *BBC Ukraine*, June 18. http://www.bbc.com/ukrainian/ukraine_in_russian/2015/06/150618_ru_s_labour_market_ukraine. Accessed 1 Oct 2017.

Sutela, Pekka. 2012. The Underachiever: Ukraine's Economy Since 1991. *Carnegie Endowment for International Peace*, March 9. http://carnegieendowment.org/2012/03/09/underachiever-ukraine-s-economy-since-1991-pub-47451. Accessed 1 Oct 2017.

Talajlo, E.A. 2010. Peculiarities of the Motivation Process in Ukrainian and Foreign Firms. *Rusnauka*. http://www.rusnauka.com/36_PWMN_2010/Economics/77127.doc.htm. Accessed 1 Oct 2017.

The Decline in Industrial Production in Ukraine Accelerated to 17.9%. *Unian*, January 19, 2015. https://economics.unian.net/industry/1033633-spad-promproizvodstva-v-ukraine-v-proshlom-godu-uskorilsya-do-179.html. Accessed 1 Oct 2017.

The Ministry of Finance. 2018. The Unemployment Rate in Ukraine. Last modified January 5. https://index.minfin.com.ua/labour/unemploy/2016. Accessed 10 Jan 2018.

The World Bank. 2017. *Ukraine*. Washington, DC: The World Bank Group. https://data.worldbank.org/country/ukraine. Accessed 1 Oct 2017.

The World Factbook. 2017. *Ukraine*. Washington, DC: Central Intelligence Agency. https://www.cia.gov/library/publications/resources/the-world-factbook/geos/up.html. Accessed 1 Oct 2017.

UNHCR. 2014. Fighting Displaces More than Half a Million People Inside Ukraine, Hundreds of Thousands More into Neighbouring Countries. *UNHCR The UN Refugee Agency*, December 5. http://unhcr.org.ua/en/2011-08-26-06-58-56/news-archive/1397-fighting-displac. Accessed 1 Oct 2017.

World Economic Forum. 2017. Ukraine: Global Competitiveness Report 2017–2018 Edition. Last modified September 26. http://reports.weforum.org/global-competitiveness-index-2017-2018/countryeconomy-profiles/#economy=UKR. Accessed 1 Oct 2017.

Part IV

Talent Management in Latin America

14

Latin America: Talent Management in the New Reality

Maria Laura MacLennan, Gabriel Vouga Chueke,
Andrei Panibratov, Svetla Marinova,
and Daria Klishevich

Latin America is generally considered to include the entire continent of South America as well as Mexico, Central America, and the islands of the Caribbean whose inhabitants speak a Romance language. This area experienced conquest and colonization by Spain and Portugal from the late fifteenth through the eighteenth century together with independence

---

M. L. MacLennan (✉)
Centro Universitario FEI, São Bernardo do Campo, Brazil
e-mail: mferranty@fei.edu.br

G. Vouga Chueke
Brazilian Multinationals Observatory, University of São Paulo,
São Paulo, Brazil

A. Panibratov • D. Klishevich
Graduate School of Management, St. Petersburg State University,
St. Petersburg, Russia

S. Marinova
Aalborg University, Aalborg, Denmark
e-mail: svetla@business.aau.dk

© The Author(s) 2018
M. Latukha (ed.), *Talent Management in Global Organizations*,
Palgrave Studies of Internationalization in Emerging Markets,
https://doi.org/10.1007/978-3-319-76418-4_14

movements against Spain and Portugal in the early nineteenth century. Now being independent states, Latin American countries claim to have experienced similar trends, but also significant differences (Encyclopedia Britannica 2017). Brazil, Argentina, Mexico, Colombia, Venezuela, Chile and Peru are among the largest economies in the region in terms of gross domestic product (GDP) (IMF 2017).

The economy of the Latin American countries continues to grow and gain more weight among the developed states. In the past three decades, the region started a process of economic liberalization and democratization, thus attracting foreign direct investment (FDI) which was encouraged by the Latin-American high-value industries such as banking and telecommunications. The developments in those years made FDI from Europe, North America and Asia possible, which was stimulated further by the signing of various international trade agreements such as NAFTA and the Trade Agreement with the European Union (Elvira and Davila 2007). Nevertheless, the business environment in this region remains rather volatile and challenging, while economic crises have a cyclic nature (Elvira and Davila 2007).

Latin America has experienced a significant negative influence of the policy-driven persistence of the Great Recession, with the consequent lagging trade growth and recovery. As the Trade and Development Report-2017 of UNCTAD shows, the short-term estimations highlight a modest recovery of the Latin American economies in 2017, after a two-year downward trend. The years before, between 2004 and 2010, demonstrated rather high rates of economic growth, with the exception of the notorious 2009 following the 2008 financial crisis (World Development Report 2017). These figures confirm the point that recent economic development of Latin America is in a constant flux, which forces business companies in the region to adapt continuously to the uncertain situation in the economy. Predictions are that potential growth will remain sluggish and threaten the region with a middle-income trap, a long-term slowdown in economic growth that countries may face when they reach middle levels of per-capita income (OECD Latin American Economic Outlook 2017).

Disregarding the cautious economic forecasts, the region has a huge potential in terms of human capital development. Indeed, the demographic opportunity of Latin America is in its young population: one quarter of the Latin American population are between 15 and 29 years old, and this promises unique chances of inclusive growth in the region (OECD Latin American Economic Outlook 2017). In light of this, the importance of talent management tools, as well as government support to increase inclusiveness in the labor market, becomes more obvious. Nevertheless, there are some challenges hindering the development of talent management in Latin America.

The labor markets in Latin America have distinctive characteristics that influence the ways in which talent management is embraced (or disregarded) by Latin American companies. They are characterized by significant inequality in professional qualifications. There is a low proportion of highly qualified workers earning substantial salaries and a lot of low-skilled and poorly paid workers. This inequality was denoted as the disparity between the "knowledge-based elite" and the "machine-minding labor masses". Thus, the relevance of talent management practices in the Latin American labor markets becomes questionable in terms of unified policies and practices (Arrau et al. 2012).

Latin American labor markets are diverse in the types of employment they offer and here, distinct modes of work are often exercised, such as temporary work which amounts to a significant part of the labor market in the region. Talent management faces challenges as temporary workers may be more difficult to motivate and engage, since they perceive their employment as something that exists for a particular period of time (Arrau et al. 2012). Nevertheless, there are companies in the region whose talent management departments are aware of such challenges and have managed to establish a system of temporary workers' recognition, for example by means of various benefits offered, both material and non-material.

The region also suffers from political instability, many countries face accusations of corruption and fraud. The incidence of corruption is common in countries such as Argentina and Brazil, and occurs at significantly lower levels in Chile. Political instability has affected Latin American countries, especially in the 1970s and 1980s when some states in the region had unstable political systems and dictatorship. This resulted in changes in labor legislation and in the ambiguous situation in the 1980s when human resource management started penetrating the region with its notions of collaboration and commitment that were discordant to the political realities of restricted freedoms and suppressed labor unions

(Arrau et al. 2012). This explains the cautious attitude toward human resource development in the first years when it was introduced and started gaining ground in the Latin American countries.

Corruption and fraud also influence the way talent management practices are implemented, as they can potentially lead to non-transparent, murky selection procedures in companies, when personal or political networks may influence decision-making and lead to the employment of less-qualified job applicants who benefit from having personal connections (Arrau et al. 2012). Along with this, informality is very much present in the labor market context, with more than a half of the labor force in the region engaged in the informal economy. Those workers are especially vulnerable to income drops and unemployment, and are usually paid less than formally employed people with the same qualification (OECD Latin American Economic Outlook 2017). According to other estimates, overall up to 70% of urban workers in Latin America may be working in the informal sector (Maloney 2004).

Among the challenges that underpin the labor market and as a result echo in the talent management reality of Latin America are discrimination and child labor, which together with inequality, corruption, high informality, fraud and political instability are typical of all Latin American countries. Though the region is often considered homogeneous, the level of development and the scale of difficulties met by different states is not the same; therefore, it makes sense to still consider the countries independently, as the following chapters will do with regards to Argentina and Chile (Arrau et al. 2012).

Similar to many other management tools, modern human resource practices arrived in Latin America in the 1980s, shortly after they had become widespread in developed countries. This was in parallel to the historical and institutional development that was taking place in the region at that time. Large Latin American firms promptly adopted the talent management tools, supposedly following their international rivals in the globalized world (Martín-de Castro 2015). Although the presence of talent management in Latin American companies is obvious, its adoption as an organizational practice has its own specifics. These are associated with the uniqueness of the local culture in Latin America that has influenced the way talent management has been perceived and adopted (Arrau et al. 2012; Rodriguez and Rios 2007).

The influence of culture is reflected in the special nature of social relationships and, by extension, their management in this region. This makes the understanding of the fundamental cultural values rooted in local culture crucial for the implementation of successful talent management practices (Elvira and Davila 2005).

Talent management in the region is also challenged by a further typical feature of the cultural context, a strong paternalism that influences the development of talent management practices. Paternalism underpins the foundation of relationships that exist in society, and the labor market is no exception. Paternalism exists as a legacy of twentieth-century labor relations when workers, originally peasants or agricultural workers, moved from the countryside to the cities in pursuit of better working opportunities. The emerging large enterprises created living quarters for them and offered low salaries, and this started the paternalistic relationships in the labor market that persist even today (i.e. a highly personalized relationship that has developed from the situation when an owner offered protection and a worker responded with loyalty). It was loyalty that was the main requirement that workers faced, not productivity (Rodriguez and Rios 2007). Paternalism does not favor the development of talent management as its focus is not on increasing the efficiency of a company, but on the personal and cultural reasoning behind the decision taken with regards to employment.

Talent management in its traditional understanding includes the development of horizontal communication channels, inspiring commitment and engagement among workers. These values are considered to contradict the traditional behavioral and cultural patterns embedded in Latin American society (Elvira and Davila 2005). This could explain the reluctance of many Latin American companies to embrace talent management. Nevertheless, the ones that are striving for better productivity, a stronger brand and better results, have acknowledged the importance of committed employees that arises from the focused work on talent attraction, development and retention.

A further characteristic of Latin American labor is the changing role of trade unions. Traditionally, being inclined toward keeping employment for their members, especially in the framework of state-owned companies, they have now started to reconsider their role in private firms and demonstrate a more open attitude toward labor market negotiations. Moreover, trade unions have revised their perception of the impact of globalization on Latin American companies and proactively offer support that can benefit both firms and the employees by means of reducing manufacturing-related costs (Arrau et al. 2012).

Talent management exercises the role of fostering knowledge management within organizational boundaries, and consequently, the processes of knowledge creation. For example, this can happen through communities of practice and learning or virtual work groups that facilitate knowledge transfer. The difficulty here is a particular perception of organizational processes, which is rather social than technological. Thus, the integration of knowledge management practices into the local working culture appears to be challenging (Arrau et al. 2012).

This part presents the cases of companies from large Latin American economies: Brazil, Argentina and Chile. The companies under investigation are large and most of them have a long working history. The way they embrace talent management practices is influenced by various factors. Previous organizational and ownership structures may affect the way talent attraction and retention is perceived. For example, former state-owned companies that on the wave of privatization liberalization in the 1980s were transformed into private companies (not a rare case for Latin American countries) may demonstrate a more hierarchical structure, which is reflected in horizontal relationships and more formalized, talent management practices. The other case is when companies merge with Western companies that bring their organizational practices to the regional companies and influence the way they consider employee-management relationships should be managed. This is evident in cases when a company either merges with a Western MNC or expands abroad by other entry modes or competes globally. It then starts incorporating new talent management practices adopted worldwide with regards to raising the commitment of employees though financial and non-material bonuses, by training and development of workers, and by attracting talented candidates at the very beginning of their professional path, once they finish universities, or even during their studies.

References

Arrau, G.P., E. Eades, and J. Wilson. 2012. Managing Human Resources in the Latin American Context: The Case of Chile. *The International Journal of Human Resource Management* 23 (15): 3133–3150.

Davila, Anabella, and Marta M. Elvira. 2007. Psychological Contracts and Performance Management in Mexico. *International Journal of Manpower* 28 (5): 384–402. https://doi.org/10.1108/01437720710778385.

Elvira, M., and A. Davila. 2005. *Managing Human Resources in Latin America: An Agenda for International Leaders (Global HRM)*. London/New York: Routledge.

Encyclopedia Britannica. History of Latin America. Last modified 28 December 2017. www.britannica.com/place/Latin-America. Accessed 2 Sept 2017.

Gregorio Martín-de Castro. 2015. Knowledge Management and Innovation in Knowledge-Based and High-Tech Industrial Markets: The Role of Openness and Absorptive Capacity. *Industrial Marketing Management* 47: 143–146. https://doi.org/10.1016/j.indmarman.2015.02.032.

IMF Report. 2017. www.imf.org/en/Publications/CR/Issues/2017/12/29/Argentina-Selected-Issues-45531. Accessed 5 June 2017.

Maloney, W.F. 2004. Informality Revisited. *World Development* 32 (7): 1159–1178.

OECD, Latin American Economic Outlook. 2017. Youth, Skills and Entrepreneurship. www.keepeek.com/Digital-Asset-Management/oecd/development/latin-american-economic-outlook-2017_leo-2017-en#page258.

Rodriguez, D., and R. Rios. 2007. Latent Premises of Labor Contracts: Paternalism and Productivity: Two Cases from the Banking Industry in Chile. *International Journal of Manpower* 28 (5): 354–368.

World Bank Group. 2017. *World Development Report 2017: Governance and the Law*. Washington, DC: World Bank. https://openknowledge.worldbank.org/handle/10986/25880. License: CC BY 3.0 IGO.

15

Brazil: Catching Up and Moving Forward

Maria Laura MacLennan and Gabriel Vouga Chueke

Brazil is the largest South American country in size and population. Its economy has remained strong despite the impact of the crisis that has ravaged companies since 2015. In this sense, Brazilian talent management has felt the recent turmoil that has transcended all aspects of the local labor market. After a period of prosperity and very low unemployment rates, the labor market in 2015 experienced massive restructuring and layoffs from companies whose revenues slumped due to the crisis. In 2017, markets began to show slight signs of recovery and talent management has gained importance in local and foreign companies operating in Brazil (Gasparin 2017).

Much is said about the recommencement of economic growth and when it occurred. The issue is controversial because for some the worst has passed and the country is on the way to economic recovery. For

M. L. MacLennan (✉)
Centro Universitario FEI, São Bernardo do Campo, Brazil
e-mail: mferranty@fei.edu.br

G. Vouga Chueke
Brazilian Multinationals Observatory, University of São Paulo,
São Paulo, Brazil

© The Author(s) 2018
M. Latukha (ed.), *Talent Management in Global Organizations*,
Palgrave Studies of Internationalization in Emerging Markets,
https://doi.org/10.1007/978-3-319-76418-4_15

others, the economic situation may continue to deteriorate. In terms of numbers, the unemployment rate in Brazil is 12.8% (for the second quarter of 2017). This number reflects a decline in the unemployment rate, if compared to prior periods. However, the growth of the informal economy is seemingly responsible for this improvement. Some measures were taken in order to boost the economy and allow it to recover. The federal government has eased labor laws in order to create greater flexibility and reduce labor costs for companies by making it easier for them to hire and fire. This novel regulation is valid as of November 2017, and among other changes, allows companies to sub-contract employees for all positions. Previously, sub-contractors were allowed only for secondary activities, mostly cleaning and security. Currently, it is possible to sub-contract all services needed by companies and any of their activities.

In order to boost economic recovery, labor law experienced some major reforms. Part-time activities and compensatory time are now regulated, as are home-office activities. Among other measures, reforms determine that the home-office should be included in the work contract, as well as in the activities of the worker. The contract must stipulate who is responsible for the costs and maintenance of all work-related material. All these changes are intended to make the Brazilian labor market more flexible and competitive. Those changes certainty may transform the way in which talent is administered, retained and stimulated, and contribute to companies' performance.

One important change in the regulations is that unions have lost some representation. Before the reform, union membership was compulsory as all workers were compulsorily syndicate. As a result of the reforms, workers may choose whether they join a union or not. The regulation also ends the obligation to contribute to the union tax, which now becomes optional. Currently, in March each year, all workers who opt to must pay the tax that is equivalent to one day of work per year, and this amount funds the union activities. On the other hand, one of the central points of the reform is that collective bargaining agreements between companies and workers' representatives may overlap with the labor laws defined in the CLT (Consolidation of Labor Laws). So, in this changing environment, companies must review their talent attraction, selection and retention strategies. Many changes can be foreseen in this new environment.

Talent management is a strong commitment of strategic human resource management to attract and develop the most talented professionals to and within the company. Human resources are committed to talent management initiatives because of the competitive need to retain high-performing teams and identify potential talent inside the organization. Therefore, it is an integrated and holistic strategy of hiring, training and retaining the best performers. And for this, talent management acts in a series of processes that aims to provide professional development, performance evaluation and talent recognition initiatives, all combined in order to offer career ascension opportunities.

As talent management is a priority in a company aspiring to improve its performance, in this chapter we analyze some of the talent management practices Brazilian companies use to attract, select and recruit talent. Mobility may increase with the new rules, as the penalties to move to other work opportunities may be decreased. In order to make the company more attractive to talent, we show three main practices used to successfully attract and retain talents: (1) develop a strong employer value proposition to attract the best; (2) administer talent retention, and (3) avoid wasteful talent management. In order to do so, some examples highlight adequate talent management practices.

We compare the experiences of Brazilian companies in attracting highly qualified specialists. One strategy—to develop a strong employer value proposition to attract the best—we use Embraer as a remarkable example. Embraer human resource strategy focuses on developing a high employer value proposition in order to attract the best available high-potential people to the aircraft manufacturing industry. This is because Embraer competes globally and needs highly qualified employees to work for it. Its Life Planning Talent Retention Program emphasizes its vibrant and challenging work environment as a leading niche company in the industry. Embraer uses its corporate positive image to develop collaboration with universities to attract outstanding students and graduates. This young talent is selected through internship and trainee programs, and allows the company to create a strong connection between the talented potential employees and the company.

On the talent retention side, another main strategy used by Brazilian companies is to implement a corporate culture based on trust and entrepreneurship. This strategy enables the company to sustain a favorable relationship with its employees. For Brazilians, to be able to foresee future opportunities is a huge career driver, so companies with a career development plan may be more successful in retaining high-performing employees.

In CCR talent retention is actively managed with several initiatives, as CCR is an infrastructure conglomerate. Its talent management strategy is to appraise and develop its staff in order to have the right person in the right position. Its leadership program is allied with several other initiatives, as an in-house university, compensation strategy and benefits are used to retain employees and reduce the employee turnover rate.

Finally, the third strategy is to avoid any waste and use the full potential of talented employees within the company. In order to illustrate this strategy, we show the case of Braskem, a petrochemical company with a worldwide presence, and CPFL Energia. CPFL Energia is a company mainly focused on employee development. This can be seen in the human resource (HR) strategies that the company uses to assist its employees to grow professionally within the firm through constant learning and competence development.

Embraer: A Strong Value Proposition in Order to Attract the Best

Any human resource manager worldwide dreams of working in a company with a strong brand name that attracts talent and keeps it motivated to deliver the best. It is no wonder that investing in a value proposition is the most important human resource priority for Embraer. This practice can reduce by half the expenditure needed to recruit a candidate, can improve employee commitment by 30% and can increase talent retention by almost 40% (Embraer Annual Report 2013).

A strong value proposition is a reality for Embraer, which is a Brazilian company that produces and sells commercial, military, executive and agricultural jet and turboprop aircraft, and provides a variety of aeronautical services. Being headquartered in Sao Paulo, Brazil, the Embraer Conglomerate has it operations in South and North America, Australia,

Europe and Asia. The number of employees working in the company is 19,373 (Embraer 2017a, b, c, d, e).

Officially called Embraer – Empresa Brasiliera de Aeronautica, the company was established in 1969. Starting its operations in 1970, the first task for Embraer was to produce turboprop aircraft that could be utilized both for military and civilian purposes. Bandeirante (a light transport aircraft) can transport up to 21 passengers, and after its successful launch the company received an order from the Brazilian government to produce advanced jet training and ground attack aircraft (Marketline 2017). The license was provided by the Italian company Aermacchi. In 1977, the company managed to widen its operations in Europe (Eckhouse 1991). In 1979, Embraer established a subsidiary in the United States. The 1970s was a milestone year as the company produced two more aircraft: the EMB 312 Tucano and the EMB 120 Brasilia. These were developed by Embraer with the help of foreign partners from Italy—Aermacchi and AerItalia. In 1980, Embraer purchased Neiva.[1] The next year, encouraged by its previous positive experience of working with Italians, Embraer made an agreement with AerItalia and Aermacchi to develop a sub-sonic fighter-bomber. In 1983, Embraer managed to launch Embraer Aviation International in France. The company also set up a service agreement with Atlantic Southeast Airlines in the United States and established a partnership with the Chinese government to start on the China-Brazil Resource Satellite Project.

The mid-1990s brought some changes to the company. Being originally founded by the Brazilian government, Embraer as well as other state-controlled Brazilian organizations, started privatization. At the end of 1994, Embraer was sold, which actually saved the conglomerate from bankruptcy (OECD 2007). In 2000, Embraer was listed on the New York Stock Exchange and the Sao Paulo Stock Exchange (OECD 2007). In 2002, Embraer opened up the College Embraer Juarez Wanderley in Sao Jose dos Campos (Instituto Embraer 2017), which became a key part of the Embraer education and research strategy. At the end of 2004, Embraer launched its Embraer 195, the largest airplane the company had managed to build so far (Instituto Embraer 2017). The corporate restructuring of Embraer took

---

[1] The Aeronáutica Indústria Neiva Ltda. was a manufacturer of aircraft and components that, after being incorporated by Embraer, had its factory park renamed Embraer—Botucatu Unit, and was responsible for Embraer's agricultural line.

place in 2006. This in its turn helped to increase liquidity for all Embraer shareholders. In 2008 the company launched an executive jet service center in Florida. In 2011, Embraer purchased 64% of the share capital of the radar division of Orbisat da Amazonia SA (Instituto Embraer 2017). In 2014 and 2015, Embraer received a National Quality Award from the National Quality Foundation (Embraer 2017a, b, c, d, e).

There are several business segments Embraer operates in. Its main competitors are Bombardier, Airbus and Boeing. Those competitors headhunt specialized employees worldwide, so talent is constantly being attracted by competitors. This segment of commercial aviation is responsible for developing, producing and selling commercial jets. The company also provides services to regional aviation. Leasing of aircrafts is also offered by Embraer. The defense and security segment is involved in design, development, production and customer support for the defense and security market. Embraer products in these segments are attack aircraft, surveillance platforms, military transport as well as different reconnaissance systems. The executive aviation segment is responsible for developing, producing and selling executive jets, and providing support services. Embraer has a line of executive jets including a variety of models with different characteristics.

In terms of talent management, the company has a rather universalist definition of talent due to its sectoral affiliation and the need for highly-qualified engineers and technicians. Indeed, talent attraction and retention is essential for a company like Embraer insofar as one of the aeronautic industry specifics is the need to attract engineering talent in the long-term due to the length of product development cycles, severe competition in the sector (apart from the two industry leaders, Airbus and Boeing, Embraer is competing with the Canadian Bombardier to conquer some of its market share), and the global labor market supplying highly qualified specialists (Embraer Annual Report 2013). Thus, Embraer insists on a lengthy selection process – which is coherent with the reduced size of its headcount compared to its top-line profit (about US$5.7billion in 2013). It has a rather well-developed and broad evaluation process, but the criteria for employee assessment remain somewhat unclear, although performance plays a key role (Embraer 2017a, b, c, d, e).

Variable remuneration is well-developed in Embraer and is highlighted by the company. It accounts for a substantial part of the remuneration for specialists. This variable remuneration is linked to corporate results and employee's individual performance compared to periodically identified and adjusted individual goals. The aim of this process is clearly to incite employees to exceed their targets (Embraer 2017a, b, c, d, e), but primarily to "attract, retain and engage" talent, to "motivate and reward individual performance". It is important to identify talent in the organization, as this group needs more intensive follow-up and support than other employees. For this, it is necessary to evaluate the professional performance of employees.

Talent retention at Embraer, beyond compensation, takes place alongside internal recruitment channels: the career development portal "Your Flight Plan at Embraer" is conceived as a framework to help employees navigate the different career options. Embraer claims that: "the developing of [their] people [and] the quality of talent within our organizations [is] the key differentiator of Embraer [...] in a highly competitive marketplace" (Embraer 2017a, b, c, d, e). Embraer offers its employees an extensive benefits package, which is considered to be one of the best in the industry. It includes a health plan, aid to parents of disabled children, a dental plan, drug store discounts, personal insurance policies, a vaccination program, a pension plan (Embraer Prev), food allowance, transportation allowance, day care, maternity leave, hospital companion benefit, transfer benefit, a credit co-op and Embraer Sports Association (Associação Desportiva Classista Embraer, ADCE).

One of the key objectives of Embraer is to create a talent organization through training and development. Out of *ad hoc* developed policies, Embraer offers tuition reimbursement in support of employees' pursuit of their education and professional development. Besides, Embraer offers lateral job rotation opportunities (a move to the same ranked positions in other departments) (Embraer 2017a, b, c, d, e). The main origin of Embraer's talent organization is the "Embraer Enterprise Excellence Program" (P3E) designed to unite all employees globally in the pursuit of results improvement and is based on the lean manufacturing philosophy. It has organized employees into more than 400 continuous improvement cells (Embraer Annual Report 2013). This is related to talent development insofar as attainment of the objectives set for each cell is the result of employee training, which is aligned to corporate needs.

There are several programs characterizing Embraer as a caring employer. The Embraer Route to Diversity Program promotes diversity among company members. Disabled people have a unique opportunity to get a two-year training position in the administrative and production functions. The diversity program has been greatly appreciated and promoted, and Embraer received a Brazilian government award for this initiative (Embraer 2017a, b, c, d, e). The Estar De Bem Program, which is translated into English as the Being Well Program, illustrates how Embraer really values its employees' well-being. The company actively promotes a healthy life-style to its employees. The program includes several initiatives oriented at supporting Embraer members along their way to improve their quality of life by developing healthy habits. Therefore, the Being-Well Programs have different objectives, depending on the individual needs of employees, for example Being Well without Drugs, Being Well without Smoking, Being Well on the Scales, Being Well with Physical Exercise, Being Well with Motherhood, Being Well with your Heart, Being Well with Stress, and a Health Week.

The list of programs is so broad that everyone could find something to suit (Embraer 2017a, b, c, d, e). The Life Planning Program assists Embraer employees with making choices that would affect their future life. The program includes several meetings with an employee, during which important subjects such as setting personal goals, healthcare, family planning and career management are covered. With the help of professionals, the company's employees can effectively organize their lives in such a way that contributes to their prosperity. Embraer is very active in participating in the program launched by the Hélio Augusto de Souza Foundation: Minor Apprentice. The program is intended to provide an opportunity for young people to learn practical work skills that would be of high demand on the market. All these initiatives are integrated in order to build a good image of Embraer as a great place to work, and so appear as a valuable choice of employer for talent.

CCR: Talent for the Future

CCR S.A. is considered to be one of the largest private infrastructure conglomerates in Latin America. Having its operations in three Brazilian states, the CCR Group employs 10,000 people in Brazil (Grupo CCR

2017a, b, c). The company is known as a leader in generating revenue. As the official annual report suggests, the net income of CCR was R$4577 billion (Grupo CCR 2017a, b, c). The company's operations cover segments of road concession, vehicle inspection services, automatic payment systems and passenger rail transport. CCR also offers automatic payment services at tollgates and parking lots (Grupo CCR 2017a, b, c). The company seeks to provide investment solutions and infrastructure services contributing to socio-economic development and to improvements in the quality of life of users of concessions managed by CCR, expanding and improving their operations in order to maximize savings (Grupo CCR 2017a, b, c).

CCR positions itself as an attractive employer capable of retaining the best professionals (CCR Annual Report 2011). In CCR's view, the term "talent" describes the best professional who is innovation-oriented, as the company claims its main goal of talent management is to do everything possible in order to cultivate talent.

As for attracting new talent, the Trainee Qualification Program is the company's main tool. The program is also referred to as the company's "talent incubator". The final purpose of the program is to develop professionals with potential to assume leading functions, ensuring the company's future growth (CCR Annual Report 2011). The selection process for this program consists of three elements: English language skills and logical reasoning; a specified set of competences; group dynamics and individual reviews. The company choses only the best talent, for example, in 2011, just 16 were accepted out of 6531 applicants. The Trainee Qualification Program offers its participants eight months of intensive training which covers all segments and sectors of the company's business (Grupo CCR 2017a, b, c).

According to the information provided on the official website of the company, the main focus of the training programs available in CCR are to qualify leaders in controlling business operations and to develop administrative and user service teams (Cemig Annual Report 2014). The Leadership Development Program (PDL) is the corporate university of CCR. This is the program that trains employees in the company's knowledge areas. Consisting of eight modules, the program transmits knowledge by means of practical sessions, workshops and lectures. The

Improving Project is complementary to the PDL course, the purpose of which is to provide continuous training to company employees (CCR Annual Report 2011). The evaluation process of employee performance takes place once a year. The company advocates continuous evaluation of its employees in order to have a clear picture of what areas of personal performance should be improved and what instruments are needed.

According to the company report (2011), CCR monitors some quality of life indicators of its employees. In its action programs and metrics, quality of life indicators show that 80% of employees exercise regularly. These indicators show an increase in regular exercise, as 66% regularly exercised in 2010 and 65% in 2009. Employees who go to the gym at the workplace increased to 42% in 2011 from 35% in 2009. CCR has dietary programs and 4% of the workforce attend them. CCR fights absenteeism and, in 2011, this was 1.25 days a year per employee. This number can be considered very positive and is certainly a reflection of the company's internal quality of life initiatives (Grupo CCR 2017a, b, c).

The evaluation procedure in CCR is conducted through a specially designed online system which demonstrates the results that were achieved by a particular employee, as well as revealing the potential and weaknesses in a person's performance. Based on the results received upon completing the evaluation, development plans are designed for each employee, so he or she knows where extra effort is needed to achieve personal professional growth. The evaluation system also assists internal recruitment due to its ability to identify high performers with potential for development.

Being an employer who is oriented to developing its people, CCR also cares about the overall well-being of its employees. There are several programs the company offers that are aimed at improving the quality of employees' life. Programs available promote a healthy life style, good habits and the right attitude toward life (Grupo CCR 2017a, b, c). Thus, the analysis of practices implemented in CCR has shown that staff development is the main focus of the talent management system developed and applied throughout the company. CCR believes that prioritizing employee development enables the company to attract and retain the best professionals.

More than 98% of CCR employees are eligible to receive benefits. From the benefits available, CCR full-time employees are eligible to medical and dental care, and group life insurance. Food and transport vouchers are also available, as well as private pension plans, loans and regular medical check-ups. Temporary and part-time employees receive fewer benefits compared to full-time ones. The benefits available for part-time and temporary employees are medical and dental care and private pension plans. From this background, it is possible to see that the company's policy can inspire employees to grow professionally within the firm.

Braskem: A Successful Case of Talent Retention in a Worldwide Industry

A well-developed value proposition is a reality for Braskem, a Brazilian petrochemical company. Its main activity is to manufacture petrochemical and thermoplastic products (Braskem 2017). The operations of Braskem are spread throughout the regions of Asia, Europe, South and North America. To date, the company has managed to set up 36 production plants, 29 of which are located in Brazil, five operate in the United States and two are in Germany (Knowledge Wharton 2013). The company produces more than 16 million tons of thermoplastic resins and other petrochemicals per year. This makes Braskem the largest petrochemical company in Latin America and one of the major players in the international petrochemical market. Braskem has a leading position in the production of biopolymers from sugarcane-based ethanol and currently operates in five segments: basic petrochemicals, polyolefin, polypropylene operations in the United States and Europe, vinyl, and chemical distribution. The first segment, basic petrochemicals, covers producing and selling basic petrochemicals at the company's Northeast and South complexes as well as those of Sao Paulo and Rio de Janeiro. The second segment involves working with polyolefin. Being produced in Brazil from renewable resources, polypropylene and polyethylene are in high demand. The third segment covers operations in Europe and the United States, which includes the production and sale of polypropylene (Braskem Annual Report 2014). The fourth segment is dedicated to producing and selling vinyl products, such as PVC, EDC and soda caustic. The fifth segment includes chemical distribution. The products manufactured by the company are distributed through main distribution channels.

Talent retention is key in Braskem's HR strategy and the company has an aggressive compensation strategy. Compared to the minimum wage, salaries in Braskem are on average 2.9 points higher in Brazil, and 3.4 points higher in the United States (based on 2014 results).

In an interview conducted by our research team, Marcelo Arantes, Vice President of People, Organization & Procurement of Braskem, claimed that currently the term "talent" is not used in the company. However, Braskem maps people that can grow into leadership roles. The company identifies those employees as "potentials". According to Mr Arantes, talent management in Braskem is defined as all organizational activities that are being conducted for the purpose of attracting, selecting, developing and integrating people in alignment with the company's culture. Braskem's talent management strategy focuses primarily on those who are defined by the company as leaders and potential leaders. The attitude of Braskem toward talent management is a belief that all "potentials" have accountability for their self-development. Braskem, from its side, is more than willing to support its employees' career ambitions. Mr Arantes stated that Braskem's strategic asset for attracting and retaining talented employees is the company's corporate culture, which is based on trust and entrepreneurship.

The core of the company strategy is its people. Braskem's main practices focus on building sustainable relationships with its employees. The trust and appreciation of an employee's willingness to grow professionally are the key principles of people management in Braskem. The company's 2014 Annual Report suggests that there are several challenges in the support area of people management in Braskem. The first challenge is to contribute to Braskem's growth and prosperity. The second challenge is to strengthen the position of the petrochemical industry as a creator of sustainable solutions to improve people's lives. Braskem emphasizes the need for the identification, development, integration and appraisal of high-performing employees.

Corporate culture (Braskem 2017) is based on the specially elaborated fundamental principles: (1) trust—the company has trust in its employees, their abilities to improve professionally, and by doing so, contribute to the company's prosperity; (2) satisfaction—the ultimate goal of all company activities is to fully satisfy customers so they remain loyal (when it comes to dealing with a customer, Braskem focuses on quality, productivity as well as socio-environmental responsibility); (3) return—Braskem values the well-being of its shareholders which is why a lot of attention is paid to increasing the value of their equity; (4) partnership—all employees are perceived as partners, whose efforts and hard work result in the current state of the company's performance; (5) self-development—the company highly appreciates a person's desire to grow personally and professionally within the organization (all the programs the company offers to its employees are aimed at assisting people in fulfilling their desire to yield better results); (6) reinvestment—Braskem is active in reinvesting for the creation of new opportunities and in community development, understanding that a bright future awaits only those who are willing to prepare for it, starting from now.

The company's expansion is largely supported by educational and development processes and its organizational culture (Braskem 2017). All training and development programs are constructed in alignment with the strategy and the business needs of the company (Braskem Annual Report 2014). Braskem employees are involved in creating an Individual Development Plan, which contains a description of the goals an employee plans to achieve by the end of attending in-company courses and training. Braskem strongly believes that human capital is the most important asset it has. There are several in-house development programs that aim at attracting and retaining new "potentials".

The company actively improves the programs oriented toward supporting the professional growth of its junior employees. Thus, in 2014, Braskem replaced its trainee program with the Associate Program, which part of the Internship Program. Ever since then, the interns at Braskem have the opportunity to become associates if their performance during the internship was evaluated as being excellent. The described opportunity is available only for those who possess Portuguese language skills. The Young Apprentice and Young Operator programs are specifically developed for technicians and have a focus on the employees who are just at the beginning of their career path. These programs are available for employees who are stationed in Brazil and Mexico.

Keeping up with the pace of global trends, Braskem has recognized the importance of having employees with entrepreneurial spirit on its team. The purpose of the Program for Developing Entrepreneurs is to nurture educational leaders at the company, the bright talented employees who will be responsible for Braskem's future prosperity and well-being. Upon completion of this program, they are expected to work toward the goal of making Braskem the best chemical company in the world. The graduates of this program are supposed to be role models for junior employees. Another program, the Expertise Development Program, was launched to improve the technical skills of employees. Leading universities are involved in conducting the program, so the quality of teaching material is high. The purpose of the Leader Workshop for Sustainable Development Program is to provide training in sustainable development. Completing the program allows employees to be fully involved in the implementation of the company strategy and have a clear vision about any future opportunities for Braskem's growth. Finally, the Horizons Program cares for retired employees. The participants of the program are eligible to receive personal and professional counseling as well as help with life challenges after their careers within the company are over. Such a program is definitely a great tool to demonstrate how Braskem treats its loyal employees. While investment in staff training is a time-consuming process, Braskem agrees that this is the path that will yield better results in the long-term. The company aims to develop people and consolidate its growth with the attraction of trained employees. This strategy avoids the inflationary spiral in the labor market that is provoked by "stealing" personnel from other companies.

The remuneration strategy (Braskem Management Report 2015) can be defined as equitable, competitive, effective and safe. The company tries to be objective when financially rewarding its employees (Braskem Management Report 2015). The payment procedure is carried out proportionally according to skills and impact on results. Braskem constantly monitors market wages to make sure that employee salaries are in line with those in the sector.

Employees' contribution to the company's goals is rewarded. Fixed remuneration and benefits are paid as a reward for short-term goal achievements. Variable remuneration is given when it comes to medium-term goal attainment. Long-term incentives are provided for those who manage to contribute to the future prosperity of the company. Such a remuneration strategy assists the company in maintaining its leading position in the industry as well as in facilitating its steady and stable growth.

According to Mr Arantes, the senior managers of Braskem are responsible for sustaining entrepreneurial spirit in the company. The leader has a fundamental role in the company's development, both with respect to technical knowledge and corporate culture. It is the leader who dedicates time, presence, example and experience to accompanying the development of young talent and guides employees on the path of career development. In this way, young managers and employees will have support from the organization for their development, but Braskem always encourages them also to be protagonists in regard to their career development. Therefore, performance and career management in Braskem imply establishing a strong relationship between the leader and team members. The purpose of this relationship is to define on a mutual basis the targets that should be achieved throughout the coming year. A so-called Action Program is developed for each team member in the company. At the end of the year, the leader evaluates the results of the work, and a further plan is devised for each member. It is indeed remarkable that each team member has an individual Action Program, which in essence is a great tool for planning one's career. The company's dedication to its employees' personal development is clearly stated in Braskem's Vision for 2020. In addition, it plans to keep working toward strengthening the relationship between company members, suppliers, clients and the communities where the company has its operations.

CPFL: Employee Assessment as a Process of Development, Evaluation and Rewarding

CPFL Energia is considered to be the largest, non-state-owned, electric energy generation and distribution group in Brazil. Being headquartered in Campinas, CPFL Energia is the third biggest Brazilian electric company (CPFL 2017). Throughout its 100 years of existence, the company has kept working toward generating knowledge. The corporation is composed of CPFL Brasil, CPFL Piratininga, CPFL Paulista, CPFL Geração, CPFL Renováveis, Rio Grande Energia and SEMESA. The company stocks are traded on the New York Stock Exchange and Bovespa. Today, CPFL Energia employs more than 8000 people. With more than 100 years of history, CPFL Energia has become an integrated energy company in distribution, generation and the commercialization of electricity and services. It has brought energy to 9.1 million clients and is among the leaders in the renewable energy sector in Brazil with a diversified matrix: from large and small hydropower plants to wind farms, biomass plants, oil thermal fuel and, more recently, the first solar power plant in the State of São Paulo (CPFL 2017).

In 2011, the company realized that it needed a transformation that would support its business sustainability. A Transformation Program was developed to make CPFL Energia a worldwide benchmark in the industry (CPFL 2017). Within the scope of this program, the company launched a new position of Business Partner, a specialist who would monitor all talent management needs within the business units. The main task of the Business Partner is to identify the areas that need to be improved in terms of managing talent and offer solutions to executive level managers (Manso 2013). Such a practice is not common among other Brazilian companies and is rather exceptional.

The CPFL Energia talent management investment is mostly focused on employee development. The variety of training avenues, the opportunity to track performance as well as the dependency of variable remuneration on the goals achieved have proved that the company has been making steady strides in encouraging its employees to grow professionally within the firm. CPFL Energia encourages its employee to learn and adopt new knowledge. The Personal Value Program was created to manage employee performance in an effective manner. The program has a tool for conducting self-evaluation of performance. Upon completing the self-evaluation procedure, the results become available to the line manager, so the employee receives feedback that would point out what in his or her performance should be improved. Based on the results and discussions, employees with their assigned superior start working toward developing an Individual Development Plan that describes in detail what should be done to improve performance and achieve professional growth (Manso 2013).

The CPFL Corporate University was established with the purpose of offering company employees training that would provide them with the knowledge and skills necessary for a particular position. It also offers online course platforms that make the process of obtaining new knowledge more accessible (Manso 2013).

The average number of hours for training varies greatly according to the functional level of an employee's position. Managers and operational and leadership levels have more training hours. Managers attend 88 hours of training per year, operational staff 78 hours and team leaders 64 hours, on average. University personnel attend 53 hours of training per year on average. Functional categories receive fewer training hours, for example, executives get 21 hours and statutory directors two hours of training per year. In 2011, the average number of hours of training per employee reached 73 (Manso 2013).

The high demand for training has forced senior management to spread the branches of the Corporate University throughout the cities of the states of Sao Paulo and Rio Grande do Sul. CPFL Energia also appreciates employee initiative in seeking knowledge outside the company. The company provides subsidies for different level of institutional education, as well as for language courses, computer courses and others (Manso 2013). As for remuneration and benefits, CPFL Energia is trying to follow the best global practices in the electricity sector. In addition to fixed salary, employees are eligible to receive variable compensation that is connected to goal attainment set in the Individual Development Plan (Manso 2013).

Another program developed by the company aims to increase employees' quality of life. The program is part of the organization's strategy to value human capital and positively and directly influence its organizational climate. The great challenge is to create tools to provide employees with the means to abandon habits that interfere with quality of life. For that, CPFL offers a gymnastics academy which stimulates and organizes groups to run and walk and provides worker gymnastics, among other health initiatives (CPFL Annual Report 2013).

* * *

Despite the advances in recent years, talent management in Brazil continues to be at a lower level than in developed countries. According to a recent poll (Nunomura 2017), nine out of ten chief executive officers in Brazil consider human capital a priority. However, one-third of the companies cannot even create a corporate strategy for managing people. Brazilian companies operate in a highly vulnerable, unpredictable and uncertain competitive environment and are challenged by the lack of well-qualified and specialized professionals. There are a number of challenges human resource departments encounter on a regular basis. Human resource managers need to develop more authentic human resource practices to motivate, engage, encourage and organize employees in order to motivate them to give their best to their company.

The cases presented above show that Brazilian companies are challenged to actively manage talent in terms of developing sustainable recruitment, training and retention practices. Currently, the Brazilian labor market does not challenge companies on the recruiting side, as there is a huge pool of unemployed people. However, as soon as the local economy grows, more sophisticated talent management strategies may be necessary. This need may be greater for high-skilled technical jobs than for unskilled ones. As there is a relationship between having better talent and obtaining better business results, organizations are increasingly looking to measure return on investment in human capital.

Rather than offering training only to develop employee-specific skills, companies are increasingly concerned about the strategic value of this strategy. It is now so much more important to evaluate how investment in training can help a company's long-term development. It makes sense to train teams to become effective in such a way as to achieve the goals and objectives of the organization. In this context, corporate universities have emerged in order assist companies in developing new knowledge and competences, as well as providing a pool of potential talent. For example, the Corporate University of CPFL Energia inaugurated in 2008 has five campuses and in 2011 registered more than 36,000 participations in courses (Manso 2013).

Expectations are that the labor reforms will benefit companies, especially regarding changes in labor lawsuits. The reform is expected to decrease contentious and opportunist claimants, who make the Labor Court a judicial lottery. For workers to benefit from the reform, there are some contentious views. The major breakthroughs in the reform process for workers are teleworking, the agreement to terminate the employment contract, the employees' commission and the vacation installment. Besides, the reform has created a limit when stipulating rights that cannot be negotiated, such as employee remuneration (with respect to the minimum wage, the thirteenth salary, minimum value of over-time at 50% higher than the normal hourly rate and the remuneration of night work to be higher than daytime), the additional risks (unhealthy and hazardous), paid weekly rest, due leave of absence, unemployment insurance, early warning, health, occupational health and safety, retirement, family pay, maternity leave, paternity and so on, which continue to be preserved by law (Vendrame 2017).[2]

Unions, on the other hand, may have to reinvent themselves. Now the compulsory union contribution has stopped, it is expected that many unions will cease to exist and some will merge. Welfare unions have a good chance of surviving, depending on the quality of their services. However, given the prevalence of bargaining in labor relations, those unions that wisely use the art of bargaining may survive (Vendrame 2017).

In this context, the above cases amply show how Brazilian companies implement evaluation and development tactics in order to catch up and move forward. The examples expounded in this chapter show that companies' actions go beyond simply looking for cost savings. All of them implement active talent management strategies, whether they refer to them as talent management or not. The core of these strategies is that they link employee incentives to company performance.

---

[2] Early warning is a communication that must be made by the employer to the employee (or vice versa), advising the end of the employment contract, within a timely period. Notice is required when dismissal of an employee has no just cause.

References

Braskem. 2017. https://www.braskem.com.br/home-en. Accessed 3 Nov 2017.

Braskem. Annual Report. 2014. http://www.braskem-ri.com.br/annual-reports/2014. Accessed 4 Nov 2017.

Braskem. Management Report. 2015. http://www.braskem-ri.com.br/annual-reports. Accessed 5 Jan 2018.

CCR Annual and Sustainability Report. 2011. http://www.grupoccr.com.br/ri2011/en/. Accessed 28 Oct 2017.

Cemig Annual Report. 2014. http://cemig.infoinvest.com.br/static/enu/relatorios_anuais.asp?idioma=enu. Accessed 15 Nov 2017.

CPFL. 2017. https://www.cpfl.com.br/Paginas/default.aspx. Accessed 9 Dec 2017.

CPFL Energia. Annual Report. 2013. https://cpfl.riweb.com.br/show.aspx?idMateria=0hIp7Kkq5lWCz+4goYsegw==&linguagem=en. Accessed 10 Dec 2017.

Eckhouse, J. 1991. *Brazil on Road Peddling State-Owned Enterprises*. The San Francisco Chronicle (final ed.) San Francisco.

Embraer. 2017a. http://www.embraer.com/en-US/pessoas/benefits/Pages/default.aspx. Accessed 5 Nov 2017.

———. 2017b. http://www.embraer.com/en-US/ConhecaEmbraer/TradicaoHistoria/Pages/default.aspx. Accessed 12 Nov 2017.

———. 2017c. http://www.embraer.com/en-US/Aeronaves/Pages/Home.aspx. Accessed 5 Nov 2017.

———. 2017d. http://www.embraer.com/en-US/pessoas/KnowPrograms/Pages/default.aspx. Accessed 6 Nov 2017.

———. 2017e. http://www.embraer.com/en-US/pessoas/ourprograms/Pages/Life-Planning.aspx. Accessed 6 Nov 2017.

Embraer Annual Report. 2013. https://ri.embraer.com.br/RAOS/RA%202013/Embraer%20Annual%20Report_2013.pdf. Accessed 22 Dec 2017.

Embraer Company Profile. www.marketline.com. Accessed 13 Nov 2017.

Gasparin, C. 2017. Para estas 5 carreiras, a crise do emprego no Brasil já passou. https://exame.abril.com.br/carreira/para-estas-5-carreiras-a-crise-do-emprego-no-brasil-ja-passou/. Accessed 10 Jan 2018.

Grupo CCR. 2017a. http://www.grupoccr.com.br/ri2011/en/training-programs.html. Accessed 28 Oct 2017.

———. 2017b. http://www.grupoccr.com.br/ri2011/en/people-management.html. Accessed 27 Oct 2017.

———. 2017c. www.grupoccr.com.br. Accessed 27 Oct 2017.

Instituto Embraer. 2017. http://www.centrohistoricoembraer.com.br/sites/timeline/en-US/Pages/default.aspx#ano/2010/2011. Accessed 12 Nov 2017.

Knowledge Wharton. 2013. Brazil's Braskem Makes a Giant Bet on North America. http://knowledge.wharton.upenn.edu/article/brazils-braskem-makes-giant-bet-north-america/. Accessed 3 Nov 2017.

Manso, U.A. 2013. Universidade corporativa da CPFL Energia tem cinco campi. https://exame.abril.com.br/carreira/universidade-corporativa-da-cpfl-energia-tem-cinco-campi/. Accessed 10 Dec 2017.

Nunomura, E. 2017. É importante saber gerir os talentos que a sua empresa têm. https://exame.abril.com.br/negocios/e-importante-saber-gerir-os-talentos-que-a-sua-empresa-tem/. Accessed 11 Dec 2017.

OECD. 2007. Territorial Reviews. Madrid. Spain. P. 258.

Vendrame, A.C. 2017. Os efeitos da reforma trabalhista. http://www.gazetadopovo.com.br/opiniao/artigos/os-efeitos-da-reforma-trabalhista-7jthiury46556y2xrs1xk7gnj. Accessed 15 Dec 2017.

16

Argentina: Learning to Tango with Talent Management

Svetla Marinova and Daria Klishevich

The economic history of Argentina is somewhat ambiguous. Once, one of the largest economies in the world (1885–1930), since the Great Depression, Argentina has been constantly falling behind the developed economies (CIA Factbook, Argentina). The country started to develop industrially by the end of the 1880s with the cornerstones of the economy being agriculture and beef exports. A century later, in the 1980s, the protectionist, import substitution economic policy was abandoned and replaced with economic liberalization, restructuring and integration into the global economy. As a result, the domestic economy and local markets were opened up to foreign goods and foreign direct investment and this brought economic stability for about a decade (Figueiredo 2005).

S. Marinova (✉)
Aalborg University, Aalborg, Denmark
e-mail: svetla@business.aau.dk

D. Klishevich
Graduate School of Management, St. Petersburg State University,
St. Petersburg, Russia

© The Author(s) 2018
M. Latukha (ed.), *Talent Management in Global Organizations*,
Palgrave Studies of Internationalization in Emerging Markets,
https://doi.org/10.1007/978-3-319-76418-4_16

However, this economic stability was short-lived and the economy fell into a spiraling increase of inflation and economic instability (Ugarte 2017). Nevertheless, to date Argentina is the third largest economy in Latin America and it has a huge unrealized potential due to its economic volatility with periods of hyperinflation and financial crises. In May 2018, the interest rate rose to 40% in order to protect the Argentinian economy from another crisis and stabilize the Argentinian currency, the peso. Nevertheless, the International Monetary Fund forecasts a stable growth for Argentinian gross domestic product in the next five years, 2018–2022 (IMF Report 2017). There are several factors that could be the reason for such a forecast. Among them is Argentina's membership of the G20, which gives certain political preferences (there is only one other country in the region, which is also a member of the G20, Brazil), large reserves of gas and oil, and the high level of exports: Argentina is the second largest exporter in Latin America after Brazil (CIA Factbook, Argentina).

The labor market conditions in Argentina are continuously improving but face serious challenges. Diverse groups of the workforce have experienced uneven recovery from the consequences of the economic crisis of 2001 that significantly influenced the country's economic development (OECD 2017).

Talent management and human resource management (HRM) development in Argentina have been influenced by the volatile economy and controversial polity, especially after 2001. Many companies had to change their HRM strategies and resort to actions such as massive downsizing, reduction or elimination of financial bonuses, voluntary retirement, and curtailment of investment in trainings and corporate events. Some international companies even transferred key employees to production facilities abroad in order to preserve their skills (Figueiredo 2005). In the case of multinational companies (MNCs) with headquarters (HQs) located outside Argentina, it was especially challenging for local subsidiaries to negotiate action plans and employee transfers with their HQs, as the latter could not grasp the gravity of the local situation. As a result, some MNCs decided to regionalize the management of these subsidiaries and created shared service centers (Figueiredo 2005), thus restructuring their operations in Argentina and the region as a whole.

The labor market in Argentina suffers from excessively rigid employment protection legislation, which is an advantage for some employees and a disadvantage for others (OECD 2017). Partly due to this rigidity and partly to societal norms, there is a rather low rate of women in full-time, long-term employment (IMF Report Argentina 2017). According to OECD data, although Argentina has more flexible labor market regulations than other Latin America countries, there is still much space for improvement that would make it easier for people to obtain employment. A combination of more flexible labor market regulation and advanced training and counseling is argued to contribute to better labor-market flexibility and increased productivity and inclusiveness (OECD 2017).

The knowledge base of Argentinian human capital has increased over the past 15 years, but still the rate of increase of secondary education completion and of college degree awards has fallen behind that of other countries in the region. Half of the students enrolled in secondary education leave school without obtaining a degree, and less than 40% of Argentinians aged 25–34 receive college, university or technical school education (IMF Report Argentina 2017). This has an effect on the knowledge base and innovation potential of Argentina's young labor force.

The employee hiring process is characterized by both conventional and modern practices. According to a PricewaterhouseCooper's report, the most popular channels to identifying potential employees are references (24%), social networks (17%), online search sites (13%) and universities (13%) (Infobae 2014). These percentages are interesting as they demonstrate the importance of relationships and networks, as well as of personal and professional trust in the employment process. Notably, universities rate poorly as a possible channel for identifying potential candidates. The above also suggests that an employer may be more interested in the specific personal characteristics of a candidate indicating "personal potential and behavior" and then experience and education. Pablo Maison, Vice President of Human Resources for Latin America at Unilever, states: "First thing potential employers look at is personality, second—work experience, third—education. An insatiable desire to become a part of the company should be clearly expressed as well" (Bistagnino 2013).

Another Argentinian feature is word-of-mouth and its well-acknowledged importance in employee recruitment, which means that an informal conversation, talking to someone or a personal call has a lot more weight than a written recommendation, which is considered as impersonal. Thus, personal referrals and word-of-mouth may be really effective in connecting a potential employee to a target employer. This situation is sometimes exacerbated by managers hiring their friends, family members and "compadres", which may affect the effectiveness of a company's operations (Recruitment Intelligence Group 2017).

An important characteristic of the labor context in Argentina is the significant informal economy and the percentage of people working but not contributing to social security. Working "black" (*en negro*), after reaching its peak in the early 2000s, has decreased but is still rather high at around 30–40% (IMF Report Argentina 2017). The factors behind the significant informal sector are considered to be high labor taxation, which is quite a major burden for individuals and families. Another reason that reinforces the informal sector could be lack of access to quality education, and rigid labor market institutions (IMF Report Argentina 2017).

One of the significant features of the labor context in Argentina is the powerful role of trade unions. This can be explained by the fact that the first resettlers mainly came from Italy and Germany, countries with powerful trade unions at that time. Since trade unions have always played a crucial role in the country's political and economic life, HR departments constantly need to negotiate with trade union representatives and adjust companies' HR strategy based on the position supported by the respective trade unions. This, of course, gives a lot of protection for workers, while employers probably wish that trade unions play less of a role in companies.

Talent management is important in such a context as Argentinian companies have to adopt practices to motivate talented employees who could drive innovation, creativity and contribute to company performance As a consequence of the globalization of production and services, many more MNCs have entered and are currently operating in Argentina. Most of them apply talent management as part of their overall management policy. This attracts talented young specialist who aspire to work for such a company on completion of their education. Local companies are thus pushed to consider introducing and development talent management practices and polity in their organizational processes. Talent management requires a move away from a focus on traditional HR management issues such as labor costs, relationships with trade unions and handling employee documentation to a much more proactive role of HRM departments in recruitment, training, emphasis on innovation and personal contribution, and on career development and employee well-being. A new generation of HR managers in Argentina has started to promote balanced scorecard methods, enhanced communication channels within the company, non-financial promotion systems and so on. Companies are starting to actively seek talented young individuals who can join their workforce on graduation, whereas a decade ago experienced workers were more desirable for the majority of companies. However, such progressive and innovative practices in HRM are currently implemented by a limited number of Argentinian companies, mostly large ones, whereas nearly 70% of the labor force is employed in small- and medium sized enterprises (SMEs), which use traditional human resource management practices (Aldao-Zapiola 2014). Yet, although adoption of talent management practices is still in its infancy and they are just creeping into business behavior, their availability has indeed increased the attractiveness of the companies using them among university graduates and young professionals because such firms can offer a more structured and predictable path to career development.

In this chapter, we discuss the talent management strategy of three relatively large Argentinian companies, which play an important role in the Argentinian labor market: Ternium, Pampa Energia and Edenor. Because of their size and partly because of their international activities, they incorporate talent management practices that are similar to those of Western MNCs but with a certain local twist. Among the common talent management strategies that the three companies use are the attraction and development of young graduates and professionals coupled with an intensive training system for existing employees, and developing a new internal communication system comprising of various channels in order to encourage feedback.

Ternium: A Search for Young Talent

Ternium is one of the main steel producers in Latin America. It was founded in 2005 as a result of the merger of Siderar (Argentina), Sidor (Venezuela) and Hylsa (Mexico). Ternium produces finished and semi-finished steel products and iron ore. It is one of the largest steel companies in the Americas in terms of capacity, technology, product quality and client base. Ternium sells its products either directly to end-users or to steel manufacturers. It is a preferred supplier to clients from different industries, such as construction, automotive, manufacturing and small components production (Techint 2017).

The business of the company is divided into steel and mining segments. The former includes sale of steel products, whereas the latter specializes in the sale of iron ore. The steel segment covers Mexico, the Southern Region and smaller markets. In Mexico, Ternium is represented by its steel production equipment, service and allocation centers, and mining processes. In the Southern Region, Ternium focuses on steel production and service centers; and in smaller markets, Ternium has steel production, service and allocation centers. Overall, Ternium operates in 16 production centers in Latin and North America (Ternium Annual Report 2016).

Ternium is most active in Mexico, having substantial manufacturing facilities and assets there (Ternium Annual Report 2009). The wide range of steel production is represented by semi-finished steel products such as round bars, billets and slabs, used in further steel production. Ternium is a producer, but also a huge supplier of steel for the development of related industries such as construction of buildings, bridges and rails, production of consumer durables such as bicycles and cars, and hospital equipment, among others. Considering its key role in the steel market, Ternium invests in technological innovation and upgrading, and has established highly innovative production facilities to minimize the negative environmental impact of its production.

The business strategy of the company is to be a sustainability leader in the steel production industry by investing in technologically superior processes, continuous product quality enhancement and customer service (Record of the Annual Meeting of Shareholders 2017). Ternium's policy on quality is based on consistent and targeted efforts for quality improvement. This corresponds to the company's efforts to offer its clients high-quality products in order to retain existing customers and further expand its customer base. Such quality improvement is achieved by investment in research and development and in eco-friendly production processes (Ternium Annual Report 2016).

The company is client needs-focused; it emphasizes its adherence to clients' needs, promoting the idea that their own success is Ternium's success. In terms of HRM strategy, Ternium cites HR practices on improving the quality of life of its employees, the quality of working spaces and equipment, and environmental protection. More precisely, its HRM is a part of the universal quality management system that includes transparent relations with workers, customers and suppliers, customer satisfaction, improvement in working conditions and high-quality production (Ternium, Quality Policy 2016). Thus external objectives of customer satisfaction are aligned with the internal focus on quality of life and the work environment.

The fundamental HRM values for Ternium are excellence and continuous development of its human resources, which reflects awareness of the importance of its workforce and the need to train and retain talented employees. The talent management strategy of Ternium refers to procedures and practices in recruitment, training and development, employee experience and welfare, building a learning organization, and communication.

Professionalism, in addition to quality, is the other value that is central in the organizational culture of Ternium, and has a great influence on the company's development. To enhance professionalism, Ternium has embraced the goal of building an agile learning organization. There are several programs in the company that focus on diverse aspects in enhancing professionalism such as professional growth programs, scholarships, and fellowships to talented undergraduate and graduate students of engineering and the applied sciences in selected countries (Deloitte Global Human Capital Trends 2017).

As Ternium is an industrial company, it values a technical culture and industrial thinking. Hence, the company invests in technological and innovation training, which are key aspects in employees' talent development. As a result, Ternium has different investment innovation and technical skills programs. Young professionals are considered an invaluable asset that can bring innovative thinking and energy into the company. In order to engage new talent, the company financially supports university programs related to the steel industry. It also funds endowment chairs at some universities (Record of the Annual Meeting of Shareholders 2017).

Talent recruitment is supported by internships that are offered to the students of various Latin American universities in Ternium's different departments. The purpose of these is to attract young people with an interest in working in steel production and services who are offered the opportunity to experience work in the company and possibly use it as a gateway to future employment (Record of the Annual Meeting of Shareholders 2017). Another specifically designed program targeting young people is the two-year Young Professionals Program in which participants obtain basic management skills for integration into professional life and possible work in Ternium. In the first year, young professionals are allocated on a rotation principle to industrial plants, with at least two months' experience in production shifts. In the second year, young professionals get a chance to obtain a vacant position adequate to their profession, profile and interests.

Another talent management program aiming to enhance professionalism focuses on developing and retaining leading managers: the Leaders Training Program. The focus here is on the development of specific skills necessary in leadership positions. Apart from that, this program intends to improve the performance results of middle management in terms of communication with staff and their commitment to employee development. In 2016, this program had an emphasis on industrial management (Record of the Annual Meeting of Shareholders 2017).

Ternium has created different courses and training programs that aim to develop leadership and employee performance and technical knowledge. These programs encourage employees from different departments to stay up-to-date in their respective field in order to boost productivity and efficiency. In addition, the company supports a teamwork culture among its workers. Various practices such as team training programs and courses were implemented in order to reach this goal (Ternium Report of Foreign Private Issuer 2014).

The company positions itself as one that really cares about its employees' well-being as this is considered an incentive for the attraction and retention of staff. In this regard, Ternium has been developing specialized training programs for the prevention of serious accidents. The issue of safety is quite important in the company's HRM policies. For example, the sub-category "Careers" on the company's webpage presents two statements: support talent and safety first (Ternium website, Careers). Ternium focuses on industrial safety by diagnosing process hazards in steelmaking and steel processing and doing its best to help workers to avoid injuries (Ternium Report of Foreign Private Issuer 2016). In 2014, the World Steel Association recognized the company for its Preventive Logistics Safety Plan (World Steel Association 2014). The safety training program includes the redesign of activities targeting factory personnel and the implementation of activities for personnel in leadership positions. Moreover, the management of the company tries to engage employees in a dialogue by encouraging feedback and information flows on occupational safety conditions, potential risks and anomalies in order to implement possible solutions (Ternium Report of Foreign Issuer 2015).

Another issue related to staff well-being is the work-life balance focus of the firm. Its policies in this aspect are built upon the Flexible Working Programs that aim to match the professional and personal needs of employees. Here the company underlines its adherence to international corporate best practice in talent management.

Ternium has been encouraging production employees to engage more actively in shaping the company's talent management processes. Yet, their participation is still limited. In addition, the company faces difficulties in expanding talent management practices due to some resistance within the firm due to internal rivalry and limited access to education and training programs (Glassdoor 2017). These aspects need to be reconsidered by the HR department and overall leadership of Ternium in order to design appropriate strategies and follow up on actions to address them.

As Ternium operates subsidiaries in six countries (i.e. Mexico, Brazil, Argentina, Colombia, the United States and Guatemala), cultural issues often emerge. Cross-cultural competence building is therefore an area that needs special attention for improvement. The management of the company is predominantly Argentinian, and this creates a sense of misrepresentation for local people working in the company's subsidiaries. In order to reduce cross-cultural tensions, the company needs to develop and deliver management development programs for its non-Argentinian branches, which may allow local employees to be introduced into the company's management. Such programs may include training activities with the Argentinian management teams in order to transfer competences and best practice to local branches. Local employees should be given more learning opportunities and flexibility in designing the most appropriate communication approaches to raise concerns, come up with new ideas and improve practice.

Pampa Energia: Toward Excellence in the Working Environment to Inspire Talent Development

Pampa Energia S.A. (hereafter called Pampa) is an Argentinian energy company with a broad scope of commercial activities that include electricity distribution, generation and transmission, oil and gas. The company is one of the market leaders in generating, transmitting and distributing electricity across Argentina. Pampa's commercial activities are not limited to Argentina alone. The company has become a regional player through its pipeline operations. In 2016, Pampa Energia became the largest integrated energy utility company in Argentina through the acquisition of a controlling stake in Petrobras Argentina S.A. and in doing so, acquired a 9184 km-long pipeline network that transports gas across parts of Latin America (Thomson Reuters 2016).

The company was established in 1945 under the name Frigorífico La Pampa S.A. Interestingly, its commercial activities before 2005 were very different from what the company does now. Its operations were originally limited to warehouse ownership and development. In 2005, the private equity firm Grupo Dolphin acquired Frigorífico La Pampa and started a process of sector reorientation. In doing so, Grupo Dolphin essentially converted the company into a vehicle for its investment goals in Argentina. The name was changed to Pampa Energia so as to embrace the direction of a newfound aspiration: "to become the largest energy company in Argentina" (Pampa Energia Annual Report 2015).

Among the company's values are "entrepreneurial spirit, ethics, excellence, innovation, and social and environmental responsibility. Pampa treats its human capital as a key asset. Productive investments, offering quality services and abiding by high ethical standards are fundamental in securing enhanced operation performance" (Pampa Energia 2017).

Talent management practices are first reflected in hiring practices. Pampa encourages potential candidates to upload their CVs by creating a personal account on the company's official website. If the CV meets all specified requirements, the HR department contacts the applicant and invites him or her for an internal exam; if successful, the applicant is invited for an interview (Pampa Energia 2017).

Pampa invests in developing policies for attracting young specialists. For instance, it has a special program, called Scholarships for more Energy, awarded in conjunction with several Argentinian universities. Within the framework of this program, Pampa selects up to 12 students who study electromechanical engineering, industrial chemistry or engineering every year as recipients of scholarships. The selection criteria are the CVs, the results from the company's exams and a final interview (Pampa Energia Annual Report 2015). The company not only pays monthly scholarships to the winners of this program, but it also finances their education and provides an opportunity to do an internship at the one of the company's plants.

Its talent management includes a strong focus on developing employee skills and competences. The importance of this issue is underlined by the fact that Pampa has employees with subject- and process-specific knowledge that needs to be constantly upgraded or maintained. To do this, the company regularly conducts specialized training sessions for its engineers and service personnel through three types of events. First, communication, leadership and teamwork sessions where employees learn more about their personalities and are able to develop soft skills as well as leadership skills. Initially, this type of training was designed only for top-managers and directors of subsidiaries, but since 2015 have also been accessible to other workers (Pampa Energia Annual Report 2015). Thus, the company underlines its commitment to developing the leadership potential of key employees. The second type of training is workshops on segment-specific activities. These are designed for particular groups of workers, and cover changes in their working processes. For instance, when a new gas turbine was installed in one of the company's factories in 2015, a special workshop was organized in order to introduce staff to the new system and its technical features. The third type of training includes coaching and mentoring sessions (Pampa Energia Annual Report 2015).

Pampa aims to boost the effectiveness of employee teamwork and regularly holds workshops and contests which can help employees learn how to work in a team effectively. For instance, during one of the contests in 2016, called Building Education Energetically, several teams worked on projects, which could help local communities improve local infrastructure. The results of this event not only contributed to the community, but also provided employees with the opportunity to work in a team and develop their soft skills.

Pampa's salary system is not disclosed but there is information about salary levels and financial bonuses for Pampa's subsidiary, Transener. Employees are divided into five categories, according to which basic salary levels are organized. In addition to basic salary, the company has implemented a system called Extra Annual Remuneration for Meeting Goals, which helps to stimulate employees to work more effectively in order to earn an extra financial bonus. The system relies on a coefficient, which is calculated in relation to the corporate goals (30%), project goals (60%) and individual goals (10%). A list of corporate goals is yearly set by the Board of Directors, based on the current financial results and corporate strategy. Project goals include the objectives of a certain department or a project, which are determined by the supervisors. Individual goals aim to measure the degree of contribution, made by every worker. This criterion is crucial, since when a worker's rating is too low ("insufficient" or "regular"), he or she will not qualify for any bonus, regardless of the corporate or department's achievements (Report of the Ministry of Labor, Employment and Social Justice 2008).

Pampa actively works to sustain the image of a socially aware company and thus provides a variety of non-financial bonuses for its employees. It aims to retain talent and give them non-financial incentives to stay in the company. For instance, it has a special program which provides scholarships for the children of employees (Pampa Energia Annual Report 2015). If a child is already a student or wants to study electrical engineering, mechanical engineering, geology and so on, there is an opportunity to apply for a special scholarship from the company. Furthermore, Pampa provides a lot of benefits for women, who have recently become mothers, in order to keep talented female staff and to provide help in reaching a better work-life balance. The company pays for childcare in daycare centers or provides its employees with an opportunity to work at home or reduce the normal working hours.

The company's corporate culture reflects the talent management practices in the code of business conduct. All in all, it focuses on the creation of an atmosphere of mutual respect. Most importantly, senior managers should behave in a way that will be an example to their subordinates. Furthermore, they should pay special attention to the motivation and development of their colleagues, delegate responsibilities, and encourage initiatives. Pampa's corporate culture includes the suppression of any cases of work discipline violation, discrimination and financial crimes. That is why the company has developed its own hotline, which can be used by employees as an information channel to alert them to topics such as conflict, fraud, theft and so on, which are related to employee behavior in the workplace (Pampa Energia 2015). Moreover, if an employee considers that particular decisions may lead to a conflict, the HRM department should be contacted immediately in order to be informed and take steps for solving the issue.

Pampa operates a corporate intranet system (Pampa Energia Annual Report 2015) designed for communication and collaboration purposes among staff and working as an information channel for corporate events. The site is used for accepting employees' ideas and projects, which can be sent via a special form. It can also be used by the HR department to get feedback from staff members on various HR initiatives.

Talent management practices are faced with challenges that relate to the use of outsourcing for handling these. This might create ambiguity about the position and importance of talent management for the firm and may challenge the position of the company's own HRM department and its expertise to handle talent management internally.

Pampa's major HRM challenges are stipulated in its Annual Report and these are identified as mastering HRM through the SAP Success Factors and working with trade unions (Pampa Energia Annual Report

2015). In 2016, Pampa bought a majority stake in Petrobras Argentina, an Argentine-based subsidiary of Petroleo Brasileiro S.A. (Petrobras), thus, taking control over the company. By executing this transaction, Pampa became one of the most important, fully integrated energy companies in Argentina (Pampa Energia Website). In this regard, it is important to understand to what degree the acquisition affected employees in Pampa. We assume that the change in ownership might lead to a change in business operations and, thus, it might affect the number of jobs in the firm. In other words, the acquisition has created a challenge for Pampa's HR department, as some of Petrobras's qualified employees might be transited from Petrobras to Pampa and the probability of layoffs is high because there are two companies operating in the same industry.

An interesting detail of Pampa's Code of Business Conduct is that it states: "employees shall provide the superior officers with proper and true information about their activities. They shall give any information related to situations, facts, misbehaviors, fraud or cheating with a customer, with Pampa, suppliers or other persons" (Pampa Energia Annual Report 2017). Latin America is a complex region when it comes to dealing with compliance and transparent business practices, and high corruption levels are the most critical problem (Kleinhempel et al. 2010). Pampa has proclaimed its commitment "to comply with any and all anti-corruption laws that may be applicable to it" (Pampa Energia Website 2017) so the company recognizes the importance of this issue.

One of the major challenges that the company faces is related to the integration of the recently acquired subsidiary of Petrobras. The possible consequences here are the emotional strain of its own employees and those who have come from Petrobras stemming from uncertainties and internal organizational restructuring. The drawback of every acquisition is inevitable downsizing and Pampa's case is no exception. However, in this particular case the rift may not be so dramatic, because Petrobras will mostly preserve its operational independence. Nevertheless the company's HR specialists have developed approaches to deal with job redundancies and further resignations as retaining staff with specific knowledge may be a serious challenge to HRM that can be addressed by designing, for example, an appropriate promotion system.

Unlike Pampa, Petrobras Argentina does not have wide experience in organizing training or workshops for its employees as most of the events were previously held in Brazil. Hence, the acquisition is also an opportunity to introduce new employee training and other joint corporate activities. Pampa can use them as one of the integration mechanisms in gaining employee commitment.

To sum up, Pampa bases its talent management strategy on supporting professionalism, equality of all employees, fairness and a positive internal climate. The company actively offers its employees education, training and corporate events. To retain talents, it focuses on both financial and non-financial benefits. These measures testify the commitment of the company to enhancing its talent management practices. In order to encourage employee feedback, Pampa actively works in co-operation with a HRM outsourcing company, which complements its internal efforts in talent management with the goal of creating a trustworthy and productive working environment.

Edenor: Talent as a Key to Success

Edenor is part of Pampa Energia and with regard to talent management it has many similar practices. Edenor was founded in 1992 as a result of the privatization of the state-owned electricity utility company, Servicios Electricos del Gran Buenos Aires (SEGBA). The then Argentinian government granted Edenor a concession for the exclusive distribution of electricity for a period of 95 years with the possibility of an extension. In 1996, the company was named Empresa Distribuidora y Comercializadora Norte S.A. (Edenor S.A.). Today Pampa Energia has full control over the company (Edenor Website 2017).

Edenor is the leader in electricity distribution in Argentina and one of the biggest companies in South America by number of customers and volume of electricity sold. Edenor distributes up to 20% of the energy in the domestic market. All company operations and customers are based in Argentina. There are several groups of customers: residential, small/medium commercial, industrial, wheeling system and others (public lighting and shanty-town customers) (CFA Institute 2015).

Edenor provides professional services and its professionalism in doing so guarantees the efficiency and effectiveness of the company's operations. As the company has a modern technological infrastructure, a very important part of its work is training its employees to maintain this, and annually a lot is spent on financing it. Overall, Edenor considers its people its key success factor, helping it to achieve pre-set financial and social targets, which are briefly presented in its mission: "Socially responsible distribution and selling electricity to improve the life of people, to develop business and society, providing growth of the company, our employees and shareholders."

Edenor promotes and supports a diverse, friendly, co-operative and productive working environment. The company's goal is to achieve transparent relationships between all employees, and develop responsibility, honesty, respect and confidence (Edenor, Code of Ethics 2015). Edenor invests in its human capital, providing training to improve specific technical skills and knowledge and leadership qualities. The majority of the employees are working under the cover of one of two unions: general employees are members of the Electric Light and Power Labor Union and middle management are members of the Association of Supervisory Personnel. Those two unions provide workers with bargaining power and, consequently, working conditions acceptable to both sides. Although the Collective Bargaining Agreements have already expired, Edenor still follows the rules set in them not only with respect to unionized workers, but to not-unionized ones as well. Bargaining power is present, for example, in salary agreements, when Edenor increased salaries by 16% in April 2016 for all its workers (Edenor Annual Report 2015).

All its employees, including top-management, should use the Code of Ethics in their work; this was first created and incorporated in 1999 and renewed in 2012. The Code of Ethics includes behavioral principles and rules which are reflected in the following statement: "A correct conduct implies a professional, honest and equitable relationship with employees, customers, suppliers, members of the Board of Directors and Audit Committee and the public in general, inspired by respect for individuals and the society we belong to" (Edenor, Code of Ethics 2015). It also adheres to standards of non-discrimination, no alcohol and drugs, equality, non-conflict of interest and no bribery policies. The Code of Ethics envisages penalties for a failure to comply with it.

Talent attraction in Edenor includes collaboration with more than 30 Argentinian universities and colleges by means of the Scholarships for Young Technicians program (Edenor Annual Report 2015). Edenor first

Argentina: Learning to Tango with Talent Management   **315**

trains recently graduated technicians and then provides them with working places. All the company's departments are open to interns: production, sales, information technology, HR, finance and so on. The compensated internship is up to a year long and requires four hours a day of work under the supervision of a tutor. Apart from that, the company always participates in university and college career forums and others career events in order to give young talent information about the company and their career prospects in it.

The development of current staff is realized through several training programs, which are included in the Annual Training Plan and consist of two main modules: a strategic development module and an operational development module. Most of the training programs were created in collaboration with external partners such as business schools and universities. The objective of operational training is to develop specific skills needed to work with new technologies, embrace safety standards and responsibility, and focus on the customer and sustainable development. One of the modules in this program is Occupational Safety – Electric Risk. The objective of the strategic module is to prepare employees for challenges related to risk and safety standards. The leadership program targets employees at all management levels and provides them with an open space for communication and debate. It is meant to develop internal recruitment. Job vacancies are first proposed to staff members as this is considered a motivational tool that can provide career progression and job satisfaction. Apart from salaries and career development, the management is trying to motivate people using corporate events, such as children's days (e.g. a photo safari for employees' children), soccer and bowling, tennis and paddle tournaments. Health policies are also addressed in Edenor. In addition to complimentary medical insurance, there are also medical examination programs and psychological support (Edenor Annual Report 2015). The program is improving both employees' lives and their attitude toward the company and the company's internal problem of absenteeism caused by sickness is becoming less of an issue.

Communication in Edenor is through the intranet and a physical and digital bulletin board, which makes it possible not only to inform employees about company news, but also to collate complaints and proposals from production workers to managers. The company has a regular magazine, *A toda luz* and the weekly "Flash Informativo Seminal" news reports. In order to improve the working environment, the company launched a large survey, outsourced to the consulting company Hay Group, enquiring about the level of commitment, the support provided by the organization and the effectiveness in achieving business results (Edenor Annual Report 2015).

The results of the survey reveal some problems and challenges, such as dissatisfaction with the work environment, surplus of managerial staff, absenteeism, retention and the reward system (Edenor Annual Report 2015). Thus, being a company that strives to be employee-oriented, Edenor has to solve various issues identified by its staff. Some of those issues are embedded in the economic context of Argentina. Other challenges may have a more complex nature. The company is likely to put effort into addressing the first issue identified: according to the survey, only about half of the employees, namely 48%, were satisfied with their work environment, whereas 24% were neutral and 28% were dissatisfied. A sense of comfort in the workplace is a multifaceted issue, as it concerns not just the physical comfort of facilities, but also emotional comfort. The latter relates to the atmosphere at work and the opportunities for employees to exchange opinions with colleagues and senior staff, which may be of particular importance to a firm's employees where the sense of community and family values is deeply rooted in social beliefs and routines.

* * *

Talent management in Argentina is an important part of company strategy—but it is still confined to mostly large enterprises who are carefully introducing it into their HRM practices. The three companies we consider in this chapter are among the leaders in their respective sector in Argentina and as such need to attract and retain talented employees who can secure the companies' competitive position. They all have some talent management practices, but their steps to developing a systematic approach to talent management are still a bit unsure and slightly off rhythm when learning to tango with talent management. A popular option is co-operation with universities, by means of which these companies establish contact with talented students and expose them to the business context via internships. The focus on young talent is present in the three studied companies, and this reflects the contemporary talent management development trend that aims to attract talented individuals from a young age and integrate them into the company environment.

Talent retainment boosts professionalism and raises the importance of following safety requirements via various training courses. Employees are offered flexible working hours and opportunities for a better work-life balance. Online and offline internal communication channels connect employees in order to ensure communication flows and allow managers to be informed about the issues that workers face.

These practices reflect the complexity in Argentina's volatile, uncertain, complex and unpredictable domestic business environment and attempt to safeguard fundamental social values, but also try to develop greater transparency in employment relations and more open and accessible job prospects for young talent in Argentina.

References

Aldao-Zapiola, C. 2014. Chapter 2: A Century of Human Resource Management in Argentina. In *The Development of Human Resource Management Across Nations*, ed. B. Kaufman, 21–45. Cheltenham: Edward Elgar Publishing.

Bistagnino, P. 2013. Pablo Maison: "La generación Y ya se adueña de todo". www.infobae.com/2014/04/07/1555646-atraer-y-retener-los-empleados-alto-potencial-es-prioridad-las-empresas/. Accessed 5 Mar 2017.

CFA Institute. 2015. https://www.ucema.edu.ar/sites/default/files/2016/ucema_edenor.pdf. Accessed 13 May 2017.

CIA Factbook, Argentina. Last modified January 17, 2018. www.cia.gov/library/publications/resources/the-world-factbook/geos/ar.html. Accessed 17 Jan 2017.

Deloitte Global Human Capital Trends. 2017. https://www2.deloitte.com/content/dam/Deloitte/global/Documents/About-Deloitte/central-europe/ce-globalhuman-capital-trends.pdf. Accessed 11 Jan 2018.

Edenor Annual Report. 2015. http://www.edenor.com/cms/files/EN/IR/financialReports/annualReports/2015AnnReport.pdf. Accessed 16 July 2017.

Edenor Code of Ethics. 2015. http://www.edenor.com/cms/files/EN/IR/P32-Code-of-Ethics.150216.pdf. Accessed 19 Mar 2017.

Edenor Webpage. About Edenor. http://www.edenor.com.ar/cms/EN/EMP/IR/ACE_contexto.html. Accessed 12 Feb 2017.

Figueiredo, R.A. 2005. Human Resource Management in Argentina. In *Managing Human Resources in Latin America: An Agenda for International Leaders*, ed. M. Elvira and A. Davila, 97–111. New York: Routledge.

Glassdoor. https://www.glassdoor.com/Overview/Working-at-Ternium-EI_IE40502.11,18.htm. Accessed 15 Aug 2017.

IMF Report. 2017. http://www.imf.org/en/Publications/CR/Issues/2017/12/29/Argentina-Selected-Issues-45531. Accessed 5 June 2017.

Infobae. 2014. Atraer y retener a los empleados de alto potencial es prioridad para las empresas. www.infobae.com/2014/04/07/1555646-atraer-y-retener-los-empleados-alto-potencial-es-prioridad-las-empresas/. Accessed 5 Jan 2018.

Kleinhempel, S., S. Nitchi, and L. Rusu. 2010. Business Process Management in Service Oriented Companies. *Informatica Economica* 14 (3): 189–198.

OECD Economic Survey Argentina. 2017. Accessed 5 Jan 2018. www.oecd.org/eco/surveys/Argentina-2017-OECD-economic-survey-overview.pdf. Accessed 12 Sept 2017.

OECD, Latin American Economic Outlook. 2017. Youth, Skills and Entrepreneurship. www.keepeek.com/Digital-Asset-Management/oecd/development/latin-american-economic-outlook-2017_leo-2017-en#page258.

Pampa Energia Annual Report. 2015. http://ir.pampaenergia.com/pampaenergia/web/conteudo_en.asp?idioma=1&tipo=23405&conta=44. Accessed 23 Dec 2017.

———. 2017. https://ri.pampaenergia.com/wpcontent/uploads/sites/18/2018/05/PESA-2017-12-EEFF-CONSOLIDADOS-memoria-IA-ICF-ingl%C3%A9s.pdf. Accessed 4 Mar 2018.

Pampa Energia Website. Vision, Mission and Values. http://www.pampaenergia.com/en/about-us/vision-mission-and-values. Accessed 4 July 2017.

Pampa Energia Website. Jobs. http://www.pampaenergia.com/en/jobs. Accessed 5 July 2017.

Recruitment Intelligence Group. 2017. www.recruitment-intelligence-group.com/how-to-recruit/in-argentina. Accessed 21 Apr 2017.

Techint. www.techint.com/en/ternium.aspx. Accessed 18 Feb 2017.

Ternium. 2017. Record of the Annual Meeting of Shareholders. https://www.sec.gov/Archives/edgar/data/1342874/000161577417001172/s105620_6k.htm. Accessed 8 Aug 2017.

———. 2016. https://terniumcomprod.blob.core.windows.net/wp-content/2017/11/EEFF-Siderar-Dic16.pdf. Accessed 7 Mar 2017.

Ternium Annual Report. 2009. https://issuu.com/ternium/docs/annual_report_2009. Accessed 20 Dec 2017.

Ternium Careers. http://www.ternium.com/en/careers/. Accessed 12 Aug 2017.

Ternium Quality Policy. 2016. https://terniumcomprod.blob.core.windows.net/terniumcom20/2016/06/ter_pol_calidad_2014_Carta-ENG.pdf. Accessed 8 Aug 2017.

Ternium Report of Foreign Issuer. 2015. https://www.sec.gov/Archives/edgar/data/1342874/000161577416005160/s103120_form6k.htm. Accessed 18 Nov 2017.

Ternium Report of Foreign Private Issuer. 2014. http://www.barchart.com/plmodules/?module=secFilings&filingid=9883527&type=CONVPDF&popup=1&override=1&symbol=TX. Accessed 10 Aug 2017.

———. 2016. https://www.sec.gov/Archives/edgar/data/1342874/000129281416004027/terniumfs2015_6k.htm. Accessed 10 Sept 2017.

Ternium, Report of the Ministry of Labor, Employment and Social Justice. 2008. http://servicios.infoleg.gob.ar/infolegInternet/anexos/150000-154999/150241/norma.htm. Accessed 29 Nov 2017

Ternium Website. About Us. http://www.ternium.com/en/about-us/. Accessed 15 Aug 2018.

Thomson Reuters. 2016. Pampa Energia Company Profile. https://www.reuters.com/finance/stocks/overview/PAM.BA. Accessed 22 Nov 2017.

Ugarte, Sebastian M.S.M. 2017. The Gender Pay Implications of Institutional and Organisational Wage-Setting Practices in Banking – A Case Study of Argentina and Chile. *International Journal of Human Resource Management* 28 (18): 2594–2621.

World Steel Association, Safety and Health Recognition Programme. 2014. https://www.worldsteel.org/en/dam/jcr:3598f733-cc73-46d8-bc55-90f45a5725b4/Safety+%2526+Health+recognition+programme+2014.pdf. Accessed 12 Nov 2018.

17

Chile: Terra Incognita

Andrei Panibratov, Maria Laura MacLennan, and Gabriel Vouga Chueke

The Chilean economy is the sixth largest economy in Latin America by gross domestic product (GDP) and the seventh largest by purchasing power parity (World Economic Outlook 2015). Chile has the highest GDP per capita in South America and is classified by the World Bank as a high-income state. It has one of the fastest growing economies in Latin America, growing at an average annual rate of above 5% since 1990. It is the only country in the region where there has been no deterioration in social conditions recently, and it is the least-corrupt country in Latin America (World Bank 2018). Although the economy has been steadily

---

A. Panibratov (✉)
Graduate School of Management, St. Petersburg State University,
St. Petersburg, Russia

M. L. MacLennan
Centro Universitario FEI, São Bernardo do Campo, Brazil
e-mail: mferranty@fei.edu.br

G. Vouga Chueke
Brazilian Multinationals Observatory, University of São Paulo,
São Paulo, Brazil

© The Author(s) 2018
M. Latukha (ed.), *Talent Management in Global Organizations*,
Palgrave Studies of Internationalization in Emerging Markets,
https://doi.org/10.1007/978-3-319-76418-4_17

growing, the fall in copper prices has had a persistent effect on GDP growth (IMF Report 2015). Moreover, after 2014 the country faced rising unemployment and fiscal imbalances. Chile is characterized by a strong and transparent financial system and is rich in natural resources (Bajpai 2015).

As the country relies on the export of commodities to a great extent and they are one of the key contributors to economic growth, Chile faces a challenging external environment. The lower demand for copper from China coupled with falling prices led to the depreciation of the Chilean peso. This has led economists to argue that the country should be more proactive in diversifying its economy and in enhancing productivity in order to be less vulnerable to external pressures (OECD Chile Policy Priorities 2015).

In recent years, Chile has shown a positive labor market performance especially in terms of unemployment rates. Despite generally optimistic statistics, the labor market is characterized by strong inequalities. Women's labor market participation is among the lowest in the Organization for Economic Co-operation and Development (OECD) and young people find it very challenging to find a first job (OECD Chile Policy Priorities 2015), although reforms and programs have been designed to improve the labor market prospects for these social groups (OECD Latin American Economic Outlook 2017). The government tries to improve the situation with regard to women's unemployment by means of different initiatives. One of them is the Bono al Trabajo la Mujer Program, which was created to increase women's engagement in the labor market (Gasparini and Marchionni 2015). In 2009, in-work benefits (Subsidio al Empleo Joven) were introduced to increase youth employment. Through this, employers could get one-third of the benefit once they hired young people between 18 and 25 years old, whose families belong to the 40% of the poorest in the country (OECD Economic Survey Chile 2013). The public employment service (Servicio Nacional de Capacitación y Empleo, SENCE) aims to provide young people with training to increase their employability. MásCapaz is another training program aimed at making the labor market more accessible to youth and women (OECD Chile Policy Priorities 2015).

The Chilean labor market is segmented, with many workers being in non-regular work arrangements. It is characterized by duality of the formal and informal sectors that widens wage inequality (IMF Report Chile 2015). Another problem is temporary employment, as this accounts for 28.7% of all employment, compared to the OECD average of 11.2% (OECD 2016). Sometimes temporary contracts can provide a source of flexibility both for firms and for workers, but if they are too many they can be a source of job insecurity, demotivating employers to invest in education and training, and causing them to avoid insurance, social and pension contributions. Such a composition of the labor market is seen as a challenge to the economic growth of the country and to talent development. Attempts have been made to increase inclusiveness and equality of the labor market and a labor market reform started in 2016. It intends to modernize labor relations and has its major focus on collective bargaining, broadening negotiable topics and implementing a female quota of at least 30% among the respective labor union representatives. The effects of the reform are still to be seen (Sustainable Governance Indicators 2017).

Human capital development is recognized by the government as an important ingredient that contributes to the economic growth of the country. Therefore, in 2014 a reform of the education system was launched to tackle the relatively low number of average schooling years of the labor force—12% lower than the OECD average (IMF Report Chile 2015). The aim of the reform is to make the educational system more inclusive and to improve the quality of education while fostering human capital development (OECD Chile Policy Priorities 2015).

Chilean society is characterized by cultural and social idiosyncrasies that influence the overall labor context and may explain the developmental path of talent management in the country. As in most Latin American countries, paternalism, which was historically related to the relationship between a landlord and tenant farmers, persists as an inherent aspect of Chilean labor relations (Rodriguez and Rios 2009). Another distinct trait is authoritarianism of the organizational culture in Chile, which results in organizational hierarchy and a lack of equality. Authoritarianism, together with increasing individualism, leads to double-talk[1] between managers

---

[1] "double-talk has been identified as a relevant aspect for understanding labour relations and HRM in Chile, where managers and employees tend to show an ambiguous image of themselves and where discourse and reality can be very different".

and employees (Arrau 2008). The Chilean context also demonstrates low levels of interpersonal trust, which is generally typical for Latin America, but especially present in Chile. Some scholars explain it as a combination of weak social bonds, the influence of past dictatorships, modernization processes and the growing subjective feeling of insecurity (Arrau et al. 2012). All these aspects influence the way human resources are treated in Chilean companies. Talent management policies in Chile are quite close to the "hard model" of talent management where cost-effectiveness is the focus. Moreover, talent management is characterized by the combination of rational human resource management (HRM) practices with a strong Chilean cultural influence. This may be attributed to the general trend observed in Latin American economies where talent management comprised of its softer issues of attracting and retaining talent gradually infiltrates talent management policies. Apart from that, talent management in Chile is highly influenced by company size: obviously, smaller organizations are associated with greater informality and personal touch coupled with lower professionalism in HRM. Human resource management is highly unequal, as is the labor market itself: along with a high proportion of low-paid and undesirable jobs, there is a professional and prestigious sector where competition for talent exists. As a result, talent management practices are very different in these two contexts (Rodriguez et al. 1999).

The general perception of the level of talent management practices in Chilean corporations is rather controversial: scholars and practitioners argue that the reason for that is the lack of concern for talent management that hinders its development. Others suggest that the prevalence of a decision-led approach, acceptance of discrimination, a low level of trust and limited understanding of the need for talent management are to be blamed.

Nevertheless, this chapter shows examples of companies that have embraced talent attraction and retention practices in order to enhance their competitiveness. Firstly, there is some optimism relating to the methods that companies are starting to use with regards to managing people. There are many examples of a transition from the authoritarian, distrustful, and paternalistic culture to a more democratic, open and less bureaucratic one (Rodriguez et al. 1999). An increase in empowerment, rising wages for high performers and the introduction of corporate social responsibility principles along with moderate changes in the culture of attracting and rewarding employees are indicative of the slow shift from more traditional to talent management HRM practices. An important symbol of this shift is the creation of awards for companies that provide better labor relations and working conditions: for example, the award of the Carlos Vial Espantoso Foundation (Fundación Carlos Vial Espantoso 2017) for small and medium enterprises that succeeded in creating fair and comfortable working environments for their employees. This process may have been encouraged by the publicly available list of the best companies to work for in Chile provided by the American Great Place to Work Institute. Nevertheless, the existence of such awards suggests that Chilean companies have started to recognize human resource strategies as important, and talent management is the very tool that aims to develop practices to make the workplace comfortable and enables companies to embrace specific approaches to attract and retain the best talent.

We provide examples of three Chilean companies that have recognized the importance of talent management in their own distinctive ways.

Banco de Chile: Talent in History

Banco de Chile is a Chilean bank and provider of financial services. Founded in 1893 through a merger of three major Chilean banks, throughout its history this bank was among the largest Chilean banks in terms of assets, revenue and profit. Nowadays it is the second largest bank in the country by assets and the largest bank by profit. The bank operates in the United States, Bolivia, Argentina, Brasil, Mexico and Hong Kong. It is controlled by Citigroup Inc. through its subsidiaries, LQ SA and LQ SimCity; the group owns 26.2% of its equity directly and 24.2% indirectly, so effectively, the bank is an arm of Citigroup Inc. (Banco de Chile Annual Report 2015). At the beginning of the twentieth century, the bank was completely consolidated in Chile and became the most important commercial bank in the country. Since its very foundation, the bank has been the most stable financial organization in the country in terms of return on assets, profitability and market capitalization.

The bank structures its business into four segments in order to meet the expectations of different groups of clients through a differentiated business model tailored to each segment and thus develops a value proposition for each customer group. The segments are retail banking, wholesale banking, treasury and money markets, and subsidiaries (Banco de Chile Annual Report 2015).

Banco de Chile's main principles are trust, strength and security. It pays a lot of attention to client security and stability of performance, claiming to be the strongest and safest bank in Latin America. The bank emphasizes its importance in the country because it has been a part of Chilean history for "more than 120 years" (Banco de Chile 2013).

The bank names fairness, loyalty, commitment, responsibility, respect and, most of all, pursuit of excellence as its corporate values. Its goal is to be known as a provider of excellent services in a high-quality workplace, and it demonstrates awareness of the need for effective talent management. In order to reach this goal, in 2014 Banco de Chile designed a three-year plan focused on four elements: ethical behavior, performance management, Banco de Chile style and human capital, for the best bank. The realization of the plan includes attracting best professionals, entry courses and processes for new employees, creating best-performing teams, and internal mobility plans (Banco de Chile Annual Report 2014).

The mission of the bank manifests in the provision of excellent financial services with creative and effective solutions for each customer segment to ensure value growth for shareholders. This illustrates what the company needs from its employees—ideas and creative input—which is included in each job description. To ensure that these criteria are met, the bank focuses on implementing an effective hiring process, which can last up to a month. Within this process, there are interviews which include psychological and specially devised tests for professional skills (for example, for information technology specialists) and an interview with a potential working group leader (Glassdoor, Banco de Chile 2017). Most of the employees have a strong academic background and have studied at Universidad de Chile, Pontifical Universidad Catolica de Chile and Universidad de Santiago de Chile, which are among the 10 best Chilean universities (Chilean University Ranking 2018).

One of the inherent parts of talent management in the company is connected to its strong brand image. Employees of Banco de Chile are introduced to the "Banco de Chile History Book" and gradually learn about the bank's history. The reputation of the bank is outstanding and employees are proud to belong to an institution that considers environmental and societal issues an integral part of its work. For instance, Banco de Chile is the major sponsor of Teletón, an annual charity event in Chile which aims to raise funds for children with disabilities (Teletón 2017).

The talent management practices of Banco de Chile pay special attention to training, coaching and workshops. The bank provides training on leadership and professional skills to 10,000 employees (more than a third of all its employees) every year, and further training mostly to middle-level managers and interns. In addition, it offers workshops on ethics and corporate culture to promote corporate values and establish better internal communication (Banco de Chile Annual Report 2015).

Among the positive features of the organization are the supportive work environment, good health insurance, complex and challenging projects, a competitive salary, professionalism of co-workers and an overall great experience at work. Many employees compare the members of their team to a family, despite a low level of interpersonal trust in the Chilean work culture (Glassdoor 2017). The bank rewards its employees with monthly bonuses for meeting pre-set goals, which is an additional motivation factor to balance their intense workload. In 2017, the bank won third place in the ratings of the companies with the best corporate reputation in Chile (Monitor Empresarial de Reputación Corporativa 2017).

Banco de Chile is an employer with a strong reputation and a large company that strives to create an excellent working environment to boost employee creativity and productivity. However, as with any big company, its size and rigidity of organizational structure may be a liability, which is typical for the banking sector when it comes to hierarchical structures and communication channels. The consequence of such a structural composition might be a lack of co-operation between employees and bottlenecks in communication. Banco de Chile puts effort in transparently communicating its results and being accountable to the public. Its establishment of a corporate social network might help facilitate internal communication and enable people from different organizational levels and departments to exchange ideas and information.

Another aspect of the talent management strategy of Banco de Chile is its focus on intern training and development of middle-level managers. All in all, Banco de Chile has a talent management strategy that involves a good system of compensation, sustaining the bank's strong brand and offering diverse development possibilities for its middle management.

CSAV: Talent Management Recognition

Sud Americana de Vapores S.A. (CSAV) is a shipping group based in Chile. The company was founded in 1872. Its main business is maritime cargo transport, mainly containers. It also transports automobiles and liquid bulk cargo. These operations are carried out directly by the company and through its subsidiaries, associates and joint ventures in different countries (CSAV Annual Report 2016). In 2014, the firm was ranked twentieth within the global container industry measured by capacity. CSAV provides container shipping services and other feeder services. The company operates through a commercial network in 115 countries, generating more than 90% of its revenue through its own agencies (CSAV Annual Report 2016).

Historically viewed, CSAV's path may be divided into four distinct periods. The first period is from its establishment till 1914. The second stage marks a time of growth and development from 1914 until the beginning of the 2000s. During this time, various historical opportunities and the merger with Sudamericana Agencias Aéreas y Marítimas S.A. (SAAM) in 1961 gave the company an opportunity to grow and expand its activities to more countries. The third period was a consequence of the crisis in 2008. The company experienced the impact of the world economic crisis, which heavily affected the global shipping industry. For the first time, there was a significant decrease in demand for shipping. Following the crisis, a new recovery period started to financially strengthen and restructure the company's operations. The most important change occurred in 2011, when Quiñenco,[2] a large Chilean conglomerate, purchased a stake in the company. CSAV was restructured and began searching for strategic partners to develop its maritime businesses. As a result, in 2014 it merged with Hapag-Lloyd AG (HLAG). In 2016, there was a further merger of HLAG with the United Arab Shipping Company S.A.G. (UASC). This transaction consolidates HLAG and CSAV as one of the five largest container shipping companies in the world (CSAV Roadmap Presentation 2017).

All in all, significant structural changes have taken place in the industry, moving toward greater joint operations between liners, a greater focus on operational efficiency and a greater percentage of owned vessels (CSAV Roadmap Presentation 2013). CSAV is now facing a new stage which includes efficiency improvement programs, several merges with partners and further restructuring, which could lead to changes in its internal and external processes.

Originally, CSAV offered shipping services for vehicles, refrigerated bulk cargo and liquid and dry bulk cargo. However, after the merger with HLAG, most of these services were transferred to HLAG, leaving CSAV to mainly focus on car carrier services. Its main markets are Chile and Peru. In addition, CSAV provides freight forwarding and logistics services throughout the world for all types of cargo through its subsidiary Norgistics. The main contribution to the company's business is provided by Norgistics, CSAV and HLAG (CSAV Annual Report 2005)

CSAV has more than 140 years of history and is one of the oldest shipping companies in the world. The mission of CSAV Group is to trade in the maritime navigation and transportation business, profitably and responsibly. Principles of conduct that CSAV adheres to are to draw the routes, guide the acts and govern the conduct of its personnel to serve the company's mission and ensure proper behavior and compliance with regulations. Having a diverse profile, CSAV needs strict control and regulations to integrate its different units so that they follow the overall strategic requirements and focus on achieving CSAV Group's core performance objectives (CSAV Group Code of Corporate Compliance and Ethics 2014).

---

[2] Quiñenco is a Chilean diversified business conglomerate that includes companies in financial, food and beverage, manufacturing, energy, transport and port services sectors. http://www.quinenco.cl/eng/nosotros.php. Accessed January 10, 2018.

Talent management in CSAV follows a common pattern in the Chilean labor market, as it lacks recognition. CSAV is a large company and is an attractive employer for the Chilean workforce. In spite of this, the talent management practices of CSAV are not very visible and remain out of public focus. The important peculiarity here is the fact that CSAV has become a truly international company with foreign subsidiaries abroad which, on one the hand, suggests that the company should enhance its level of control to be able to handle multiple processes. This, in turn, leads to a more hierarchical organizational structure that does not tend to develop the horizontal linkages vital for talent management. On the other hand, the recent mergers are likely to bring new talent management practices into the company and influence the way it treats its employees.

In light of these assumptions, we discuss the talent management practices of CSAV together with the approaches used in one of its international subsidiaries, HLAG, since the latter represents a significant part of the CSAV group in its current organizational format. CSAV itself supposedly allocates the preliminary part of the hiring process to recruitment agencies as information on possible career opportunities is not presented on the company's website. Employee feedback suggests that the recruitment process in CSAV is easy and relatively quick (Glassdoor 2014). The hiring process in HLAG is transparent: potential candidates are invited to apply by uploading a CV onto the company's sites. The process of finding appropriate information and figuring out the whole application procedure is comprehensible and easily accessible, which shows a positive attempt to attract new talent.

In contrast to Banco de Chile where there are not many communication channels, in CSAV this aspect is given much room though with caveats. The communication structure in CSAV includes several elements. Firstly, there are meetings organized by the CSAV Group on a regular basis, at least once a month. In 2015, the company organized 14 meetings related to various aspects of the company's working life such as the approval of the annual report, selecting external audit firms, reviewing the organizational structure of the Internal Control Department, reviewing employee remuneration and compensation plans and so on. In all cases, the briefings were held by the board of directors and the chief executive officer. There was no participation by representatives from the functional levels or any CSAV departments, which actually mirrors the hierarchical structure of the company.

Secondly, there are more participative channels of communication in CSAV that have one particular focus: they all aim to give the various stakeholders in the company a tool to communicate information about events or behavior that are illegal, irregular, unethical or may give rise to conflicts of interest. This function is allocated to the Ethical Line, a particular email address which can be used by employees. The Grievance System on the company's website is designed to make a room for any person to articulate or report on inappropriate or illegal behavior in CSAV (CSAV Code of Ethics 2014; CSAV Grievance System 2018). Thus, communication in the company has a very distinct focus on the prevention of any cases of misbehavior, any illegal practices or conflicts of interest.

Employee feedback suggests that the working environment does have positive characteristics and they concern the work-life balance as well as friendly colleagues. The comfortable working environment and good working opportunities are highly appreciated (Glassdoor 2016). These aspects, together with a reputable company brand, are key tools used in recruitment and employee retention.

In comparison to the practices of CSAV, its subsidiary HLAG demonstrates another talent management strategy that is more visibly presented and communicated to employees. HLAG fosters a more open culture and encourages employees' engagement using benefits concerning various aspects of employees' lives, such as providing insurance, caring about health and wellness, as well as their financial state and retirement, and providing conditions for a family-work balance. This may be attributed to the fact that the original German company orients itself toward Western talent management practices of raising commitment, ensuring well-being and enhancing the image of the company as being of added value for potential employees. It remains to be seen whether CSAV will adopt some of the more-transparent and less-formalized talent management strategies inspired by its subsidiary or stick to its own culturally embedded approach.

Concha y Toro: Your Well-Being – Our Global Lead

Viña Concha y Toro (also referred to as Concha y Toro) was founded by Don Melchor Concha y Toro (a Chilean politician and businessman). In 1933, its shares were traded on the Santiago Stock Exchange, and its first exports were made to Holland. In 1957, a complete modernization of the company was initiated by Eduardo Guilisasti Tagle who set the production base needed for the company's expansion. The 1990s marked the beginning of a strong international expansion, still relevant today. It involves the acquisition of vineyards, increasing production capacity and introducing the most modern wine-making and cellar processes aiming to get the best quality in all lines of wine. In 1994, Viña Concha y Toro became the first winery in the world to trade its shares on the New York Stock Exchange. In 1996, the company expanded its business to Argentina with the foundation of Trivento Bodegas y Viñedos in Mendoza. In 1997, Concha y Toro signed an agreement on the creation of a joint venture with the French winery Baron Philippe de Rothschild to produce Almaviva, a wine category equivalent to the French Grands Crus Classes. The years 2008 and 2009 witnessed the creation of VCT Brasil and VCT Nordics (Concha y Toro History 2017).

The business strategy of the company aims at an increase in sales, participation and market share. The vision of Viña Concha y Toro is being a leading global brand wine company and thus, the idea of its global positioning underpins the strategy of the company which is articulated in one sentence: "Concha y Toro is the largest Latin American wine producer and the seventh largest in the world". Export activities of the company represent 68% of all sales (Concha y Toro 2014). The greatest success here is attributed to Casillero del Diablo, the company's brand that has world recognition and has entered a strategic alliance with Manchester United as an official wine partner of the team (Concha y Toro 2014). The other milestone of the company is the creation of a vertically integrated model from planting to marketing. The company has developed a broad portfolio of multiorigin wines from Chile, Argentina and the United States in order to meet the needs of diverse and demanding customer profiles and to be present at several price-points in the markets in which it participates

Concha y Toro has been successful internationally, becoming a symbol of Chilean wine in the world. It is recognized by the most prestigious publications. It has 16 awards as the Winery of the Year in *Wine & Spirits* and became the Most Powerful Wine Brand, according to Intangible Business (June, 2014). The sustainability strategy of the company embraces three areas: economic aspects (business value chain, supply chain, products and customers), social aspects (Concha y Toro employees and society) and environmental aspects (the environmental pillar) (Concha y Toro Sustainability Strategy 2018).

The talent management practices of the company are based on its strong brand and the desire to expand its operations globally. It is noticeable that the company is aware that the sound brand itself is able to attract talented employees but it can hardly help in retaining talent. That is why in its human resource management the company cares about its employees in order to create long-term relationships with them. Concha y Toro understands the importance of attracting and retaining talented and committed people. It constantly tries to improve talent management by providing employees with training and education, 360-degree analysis of individual contributions, assessment of the co-operation between employees and its influence on the success of the company.

The recruitment process at the company includes various approaches. Potential employees can use the direct application procedure on the official website, or they can apply by addressing the specialized recruiting portals. The recruitment process depends on the position a person applies for. Most often, it consists of a CV screening and several rounds of interview. Apart from that, for some positions (e.g. sales manager), the process includes a psychological test. Concha y Toro also uses the services of a head-hunting agency to find and select new talent, and it illustrates the active approach of the company to talent management as it relies on diversified methods for attracting new employees.

The focus of talent management in Concha y Toro is on the well-being of employees and their families that results in high levels of commitment toward the company. The well-being of employees is targeted by various programs that aim to make employees happier with their work through different tools.

The well-being of staff is secured through respect for the rights of individuals and non-discriminatory policies that are stated in the new version of the company's Code of Ethics and Conduct introduced in 2012. The main principles outlined in this document are respect for fundamental human rights, non-discrimination, orientation of the company toward quality, the importance of comfortable working conditions and environmental protection. The Code of Ethics and Conduct fosters an atmosphere of mutual respect and recognition that leads to stronger commitment. Thus, the company promotes equality of opportunity and treatment within the organization, regardless of ethnicity, gender, religion, nationality, marital status, age, political beliefs, sexual orientation or disability. All employees have access to the corporate intranet, which creates an opportunity to communicate with everyone, including the company's management.

The well-being of employees is secured by means of various programs that seek to individually approach every worker given his or her needs and concerns. The programs are sports championships, vacation programs and competitive funds. Apart from that, the well-being of workers is fostered by means of ensuring their health and operational safety. Concha y Toro co-operates with the Chilean Safety Association (ACHS) and conducts training on safety and health measures (Concha y Toro People 2017).

The company aims to have close relations with its employees on the basis of mutual respect and open communication in order to create and sustain a comfortable work environment. With this goal, the company has designed a labor relations strategy that facilitates dialogue and understanding within the organization, and employees themselves are encouraged to express their suggestions toward improvements in organizational practices. The principles of this strategy are direct communication between employees and managers, enhancing leadership and identifying room for improvement (Concha y Toro People 2017). In 2014, the company implemented the Corporate Leadership Program, aiming to equip employees with various tools to enhance their leadership skills and lead teams efficiently to achieve the organizational goals.

The programs that are designed to support the well-being of employees are multifaceted. They include the medical dimension of well-being and offer employees support in crisis situations. A distinctive one was implemented in 2014 and was called the Communicate Program, which focused on the emotional stability of workers. It provided telephone psychotherapy to company staff and families with nationwide coverage for situations of low or medium complexity. Another program with such a profile is the Alcohol and Drugs Program, implemented in 2014. This program is a logical continuation in the series of care initiatives of the company given its production specificity as a leading wine producer. Not surprisingly, the company promotes awareness regarding the consequences of alcohol and/or drug abuse among employees and its effects on their life in the family and at work (Concha y Toro People 2017).

Training and development are recognized by Concha y Toro as a vital part of the talent management strategy. The company offers many different training courses and invests substantial resources into the development of its employees. Training programs are adjusted to the working reality and the specificity of a certain job position. The focus here is on development of skills, continuous education and increasing employability. Convinced of the transforming power of education, the company inaugurated a Concha y Toro Knowledge Centre (CDC is its acronym in Spanish) in 2013, a school providing internal training, with curricula and courses designed by specialists, for each management sector and for each particular position. In 2014, the Center increased its training programs from four to 10, on subjects such as Pneumatics, Food Defense, Introduction to Warehouse Management, Industrial Electricity, Lubrication, Metrology, and Winemaking Cellars Management, among others (Concha y Toro People 2017).

Concha y Toro bases its talent management practices both on the material and non-material appraisal of workers. There is a bonus system and an annual bonus is equivalent to 4.5% of net income, in proportion to the remuneration of employees. It relates to all the permanent workers (but not temporary employees and those who are on commission) and corresponds to at least a one-month salary, proportionate to the salary and date of entry into the firm in the calendar year (Concha y Toro Annual Report 2015). The company claims to have a comprehensive system of bonuses to support and strengthen employee commitment, and the loyalty of their family members too, as they benefit from some of the bonuses, for example bonuses at certain periods of the year, a shuttle bus service for employees working on shifts where there is little public transport, as well as work clothes for some categories of workers, depending on the nature of work (Concha y Toro People 2017).

A further bonus introduced in 2013 is the so-called Operations and Enology Excellence Bonus. The goal of this bonus as a tool for performance evaluation is to achieve improvements in day-to-day activities for the growth of the whole company. This is a percentage increase in monthly salary (up to 15%). There are different parameters that are given to different departments to evaluate, on a daily basis, the results of a job. This bonus is designed to promote the idea of improving employee performance, which as a result contributes to the company's mission of excellence (Concha y Toro Annual Report 2013).

The company's communication channels include the internal magazine *Nuestra Viña*, the Sustainability Report, and an interesting tool—breakfasts with employees, introduced in 2013 to provide more chances for employees and managers to articulate their concerns and improve communication (Concha y Toro Sustainability Report 2013). A further, impersonalized communication tool is an anonymous complaint system called the Whistle Blower Channel, designed to help various groups with making confidential, anonymous complaints on issues related to accounting, fraud, asset safeguarding, auditing matters or any other matters related to the company's internal control (Concha y Toro Whistle-Blower 2017).

The key point underlined by the company in its various talent management practices is raising commitment as a result of all measures taken. It is important to note that Concha y Toro not only implements the programs but also analyzes the results, which shows its mature approach toward talent management. According to a regular survey assessing the level of commitment, in 2016, 84% of the regular employees took part in the study, and the overall level of commitment was 68%, which is a 6% improvement in comparison to the previous year's results. Among the recognized positive achievements of Concha y Toro as an employer were a positive work environment, diversity, inclusion and ecological awareness, as well as its strong reputation. Some room for improvement was identified with regards to communication between managers and departments, and recognition (Concha y Toro Sustainability Report 2016).

Concha y Toro demonstrates its awareness of the current topical issues within the labor market and strives to address them directly. To do so, the company responds to the issue of wage inequality between female and male employees, for example. It explicitly states that gender does not play a role in determining the base salary or average wage, which includes different bonuses. Another burning issue in Chile concerns temporary employment, and Concha y Toro addresses this, too. The company admits that due to the particularities of the wine-making process it has to rely on a seasonal workforce but temporary employees are treated with respect and provided with various bonuses, including an affiliation to the Compensation Fund, bonuses for Christmas and national holidays. Apart from that, the workers involved in harvesting obtain a weekly performance bonus, an end-of-harvest voucher, a monthly gift card between March and June, night shift bonuses, food benefits at the company's cafeteria, and shuttle bus services or a payment for public transport (Concha y Toro Sustainability Report 2016).

Thus, the company obviously follows the trends in the labor market and the overall country context to create an image of a responsible and caring employer that appreciates its employees as its key resource. All in all, its talent management strategy may be denoted as one that focuses on the well-being of employees and strives to meet any needs they may have. The company provides employees with various development and support opportunities, with material and non-financial bonuses, with training, counselling and even with telephone psychotherapeutic advice. Such an all-embracing strategy may be explained by the global expansion of the firm, where the company faces local standards in human resource management and has the opportunity to adopt and adapt some talent management practices.

*   *   *

Chilean companies have slowly admitted the relevance of talent management for their success. The experience of international expansion appears to be a factor that can positively influence the attitude of a company toward the importance of talent attraction and retention. International exposure may moderate the enthusiasm of companies to invest in human relations, depending on their organizational history and structure, and the nature of their internationalization. Concha y Toro may be regarded as an example of an enthusiastic proponent of talent management implementation, and this correlates with the global aspirations of the company to become the leading brand in its category worldwide. Thus, the company embraces modern transparent HRM and talent management practices in its desire to retain talented employees by offering them various benefits and assuring their well-being.

On the other hand, there are companies that do not expose their tools and work practices with talented employees, notwithstanding internationalization. The example here is CSAV that has international subsidiaries that do show inclusive practices of talent management, but CSAV itself keeps to quite a formal, hierarchical, organizational structure with the main focus on delivering profitable services responsibly. This is reinforced by the particular type of transparency that the company underlines: its communication strategy with its stakeholders, including employees, is oriented toward combating the possible cases of illegal practices and misbehavior that can be articulated using various tools. Such awareness may be attributed to the context specificity of Chile where corruption and fraud are somewhat of a problem in some cases. At the same time, CSAV has recently merged with foreign companies that place value on talent management practices and eventually the focus of the company from its investigation of illegal practices and ensuring quality of service may move a bit in the direction of employee inclusion.

Last but not least, the Chilean context shows evidence of companies that do justify the role talent plays in the organization and the contribution talented employees make. Yet, these companies implement attraction and retention tools in their specific ways, which are affected by organizational and contextual particularities. Banco de Chile is an example of such an approach: the company focuses on employee development and retention through training and other educational measures, and through the initiation of workers into the rich history of the company.

The cases presented in this chapter illustrate the modern realities of talent management in Chile, where talent attraction and retention are embraced with various degrees of excitement, and implemented differently, depending on internal and external factors, with the latter being rather influential. The years to come are likely to witness further professionalization of talent management tools and the recognition of talent management not just in large companies like CSAV, Concha y Toro and Banco de Chile, but in small- and medium-sized companies, where its role has started to be reinforced, as seen in the adoption of professional awards in this sphere focused particularly on smaller enterprises.

References

Arrau, P.G. 2008. Gestion de Recursos Humanos en el Contexto Social y Cultural Chileno. *Asian Journal of Latin American Studies* 21 (1): 65–95.

Arrau, P.G., E. Eades, and J. Wilson. 2012. Managing Human Resources in the Latin American Context: The Case of Chile. *The International Journal of Human Resource Management* 23 (15): 3133–3150.

Bajpai, Prableen. Emerging Markets in Latin America: Chile, Brazil, Colombia, Peru, Mexico. 2015. http://www.nasdaq.com/article/emerging-markets-in-latin-america-chile-brazil-colombia-peru-mexico-cm531709. Accessed 12 Nov 2017.

Banco de Chile. 2013. About Us. http://www.bancochile.com/wps/wcm/connect/Internacional/Portal/About-Us/. Accessed 9 July 2017.

Banco de Chile Annual Report. 2014. https://ww3.bancochile.cl/wps/wcm/connect/4d0b540047952045975eb7137599e294/BCH_annual+report2014+FINAL.pdf?MOD=AJPERES&CONVERT_TO=url&CACHEID=4d0b540047952045975eb7137599e294. Accessed 18 Nov 2017.

———. 2015. http://ww3.bancochile.cl/wps/wcm/connect/9fa2ff804c920dc7bd47fd60b15dc6b2/20F2015_asfiled-opfinal.pdf?MOD=AJPERES&CONVERT_TO=url&CACHEID=9fa2ff804c920dc7bd47fd60b15dc6b2. Accessed 10 Mar 2017.

Banco de Chile Internacional. http://www.bancochile.com/wps/wcm/connect/internacional/portal/latam/en/trust. Accessed 11 Feb 2017.

Chile Policy Priorities for Strong and More Equitable Growth. 2015. https://www.oecd.org/chile/chile-policy-priorities-for-stronger-and-more-equitable-growth.pdf. Accessed 9 July 2017.

Chilean University Ranking. 2018. http://www.4icu.org/cl. Accessed 5 Aug 2017.

Concha y Toro Annual Report. 2013. https://www.conchaytoro.com/wp-content/uploads/2014/07/Concha-y-Toro-Annual-Report-2013.pdf. Accessed 10 Sept 2017.

Concha y Toro History. 2017. https://www.conchaytoro.com/concha-y-toro-holding/quienes-somos-cat/history/. Accessed 11 Sept 2017.

Concha y Toro Whistle-Blower. 2017. https://www.conchaytoro.com/concha-y-toro-holding/informacion-legal-cat/whistle-blower/?lang=en_us. Accessed 10 Sept 2017.

CSAV Annual Report. 2005. http://www.csav.com/special-services/en/InvestorRelations/Reports/Documents/2005%20-%20Annual%20Report.pdf. Accessed 7 Nov 2017.

———. 2016. http://www.csav.com/special-services/en/InvestorRelations/Reports/Documents/2016%20-%20Annual%20Report.pdf. Accessed 18 Nov 2017.

CSAV Grievance System. 2018. http://www.csav.com/special-services/en/aboutus/pages/greavancesystem.aspx. Accessed 3 Oct 2017.

CSAV Group Code of Corporate Compliance and Ethics. 2014. http://www.csav.com/special-services/en/InvestorRelations/Documents/CSAV%20Group%20Code%20of%20Corporate%20Compliance%20and%20Ethics.pdf. Accessed 3 Oct 2017.

CSAV Roadmap Presentation. 2013. http://www.csav.com/special-services/pt/InvestorRelations/Documents/2011-%20December%20CSAV%20Roadshow%20Presentation.pdf. Accessed 24 Oct 2017.

———. 2017. http://www.csav.com/special-services/en/InvestorRelations/Documents/2017-10-13%20%20CSAV%20Roadshow%20Presentation.pdf. Accessed 16 Nov 2017.

Fundación Carlos Vial Espantoso. 2017. https://www.fundacioncarlosvial.cl/. Accessed 10 June 2017.

Gasparini, Leonardo, and Mariana Marchionni. 2015. Bridging Gender Gaps? The Rise and Deceleration of Female Labor Force Participation in Latin America. http://labor-al.org/participacionfemenina/wp-content/uploads/2016/01/Chapter-8_Policies.pdf. Accessed 30 June 2017.

Glassdoor CSAV Interview Questions. 2014. https://www.glassdoor.co.in/Interview/CSAV-Agency-Interview-Questions-E279733.htm. Accessed 29 May 2017.

Glassdoor CSAV. 2016. https://www.glassdoor.com/Overview/Working-at-CSAV-EI_IE109779.11,15.htm. Accessed 15 July 2017.

Glassdoor, Working in Banco de Chile. 2017. https://www.glassdoor.com/Reviews/Banco-de-Chile-Reviews-E23934.htm. Accessed 15 July 2017.

Great Place to Work Institute. http://www.greatplacetowork.cl/index.php.

https://www.conchaytoro.com/wp-content/uploads/2014/10/Sustainability-Report-2013.pdf. Accessed 12 Nov 2017a.

https://www.glassdoor.com/Interview/CSAV-Interview-Questions-E109779.htm. Accessed 8 Dec 2017b.

https://www.imf.org/external/pubs/ft/weo/2017/02/weodata/weorept.aspx?sy=2017&ey=2017&scsm=1&ssd=1&sort=country&ds=.&br=1&c=311%2C336%2C213%2C263%2C313%2C268%2C316%2C343%2C339%2C273%2C218%2C278%2C223%2C283%2C228%2C288%2C233%2C293%2C238%2C361%2C321%2C362%2C243%2C364%2C248%2C366%2C253%2C369%2C328%2C298%2C258%2C299&s=NGDPD%2CNGDPDPC&grp=0&a=&pr.x=59&pr.y=10. Accessed 21 Nov 2018.

IMF. Selected Issues, Chile. 2015. http://www.imf.org/en/Publications/CR/Issues/2016/12/31/Chile-Selected-Issues-43183. Accessed 15 Nov 2017.

IMF. World Economic Outlook. http://www.imf.org/en/Publications/WEO/Issues/2016/12/31/Adjusting-to-Lower-Commodity-Prices.

Latin American Economic Outlook. 2017. Youth, Entrepreneurship and Skills. http://www.oecd.org/dev/americas/E-Book_LEO2017.pdf. Accessed 12 Dec 2017.

Monitor Empresarial de Reputación Corporativa. 2017. http://merco.info/cl/actualidad/resultados-merco-empresas-y-lideres-chile-2017-8edicion-bci-banco-de-chile-y-falabella-las-tres-emp. Accessed 12 Jan 2018.

OECD Economic Survey Chile. 2013. https://books.google.ru/books?id=OQySAQAAQBAJ&pg=PA54&lpg=PA54&dq=Chile+employer+training&source=bl&ots=xDikfNE3QG&sig=JfXc1t4mjAxgaAoStQCDVIWMaT8&hl=ru&sa=X&ved=0ahUKEwiqzJaHnPPYAhWEDCwKHfZeC8YQ6AEITzAF#v=onepage&q=%20training&f=false. Accessed 16 Aug 2017.

OECD, Temporary Employment. 2016. https://data.oecd.org/emp/temporary-employment.htm#indicator-chart. Accessed 11 Oct 2017.

Rodriguez, D., and R. Rios. 2009. Paternalism at the Crossroads: Labour Relations in Chile in Transition. *Employee Relations* 31 (3): 322–333.

Rodriguez, D., C. Bozzo, and M. Arnold 1999. *Cultura Organizational e Innovacion. in Cultura en Organizaciones Latinas*, ed. Anabella Davila and Nora H. Martinez. Mexico: Siglo XXI.

Sustainable Governance Indicators. 2017. http://www.sgi-network.org/2017/Policy_Performance/Economic_Policies/Labor_Markets/Labor_Market_Policy. Accessed 10 Dec 2017.

Teletón. http://www.teleton.bancochile.cl/. Accessed 27 Oct 2017.

World Bank Chile. 2018 https://data.worldbank.org/country/chile. Accessed 12 Jan 2018.

18

Creating a Talent Management Agenda for a Global Environment

Marina Latukha, Anna Veselova, Liudmila Veselova,
József Poór, János Fehér, Victoria Tikhonova,
Louisa Selivanovskikh, Maria Laura MacLennan,
Gabriel Vouga Chueke, Svetla Marinova,
Andrei Panibratov, and Daria Klishevich

M. Latukha (✉) • A. Veselova • V. Tikhonova • L. Selivanovskikh •
A. Panibratov • D. Klishevich
Graduate School of Management, St. Petersburg State University,
St. Petersburg, Russia
e-mail: marina.latuha@gsom.pu.ru; a.s.veselova@gsom.pu.ru; tikhonova@
gsom.pu.ru; l.selivanovskih@gsom.pu.ru

L. Veselova
School of International Relations, St. Petersburg State University,
St. Petersburg, Russia

J. Poór
Szent István University, Gödöllő, Hungary
e-mail: poorjf@t-online.hu

J. Fehér
Károli Gáspár University of the Reformed Church in Hungary, Budapest,
Hungary
e-mail: feherdr@t-online.hu

© The Author(s) 2018
M. Latukha (ed.), *Talent Management in Global Organizations*,
Palgrave Studies of Internationalization in Emerging Markets,
https://doi.org/10.1007/978-3-319-76418-4_18

M. L. MacLennan
Centro Universitario FEI, São Bernardo do Campo, Brazil
e-mail: mferranty@fei.edu.br

G. Vouga Chueke
Brazilian Multinationals Observatory, University of São Paulo,
São Paulo, Brazil

S. Marinova
Aalborg University, Aalborg, Denmark
e-mail: svetla@business.aau.dk

Intensive market growth and integration into the global economic environment significantly increase the relevance of valuable human resources; however, countries and companies react differently in bringing about changes in their talent management systems at a varied pace and with different scope. The economic and cultural differences between countries, among other factors, strongly influence the way their companies develop and implement talent management practices. In most cases, we see some sort of intertwining of tradition and innovation in human resource management systems and talent management practices.

Chinese talent management is strongly determined by a specific historical path and cultural idiosyncrasies. Through consideration of talent management practices in Geely, China Mobile and Fosun, we see how Western talent management practices are carefully adapted and aligned with the deeply rooted and nurtured traditional values and beliefs in the Chinese culture and integrated into a company's management system. Despite quite a huge diversity in talent management approaches, there are many similar features. In most Chinese companies, employees are considered as a part of a large "family", which increases their loyalty and makes talent retention easier as employees feel respect and moral obligations to their employers. However, the modern generation of talented employees in China is more likely to change its work behavior. Being more open to innovation, apart from moral incentives many young talented Chinese feel it is important to have a transparent promotion and a clear bonus system in developing their career. Chinese companies have initiated various contests and programs to stimulate and motivate their employees, to strengthen the sense of belonging and commitment, to develop new skills and competences and to retain talented employees. Quite an extensive pool of domestic talent in India attracts many foreign companies and stimulates them to set up research and development facilities in the country. In terms of career path, Indian talent management systems provide rather limited opportunities for young talented employees. This is determined by a deeply instilled strict hierarchy and paternalism and a still widespread caste system. However, we see extensive efforts in enhancing education and competences in India through co-operation with leading international universities. South Korea experienced even stronger pressure than China and India to create efficiency-driven talent management systems, which could meet the expectations and requirements of the global competitive business environment. Hyundai Motors, Samsung and Ssang Yong, being leading Korean companies, have quite advanced talent management practices and yet, they are still very paternalistic and strongly influenced by Confucian values associated with collective vision and trustful horizontal relations between colleagues. The presented Korean companies show a unique capability in combining a traditional hierarchical order of vertical communication with an internal environment based on harmony. Modern Korean companies are eager to attract talented employees, so they apply active recruitment approaches using publicly advertised job openings. They also intensify and diversify talent attraction and retention practices to provide higher job security and development for permanent employees and more flexibility for temporary ones. However, they still lack advanced individual performance appraisal instruments, which on the one hand may demotivate some employees and create a threat of talent outflow, but on the other hand may maintain harmony in a society defined by the cultural values of Korean society. Being in search of a balance between the traditional Korean management system and modern, efficiency-based, talent management strategies, Korean companies have found themselves in a position in which they have to consider their own unique ways to select, adopt and adapt Western talent management approaches. However, the most important challenge faced by most Asia-Pacific countries is the potential loss of their home-grown talent, which requires a persistent talent management agenda.

Talent management practices in Central and East European (CEE) countries are influenced by the regional and country-specific environment. Hungary, Poland and the Czech Republic produce successful results in transforming their economies into knowledge-based and free market-led ones in terms of macro-economic indicators through replication of Western approaches toward talent management and better application of some relevant approaches from the past. Yet, compared to the Asian-Pacific countries, CEE companies seem to have adopted Western talent management practices more indiscriminately and without a thought to the adaptation of these practices considering fundamental, local, cultural values. The countries represent hierarchical, centralized societies, where the government's role is still important, but less so than in the past, and collective aspiration has shifted mostly to individual private gain. There is awareness of the need for better talent management, but there is a lack of specific, locally differentiated talent management expertise. However, our examples show some interesting perspectives creating new development paths for talent management in the CEE context. For example, management practices in Polish companies are changing year by year in terms of functional expansion and growing importance of the talent management role. Ongoing reforms targeted at reducing corruption, attracting investments, improving social welfare and removing labor market rigidities in the Czech Republic indicate new possibilities for talent management in Czech companies. Hungary has come a bit further than other CEE countries in transforming its economy toward being a knowledge-based one. Its market regulations and favorable climate for entrepreneurs have boosted the development of innovation activity in the country and helped it to become the largest producer of electronics in the CEE. This has increased the need for targeted talent attraction, development and retention. To be the best in talent recruitment, Polish and Czech organizations, just like their Asia-Pacific counterparts, are greatly involved in co-operation with universities to create new competences and knowledge and to train and develop new talent. In the process of transition toward a knowledge-based economy, companies from the CEE region try to adopt a more flexible organization structure that makes the process of knowledge transfer easier. Czech companies also represent a good example of promoting innovation by implementing e-learning platforms as another knowledge flow platform within the company. The Polish company Tyskie uses innovative approaches in marketing and advertising of its products and this requires nurturing creativity and originality in the company. An important aspect of talent management in the CEE context is the motivation system in firms that supposes the use of financial and non-financial benefits for employees and their families in order to retain professional staff. The latter were well-developed in the recent past of the region and to date are recognized as needed for a more wholesome and differentiated talent management system. Companies in the CEE are interested in talent management that is still based on the adaptation of Western experience, but have also realized that they have come to recognize the need for their own uniqueness in talent management, which can contribute positively to their competitive position in international and domestic markets.

The examples from Kazakhstan, Belarus and Ukraine illustrate how different companies from the specified countries in the Commonwealth of Independent States (CIS) region deal with attraction, recruitment, development, motivation and retention of talented employees. We see that talent management is influenced by a number of factors, some of which are rather specific to Kazakhstan, Belorussia and Ukraine, but at the same time can be featured as common in the CIS context. The specificity of talent management in these countries is generally determined by the historical legacy of the Soviet past (e.g. highly centralized organizational structure, strict hierarchy, high power distance, authoritarian leadership style). Therefore, a common feature of organizations from the region is the generally higher formalization of talent management policies, especially when compared to that of Western and some CEE companies, but not so different when compared to the formalization in the presented companies from the Asia-Pacific region. Talent management practices in CIS countries are still in dynamic transition, trying to find their own unique ground. On the one hand, they are path-dependent on history and, on the other hand, changes are driven by Western multinational corporations (MNCs) that transfer human resource knowledge. It remains to be seen how local talent management will align these with local norms, traditions, cultures, and behavior. Kazakhstan is the only country out of the three which managed to create a "hybrid" form of practices that shares the characteristics of both Western and local talent management systems. Examples from Belorussian companies show that talent management practices there have much more potential for development in comparison with Russian and Ukrainian firms due to the idiosyncrasies of the political and economic environment. We see that the specifics of talent management in Belorussia, Russia and Ukraine have the marks of the Soviet past, but some new practices are a natural response to the economic and political situation in each country.

Latin American countries are rarely studied in the context of talent management development. This may be partially explained by the fact that the region has experienced the intervention of talent management as an imported tool used by Western MNCs operating in the region or by local large enterprises that went global, with the assumption that such imported management practice should be working in Latin America as elsewhere. Latin American countries, however, have demonstrated that local contexts that shape the impact of external factors matter in the implementation of formalized management systems such as talent management. The reason is that talent management inevitably experiences the influence of embedded structures that determine how talent management practices, if indeed accepted and recognized, are going to be implemented in companies. Latin America has a rather turbulent and changing economic environment that affects the operations of firms and the resources they can use for talent management. The countries in this region have a number of similarities that determine the way companies work, how they see their strategies and how much importance they allocate to human resource management in organizations. Among the distinct characteristics of the Latin American society are the significant level of inequality, informality and rather diverse constellations on the labor market such as temporary employment, influence of political instability, corruption, paternalism and limited access to employment for women and young people. In this reality, talent management evolves at the intersection of global tools and local cultural influence.

The presented company experiences in talent management from Brazil, Argentina and Chile are developed by large and successful companies, but they illustrate its limited scope. Indeed, talent management is used mostly by larger companies, some of which embraced talent management as a part of the organizational strategy in the late 1980s and 1990s when Latin American state-owned companies went through a process of privatization accompanied by liberalization, which stimulated the expansion of Western MNCs into the region. As for smaller enterprises, they are still on the way to identifying and accommodating talent management practices. Companies demonstrate various levels of recognition of the need for talent attraction, selection and retention, and use different tools to make workers aware of the advantages and prospects they get by working for a company. Some employers tend to focus on building a strong brand that works as an attraction for potential employees in itself. Some Latin American companies focus on talent attraction via the introduction of young talent to the company, thus winning these individuals at a very early stage of their career development. Other enterprises focus on retaining their existing employees and avoiding high turnover by the provision of versatile benefits and educational and development bonuses that aim to increase employee well-being. All in all, these initiatives appear to be shaped by the external and internal factors that determine the way they are implemented. The Latin American context is still not well-developed in terms of talent management but the cases presented here illustrate that awareness of the importance of talent management is growing, especially among the larger companies, although small and medium-size companies still have a long way to go.

We see that the exploration of talent management practices in companies around the world shows their unique experiences, which are very varied. They range from the limited application of practices for talent attraction, development and retention to well-integrated and organized talent management systems. It has become evident, though, that all case firms have recognized the importance of talent management, of talented employees with knowledge, innovation and creative potential that are so much needed for the long-term competitive success of each company in a global, ever more vulnerable, unpredictable, competitive and uncertain business environment.

Index[1]

A

Absenteeism, 315, 316
  rates, 286
Accident prevention, 184
Accountability, 16, 48, 50, 195, 288
Achievements recognition, 192
Acquisition, 16, 20, 45, 46, 49, 51,
  55, 56, 80, 91, 154, 156, 172,
  188, 243, 308, 312, 313, 332
Action program, 148, 286, 291
Adaptation
  period, 223, 247
  process, 121, 216–217
  trainings, 217
ADCE, *see* Associação Desportiva
  Classista Embraer
Ad Exchange, 250
Adhocracy, 22
Ad Japon, 250

Advanced training, 33, 35, 191,
  222, 301
Aeritalia, 281
Aermacchi, 281
Aeronautical service, 280
Aeronautic industry, 282
  See also Aeronautics
Aeronautics, 280
Agriculture, 177, 209, 299
Agrochemical products, 130
AIIB, the, 143
Airbus, 282
Aircraft industry, 279
Aircraft leasing, 282
Airline Nordica, 107
Airplane, 92, 106, 281
Aktogay, 180, 181
A La Ding, 32
Albania, 89, 90

---

[1] Note: Page numbers followed by 'n' refer to notes.

© The Author(s) 2018
M. Latukha (ed.), *Talent Management in Global Organizations*,
Palgrave Studies of Internationalization in Emerging Markets,
https://doi.org/10.1007/978-3-319-76418-4

351

352   Index

Alcohol and Drugs Program, 335
Al Jazirah Enterprise, 254
Allocation center, 304
Almaviva, 332
Annual report, 181, 285, 288, 311, 330
Annual Training Plan, 76, 315
Anti-discrimination amendments, 240
Anxiety prevention, 249
Anytime-anywhere learning opportunities, 229
Applicant, 17, 70, 75, 76, 131, 150, 251, 272, 285, 309
Applied science, 305
Appraisal system, 18, 28, 47, 109, 115, 126, 139, 199, 200, 258
Aptitude test, 196
Arantes, Marcelo, 288, 291
Argentina, 8, 270, 272, 274, 299–317, 325, 332, 348
Argentinian economy, 300
Argentinian GDP, 270, 300
Argentinian government, 313
Argentinian university, 309, 314
Articles of Association of the organization, 226
Asia, 49, 63, 78, 250, 270, 281, 287
Asian Development Bank, 176
Asset, 20, 30, 31, 45, 47, 54, 100, 111, 126, 134, 155, 158, 169, 170, 180–182, 185, 188, 191, 195, 207, 221, 288, 289, 304, 306, 309, 325, 336
Associação Desportiva Classista Embraer (ADCE), 283
Associate Program, 289

Association of Supervisory Personnel, 314
Atlantic Southeast Airlines, 281
A toda luz, 316
Attracting factor, 190, 197, 216, 221, 222
Attractiveness, 16, 123, 135, 201, 303
Audit Committee, 314
Australia, 46, 68, 219, 225, 280
Austria, 154
Authority, 11, 17, 74, 105, 121, 131, 170, 185, 208, 226, 240
Autocratic leadership style, 241
Automatic payment services, 285
Automobile, 19–25, 69, 78, 92, 120, 122, 123, 328
Automotive industry, 79, 208
Average annual rate, 321
Average wage, 183, 257, 337
Aviation fuel, 101, 155
Azovstal, 242–249, 253, 260

B

Balanced scorecard method, 303
Baltic states, 89, 90
Banco de Chile, 325–328, 330, 338, 339
Bandeirante, 281
Bangkok, 107
Banking, 30, 95, 270, 326, 327
Bank loaning system, 176
Bankruptcy, 66, 106, 239, 281
Baron Philippe de Rothschild, 332
Basic employee training and development, 221
Basic petrochemicals, 287

Basic salary systems, 169
Beef export, 299
Behavioral aspects, 201
Behavior Based Safety Program, 197
Beijing, 23, 107
Being Well on the Scales Program, 284
Being Well Program, 284
Being Well with Motherhood Program, 284
Being Well without Drugs Program, 284
Being Well without Smoking Program, 284
Being Well with Physical Exercise Program, 284
Being Well with Stress, Health Week Program, 284
Being Well with your Heart Program, 284
Belarus, 23, 97, 169, 172, 201, 207–231, 237, 239, 347
Belarusian Autoworks, 214
Belarusian labor law, 172
BELAZ, 213–218, 231
BELAZ Young People 2016–2020, 218
Benchmark, 79, 292
Benefit package, 113, 183, 198, 257, 283
Benzina, 130
Best practices, 32–34, 45, 73–78, 100, 104, 113, 120, 138, 183, 188, 198, 213, 253, 257, 307, 308
Best talents, 6, 18, 43, 46, 285, 325
Biased promotion, 200

Biased recruitment, 200
Bilateral contracts, 228
Biomass plant, 292
Biopolymers, 287
Bitumen, 155
B-level employee, 259
Board of directors, 130, 310, 314, 330
Boeing, 282
Bolivia, 325
Bombardier, 282
Bonuses, 80, 121, 136, 148, 186, 192, 217, 218, 221, 239, 246, 252, 274, 300, 310, 327, 335–337, 349
Bovespa, 292
Bozshakol, 180, 181, 185
Bozymchak, 180, 181
BP Plc, 102
Brain drain, 97, 210, 240
    phenomena, 240
Brain waste, 239
Brand, 19, 21, 29, 46, 68, 69, 73, 78, 81, 101–103, 108–110, 112, 122, 123, 125, 126, 154, 218, 222, 247, 252, 273, 280, 327, 328, 331–333, 338, 349
    recognition, 222, 252
Braskem, 280, 287–291
Brazil, 270, 274, 277–295, 300, 307, 313
Brazilian companies, 8, 279, 280, 292, 294, 295
Brazilian crisis, 277
Brazilian government, 281, 284
Brazilian labor market, 278, 294
Budgetary deficit, 176
Budget-funded institutions, 256

354 Index

Building Education Energetically, 310
Bulgaria, 89, 90, 219
Bureaucracy, 90, 125, 170
Bureaucratic procedures, 178
Business
  climate, 120, 208
  communications, 257
  decisions, 247, 259
  education, 170
  entities, 208
  environment, 34, 57, 72, 81, 90, 99, 103, 207, 218, 259, 270, 317, 345, 349
  model, 30, 31, 45, 74, 255, 326
  partner, 31, 132, 194, 292
  processes, 44, 98, 103, 185, 228
  relations, 58, 221
  results return on investment, 294 (*see also* Return on investment)
  segment, 130, 282
  strategy, 28, 123, 130, 160, 181, 244, 304, 332
Byelorussian Steel Works (BSW), 213, 224–231

C

Cadre reserve, 229
California, 160
Campinas, 291
Canada, 102, 172, 219
Capacity, 30, 48, 175, 181, 187, 213, 242, 243, 248, 304, 328, 332
Capital intensive economy, 177
Capital intensive project, 244
Cardiovascular products, 149

Career, 18, 23, 27, 35, 46, 55, 66, 76, 77, 108, 127, 128, 147, 148, 150–152, 156, 157, 183, 184, 195, 196, 199, 216, 227, 228, 242, 259, 279, 290, 291, 315, 344
  agencies, 216
  ambition, 288
  development, 5, 8, 18, 25, 31, 35, 42, 72, 77, 80, 108, 148, 152, 157, 170, 189, 193, 218, 221, 227, 253, 291, 303, 315, 349
  development plan, 126, 280
  development portal, 283
  driver, 280
  growth assistance, 198
  ladder, 211
  management, 137, 148, 284, 291
  management system, 157, 245, 247
  opportunities, 125, 136, 196, 242, 330
  option, 283
  path, 76, 77, 80, 125, 131, 157, 289, 345
  path development, 247
  promotion policy, 245
  prospects, 35, 66, 211, 315
  starting positions, 196
Caribbean, 269
Caste system, 42, 58, 345
Caustic soda, 287
CCR Group, 280, 284–287
  See also CCR S.A.
CCR S.A., 284
CDC, *see* Concha y Toro Knowledge Centre
CEE, *see* Central and Eastern Europe

Index **355**

Center of Excellence, 56
Central and Eastern Europe (CEE),
5, 7, 89–92, 101, 106, 107,
119, 129, 144, 149, 154, 155,
172, 208, 240, 346, 347
economies, 208
Central Asia, 175, 182, 193
Central Asia Regional Economic
Cooperation, 176
Centralized economy, 171
Centralized leadership, 170
CEO, *see* Chief Executive Officer
Certificates of Appreciation, 192
CEZ, 122, 133–139, 154
Chaebols, 63, 64
Change management, 125, 221
Chemical distribution, 287, 288
Chevron, 193, 194, 196
Chicago, 107
Chief Executive Officer (CEO), 161,
162, 246, 251, 294, 331
Chile, 8, 270, 272, 274, 321–339,
348
Chilean economy, 321
Chilean labor market, 323, 330
China, 6, 9–11, 15–36, 46, 57, 58,
64, 65, 68, 81, 120, 122, 149,
172, 175, 181, 193, 249, 322,
344, 345
China-Brazil Resource Satellite
Project, 281
China Development Bank
Corporation, 180
Chinese government, 11, 16, 17, 19,
281
Christmas hamper, 98
Citigroup Inc., 325
Clan, 63, 66

Clanism, 179, 200
Clickburner, 250
Clickky, 242, 249–254, 260
Client, 44, 45, 48, 112, 257, 291,
292, 304, 305, 326
C-LIFE, 48
CLT, *see* Consolidation of Labor
Laws
Coal, 134, 243
Code of business conduct, 311, 312
Code of conduct, 74, 105,
124, 191
Code of Ethics, 113, 314, 331, 334
Collaboration with universities, 257,
279
Collaborative relationships, 195
Collapse of the Soviet Union, 170,
176, 180, 208
Collective bargaining agreements,
278, 314
Collective spirit, 212
Collectivism, 64, 70, 170
College Embraer Juarez Wanderley,
281
Colombia, 270, 307
Commercial aviation, 282
Commercial products, 225
Commitment, 21, 26, 29, 31, 35,
47, 55, 65, 67, 82, 103, 107,
112, 113, 126, 130, 149, 150,
156, 182, 188, 249, 251, 260,
271, 273, 274, 279, 280, 306,
309, 312, 313, 316, 326, 331,
333–336, 345
Commodity market, 244
Commonwealth of Independent
States (CIS), 5, 7, 90, 149,
155, 169–173, 177, 201, 208,

212, 213, 215, 218, 219, 222, 224–226, 231, 240, 347
managerial practices, 171
Communicate Program, 335
Communication channel, 250, 273, 303, 317, 327, 330, 336
Communistic system, 95
Community, 10, 16, 30, 104, 134, 155, 181, 182, 188, 194–196, 274, 291, 310, 316
development, 52, 289
investment program, 194
and stakeholder engagement, 195
Company, 3, 10, 16, 41, 64, 90, 95, 120, 145, 169, 178, 209, 239, 270, 277, 300, 324, 344
culture, 57
growth, 102, 111, 185, 201
performance, 24, 28, 29, 80, 91, 111, 171, 218, 295, 302
Company Sud Americana de Vapores S.A. (CSAV), 328–331, 338, 339
Compensation
package, 17, 227
strategy, 280, 288
system, 71, 147, 171, 211, 224, 231
Compensatory time, 278
Competences, 16, 33, 46, 47, 49–52, 55, 56, 66, 72, 76, 99, 108, 111–113, 127, 131, 132, 137, 138, 170, 191, 216, 222, 228, 250, 259, 280, 285, 295, 307–309, 345, 346
Competency model, 246
Competition, 4, 5, 10, 17, 24, 26, 42, 58, 71, 73, 75, 99, 112, 122, 133, 156, 179, 192, 212,

217, 218, 223, 229–231, 243, 245, 254, 282, 324
Competitive ability, 227
Competitive advantage, 3, 6–8, 11, 20, 36, 49, 50, 54, 58, 78, 81, 91, 120, 139, 150, 171, 177, 179, 182, 186, 189, 197, 215, 224, 226, 230, 240, 244, 259, 260
Competitive environment, 80, 96, 294
Competitive marketplace, 283
Competitiveness, 4, 44, 45, 66, 77, 121, 125, 136, 139, 152, 196, 226, 240, 248, 324
Competitive salary, 183, 199, 221, 249, 327
Compliance assurance, 195
Computer courses, 293
Concession, 285, 313
Concha y Toro Knowledge Centre (CDC), 335
See also Viña Concha y Toro
Confidential communication, 185
Conflict, in Donetsk and Luhansk, 245
Confucian values, 17, 64, 82, 345
Conglomerate, 19, 53, 63, 73, 102, 129, 280, 281, 284, 329, 329n2
Consolidation of Labor Laws (CLT), 278
Consumer, 110, 123, 161, 214, 245, 254, 255, 304
good, 90
Consumption, 30, 97, 244
Context-specific managerial practices, 215

Index **357**

Continuous improvement cells, 283
Continuous professional education
system, 229
Contract management, 221
Control systems, 21, 113, 241
Convergence, 17, 100
Copper, 180, 181, 187, 322
Copper mining and smelting
activities, 186
Core personnel, 256
Corporate
activities, 192, 221, 313
awarding, 229
communication, 28, 108, 328
culture, 21, 22, 26, 28,
32, 45, 65, 66, 72, 74,
103–105, 108, 109,
134, 135, 137, 138,
149, 151, 186, 192,
212, 227, 229, 251,
252, 254, 279, 288,
291, 311, 327
environment, 33, 56, 257
event, 300, 311, 313, 315
goals, 30, 69, 185, 199, 201, 246,
310
image, 279
mission, 226, 253
objective, 111, 133, 188, 224,
230, 253, 259
policy, 32, 227
results, 282
social program, 282
Corporate social responsibility
(CSR), 103
commitments, 188
Corporate strategy, 33, 34, 45, 111,
182, 188, 226, 249, 310

for managing people, 294
Corporate university, 23, 24, 47, 51,
126, 127, 191, 257, 285, 294
Corporate values, 21, 31, 52, 130,
185, 188, 195, 254, 326, 327
Corporate vision, 199
Corporation, 20, 25, 36, 44, 49, 66,
78, 100, 106, 156, 184, 193,
292, 324
Corruption, 96, 120, 132, 171, 176,
188, 189, 271, 272, 312, 338,
346, 348
Corruption-prone regulated
environment, 255
Costa Rica, 107
Cost control, 186
Cost-cutting programs, 246
Cost-effective organization, 103
Cost saving, 295
Counseling, 290, 301
Country of origin, 183
Country-specific environment, 5, 7,
92, 139, 172, 346
Country status, 176
Course, 27, 28, 32, 34, 35, 56, 69,
72, 76, 105, 107, 109, 111,
112, 126, 127, 129, 131, 137,
158, 207, 217, 222, 238, 244,
247, 252, 257, 286, 289, 293,
295, 302, 306, 317, 326, 335
CPFL, 291–295
See also CPFL Energia
CPFL Brasil, 292
CPFL Corporate University, 293, 295
CPFL Energia, 280, 291–293, 295
CPFL Geração, 292
CPFL Paulista, 292
CPFL Piratininga, 292

358   Index

CPFL Renováveis, 292
CRANET, 145
Creative work, 256, 258
Creativity, 5, 48, 67, 75, 78, 162, 163, 189, 222, 251, 302, 327, 347
Credit co-op, 283
Crimea, 238, 243, 255
CRM, *see* Customer relationship management system
Croatia, 89, 154
Cross-cultural management, 33, 200
Crude oil, 49, 101, 129, 130, 155, 193
CSAV, *see* Company Sud Americana de Vapores S.A.
CSR, *see* Corporate social responsibility strategy
Cuba, 23, 107
Cultural adjustment, 185
Cultural distance, 172
Cultural heritage, 119
Cultural Revolution, 16
Cuprum Holding, 180
Currency
  crises, 209
  depreciation, 238
  fluctuations, 220
Customer relationship management (CRM) system, 253
Customer(s), 21, 25, 31, 44, 45, 48, 68, 69, 75, 79, 102–104, 111, 112, 115, 123, 130, 134, 149, 155, 161, 181, 194, 214, 222, 226, 250, 255, 289, 304, 305, 312–315, 326, 332, 333
  satisfaction, 21, 69, 305
  support, 161, 282
CV screening, 251, 256, 333

D
Damage control, 221
Day care, 283
DCFTA, *see* Deep and Comprehensive Free Trade Area
Decision-making process, 125, 170, 216, 231, 258
Deep and Comprehensive Free Trade Area (DCFTA), 238
Degree of individualism, 240
Deloitte, 101
Democracy, 144
Democratic leadership style, 241
Demographic security, 209
Dental plan, 283
Destabilization, 244
Devaluation, 186, 255
Developed countries, 5, 9, 100, 177, 185, 272, 294
Developed economies, 5, 119, 299
Developed markets, 5, 6, 193, 201
Development plan, 157, 197, 286
Development policy, 189
Development strategy, 189, 240
Diesel engine, 78, 123
Dietary programs, 286
Differentiation, 21, 169, 171, 249
Digitalization, 101
Disability discrimination, 75
Disabled children, 283
Disabled people, 22, 190, 284
Disputes with Russia, 238, 254
Distance learning system, 191
Distribution channels, 288
Distribution network, 219
Divergence, 17
Diversification stage, 214

Diversity, 4, 9–12, 21, 57, 92, 104, 123, 125, 132, 158, 159, 182, 195, 200, 283, 336, 344
Diversity program, 284
Dollar-equivalent salary, 217
Domestic migration, 242
Domestic production, 255
Dominant coalition, 256, 258
Don Melchor Concha y Toro, 332
Downsizing, 300, 312
  and layoffs, 171

E

Early warning, 295
Ease-of-doing-business report, 95
Eastern Europe, 106, 219, 249
East European political reforms, 171
East Kazakhstan region, 187, 190
Eco-friendly, 20
Ecological safety, 186
Economic
  barrier, 193
  context, 316
  crisis, 64, 66, 212, 270, 300, 328
  decline, 208
  development, 30, 96, 177, 182, 240, 270, 300
  downturn, 242
  environment, 15, 238, 257, 344, 348
  growth, 6, 8, 10, 15, 63, 119, 176, 177, 179, 200, 210, 270, 277, 323
  heterogeneity, 89
  inequality, 210
  integration, 176
  policy, 299

reform, 15, 237
situation, 96, 220, 230, 254, 278
status, 215
system, 4, 90, 171
transformation, 16, 95, 96, 145, 208
turbulence, 238
Economy, 5, 6, 8–10, 16, 19, 30, 41, 42, 53, 63, 64, 90, 91, 95–97, 99, 102, 106, 114, 115, 119, 120, 132, 139, 144, 171, 175, 176
EDC, 287
Edenor, 303, 313–317
  See also Empresa Distribuidora y Comercializadora Norte S.A. (EDENOR S.A.)
Educational program, 17, 23, 108, 198
Educational project, 104, 247
Educational establishments, 228
Education quality, 23, 240, 323
Effectiveness, 3, 34, 51, 72, 91, 107, 226, 228, 230, 231, 240, 258, 302, 310, 313, 316
Efficiency, 3, 19, 21, 23, 29, 34, 72, 73, 91, 107, 108, 113, 115, 130, 137, 177, 182, 186, 188, 189, 191, 193, 195, 221, 225, 228, 229, 244, 246, 253, 255, 273, 306, 313, 329
  management, 229
E-learning
  platform, 137, 139, 347
  program, 131
Electric energy
  distribution, 291
  generation, 291

360   Index

Electricity
  distribution, 308, 313
  generation, 134, 308
  transmission, 308
  utility company, 313
Electric Light Labor Union, 314
Electric sector, 293
Elitist talent definition, 172, 183
EMB 120 Brasilia, 281
EMB 312 Tucano, 281
Embraer, 279–284
  See also Empresa Brasiliera de
    Aeronautica
Embraer Aviation International, 281
Embraer Conglomerate, 280
Embraer Enterprise Excellence
    Program (P3E), 283
Embraer Prev, 283
Embraer Route to Diversity
    Program, 283
Embraer Sports Association
    (Associação Desportiva
    Classista Embraer), 283
  See also Associação Desportiva
    Classista Embraer (ADCE)
Emergency management, 195
Emerging market firm, 5
Employee
  assessment, 54, 127, 282,
    291–295
  benefits packages, 198
  commitment, 212, 280, 313, 335
  dedication, 52, 53, 291
  involvement, 112, 138
  motivation systems, 71, 227
  promotion, 71, 75
  recruitment, 75, 221, 302
  remuneration, 182, 295, 330

  rotation, 157
  satisfaction, 35, 226, 229
  training and development, 58, 66,
    221, 257
  turnover, 199, 211, 224, 231,
    252, 257, 280
  welfare, 11, 26, 27, 50, 51, 125,
    226, 229, 305
  well-being, 27, 153, 230, 284,
    286, 303, 307, 333–335, 337,
    338
Employee-specific skills, 294
Employer, 11, 22, 27, 29, 31, 43, 46,
    53, 54, 66, 72, 75, 100, 101,
    105, 108, 110, 124, 135, 136,
    145, 153, 163, 196, 197, 199,
    210, 211, 217, 222, 239, 244,
    248, 249, 251, 256, 283–286,
    301, 302, 322, 323, 327, 330,
    336, 337, 344, 349
  value proposition, 279
Employer-worker relationship, 179
Employment, 10, 53, 64–66, 90, 91,
    126, 132, 144–146, 150, 152,
    154, 158, 163, 170, 177, 190,
    196, 209, 210, 212, 228, 247,
    252, 271–273, 301, 306, 322,
    323, 337, 348
  contract, 150, 295
  elasticity, 177
  policy, 245
  practices, 171
  preservation, 241
  protection legislation, 301
  relationships, 136, 138,
    240, 317
Empresa Brasiliera de Aeronautica,
    281

Empresa Distribuidora y
Comercializadora Norte S.A.
(EDENOR S.A.), 303,
313–317
Endowment, 306
End-user, 134, 304
Energy company, 292, 308, 312
Energy conglomerate, 102
Energy efficient technology, 244
Energy Management standard, 187
Engineering, 23, 44, 46, 50, 53–55,
57, 127, 156, 191, 194, 196,
213, 214, 225, 247, 282, 305,
309–311
English language, 70, 128, 285
proficiency, 252
Enterprise management, 212
Entrepreneurial skills, 96
Entrepreneurial spirit, 176, 290,
291, 309
Entrepreneurship, 21, 97, 137, 161,
280, 288
Environment, 10, 12, 15, 17, 18, 23,
26, 29–31, 33, 34, 41, 43, 44,
46, 48, 50, 51, 53, 54, 56, 57,
65, 69, 72, 75, 79–82, 90, 91,
96, 99, 102–104, 108, 113,
114, 128, 130, 139, 152, 153,
159, 161–163, 179, 181–183,
186, 188–191, 193–195, 197,
199, 207, 216, 218, 222, 223,
227, 237, 238, 242, 246, 249,
252, 255, 257, 259, 260, 270,
278, 279, 305, 308–314, 316,
317, 325, 327, 331, 334, 336,
344–346, 348, 349
contamination, 226
safety, 112, 123

Environmental
impact, 188, 226, 244, 304
issues, 190
laws, 181
protection, 31, 102, 104, 151,
175, 190, 305, 334
responsibility, 309
safety, 226
stewardship, 195
Environmentally-friendly product,
31, 102
Equality, 26, 98, 158, 177, 182, 196,
212, 216, 221, 228, 256, 258,
313, 314, 323, 334
Equal opportunities employer, 257
Equal rights, 114, 193, 230
Equipment, 20, 53, 54, 181, 183,
213, 214, 220, 221, 243, 244,
304, 305
Equity, 30, 122, 289, 308, 325
Estar De Bem, 284
See also Being Well Program
Estonia, 89, 90, 102
Ethical standards, 74, 134, 195, 212,
309
Ethnic discrimination, 334
Ethnic diversity, 200
EU, see European Union
Eurasian Economic Union (EAEU),
210, 239
Europe, 19, 78, 80, 98, 106, 107,
110, 119, 133, 134, 143, 175,
181, 193, 214, 219, 221, 225,
244, 249, 250, 254, 255, 270,
281, 287
European Commission, 96, 97, 106,
107, 134, 238, 242
European labor market, 242

362 **Index**

European Union (EU), 95–97, 119, 120, 143, 145, 220, 238, 239, 270
  labor law, 240
Evaluation, 7, 23, 24, 29, 43, 67, 77, 80, 92, 113, 121, 124, 155, 159, 212, 229, 230, 279, 282, 286, 291–295, 336
Executive aviation, 282
Executive jets, 282
Executive level manager, 292
Expansion, 19, 20, 45, 49, 68, 69, 72, 107, 122, 148, 219, 247, 250, 289, 332, 337, 346, 349
Experience-building training, 197
Expertise, 32, 33, 45, 48, 52, 80, 90, 120, 130, 137, 157, 158, 182, 184, 195, 227, 311, 346
Expertise Development Program, 290
Export-oriented enterprise, 64, 176, 213
Export possibilities, 220
External environment, 8, 27, 74, 103, 251, 260, 322
External labor market, 24
External recruitment, 196
External shocks, 176
Extra Annual Remuneration for Meeting Goals, 310
Extrinsic motivation, 254
Exxon Mobil Corporation, 102

F

Facebook, 251
Fair hiring, 178
Fair remuneration, 183

Family-like organizational culture, 215
Family pay, 295
Family planning, 284
Fast career start, 216
Fastest growing economy, 96, 321
Fast-growing markets, 172, 175
Fast-track promotion, 11
FDI, *see* Foreign direct investment
Feedback, 25, 47, 67, 111, 113, 121, 132, 138, 150, 152, 155, 221, 253, 292, 303, 307, 311, 313, 330, 331
  systems, 193
Fellowship, 305
Female involvement, 216
Financial
  bonuses reduction, 300
  crisis of 2008–2009, 176, 189, 254, 270
  distress, 78
  liquidity, 255
  loss, 181
  performance, 101, 103, 105, 136, 181
  service, 30, 325, 326
  stability, 223
  system, 322
Finished steel products, 304
Fixed remuneration, 290
Fixed salary, 71, 293
Flash Informativo Seminal, 316
Flexibility, 67, 74, 75, 107, 112, 121, 161, 248, 258, 278, 301, 308, 323, 345
Flexible Working Programs, 307
Florida, 282
Fluctuations

in exchange rates, 181
in oil prices, 176
Follow-up, 283
Food allowance, 283
Food processing industry, 220
Food vouchers, 287
Foreign currency, 255
Foreign direct investment (FDI), 90,
95, 96, 114, 208, 240, 270,
299
Foreign investor, 95, 201
Foreign language proficiency, 257
Foreign partner, 42, 281
Foreign talent, 11, 72, 183
Formal sector, 323
Former socialistic countries,
89, 90
Former Soviet republics, 169, 172,
175, 207
Fo-star Program, 33
Fosun Pay, 32
Four Modernizations, 16
France, 281
Fraud, 271, 272, 311, 312,
336, 338
Free market, 95
French Grands Crus Classes, 332
Frigorífico La Pampa S.A., 308
Front-line network employee, 29
Fuel and energy complex, 254
Fuel market, 102
Full-time employee, 152
Functional excellence, 194
Functionalist approach to defining
talent, 259
Future Growth Project-Wellhead
Pressure Management Project
(FGP-WPMP), 194

G
G20, 300
Gasoline, 68, 78, 154
Gazprom, 255
Gear unit, 123
Gender
composition, 227
discrimination, 144
distribution, 239
equality, 98, 177, 196, 212, 216
issues, 182
Generalists, 65
Geopolitical turbulence, 238
Germany, 90, 102, 120, 190, 208,
219, 225, 287, 302
Glassdoor, 307, 326, 327, 330, 331
Glencore, 187
Global Competitiveness Index, 240
Global crisis, 177
Global environment, 3–8, 41, 44,
91, 344–349
Global expansion, 250, 337
Global financial crisis, 96, 238
Globalization, 3, 20, 179, 224, 230,
274, 302
Global market, 73, 91, 215
Global practice, 293
Global talent, 4, 5, 15–36, 50, 75,
249–254
pool, 190
Global trends, 290
Government, 11, 16, 17, 19, 28, 35,
63, 64, 96, 106, 114, 120,
122, 133, 170, 171, 178, 180,
181, 207, 209, 210, 217, 243,
248, 271, 278, 281, 284, 313,
322, 323, 346
corruption, 176

364 Index

Government (*cont.*)
  debt, 96
  objectives, 209
  targeted intervention, 177
Governmental control, 207, 231
Government-set environmental
  targets, 186
Graduate, 23, 33, 42, 50, 54, 65–67,
  69, 70, 104, 125, 127, 128,
  131, 135, 151, 156, 163, 179,
  189, 196, 210, 211, 217, 223,
  279, 290, 303, 305, 315
Great Depression, 299
Greenfield and brownfield
  exploration, 188
Greenfield project, 180
Grievance system, 331
Gross domestic product (GDP), 119,
  120, 143, 144, 176, 177, 208,
  215, 238, 254, 270, 300, 321,
  322
  growth, 119, 176, 208, 254, 322
Group dynamics, 285
Group life insurance, 287
Growth, 6, 8–10, 15, 22, 23, 27, 30,
  32, 33, 35, 41–58, 63, 73, 74,
  78–82, 95–97, 102, 106–108,
  111, 114, 119, 123, 129–131,
  137, 157, 158, 161, 176, 177,
  179, 183, 198–201, 208–210,
  223, 225, 238, 244, 251–254,
  256, 258, 270, 271, 277, 278,
  285, 286, 288–291, 293, 300,
  305, 314, 322, 323, 326, 328,
  336, 344
  projects, 180–183, 185
  strategy, 27, 107
Grupo Dolphin, 308

Guatemala, 307
Gynecological products, 149

H

Hapag-Lloyd AG (HLAG), 329–331
Happiness 1+1, 27
Hay Group, 316
Headhunting agencies, 179
Headquarter (HQ), 47, 53, 73, 106,
  148, 160, 224, 300
Health and safety incidents, 181,
  183
Health and safety performance, 182,
  186
Health care, 120, 136
Health, environment and safety
  practices, 194
Health plan, 283
Health protection, 191
Healthy life style, 284, 286
Heating oil, 101, 154
Hélio Augusto de Souza Foundation,
  284
Herzberg theory of motivation, 192
Hierarchical organizational structure,
  109, 170, 330, 338
Hierarchy, 58, 64, 66, 72, 74, 100,
  121, 178, 213, 221, 248, 323,
  345, 347
Higher education, 70, 185, 189,
  191, 227, 247
High-income state, 321
Highly-qualified personnel, 189
High performers, 45, 46, 189, 199,
  221, 286, 324
High-potential employees, 178, 252
High-quality production, 222, 305

Highly-skilled graduates, 211
Highly-skilled workforce, 182
Hiring process, 75, 251, 259, 301, 326, 330
Historical legacy, 200, 347
HLAG, *see* Hapag-Lloyd AG
Hofstede 6-D Model, 121
Home office, 278
Hong-Kong Stock Exchange, 180
Horizons Program, 290
Horizontal knowledge flow, 248
Hospital companion benefit, 283
Host-country, 251
  nationals, 221
HR brand, 213
HR brand award of Belarus, 213
HRM, *see* Human resource management
HR-related expenses, 242
HR strategy, 288
Human capital, 9, 11, 22, 30, 49, 103, 170, 177, 189, 256, 270, 289, 293, 294, 301, 309, 314, 323, 326
  investment, 58, 229, 230, 294
  quality, 185, 222
Human Development Index, 144
Human resource management (HRM), 5, 7, 9, 10, 15–17, 22, 42, 50, 75, 99–101, 109, 120, 121, 124, 139, 145, 146, 171, 172, 196, 201, 213, 223, 224, 231, 246, 249, 256–259, 271, 279, 300, 303, 305, 307, 311–313, 316, 324, 325, 333, 337, 338, 344, 348
  activities, 170

department, 201, 246, 256, 303, 311
policies, 100, 224, 231, 307
practices, 5, 16, 50, 100, 171, 201, 223, 249, 303, 316, 324, 325, 338
strategy, 9, 171, 257, 279, 300, 305
system, 15, 16, 224, 231, 258, 259, 344
Human resources (HR)
  department, 70, 75, 99, 100, 146, 184, 185, 211, 212, 221, 231, 294, 302, 307, 309, 311, 312
  expertise, 32, 90, 120
  function, 10, 46, 91, 109, 145, 201, 212, 258
  manager, 46, 70, 100, 121, 150, 210, 213, 231, 294, 303
  motivation system, 257
  objectives, 124, 256
  provision, 228
  specialist, 70, 215, 256, 312
  staff, 220, 231
  standards, 212
  strategy, 8
  training programs, 228
Hungary, 7, 89, 90, 143–163, 225, 237, 240, 346
Hybrid environment, 45
Hybrid form of talent management, 200, 347
Hydrocarbon, 102
Hydropower plant, 292
Hylsa, 304
Hyperinflation, 96, 300

366 Index

IATA, *see* International Air Transport Association

Ideological control, 210

Ilyich Iron and Steel, 243, 248

Image, 20, 34, 53, 68, 75, 122, 186, 228, 279, 284, 310, 327, 331, 337

IMF, *see* International Monetary Fund

Improving Project, 286

Incentive mechanisms, 27, 29, 246

Incentive system, 71, 99

Inclusive talent definition, 195

Income inequality, 177, 208

India, 6, 9–11, 41–58, 68, 122, 126, 127, 249, 345

Individual Development Plan, 157, 289, 293

Individualism, 90, 122, 240, 323

Individual performance, 43, 50, 81, 148, 159, 184, 283, 345

Individual review, 285

Industrial
associations, 243
capacity, 242, 243
plant, 306
production, 238
psychology, 247
safety, 186, 197, 200, 258, 307
safety programs, 184
sector, 243

Industry, 4, 17, 19, 30, 31, 44–46, 48, 52, 53, 69–71, 73, 74, 76, 78, 79, 92, 98, 105, 114, 120, 127–129, 131, 149, 150, 154–156, 163, 180, 183, 186, 188, 190–192, 197, 198, 208, 209, 213, 215, 220, 224, 238, 242–244, 246, 250, 252, 254, 259, 279, 282, 283, 287–292, 304, 306, 312, 328, 329

Inflationary spiral, 290

Inflation growth, 208, 300

Inflation rate, 96

Informality, 272, 324, 348

Informal sector, 272, 302, 323

Information technology (IT), 315

Infoscions, 47

Infrastructure, 42, 44, 47, 49, 53, 54, 56, 58, 90, 96, 98, 175, 194, 225, 245, 280, 284, 310, 313
development, 190
service, 285

In-house development program, 289

In-house trainings, 56, 72

Innovation, 5, 21, 27, 31–32, 44, 45, 47, 48, 50, 57, 58, 64, 69, 73–75, 79, 82, 91, 103–105, 108, 115, 120, 123, 133, 139, 149, 152, 158, 160–163, 189, 209, 227, 240, 252, 301–306, 309, 344, 346, 349

Innovation-driven company, 130

Innovation-oriented, 285

Innovative facility, 304

Innovative managerial solutions, 179

Innovative practice, 36, 99, 303

INSEAD, 247

Institutional distance, 251

Institutional education, 293

Instrument, 162, 209, 286, 345

Integration, 5, 9, 11, 16, 20, 23, 32, 44, 49, 81, 91, 172, 176, 223, 244, 274, 288, 299, 306, 312, 313, 344

Intellectual competition, 254

Internal communication, 32, 200, 259, 303, 317, 327, 328
Internal consumption, 244
Internal recruitment, 103, 146, 196, 283, 286, 315
Internal talent, 190
International accreditation, 243
International Air Transport Association (IATA), 106
International company, 109, 330
International competition, 212, 223
International experience, 196, 215, 221, 257
International human resource management standards, 212
International industry standards, 191
Internationalization, 32, 33, 57, 158, 193, 252, 338
Internationalized operations, 215
Internationalized organization, 259
International markets, 3, 58, 78, 82, 102, 122, 154, 193, 221, 226
International Monetary Fund (IMF), 176, 177, 238, 270, 300
International petrochemical market, 287
International quality standards, 260
International recruitment channel, 23, 283
International specialists, 184, 215
International standards, 21, 109, 182, 194, 222, 226, 231, 244
International talent, 156
International working experience, 198
Internet job boards, 196
Internship, 67, 104, 125, 128, 139, 247, 252, 257, 279, 289, 306, 309, 315, 317
Intra-organizational teams, 189

Intra-workforce cooperation, 212
Investment
  decision, 194
  solution, 285
  in staff training, 290
Investor, 44, 181
Iron bowl, 12
Iron ore, 243, 304
IT, *see* Information technology
Italian company, 281
Italy, 154, 225, 281, 302
iTech Capital, 250

J

Jet
  agriculture, 280
  commercial, 280, 282
  executive, 280, 282
  military, 280–282
Job
  center, 210, 216
  creation, 177
  evaluation, 159, 230
  fair, 35, 104, 196
  opportunities, 97, 249
  position, 48, 72, 135, 196, 198, 335
  referral, 170
  requirements, 252
  rotation opportunities, 283
  rotation principles, 245
  security, 67, 171, 212, 345
JobSearch, 216
Joint-stock company, 130, 133, 180
Junior employee, 289, 290
Just compensation, 191

368 Index

K

Kazakhmys, 180
Kazakhstan, 7, 79, 169, 172, 173, 175–201, 219, 224, 239, 347
Kazakhstan Stock Exchange, 180
KAZ Minerals, 179–186, 192, 197, 200
Kazzinc, 179, 187–193, 195, 197, 200, 201
Key performance indicators (KPI), 24, 29, 188, 212, 253
Kim, Vladimir, 180
Knowledge, 6, 11, 16, 18, 22, 27, 32, 34, 42, 45, 46, 48, 49, 51, 52, 55, 56, 58, 65, 67, 70, 91, 96, 103, 110, 112, 120, 127, 148, 158, 161–163, 184, 185, 189, 190, 198, 201, 223, 227, 230, 247, 252, 256, 257, 274, 285, 292–294, 301, 314, 346, 347, 349
  area, 285
  economy, 139
  exchange, 229
  flow, 248, 347
  management, 101, 274
  society, 227
  transfer, 33, 139, 159, 189, 198, 274, 346
Koksay, 181
Kompania Piwowarska, 109, 110
KPI, *see* Key performance indicators

L

Labor
  activity, 229
  collective, 138, 230, 278, 323
  cost, 97, 98, 220, 278, 303
  force, 11, 18, 41, 42, 97, 98, 176, 209, 239, 240, 272, 301, 303, 323
  law, 129, 217, 231, 240, 278
  litigations, 221
  monotony, 228
  productivity, 64, 185
  protection, 184, 209
  relations, 5, 146, 209, 224, 240, 273, 295, 323, 325, 334
  safety, 227
  stimulation, 230
  unions, 138, 181, 271, 323
  Labor Code, 212, 239, 240
Labor market, 64, 90–92, 96–98, 105, 114, 120, 125, 135, 136, 144, 145, 148, 169, 177, 183, 188, 195, 209–212, 218, 224, 231, 239, 240, 271–274, 277, 282, 290, 300–303, 322–324, 337, 346, 348
  dynamics, 64, 239
  effectiveness, 240
  efficiency, 177
  instability, 169, 272
  regulation mechanisms, 177
  trends, 239, 243, 249, 337
Labor-regulating documentation, 241
Language course, 109, 126, 129, 131, 151, 252, 293
Language skills, 70, 252, 285, 289
Latvia, 89, 90, 207, 208, 219
Leadership, 5, 25, 33, 35, 43, 44, 46–48, 54, 56, 57, 65, 72, 82, 99, 110, 111, 115, 155, 157, 207, 246, 293, 306, 307, 309, 314, 327, 334, 347

accountability, 195
program, 51, 76, 151, 157, 280, 315
role, 288
skills, 56, 76, 100, 246, 259, 309, 334
Leadership Development Program, the (PDL), 33, 55, 56, 105, 285
Leaders Training Program, 306
Leader Workshop for Sustainable Development program, 290
Lean manufacturing philosophy, 283
Leap-frogging strategy, 25
LearnBMZ, 229
Learning organization, 305
Legal norms, 228
Legal obligation, 178
Legal requirement, 186
Legislation, 181, 228, 271
Legislative and regulatory advocacy, 195
Life Planning Talent Retention Program, 279
Life-time employment, 65
Life/work balance, 51, 77, 100, 229, 241, 307, 311, 317, 331
Linear-functional organizational structure, 220
LinkedIn, 251
Liquefied petroleum gas (LPG) products, 155
Liquidity crisis, 255
Lithuania, 89, 90, 101, 207
Loan, 52, 105, 107, 113, 132, 153, 175, 176, 199, 255, 287
Local communities, 181, 182, 195, 196, 310
Local context, 224, 348
Local currency, 186

Local economy, 294
Local employers, 11, 210
Localization perspective, 172
Local labor market peculiarities, 330
Local management style, 253
Local market, 4, 231, 299
Local specialists, 216
Local talent, 22, 182, 184, 198, 216, 347, 348
pool, 184, 251
London Stock Exchange, 180
Long-haul flight, 107
Long-term orientation, 240
LOT Flight Academy, 108
LOT Polish Airlines, 106
Low-cost country, 97
Low-level job position, 216
Low-out monitoring and breaking system, 21
Low-skilled workers, 210, 216
Loyalty rent, 208
LQ SA, 325
LQ SimCity, 325
Lubricating oil, 130
Luncheon session, 34

M

M&A, *see* Mergers and acquisitions
Machine-building complex, 208
Macro-economic adjustment, 176
Macro-economic environment, 237
Macro-economic fluctuations, 220
Maison, Pablo, 301
Management
effectiveness, 228
efficiency, 91, 195, 229
functions, 10, 209
practices adaption, 200

370 Index

Management (*cont.*)
  principles, 228
  standards, 111, 187, 212, 226
  succession, 228
  system, 15, 16, 22, 29, 31, 42, 48, 56, 67, 71, 75, 78, 80, 113, 189, 213, 221, 224, 226, 230, 231, 253, 256, 258, 259, 344, 345, 348
  team, 58, 80, 103, 214, 308
  techniques, 90, 158, 188, 212
Manager, 3–8, 10, 11, 17, 18, 24, 29, 33, 42, 43, 46–48, 55, 56, 58, 75, 76, 80, 91, 100, 105, 111–113, 121, 124–126, 130, 136–138, 145–148, 150, 151, 157, 170–172, 179, 184–186, 191, 193, 198, 200, 201, 209–213, 216, 218, 220, 224, 231, 240, 241, 243, 248, 251, 253, 256, 280, 291–293, 302, 303, 306, 311, 316, 317, 323, 327, 328, 333, 334, 336, 337
Managerial
  activities, 224
  competence, 137, 138, 170
  position, 70, 210, 215, 249
  practices, 3, 16, 78, 82, 171, 201, 215, 218, 242, 258
  procedures, 224
  thinking, 91
Mandatory allocation period, 211
Mandatory placement, 210
Manufacturing operation, 53
Maritime cargo transport, 328
Mariupol Metinvest, 243
Market
  capitalization, 179, 325
  competition, 91, 96

  economy, 6, 106, 119, 171
  instability, 258
  institution, 302
  reforms, 208, 323
  share, 42, 68, 102, 122, 282, 332
  stagnation, 239
  system, 171
  uncertainty, 212
Market-oriented management skills, 91
Maslow's hierarchy of needs, 192
Massive layoffs, 169, 239, 243
Material liability, 229
Maternity leave, 144, 283, 295
Maternity protection, 230
Medium-term goal attainment, 290–291
Memorandum of co-operation, 187
Mentoring program, 101, 185
  See also Mentorship program
Mentorship program, 223, 257
Mentorship system, 217
Merger, 133, 187, 191, 214, 304, 325, 328–330
Mergers and acquisitions (M&A), 41, 80, 154, 188
Merit-based promotion, 211
Merit-based remuneration, 159
Metallurgical research center, 227
Metallurgical training center, 227
Metallurgist Palace of Culture, 230
Metinvest Holding, 242–244
Metallurgist Day, 192
Mexico, 107, 269, 270, 289, 304, 307, 325
Middle East, 19, 78, 80, 154, 155
Middle East and Africa, 225
Migrant, 97, 99
Migration, 11, 120, 183, 199, 210

Military
conflict, 238–240, 248
operations, 243
service, 240
transport, 282
Military-style-efficient execution, 21
Millions of Talents Plan, 28
Minimum wage, 144, 288, 295
Mining, 133, 134, 180, 181, 183,
184, 188, 190, 191, 208, 213,
214, 242, 304
segment, 304
Mining and metallurgy industry,
188, 190, 191, 244–246
Minor Apprentice, 284
Miracle on the Han River, 63
Mission, 25, 110, 123, 130, 138,
160, 161, 194, 217, 226, 253,
256, 314, 326, 329, 336
MNC, *see* Multinational companies/
corporations
Mobile advertising, 249, 250
Mobile monetization, 249
Mobile Starts School, in Odessa, 252
Mobility, 4, 44, 47, 48, 66, 67, 103,
121, 123, 241, 279, 326
Modern competitive market rules,
255
Modernization, 49, 244, 249, 324,
332
Modern technology, 22, 244, 313
Mogilev Autoworks, 214
Mogilev Railway Car Building Plant,
214
MOL Group, 154–159
Monetary incentive, 199
Monetary remuneration, 239, 257
Monitor Empresarial de Reputación
Corporativa, 327

Moral climate, 227
Moral education, 18
Moral stimulation, 229
Moshensky, Mikhail, 219
Motivation, 24, 28, 48, 52, 58, 80,
91, 108, 112, 121, 125, 130,
135, 137, 157, 162, 163, 178,
192, 193, 199, 211, 212, 221,
222, 229, 230, 239, 241, 246,
251, 252, 254, 257, 311, 327,
347
system, 71, 139, 163, 191, 193,
199, 227, 241, 257, 347
techniques, 241
Multi-level personnel reserve, 228
Multinational companies/
corporations (MNC), 91, 145,
274, 300, 302, 303
Multi-origin wine, 332
Mutual interest, 76, 227
Mutual trust, 132, 185

N

Naftogaz, 242, 254–260
National borders, 224
National currency, 217, 238
National language, 251
National laws, 226
National Press Center, 222
National pride motives, 215
National Quality Award, 282
National Quality Foundation, 282
National survey, 222
NATO, 143
Natural resources, 130, 176, 177,
181, 182, 188, 201, 322
industry, 180
production, 238

372   **Index**

Neiva, 281
Nepotism, 17, 170, 179
Nerve-like management, 21, 22
Net income, 285, 335
Net migration rate, 239
Network-based recruiting practices, 17
Networking, 21, 25, 45, 101, 102, 107, 127–129, 135, 155, 158, 176, 196, 210, 215, 230, 250, 272, 301, 308, 328
Newly-hired employee, 184, 185, 217
New product launch, 250
New York, 107
New York Stock Exchange, 281, 292, 332
Non-financial encouragement, 192
Non-monetary benefits, 171, 211, 217
Non-monetary compensation, 211, 224, 231
Non-monetary motivation schemes, 241
Non-monetary remuneration system, 217
Non-state-owned group, 291
Norgistics, 329
North America, 106, 214, 225, 250, 270, 280, 287, 304
North Sea, 154
Norway, 155

O

Occupation, 81, 122, 183–185, 222, 243, 247, 249
Occupational
  disease, 183, 226
  health, 295
  injury, 188, 190
  position, 217
  safety, 184, 190, 191, 307
  training, 247
Occupational health and safety management system (OHSMS), 153
Occupational Safety – Electric Risk, 315
OECD, *see* Organization for Economic Cooperation and Development
Official site, 196, 251, 285, 309, 333
Off-site seminars, 230
OHSMS, *see* Occupational health and safety management system, 153
Oil and natural gas reserves, 176
Oil derivatives, 101
Oil thermals fuel, 292
OMV Group, 102
One Thousand Talents Plan, 28
Online courses platform, 293
On-the-job accident, 226
On-the-job training, 24, 148
Open dialogue system, 223
Open-Door policy, 16
Operating costs, 181, 183
Operating environment, 183
Operating license, 181
Operating staff, 184–186
Operational excellence, 130, 195
Operational Excellence Management System (OEMC), 194
Operations and Enology Excellence Bonus, 336
Optimization program, 182
Optimized production, 220

Orange Polska, 101
Orbisat da Amazonia SA, 282
Organization, 3, 4, 6–8, 11, 18, 19,
    22, 29, 34, 36, 42, 45, 65, 82,
    91, 99, 101, 103, 104, 109,
    121, 132, 135, 139, 146–148,
    150–153, 160, 162, 163, 170,
    172, 178–180, 182, 185, 189,
    190, 192, 193, 199–201, 210,
    211, 215, 218, 221–223, 226,
    228–231, 238, 241, 243, 247,
    248, 250, 252, 253, 256–260,
    279, 281, 283, 289, 291, 293,
    294, 305, 316, 324, 325, 327,
    334, 338, 346–348
Organizational
    activity, 288
    behavior, 5, 22, 139, 212, 241
    culture, 49, 80, 90, 105, 113,
        124, 130, 131, 134, 144, 145,
        215, 244, 289, 305, 323
    culture building, 259
    environment, 51
    hierarchy, 100, 323
    improvement model, 172
    inertia, 258
    skills, 90
    structure, 26, 74, 75, 125, 161,
        178, 215, 241, 327, 330, 338,
        347
Organization for Economic
    Cooperation and
    Development(OECD), 64, 89,
    270–272, 281, 300, 301, 322,
    323
ORLEN, 101–105, 114, 115, 129,
    131, 133
Outsourcing, 41, 44, 67, 100, 146,
    311, 313

Outstanding Talent Engineering, 27
Ownership structure, 169, 180, 201,
    241, 274

P

P3E, *see* Embraer Enterprise
    Excellence Program
Pakistan, 68, 155
Pampa, 308–313
Pampa Energia S.A., 303, 308–313
    See also Pampa
Part-time employees, 287
Party membership rewards, 171
Passenger rail transport, 285
Paternalistic culture, 11, 324
Paternity, 295
Pause or no-change strategy, 244
Payment delays, 239
Pay review, 246
PDL, *see* Leadership Development
    Program, the
Pension plan, 283
People management, 288
Performance, 5–7, 16, 18, 19, 21,
    22, 24, 26, 29, 32, 33, 35, 43,
    44, 46, 47, 50, 53, 55, 57, 58,
    66, 71, 77, 78, 80, 91,
    99–101, 105, 111, 113, 121,
    122, 126, 136, 137, 139, 146,
    147, 149, 151, 152, 157, 159,
    162, 171, 180–182, 184, 186,
    188, 189, 194, 195, 197, 199,
    200, 209–212, 215, 216, 218,
    222, 225, 243, 244, 246, 250,
    253, 255, 258, 278, 279, 282,
    283, 286, 289, 291–293, 295,
    302, 306, 309, 322, 326, 329,
    336, 337, 345

374   Index

Performance(*cont.*)
  appraisal procedures, 178
  assessment system, 192
  management, 11, 29, 48, 57, 71,
    80, 113, 212, 221, 258, 326
  results, 171, 194, 306
  reviews, 134, 253
Performance appraisal systems (PAS),
  18, 71, 146, 147, 172, 199
Performance-based remuneration,
  28, 43, 52, 172, 199, 210
Performance-related pay, 148
Personal
  accounts, 136, 309
  connections, 211, 212, 216, 272
  goals, 199, 284
  insurance, 283
  relations, 90
Personality inventory test, 69
Personal Value Program, 292
Personnel
  administration, 170
  compensation, 221
  departments, 240
  development, 212
  moral responsibility, 229
  outflow, 245
  performance, 248
  policy, 228
  recruitment and selection, 224
  training programs, 222
  well-being, 210
Petrobras Argentina S.A., 308, 312
  See also Petroleo Brasileiro S.A.
    (Petrobras)
Petrochemical company, 129, 280,
  287
Petrochemical industry, 129, 208,
  288

Petrochemical products, 101, 102,
  129, 130
Petrol, 101
Petroleo Brasileiro S.A. (Petrobras),
  312
Pharmacovigilance training
  programs, 151
Physical training, 184
Pipeline operations, 308
Plastics, 101, 129
Poland, 7, 89, 90, 95, 120, 207, 208,
  237, 240, 346
Policy instruments, 209
Political
  alliances, 208
  inertia, 237
  instability, 181, 271, 272, 348
  intervention, 237
Polski Koncern Naftowy Orlen SA,
  see ORLEN
Polyethylene, 287
Polyolefin, 287
Polypropylene, 287
Pontifical Universidad Catolica de
  Chile, 326
Pools, 20, 34, 45, 46, 51, 52, 55, 77,
  80, 105, 153, 156, 163, 178,
  184, 187, 190, 201, 217, 222,
  231, 247, 251, 256, 294, 295,
  345
Population density, 176
Portuguese language, 289
Positive company image, 34, 53, 186
Post-acquisition social integration,
  172
Post-communist countries, 208
Postgraduate degree, 105
Post-Soviet approach to HRM, 256
Post-Soviet countries, 193

Potential leaders, 47, 100, 288
Potential talent, 156, 163, 279, 295
Power distance, 10, 18, 74, 178, 185, 193, 200, 201, 240, 248, 347
Power Labor Union, 314
Practical sessions, 285
Pre-hire outcomes, 17
Pre-hiring special tracks with partner-universities, 189
Preliminary interviews, 196
Presidium of Supreme Soviet of the National Economy, 243
Preventive Logistics Safety Plan, 307
Price/wage deregulation, 171
Private infrastructure conglomerates, 284
Private organizations, 19, 145
Private pension plans, 287
Private sector, 97, 145–148, 176, 177
Privatizations, 90, 91, 95, 96, 114, 129, 154, 169, 171, 180, 274, 281, 313, 349
Problem-solving skills, 21, 24, 251
Product
    competitiveness, 215
    development cycles, 282
    quality, 226, 304
    stewardship, 195
Production
    activity, 226
    capability, 220
    capacity, 187, 243, 332
    cycle, 187, 214, 243
    disruption, 181
    efficiency, 186, 244
    facility, 219, 223, 225, 246, 300, 304

flows, 225
lines, 223, 243, 244, 249
plants, 220, 287
process optimization, 249
stability, 189
supervision, 221
Production-and-training center, 247
Productivity growth, 209
Productivity honorarium scheme, 51
Professional
    activities, 223
    ambitions, 229
    competences, 222
    degradation, 239
    development, 43, 55, 71, 72, 78, 105, 131, 153, 162, 184, 186, 199, 252, 279, 283
    growth, 198, 223, 286, 289, 293
    growth programs, 305
    knowledge, 227
    qualifications, 135, 171, 247, 257, 271
    schools, 247
    skills, 150, 184, 185, 222, 227, 257, 326, 327
    training, 18, 27, 33, 128, 129, 191, 212, 222, 227–229, 245–247
Professionalism, 54, 195, 227, 305, 306, 313, 317, 324, 327
Profit, 22, 130, 148, 155, 194, 244, 253, 282, 325
Profitability, 99, 255, 325
Program for Developing Entrepreneurs, 290
Project development, 112
Project management, 56, 112

376   Index

Promotion, 11, 16, 18, 26, 27, 33, 35, 42, 44–49, 52, 66, 69, 71, 72, 75, 78, 108, 129, 158, 178, 179, 196, 200, 211, 227, 228, 245, 303, 312, 344
Proprietorship, 209
Psychological climate, 227
Psychological contracts, 240
Public policy, 209
Public sector, 145–148, 177
Purchasing power, 321
PVC, 287
Pyramid of motivation, 192, 193

Q

Qualification
  characteristics, 228
  degrees, 229
  rank, 223
Quality, 21, 23, 24, 27, 29, 30, 57, 64, 67–69, 72, 99, 102, 103, 112, 120, 123, 135, 151, 161, 162, 185, 188, 194, 199, 214, 215, 221–223, 226, 227, 229, 231, 240, 247, 283–286, 289, 290, 293, 295, 302, 305, 309, 314, 323, 332, 334, 338
  department, 221
  of life indicators, 286
  management systems, 187, 305
  standards, 215, 260

R

R&D, *see* Research and development
Racial discrimination, 75, 240
Rebranding, 102

Recession, 208, 238
  in economy, 96
Reconnaissance systems, 282
Record-keeping, 170
Recovery, 194, 239, 260, 270, 277, 278, 300, 328
Recruitment
  agencies, 146, 189, 330
  channels, 23
  policy, 32, 103, 131
  practices, 17, 128, 178
  procedures, 80, 218
  process, 17, 23, 69–71, 103, 108, 121, 124, 131, 150, 152, 158, 178, 179, 190, 224, 257, 330, 333
Refinery products, 129, 130
Regional
  aviation, 282
  instability, 254–255
  player, 308
  trade, 176
Regulatory requirements, 182
Reinvestment remuneration, 161
Relocation costs, 183
Remittances, 210
Remote electronic system of module training, 229
Remuneration gap, 210
Remuneration systems, 28, 126, 136, 217
Renewable energy, 53, 292
Renewable resources, 287
Renovation, 44, 179
Reputation, 21, 115, 181, 200, 214, 226, 327, 336
Reputational damage, 181
Requalification, 196

Research and development (R&D), 20, 21, 49, 57, 151, 188, 215, 345
 investments, 226, 305
Research centers and laboratories, 190
Reserve establishment honorarium, 51
Respect for authority, 185
Responsibility, 22, 26, 31, 52, 55, 95, 100, 104, 108, 113, 124, 130, 134, 136, 138, 157, 184, 196, 198, 211, 222–224, 227, 229, 255, 289, 309, 311, 314, 315, 325, 326
Restoration of National Economy, 213
Restructuring, 30, 42, 66, 71, 75, 90, 95, 107, 145, 180, 201, 224, 256, 258, 277, 281, 299, 300, 312, 329
Retention, 4, 7, 8, 10, 11, 18, 29, 33, 35, 42, 46, 51, 53, 55, 57, 67–72, 91, 103, 109, 135, 139, 159, 163, 172, 185, 192, 198, 201, 212, 224, 227, 229–231, 239, 242, 250, 256, 273, 274, 278–280, 282, 283, 287–291, 294, 307, 316, 324, 331, 338, 344–347, 349
 mechanisms and techniques, 218
Retirees, 77, 186
Retirement, 24, 52, 91, 136, 295, 300, 331
 planning, 221
Retraining, 191
Return on investment (ROI), 294
Revenue, 285

Revenues, 42, 44, 68, 69, 120, 149, 176, 254, 259, 277, 325, 328
Reward system, 77, 200, 316
Rio de Janeiro, 287
Rio Grande do Sul, 293
Rio Grande Energia and SEMESA, 292
Risk
 assessment, 247
 awareness, 183
 management program, 194–195
Risk-averse cultural environment, 18
Road concession, 285
Rogovskiy, Vadim, 250
ROI, *see* Return on investment
Role models, 123, 290
Romania, 89, 90, 106, 154, 237
Russia, 20, 23, 79, 149, 154, 169, 175, 177, 190, 191, 193, 207, 208, 210, 213, 214, 218–220, 224, 237–240, 248, 249, 254, 255, 258
Russian-Ukrainian conflict, 242, 253
Russian-Ukrainian relationship, 241

S
Safe Driving Academy, 105
Safety, 21, 75, 79, 103, 108, 112, 123, 139, 151, 153, 155, 156, 163, 181–184, 186, 188, 190–192, 194, 197, 200, 226, 227, 242, 248, 257–260, 295, 307, 315, 317, 334
 culture, 105, 138, 183
 issues, 192, 197
 management systems, 221

378 Index

programs, 186
regulations, 186
SafeWork, 190, 191
Salary, 51, 71, 75, 77, 80, 97–99,
109, 120, 121, 147, 148, 159,
169, 177, 179, 183, 192, 197,
199, 209–211, 217, 218, 221,
228, 230, 239, 241, 246, 248,
249, 252, 257, 271, 273, 288,
290, 293, 295, 310, 314, 315,
327, 335–337
differentiation, 171
Sanctions, 220
Sanitary registration, 221
Santa Bremor, 213, 219–224, 231
Santiago Stock Exchange, 332
Sao Jose dos Campos Embraer 195,
281
Sao Paulo, 280, 287, 292, 293
Sao Paulo Stock Exchange, 281
SAP Human Capital Management,
218
SAP Success Factors, 311
Scholarship, 67, 69, 133, 305,
309–311, 314
Scholarships for more Energy, 309
Scientific and technical conference,
228
Secondary school education, 177
Security, 67, 73, 103, 104, 155, 171,
195, 209, 212, 214, 221, 278,
282, 326, 345
SEGBA, *see* Servicios Electricos del
Gran Buenos Aires
Selection, 5, 21, 24, 26, 28, 29, 32,
36, 55, 58, 66, 69, 108, 131,
135, 137, 146, 150, 222, 224,
227, 259, 272, 278, 309, 349

process, 46, 51, 55, 66, 69, 70,
150, 178, 282, 285
Selective approach to defining talent,
259
Self-development, 256, 258, 288,
289
Self-evaluation procedure, 292
Self-improvement, 31, 32, 228
Self-motivated employee, 253
Self-realization possibilities, 192
Semi-finished steel products, 304
Seminars and training programs, 221
SENCE, *see* Servicio Nacional de
Capacitación y Empleo
Seoul, 73, 107
Service
agreement, 281
management staff, 221
quality, 29, 215
sector, 64, 209
Servicio Nacional de Capacitación y
Empleo (SENCE), 322
Servicios Electricos del Gran Buenos
Aires (SEGBA), 313
Sexual orientation discrimination,
75, 240
Share capital, 282
Shared services centers (SSC), 98
Shareholders, 29, 75, 129, 130, 180,
182, 188, 256, 282, 289, 304,
306, 314, 326
Share Option Scheme, 29
Shipping company, 329
Short-term goal, 224, 290
Short-term orientation, 240
Siderar, 304
Sidor, 304
Simulation machine, 186

Index **379**

Singapore, 106
Skilled personnel, 181, 183
Skills and competences, 46, 216, 250, 259, 309, 345
Skill shortages, 182
Škoda, 122–129, 139
Slovak Republic, the, 89
Slovenia, 89
Small and medium size firms, 178
Small-medium enterprise (SME), 325
Social app monetization network, 250
Social benefits package, 183, 257
Social capital, 104, 179, 251
Social commitment, 182, 249
Social contract, 208
Social development, 190, 209
Social equality, 228
Social infrastructure projects, 194
Social integration, 172
    mechanisms, 172
Social investment program, 194
Socialist system, 169
Social license, 181
Socially oriented reforms and policies, 208
Socially responsible organization, 223
Socially-vulnerable groups, 190
Social orientation, 201
Social package, 154, 192, 217
Social partnership, 227
Social policy effectiveness, 230
Social protection, 210, 240
Social-psychological climate, 228
Social respect, 227
Social security, 50–52, 209, 210, 302

Social stability, 245, 257
Social welfare, 120, 145, 211, 346
Socio-cultural context, 89
Socio-economic development, 52, 182, 285
Socio-environmental responsibility, 289
Solar power plant, 292
South Africa, 107
South America, 19, 78, 80, 214, 225, 269, 277, 313, 321
South Asia, 175
Southeast Asia, 225
Southern Europe, 154
Soviet authoritarian style, 260
Soviet command economy, 177
Soviet era, 179, 200, 207, 230, 237
    traditions, 230
Soviet heritage, 169–173, 178, 201
Soviet legacy, 200, 217, 259
Soviet management system, 170
Soviet recruitment practices, 178
Soviet republics, 169, 172, 175, 207
Soviet system, 145, 259
Soviet times, 210–212
Soviet Union, 144, 169, 170, 176, 180, 208, 237
    heritage, 170
    legacy, 200, 217, 259
Special adaptation program, 216
Special education, 108
Specialization, 41, 101, 127, 221, 222, 252
Specialized human resource units, 224
Specialized training, 34, 184, 307, 309
Specific knowledge, 312

380   **Index**

Sri Lanka, 107
SSC, *see* Shared services centers
Stability, 74, 110, 131, 149, 188,
     189, 199, 208, 223, 238, 244,
     248, 249, 259, 260, 299, 300,
     326, 335
Stable production, 223
Staff development, 286
Staff turnover, 35, 185, 229, 251
Stakeholders, 21, 26, 69, 74, 102,
     103, 124, 130, 180–182, 194,
     195, 331, 338
Standard industrial safety
     measurements, 197
Standardized appraisal system, 258
Standard of living, 228
State
   assets, 185, 207
   certificate, 223
   coup, 239
   ownership, 207, 231
   policies, 223, 231, 258
   quotas, 178
   reform, 255
State-appointed executives, 210
State-controlled organization, 281
State-owned company, 90, 95, 96,
     105, 110, 114, 179, 210, 224,
     225, 241, 254, 273, 274, 313,
     349
State-owned enterprise, 17, 209, 258
Statistics, 322
Statoil ASA, 102
Steel
   market, 226, 304
   melting production, 225
   producer, 242, 244, 259, 304
   production, 243, 244, 304, 306

   segment, 304
Strategic asset, 288
Strategic human resource
     management, 171, 279
Strategic Leadership Development
     Program, 247
Strategic planning, 198
Strategic value, 294
Strategy, 9, 20, 22, 25, 27, 28, 31,
     32, 34, 35, 45, 48, 54, 67, 69,
     73–75, 78, 80, 90, 102, 103,
     105, 107–111, 120, 123, 127,
     129–131, 133, 139, 154, 159,
     160, 179–186, 188, 189, 194,
     225, 226, 229, 240, 244, 249,
     253, 257, 259, 279–281,
     288–291, 293–295, 300, 302,
     304, 305, 307, 310, 316, 325,
     332–334, 337, 338, 348, 349
Structural reform agenda, 177
Student allocation, 216
Subcontract, 70, 278
Subsidiary, 23, 47, 66, 68, 70, 72,
     73, 78, 102, 126, 128, 135,
     138, 149, 185, 187, 219,
     242–245, 251, 281, 300,
     307–310, 312, 325, 326,
     328–331, 338
Substitution of import, 299
Success factor, 98, 175, 253, 314
Sugarcane-based ethanol, 287
Sulfur, 155, 190
Supervisor, 24, 76, 198, 200, 229,
     310
Supplementary health improvement
     opportunities, 227
Suppliers, 21, 111, 181, 197, 198,
     226, 291, 304, 305, 312, 314

Index   **381**

Support payments, 217
Support service, 282
Surveillance platform, 282
Sustainability, 26, 44, 51, 244, 248, 292, 304, 333, 336
Sustainable competitive advantage, 7, 78, 182
Sustainable development, 25, 26, 31, 103, 214, 290, 315
Sustainable growth, 176, 177, 244, 256
Sustainable relationships, 288
Sustainable solution, 288
System of bonuses,
  221, 335

Talent, 3–8, 15–36, 42, 68–72, 78–82, 89–92, 109–115, 121, 143–163, 177, 193–200, 210, 224–231, 239, 249–254, 269–274, 284–287, 299–317, 323, 325–331
  decisions, 186
  incubator, 285
  organization, 283
  procedures, 248
  recognition, 279
  recruitment, 91, 135, 200, 259, 306, 346
  scarcity, 257
  status, 199, 245
  value, 193–200
Talent attraction, 4, 7, 8, 17, 21, 28, 29, 36, 51, 52, 67–72, 91, 92, 161, 170, 178, 201, 216, 222, 224, 230, 256, 273, 274, 278,

282, 314, 324, 338, 345, 346, 349
  issues, 228
  practices, 197, 222, 231
  processes, 17
  tools, 4, 325, 339, 348, 349
Talent development, 7, 28, 30–36, 47, 52, 57, 58, 76, 121, 127, 137, 157, 161, 162, 191, 197, 212, 283, 305, 308–313, 323
  practices, 173, 178
Talent-echelon-pyramid, 33
Talented employee, 4, 6, 17, 27, 32, 33, 43, 45, 54, 57, 65, 114, 139, 152, 156, 196, 198, 211, 224, 241, 280, 288, 290, 302, 305, 316, 333, 338, 344, 345, 347
Talent management, 3–12, 15, 16, 18–25, 31, 35, 46, 49–58, 64–67, 69, 71, 75, 79, 81, 82, 89–92, 99, 101, 103, 104, 109, 111, 113, 114, 124, 129, 145, 156, 158, 160–163, 170, 172, 173, 185, 200, 201, 212, 213, 215, 224, 227, 231, 242, 248, 249, 258–260, 269–274, 277, 279, 282, 285, 288, 292, 294, 295, 299–317, 323–331, 333, 336–339, 344–349
  agenda, 245, 248, 260, 344–349
  components, 19, 134, 136, 237
  concept, 171
  environment, 3–8
  field, 213
  implementation, 58, 132, 179, 231, 260, 338
  initiatives, 279

382 Index

Talent management (*cont.*)
 investments, 292
 issues, 178
 landscape, 99, 177
 objective, 186, 199, 245, 258
 practices, 3, 5–8, 10–12, 17, 18,
  31, 34, 35, 42, 43, 50, 53,
  56–58, 66, 75, 81, 91, 92, 99,
  124, 139, 156, 161, 163,
  170–172, 179, 182, 183, 189,
  200, 201, 210, 221, 223, 224,
  227, 242, 257, 259, 260,
  271–274, 279, 303, 307, 309,
  311, 313, 316, 324, 327, 330,
  331, 333, 335–338, 344–349
 strategy, 4–6, 8, 15, 22, 43, 53,
  78, 131, 153, 163, 215, 253,
  280, 288, 294, 295, 303, 305,
  313, 328, 331, 335, 337, 345
 system, 4, 5, 22, 27, 34, 42, 66,
  99, 101–105, 111, 125, 138,
  157, 161, 170, 179, 186, 192,
  193, 195, 201, 213, 240, 241,
  245, 286, 344, 345, 347–349
 trends, 216
Talent motivation, 43, 57, 191
 systems, 257
Talent pool, 20, 55, 156, 184, 190,
  201, 217, 222, 231, 247, 251,
  256
 expansion, 247
Talent retention, 7, 10, 18, 52, 57,
  72, 198, 279, 280, 283,
  287–291, 344
 mechanism, 231
 practices, 172, 185, 242
 strategy, 229
Tallinn, 107
Tariff rates, 192, 230

Task orientation, 201
Taxation policy, 95
Team
 climate, 191
 leader, 161, 293
 member, 291
 spirit, 155
 work, 32, 52
Team-building activity, 239, 252
Technical competences, 50, 216
Technical culture, 305
Technical knowledge, 150, 163, 291,
  306
Technical skills, 127, 216, 217, 290,
  306, 314
Technological infrastructure, 313
Technological progress challenge,
  215
Teletón, 327
Temporary employee, 70, 287, 335,
  337
Temporary employment, 323, 337,
  348
Temporary International Assignment
  Program, 198
Tengiz, 193, 194, 196
Tengizchevroil, 179, 193–201
Ternium, 303–308
Terra Incognita, 321–339
Thailand, 107
Thermal energy, 101
Thermoplastic product, 287
Thermoplastic resins, 287
Third-country national, 221
Thousand Talents Plan, 11
360 degree technique,
  178
Tokyo, 107
Top-level positions, 216

Top management, 24, 43, 55, 58, 80, 99, 100, 105, 120–121, 135–137, 157, 188, 248, 253
team, 214
Top-manager, 229, 309, 314
Toronto, 107
Trainee program, 128, 131, 279, 289
Trainee Qualification Program, 285
Training, 5, 7, 11, 18, 22–24, 27, 28, 31–36, 46–48, 51, 55–58, 67, 71, 72, 76, 99, 104–106, 109–115, 125–129, 131, 133, 137, 139, 145–148, 151–154, 158, 161, 170, 177, 178, 182, 184–186, 189, 191, 196–198, 201, 212, 216, 217, 221–224, 227–229, 245–247, 252, 257, 279, 281, 283–286, 289, 290, 292–294, 300, 301, 303, 305–310, 312–315, 317, 322, 323, 327, 328, 333–335, 337, 338
center, 47, 72, 127, 191, 227, 229, 247, 257
process, 228
session, 33, 99, 217, 223, 252, 309
system, 33, 71, 76, 177, 245, 247, 303
Training and development, 5, 11, 33, 51, 58, 92, 109–115, 146, 147, 182, 185, 191, 221, 224, 247, 257, 274, 283, 289, 335
activities, 131, 147, 178
programs, 46, 127, 137, 196, 289
system, 222
Transener, 310
Transfer benefit, 283

Transformation Program, 292
Transition, 8, 67, 91, 92, 99, 114, 139, 144, 145, 157, 171, 179, 200, 259, 324, 346, 347
process, 91, 92, 144, 259
Transparency policy, 254
Transportation allowance, 283
Transport vouchers, 287
Treasury, 152, 198, 326
Trivento Bodegas y Viñedos in Mendoza, 332
Tuition reimbursement, 283
Turbo machinery, 124
Turboprop aircraft, 280, 281
Turnover rate, 147, 252, 280
Tyskie, 101, 109–115, 347

U

Ukraine, 7, 79, 97, 120, 122, 169, 172, 173, 201, 207, 208, 219, 237–260, 347, 348
Ukrainian context, 242, 258, 259
Ukrainian economy, 237, 238, 245
Ukrainian labor market, 239, 243, 249, 257, 258
Ukrainian market, 213
Ukrainian mentality, 241
Unbiased business decisions, 259
Uncertainty avoidance, 98, 240
Unconventional motivation techniques, 193
Unemployment
insurance, 295
rates, 97, 119, 120, 144, 176, 239, 240, 277, 278, 322
Unified workers wage tariff system, 230

384 Index

Unilever, 301
Union membership, 278
Unipetrol, 102, 122, 129–133, 139
United Kingdom (UK), 46, 97, 155, 208
United Nations (UN), 143, 245
United States (U.S.), 46, 68, 96, 157, 178, 201, 219, 220, 249, 250, 281, 287, 288, 307, 325, 332
Universalist definition of talent, 189
Universalist talent definition, 172
Universalist talent management approach, 227
Universal quality management system, 305
Universidad de Chile, 326
Universidad de Santiago de Chile, 326
University, 16, 17, 20, 23, 33, 35, 42, 46, 47, 50, 55, 56, 58, 69, 71, 72, 98, 100, 104, 115, 126–128, 133, 135, 137, 139, 152, 156, 170, 189, 191, 196, 210, 216, 247, 256, 274, 280, 290, 293, 301, 303, 306, 315, 316, 326, 345, 346
collaboration, 257
Up-and-down job movement, 29
USSR dissolution, 207

V

Value chain, 30, 155, 333
Value creation, 102
Variable remuneration, 80, 282, 290, 292
VCT Brasil, 332

VCT Nordics, 332
Vehicle inspection services, 285
Venezuela, 270, 304
Venture company, 122, 198, 254, 328, 332
Vertical integration, 20, 244
Vertical organizational structure, 178
Vice President of People, Organization & Procurement, 288
Vietnam, 107
Viña Concha y Toro, 332
Vineyard, 332
Vinyl, 287
Vision for 2020, 291
Vkontakte, 251
Vocational and training system, 177
Volatile economic background, 238, 270, 300
Volkswagen Group (VW), 122–129
Voluntary layoffs, 248, 249
Voluntary retirement, 300
VW, *see* Volkswagen Group

W

Wage
inequalities, 323, 337
rates, 171
scales, 209
Warehouse, 308
War for talent, 70, 242
Warsaw Stock Exchange, 101
Wasteful talent management, 279
Well-qualified professional, 294
Western Europe, 96, 149, 175, 219

Westernization perspective, 172
Western-like managerial practices, 258
Western management practices, 75, 91, 231
Western management style, 260
Western practices and traditions, 70
West-European approach to HRM, 240
West-style democracy, 144
Whistle Blower Channel, 336
Wholesale and retail trade, 219
Wholesale banking, 326
Wind farms, 292
Wine cellar, 332
Workers' allocation process, 170
Workers' Amenities program, 246
Work ethics, 240
Workforce, 10, 22, 51, 52, 64, 66, 67, 98, 105, 126, 145, 152, 153, 158, 159, 182, 184, 185, 195, 198, 209, 211, 216, 218, 227, 240, 253, 286, 300, 303, 305, 330, 337
    development, 194, 197
Working atmosphere, 78, 223
Working capital, 180
Working conditions, 91, 115, 139, 153, 161, 163, 182, 183, 191, 192, 215, 218, 223–231, 249, 305, 314, 325, 334
Working environment, 29, 43, 48, 53, 65, 108, 113, 128, 155, 179, 186, 190, 193, 199, 216, 246, 249, 252, 308–314, 316, 325, 327, 331
Working experience, 65, 184, 198, 259

Working relations, 170
Working requirements, 184
Working teams, 227, 228
Work-life balance, 51, 77, 100, 229, 241, 307, 311, 317, 331
Workload, 252, 327
Workplace
    conflicts, 211
    culture, 182
    diversity, 182
    equality, 221
    fairness, 256
    injury, 197, 226
    productivity, 100
    safety, 190, 257
    transparency, 227
Workplace-based voluntary benefits, 11
Work quality, 199
Workshops, 33, 104, 105, 111, 112, 131, 135, 138, 285, 309, 310, 312, 327
World Bank, the, 95, 143, 144, 175, 176, 208, 209, 238, 239, 321
World Steel Association, 307
World Trade Organization (WTO), 143
Worldwide industry, 287–291

Y

Young Apprentice program, 289
Young employees, 32, 58, 125, 151, 153, 217
Young Operator program, 289
Young Professionals Program, 306

Young specialists, 154, 163, 170, 217, 218, 249, 257, 302, 309

Young talent, 67, 151, 156, 159, 218, 228, 239, 279, 291, 304–308, 315, 317, 349

Your Flight Plan, at Embraer, 283

Youth employment opportunities, 64, 322

Youth unemployment, 176

Z

Zhezkazgan, 180

CPSIA information can be obtained
at www.ICGtesting.com
Printed in the USA
LVHW05*1909041018
592416LV00009B/456/P